Nostradamus

FOR

DUMMIES®

W9-DET-254

Nostradamus

FOR

DUMMIES®

by Scarlett Ross

WILEY

Wiley Publishing, Inc.

Nostradamus For Dummies®

Published by
Wiley Publishing, Inc.
111 River St.
Hoboken, NJ 07030-5774
www.wiley.com

Copyright © 2005 by Wiley Publishing, Inc., Indianapolis, Indiana

Published simultaneously in Canada

No part of this publication may be reproduced, stored in a retrieval system, or transmitted in any form or by any means, electronic, mechanical, photocopying, recording, scanning, or otherwise, except as permitted under Sections 107 or 108 of the 1976 United States Copyright Act, without either the prior written permission of the Publisher, or authorization through payment of the appropriate per-copy fee to the Copyright Clearance Center, 222 Rosewood Drive, Danvers, MA 01923, 978-750-8400, fax 978-646-8600. Requests to the Publisher for permission should be addressed to the Legal Department, Wiley Publishing, Inc., 10475 Crosspoint Blvd., Indianapolis, IN 46256, 317-572-3447, fax 317-572-4355, or online at http://www.wiley.com/go/permissions.

Trademarks: Wiley, the Wiley Publishing logo, For Dummies, the Dummies Man logo, A Reference for the Rest of Us!, The Dummies Way, Dummies Daily, The Fun and Easy Way, Dummies.com and related trade dress are trademarks or registered trademarks of John Wiley & Sons, Inc. and/or its affiliates in the United States and other countries, and may not be used without written permission. All other trademarks are the property of their respective owners. Wiley Publishing, Inc., is not associated with any product or vendor mentioned in this book.

LIMIT OF LIABILITY/DISCLAIMER OF WARRANTY: THE PUBLISHER AND THE AUTHOR MAKE NO REPRESENTATIONS OR WARRANTIES WITH RESPECT TO THE ACCURACY OR COMPLETENESS OF THE CONTENTS OF THIS WORK AND SPECIFICALLY DISCLAIM ALL WARRANTIES, INCLUDING WITHOUT LIMITATION WARRANTIES OF FITNESS FOR A PARTICULAR PURPOSE. NO WARRANTY MAY BE CREATED OR EXTENDED BY SALES OR PROMOTIONAL MATERIALS. THE ADVICE AND STRATEGIES CONTAINED HEREIN MAY NOT BE SUITABLE FOR EVERY SITUATION. THIS WORK IS SOLD WITH THE UNDERSTANDING THAT THE PUBLISHER IS NOT ENGAGED IN RENDERING LEGAL, ACCOUNTING, OR OTHER PROFESSIONAL SERVICES. IF PROFESSIONAL ASSISTANCE IS REQUIRED, THE SERVICES OF A COMPETENT PROFESSIONAL PERSON SHOULD BE SOUGHT. NEITHER THE PUBLISHER NOR THE AUTHOR SHALL BE LIABLE FOR DAMAGES ARISING HEREFROM. THE FACT THAT AN ORGANIZATION OR WEBSITE IS REFERRED TO IN THIS WORK AS A CITATION AND/OR A POTENTIAL SOURCE OF FURTHER INFORMATION DOES NOT MEAN THAT THE AUTHOR OR THE PUBLISHER ENDORSES THE INFORMATION THE ORGANIZATION OR WEBSITE MAY PROVIDE OR RECOMMENDATIONS IT MAY MAKE. FURTHER, READERS SHOULD BE AWARE THAT INTERNET WEBSITES LISTED IN THIS WORK MAY HAVE CHANGED OR DISAPPEARED BETWEEN WHEN THIS WORK WAS WRITTEN AND WHEN IT IS READ.

For general information on our other products and services, please contact our Customer Care Department within the U.S. at 800-762-2974, outside the U.S. at 317-572-3993, or fax 317-572-4002.

For technical support, please visit www.wiley.com/techsupport.

Wiley also publishes its books in a variety of electronic formats. Some content that appears in print may not be available in electronic books.

Library of Congress Control Number: 2005923235

ISBN-13: 978-0-7645-8412-1

ISBN-10: 0-7645-8412-X

Manufactured in the United States of America

10 9 8 7 6 5 4 3 2 1

1B/RS/QU/QV/IN

WILEY

About the Author

Scarlett Ross is a writer (and English teacher) who has spent 18 years actively participating in and researching the New Age and Metaphysical movement. She has worn many hats over the years, including personal guide, community leader, and chef of the heart. She has developed and supported spiritual events, including building a school for kids to see the next stage of humanity's growth toward enlightenment.

For fun, Scarlett has developed and presented workshops on personal spirituality in the everyday (dishes and all), connecting with the divine, personal responsibility, symbolism in spiritual growth, divination, prophecy, and dreams because these are the things that fascinate and motivate her to look at the world with a tilted head and a questioning look. Teaching high school English and literature interpretation in two out-of-the-box schools hasn't hurt that tendency. A lifelong student of language, wordplay, and symbolism, Scarlett takes her workshops to a variety of locations throughout the eastern United States and has published *Dreams of the Goddess* (New Page Press), a guided personal journal workbook for spiritual dreaming.

Off time is very precious when it comes, and Scarlett is most likely to be found behind a good book — whether it's reading, scrapbooking, or telling stories to teach the next generation. Her favorite activities include cooking for anyone who'll sit still, dancing, black-and-white photography, camping with friends, and hopefully, keeping up with her young son, cat, and, family.

Dedication

To the guiding lights who've taught me to fly and breathe deeply — my husband, John; my sunshine and son, Ian; my best friend, Brian; and the rest of my heart family that have been unbelievable and supportive (even pushy) when I doubted. *From my heart to your hearts,* I offer you thanks and blessings

To my mother and Jere, who have taught me the meaning of perseverance, following my own path, and living life fully. Live without regrets.

To you, the reader, for reminding me that everybody needs a little bit of prophecy. I hope Nostradamus and I can shed some light for your future.

Author's Acknowledgments

A hearty thank you and nod of appreciation to those research-assistant mice who scrambled quietly in the background, including Lee Watts, Rebecca Emberger, Joe Hancammon, Clove Tolbert, Professor Puckett, and Alexander Baghira.

Sandy Blackthorn gets the Coffee Cup Award of Patience and Sanity for her overwhelming support and coaching.

To the writers who've encouraged me and walked the hard road before me, my thanks to Carl McColman and the writers who continually inspire me including Trish Telesco, Dorothy Morrison, and MR Sellers.

In the end, there are the behind-the-scenes busy bees at Wiley; I appreciate the patience of acquisitions editor Tracy Boggier, project editor Mike Baker, copyeditor Trisha Strietelmeier, technical reviewer Troy Guthrie, and the rest of the staff who've helped design and guide this book.

Thanks to my agent Ron Formica at New England Publishing Associates for the guidance and help in reaching my goals and keeping sanity.

Publisher's Acknowledgments

We're proud of this book; please send us your comments through our Dummies online registration form located at www.dummies.com/register/.

Some of the people who helped bring this book to market include the following:

Acquisitions, Editorial, and Media Development

Publisher's Acknowledgment: Sandy Blackthorn, Consultant

Project Editor: Mike Baker

Acquisitions Editor: Tracy Boggier

Copy Editor: Trisha Strietelmeier

Editorial Program Assistant: Courtney Allen

Technical Reviewer: Troy Guthrie

Senior Permissions Editor: Carmen Krikorian

Editorial Manager: Christine Meloy Beck

Editorial Assistant: Hanna Scott, Melissa Bennett

Cover Photos: © Chris Nurse/AOE Fotostock

Cartoons: Rich Tennant (www.the5thwave.com)

Composition Services

Project Coordinator: Maridee Ennis

Layout and Graphics: Joyce Haughey, Stephanie D. Jumper, Lynsey Osborn, Melanee Prendergast, Heather Ryan, Mary Gillot Virgin

Proofreaders: David Faust, TECHBOOKS Production Services

Indexer: TECHBOOKS Production Services

Publishing and Editorial for Consumer Dummies

> **Diane Graves Steele,** Vice President and Publisher, Consumer Dummies
>
> **Joyce Pepple,** Acquisitions Director, Consumer Dummies
>
> **Kristin A. Cocks,** Product Development Director, Consumer Dummies
>
> **Michael Spring,** Vice President and Publisher, Travel
>
> **Kelly Regan,** Editorial Director, Travel

Publishing for Technology Dummies

> **Andy Cummings,** Vice President and Publisher, Dummies Technology/General User

Composition Services

> **Gerry Fahey,** Vice President of Production Services
>
> **Debbie Stailey,** Director of Composition Services

Contents at a Glance

Table of Contents

Introduction

L ike leafless trees illuminated by a full moon on a cool fall night, merely uttering the name Nostradamus can evoke an eerie sense of mystery and the possibility of danger for some, while others quickly adopt a skeptical attitude. But one thing is certain, after nearly 500 years, the name Nostradamus still elicits a reaction and creates controversy in most circles — a considerable accomplishment for an average, run-of-the-mill doctor from the 1500s. Well, average and run-of-the-mill with the added twist that his specialty was writing down prophecies by moonlight that would attempt to predict some of the most significant, earth-shattering events of the next 2,000 years.

It's the mystery surrounding how prophecy works — and whether it really works at all — that has kept Nostradamus in the public eye for all these years. But for Nostradamus, viewing the future was serious business, and it wasn't an easy profession. Night after night, he contemplated the fate of the world and then tried to record his visions in a way that only a select few could decipher.

About This Book

Even though Nostradamus is still a celebrity in the 21st century, most folks don't know much about the man himself, let alone what made him tick. That's where I come in. *Nostradamus For Dummies* is my way of giving you a peek inside the fascinating world of Nostradamus. I introduce you to the personal side of Nostradamus and delve into the history and culture of his times, uncovering many of the influences on Nostradamus, his writing, and his predictions.

My take (and the premise of this book) is that prophecy *is* possible and that it's one of the talents Nostradamus displayed. But I don't think that every prophecy he wrote was truly a vision of the future. I believe that at times, Nostradamus was simply writing commentary on his own world and about the future as well.

From this point of view, *Nostradamus For Dummies* explains the basics of Nostradamus's prophecies — in plain English. I offer interpretations of some of his predictions that I believe match (or don't match) particular events in history. I also cover some of his predictions that I believe fit into a larger pattern of human history and provide a positive outlook of the future — it's not all doom and gloom. I help you decipher these predictions by explaining the history surrounding Nostradamus's writings, picking apart some of the writings themselves, and performing a fair amount of detective work. Along the way, I also give you a few tools to start investigating the meaning within Nostradamus's works on your own, should you be interested in really getting into this stuff.

This book is the result of years spent immersed in prophecy, cultural study, and the power of symbols and language to motivate and influence people. My approach is one that tries to look at the larger picture of human history instead of focusing on the details of a specific event. Other authors present very academic and detailed analyses of Nostradamus's prophecies. That approach works, but not for me in this book. Sometimes you'll find that my interpretation varies wildly from those of other interpreters and experts, but I think that's part of the beauty of the work — the interpretations of his writings are never quite the same twice. This gives Nostradamus's predictions a sense of timelessness.

If you're looking for a specific quatrain that you've heard about or that relates to an issue that's fairly recent, you'll probably find it here, but note that I don't cover each and every quatrain in this book. I've only included some of them to give you a sampling of the flavor and scope of Nostradamus and his works.

Conventions Used in This Book

The benefit of picking up a *For Dummies* book is that you know what to expect — an informal, easy-to-understand book that you can read any way you want (cover to cover or simply by topic of interest). This book is the same in that regard, but *Nostradamus For Dummies* is just a shade different in one aspect, thanks to writings of the star of the show.

As you read through the chapters, you notice that some lines are indented. These lines are *quatrains* — Nostradamus's four-line predictions in poetic form. Nostradamus wrote the original quatrains in a combination of French and several other languages, but I stick to the English translations so you can avoid serious language headaches and get right to understanding what the quatrains mean and how they relate to you. (If you want to go back to the original text, I provide some good pointers for doing so in Chapter 22.)

With any kind of translation from one language to another, there are bound to be different versions, and translating Nostradamus's words is no different. But in this book, I keep this kind of academic talk to a minimum and only mention a different translation when I think something is important for your understanding of the quatrain. If a word or phrase has an alternate translation, you find it within brackets in the quatrain [like this].

Likewise, at times, translators have struggled and ultimately failed to figure out what Nostradamus was getting at with a particular word or words in a quatrain. To signal these untranslated direct quotes from Nostradamus, I've set them inside of quotation marks in the quatrain, "like this."

At the end of each quatrain, you find some numbers and letters in parentheses that look like this: (C III – 42). Nostradamus wrote nearly 1,000 quatrains, so he kindly gave us a system for sorting out which one is which. He divided the quatrains into groups of 100, each called a *century* — that's what the C stands for — and he gave each century a Roman numeral to note which one of the ten centuries it is. In addition, he gave each quatrain within each century a number, so C III – 42 represents Quatrain 42 in Century III. This info is helpful if you ever want to compare this book with another interpretation of Nostradamus's writings.

Finally, to help you navigate through this book, I use the following typographical conventions when I'm not presenting a quatrain:

- ✔ *Italic* is used for emphasis and to highlight new words, terms that are defined in the text, or words that are quoted directly from a quatrain when I refer to them in the course of my interpretation.

- ✔ **Boldfaced** text is used to indicate keywords in bulleted lists or the action parts of numbered steps.

- ✔ `Monofont` is used for Web addresses.

- ✔ Sidebars are shaded gray boxes that contain text that's interesting to know but not necessarily critical to your understanding of the chapter or section topic.

What You're Not to Read

Sometimes the full story is just too much, and you may want information broken down to the shorthand version. If you're short on time (or attention), feel free to skip the text marked by a *Technical Stuff* icon and the text formatted in a sidebar (paragraphs inside shaded boxes), because you don't necessarily need to know this info. Yes, it's interesting — hey, I wrote it, what do expect me to say? — but you can still understand the subject at hand without reading it.

Foolish Assumptions

Before writing this book, I carefully considered you, the reader. Yes, I've been looking into my crystal ball and have come to some conclusions about you. If any of these descriptions rings a bell, you've come to the right place:

- ✔ You've heard about Nostradamus and some of his predictions. Now, you'd like to find out more about him, uncover additional facts and myths, and see how some of his other predictions panned out. You have a curious spark in your eyes to discover just what all the mystery is about and what the predictions really mean.

- ✔ At some point, you've wished that you could look ahead to tomorrow and know what's going to happen (even if it was just on Christmas Eve when you were 7 years old).

- ✔ You're not an expert at translating French, interpreting literature, or understanding symbolism. You want to step around these roadblocks long enough to take some of the mystery out of Nostradamus's prophecies.

- ✔ You haven't been hiding in a hole, so countries, world religions, and major events like World Wars are at least familiar to you, if only by name. If some terms are unfamiliar, don't worry. I straighten them out.

- ✔ You're willing to explore the idea of predicting events in the future with an open mind and the possibility that Nostradamus did something real (his quatrains weren't the result of lunatic ravings).

- ✔ You aren't looking to be an expert on Nostradamus and interpret his writings after one book. If you are, then I'll risk my hand at some fortune telling and suggest that you won't find all the answers here.

- ✔ You're the kind of person who looks at the big picture instead of getting lost in the day-to-day grind. This mindset is helpful, because you have something in common with Nostradamus.

How This Book Is Organized

For you to get a firm hold on the slippery ideas of Nostradamus, the Renaissance, astrology, alchemy, and prediction (all terms that I define and explain within these pages), I broke the book up into parts that give you one piece of the puzzle at a time and together give you a full picture. Parts I and II provide you with the foundation, and Parts III through V contain quatrains that are organized loosely by time, moving from the past to the present and then on into the future. Part VI provides some bonus info to help with your understanding of Nostradamus and his works. Here's a brief description of the parts of this book.

Part 1: Nostradamus, This Is Your Life

Every journey begins with a starting point (you're here) and a destination (in this case, information and insight on Nostradamus and his writings). In this part, I begin by giving you a bird's eye view of the subject at hand, mapping it out like a journey. Then I dive in and start at the beginning with Nostradamus's birth, working my way forward through his adventures and misadventures on the long road toward fame as a prophet. You can't talk about Nostradamus or his writings without understanding the frame around the portrait, so I also take a brief peek at the time period when Nostradamus lived — near the end of the Renaissance.

Part 11: The Big Influences on Nostradamus

Nobody lives in a vacuum, so this part helps you understand how the intellectual movements and metaphysical movements (alchemy, astrology, numerology, mysticism, and superstition) of Nostradamus's time helped to define and shape him. Nostradamus's early education, the influences of his Jewish conversion to Christianity, Christianity itself, his study of alchemy and astrology, and even the Black Plague all stimulated his insight into mankind. This part also gives you some history on prophecy, how it works in general, and how it worked specifically for Nostradamus.

Part 111: The Prophecies From Nostradamus's Time to Napoleon

Nostradamus wouldn't be so popular now if he hadn't developed a reputation during (and just after) his lifetime as a man whose words could predict the future. In this part, I explore some stories about his early experiences with prophecy and the distinction it earned him at the time, which wasn't always a good thing. I also discuss the first published prediction that created a stir, address Nostradamus's concerns with the Church, and introduce the influential queen of France, Catherine de Medici, and her family.

Then I really get into some thrilling quatrains that I believe predicted and commented on the French Revolution and the notorious Napoleon Bonaparte. Nostradamus's visions of these years included the cloak and dagger intrigue that plagued the French court, the trouble that would lead to the French Revolution, and the quick rise and fall of Napoleon's power, which ended at the famous (and predicted) Battle of Waterloo. Nostradamus was a Frenchman by heart, and his concerns often focused on the future of his own country, so I take a moment to honor his concerns for France in this part of the book.

Part IV: The Prophecies of the Modern Era

If the distant past isn't your thing, then the quatrains in this part will be more to your taste. I begin this part with quatrains from around the year 1800 and sweep all the way forward to the millennium. I believe Nostradamus expanded his focus from his own homeland of France to include Europe and the New World. I also think he begins to sound like a severe pessimist, and I explore quatrains and interpretations that are connected with both World Wars, the Holocaust and Hitler, antichrist figures, and the end of the millennium. I also cover quatrains on technology and space travel. And if you're interested in quatrains popularly believed to predict the lives and unfortunate deaths of famous people like Princess Diana and John F. Kennedy, then this is the part for you. Don't worry: After you get past all the wars and death, it's not really that bad when you get to the end of the millennium. But you have to read this part to find out why.

Part V: The Prophecies of a Future Era

Bring your time traveler's passport when you approach this part, because you're going forward into time. This part contains the quatrains that are still hotly debated. They're the ones that touch on what will happen in the future, including changes in religious and family values, natural disasters and events during the Age of Aquarius — an astrological shift that Nostradamus saw as the light at the end of a dark tunnel of wars.

Part VI: The Part of Tens

If you only read one part before you pick up another Nostradamus book, make it this one. I provide the keys to the quatrains by giving you the basics on how to understand a quatrain on your own. I also spend some time on biographical points of interest that help you really get to know Nostradamus the man and explore his everyday life. Finally, I provide a few guidelines on continuing to explore Nostradamus if you haven't had your fill of him and his prophecies by the end of *Nostradamus For Dummies*.

Appendix

Just for the sake of clarity, this appendix presents a timeline of events for Nostradamus's life, as well as events that surrounded his life and were important to his work.

Icons Used in This Book

This book comes conveniently labeled to help you find your way around, and along the way (in the margins), you find road signs that point you to various types of information. Here are the icons used in *Nostradamus For Dummies* and their accompanying meanings:

This icon points out suggestions for interpreting quatrains and getting to the heart of Nostradamus's meanings. Consider the accompanying paragraphs as your self-service, how-to guide to identifying some of the specific techniques Nostradamus used to write his prophecies.

This icon highlights insights and information to keep in mind that are essential to understanding Nostradamus or his works.

This icon indicates a red flag for a possible landmine within the text or as part of an interpretation. Most often these warnings occur when assumptions and myths may lead you to be misinformed or to misunderstand a quatrain.

This icon points out in-depth interpretive techniques or historical background that's interesting and/or relevant to the interpretation or discussion but isn't absolutely necessary for you to read if you'd like to skip it.

This icon points out where history and Nostradamus's predictions still intersect and affect the lives of people — you and me — today.

Where to Go from Here

Alright, you've taken the first step by picking up *Nostradamus For Dummies*. From here it's up to you, because you determine how you use this book. I'm not going to give you reading assignments or look over your shoulder, so feel free to read over the Table of Contents or consult the Index to find a topic that's interesting to you. Your curiosity is a very strong force, and after you've found a topic that interests you, I'm sure your own questions about prophecy and about the past, present, and future will lead you on your own personal and thorough tour of the book.

If you'd like a complete tour of Nostradamus's inner workings, his surrounding world, and his writings (or at least the ones I could squeeze in here), and you don't want to miss a thing, I suggest you read from start to finish. Like a guide in a museum, I take you through the process of understanding the people, places, and events and how they helped form Nostradamus's prophecies both then and now.

My suggestion is to at least skim Chapter 2 or Chapter 3 before you begin to really get into the quatrains. Nostradamus was a product of his times, and many of the quatrains reflect that strongly, so find out what his life was like, and then have at it.

Part I
Nostradamus, This Is Your Life!

The 5th Wave   By Rich Tennant

"I've arranged for you to have lunch with Nostradamus, Your Highness, a scholar and man of extraordinary abilities."

In this part . . .

I hope you have your passport handy, because you're about to journey into the world of Nostradamus. It may feel like foreign territory, but don't worry — you're in good hands. In this part, I give you two tours. One is a general overview — a kind of global picture — of the way Nostradamus's mind worked. The other is a detailed view of his life and the world that surrounded him. This part of the book is your personal portrait of Nostradamus, and the Renaissance is the frame and background. Understand the issues of his day, and you begin to understand the man himself and the reasons he was concerned for the future.

Chapter 1

The Stuff Legends Are Made Of

The future is a funny business. Finding out what's going to happen is never easy, and even if you do, there's a fair chance that your views will never see the light of day. But Nostradamus took his predictions very seriously and published them to make sure that people got the message. For a man who's dead and who only achieved a fair amount of fame in his native France while alive, he's left quite the lasting impact. During his lifetime, the small section of his prophecies that were published gained him notoriety, mainly among those people wealthy enough to purchase his publications. Today, his voice is still heard loud and clear — by *many* more people — throughout the world in the multiple books published in various languages that present his prophecies and attempt to interpret them. For most people, though, Nostradamus is just the name of a famous person who supposedly predicted the future, but beyond that, the information is a bit sketchy.

Nostradamus was a fascinating fellow, and I'd like for you to see him in his element. He was a doctor, a writer, a fair cook (rare for a man during the Renaissance), an apothecary (what you'd think of as an early pharmacist/ herbalist), and a humanitarian. His words focused on the lives of people he'd never meet and the fates of countries he'd never see. From the past, he still reaches out today, handing us a gift of insight and hope that a positive change will occur within humanity.

Meeting Nostradamus

Getting to know Nostradamus isn't easy. It's been almost 450 years since he last sat down to record a prediction, and that much time obscures even the flashiest of folks. But an even greater challenge facing anyone who sets out to chronicle this writer is that Nostradamus's writings rarely focus on

Nostradamus, personally, and only rarely include an indication of his opinions. But more than writings make the man, and knowing some of the details of his life and times can help you understand just who this guy was and why he still fascinates many people today. (Start things off by checking out Figure 1-1 for a glimpse of what he looked like.)

Figure 1-1:
Walking a
mile in
Nostrada-
mus's
shoes.

Scala / Art Resource, NY

The man

Nostradamus was born under the Zodiac sign of Capricorn (for an explanation of the Zodiac and astrology, see Chapter 6), which may not mean much to you. But to an astrologer (who studies how stars influence people's lives) like Nostradamus, his sign revealed a great deal about his overall character. In many ways, he was a typical Capricorn — a determined man who felt a sense of responsibility and was cautious not to be too rash in words or actions.

Now, you may think that the term *caution* wouldn't be associated with anyone who predicted the coming of the antichrists (yep, you meet these characters in Chapter 13) and global destruction (Chapter 18 is pretty intense), but consider this: He waited to publish the second portion of his most famous predictions, *The Prophecies,* until *after* his own death. Folks in the 1500s weren't

Check Out Receipt

Saratoga Springs Public Library
518-584-7860
http://www.sspl.org/

Tuesday, June 7, 2016 4:54:33 PM
77052

Title: Numbers and you : a numerology guide for
everyday living
Material: Book
Due: 07/05/2016

Title: So you want to be psychic?
Material: Book
Due: 07/05/2016

Title: Nostradamus for dummies
Material: Book
Due: 07/05/2016

Thank You!

one regard — predictions of
ys welcomed with open arms.

a Zodiac sign to understand
purpose: You can't define a
le are complex, so you have to
tand Nostradamus, and his pre-
ou have to try to see the world as

product of his times — the
hrough Europe during the 14th,
t the calendar, think late 1300s,
to describe the Renaissance, in
h more than one word describing

an Church had control over learn-
ers and priests were just about
royalty. But then translators and
o the hands of more people, and
sult, more folks began to think,
value people placed on the human
t idea turned into a revolutionary
umanism suggested that there was
an potential to create. Previously,
limited to a divine source, largely

, writing, creating music, reading
veloping a scientific examination of
first, what you believed helped
ice progressed, what you believed
ning was exciting but also uncom-
n't all likely to come to the same
uo started all kinds of struggles
eas and approaches to life clashed
ed a threat to its previously unques-
tioned p

Add in the sweeping political and economic changes that rocked the world —
well Europe, but the people there thought it was the whole world — and you
have a swirling, shifting mixture that's just ripe for mankind to pick a new
direction into the future. Standing right in the middle of this commotion was
Nostradamus who saw the patterns of change emerging and hoped to use his
predictions to warn, guide, and influence the direction of people's lives.

His life

If I say *Nostradamus,* the first thing you probably think of is *future predictions,* and for good reason — they were his major claim to fame. But like his predictions, there's more to Nostradamus than meets the eye. Though *professional future predictor* would've fit on his business card, Nostradamus wore many hats during his lifetime, including student, teacher, astrologer, doctor, pharmacist (*apothecary* was the term of the day), advisor, father, husband, friend, humanitarian, philosopher, alchemist, prophet, and author. Not bad for 62 years of life. (I explore his complete life story in Chapter 3.)

Nostradamus's early education in the standard subjects of the day (such as Latin) helped lay a foundation and provide him with the tools he'd use throughout his life. But, he was exposed to other, shall I say, nonstandard subjects as well, like astrology and the mystical components of the Jewish faith (from which his family converted to Christianity when he was young). I cover many of the key influences on Nostradamus in Chapter 4.

After attending college, Nostradamus took up a career in medicine and made a name for himself by helping the victims of the Black Plague, an incurable disease that spread through Europe, wiping out large populations quickly. Traveling from town to town, he was widely recognized for his work, yet widely criticized among his peers for his unorthodox methods.

After his time as a wandering healer, and after a brief, happy stint as a husband and father, Nostradamus lost both his reputation and his family. He reacted by picking up his doctor's bag and wandering again, but this time he began to look within for answers to life's questions and experience what he believed was the strange power of seeing the future. Nostradamus settled down in Salon, France, and began to acquire a new reputation as a doctor, apothecary, and astrologer who possessed additional skills.

The predictions

If Nostradamus had been content to spend his remaining years as a doctor, apothecary, astrologer, and family man, you and I would've never heard of him. But something clicked as he wandered the countryside, and rumors of his power for prophecy began. But he didn't provide us with written evidence of his insights into the future until he later began publishing *The Almanacs.*

Beginning with yearly publications called *The Almanacs,* Nostradamus used his knowledge of the stars to predict weather and crops. Included in these yearly publications were four-line poems called *quatrains,* in which he predicted events for the year. These yearly publications became so popular that Nostradamus embarked on a larger project of writing predictions for years into the future, up until the year 3737 to be exact. He published these predictions in a separate volume he called *The Prophecies*. Today, the predictions of *The Prophecies* get the most attention of Nostradamus's works, because there are a total of 942 of them.

But after the first three and a half sections of *The Prophecies* were published, Nostradamus decided that although he'd written the rest of this masterwork, it might be better to keep it unpublished until after his death. The Renaissance was a turbulent time, and Nostradamus knew that the Church, French government (especially the royal family who has its own place in Chapter 8), and certain individuals mentioned in the quatrains may not find the predictions for the future flattering, and as a result, they may decide to bring him up before the Inquisition (a kind of Church court that prosecuted enemies of the Church — real and imagined — that you can read about in Chapter 2).

Nostradamus's predictions range from 1555 to 3737 — a terrific scope of vision. He looked around his native France, predicting the immediate future of Queens, countries, and politics for his own corner of the world (Chapters 7 and 8); the French Revolution (Chapter 9); and Napoleon's career (Chapter 10). As Nostradamus looked farther into the future, he saw a wider world and wrote prophecies that embraced his expanded perspective. His worldview of the years ahead included the horrors that would be the World Wars (Chapters 11 and 12), the changes surrounding the millennium (Chapter 16), changes wrought by natural disasters (Chapter 18), and the light at the end of the tunnel — the hope of the Age of Aquarius (Chapter 19). He even foresaw the people of the future, including the royalty of our own age like Prince Charles and Lady Diana (Chapter 14), and changes in the institution of the family (Chapter 17).

Nostradamus continued to write prophecies and draw up astrological charts for predicting people's lives until his death in July 1566. He even predicted his own death, according to one of the many stories told about him, though some stories bear only a passing resemblance to the truth. (See Chapter 3 for a rundown on all of the works Nostradamus published and tales of his death.)

Or should I say, the prophecies?

The art of telling the future is as old as mankind. People are naturally curious and want to know what the future holds. Most of the time, the act of seeing into the future is referred to as *predicting*, or *making a prediction*. That's fine, but it's really not specific enough — meteorologists *predict* the weather, after all. With Nostradamus, things worked a bit differently, and that difference — the influence of a divine force — changes what may be a *prediction* into a more lofty-sounding *prophecy*. My feeling is that Nostradamus used two rather specific ways to look into the future:

> ✔ **Divination:** Some divination systems you may be familiar with are the tarot deck, the patterns in the stars, and all manners of coins, sticks, and stones. Each system involves using *symbols,* a process where one thing

represents another thing (a picture of a heart may represent love, for example), and a person who has studied the symbols and the system interprets them. Divination often focuses on obtaining answers about one person's life.

✔ **Prophecy:** *Prophecy* is a way of performing divination with some form of divine assistance, or aid from a higher power, and often includes meditation or prayer. The purpose for prophecy is likely religious and is generally for the good of all humanity, instead of focusing on one person's life. Skeptics raise even more concerns about prophecies than divinations, because people giving prophecies predict the future *and* claim that the info came in on the divine hotline.

Nostradamus used both divination and prophecy, and in his case, the Christian God was the divine assistance he sought to guide his writings and insights. So, the works Nostradamus produced were technically *divinations* and *prophecies,* but I often use the term *predictions* throughout this book as well, because it's so common. But when I feel Nostradamus must have been particularly hooked up with a higher power to produce such an accurate view into the future, I make sure to point it out — just like I point out instances when lack of sleep seems to have caught up to him and he turned out a real clunker. (I cover the business of predicting the future in detail in Chapter 5.)

The idea that God gave Nostradamus visions helped to give his writings a bit more believability among the very religious population of the Renaissance, and it helped keep him out of trouble with the local Church when push came to shove. Well, okay, it only *mostly* kept him out of trouble (see Chapter 3 for more on Nostradamus's run-in with the Church). The Church didn't really like when people claimed to speak directly with God. That was their job, and they weren't about to be downsized.

So, how'd he do it?

Nostradamus sat at night in the third-floor study of his home in southern France meditating and contemplating the future. He used all the mystical methods he'd encountered, including pieces from Pagan religions, alchemy (see Chapter 6), the Kabbalah (mystic tradition of Judaism), and Christian mysticism (I discuss these last two in Chapter 4). To clarify his visions, he used calculations of how the planets and stars influenced people and countries he saw (check out Chapter 6). After he made his notes (probably in Latin, the language of the learned men of the Renaissance), Nostradamus wrote quatrains in French about the future he saw.

The quatrains were written largely in Provençal French, the language of the region where Nostradamus lived and grew up. But he added in so many puns, symbols, and tricks to confuse the average reader that interpreting his quatrains is difficult even for scholars (I cover the reasons behind this obscurity and some of the tricks he used to blur the lines in Chapter 6). He was trying to communicate, but he went to great lengths to make his writings hard to understand. Negative or wrong predictions could've gotten him killed (see "The predictions" section earlier in the chapter for more on the societal forces confronting him), and not everything came up roses in his visions, so he walked a fine line between telling the truth and pleasing the people who had power. (For more on the form and function of his writings, and an exploration of the quatrains in which he describes the scene of his nightly prediction sessions, see Chapter 5.)

Finding the Key to His Lasting Fame

Nostradamus was a strong believer in the Christian faith, a fact that may surprise you, because many people think of him as a fortuneteller of sorts. But Nostradamus has achieved a different kind of immortality from the kind typically offered through Christianity. His prophecies have been continuously in print since his death, with five to ten new interpretation books per year in the modern era, a record shared only by the Bible. As long as his prophecies are in print, he and his legacy will remain an active part of human life. The trick to achieving this kind of notoriety is to find out what keeps people interested in Nostradamus and returning to his quatrains for answers.

There you have it. Go back and read the last sentence again. That's the key: People want answers. We want to participate in life, but we also want to hedge our bets a bit and know what the future holds. But beyond a glimpse of the pattern of the future, I believe that people want some reassurance that there's a bigger picture, whether it's a divine plan for things or simply a logic for the way the world works. I think that deep within the heart of the individual lies the subconscious need to be connected to the pattern of the universe, or put another way, people don't want to be alone and responsible for all this mess (that humanity has made during the course of our history).

So how does this deep longing to find a pattern relate to Nostradamus? If he was correct with his predictions and was able to connect with a divine power and the pattern that connects all of life, then it's true (or at least possible) that both the divine and the pattern are real. In other words, I think that if Nostradamus was indeed able to predict future events, his feat gives some real foundation to the idea that we're all part of a bigger pattern in the universe, that we belong and are important to that system, and that the pattern has a purpose. We're not just randomly wandering around until wars, disease, and our own technology make us obsolete. Nostradamus's ability to predict the future gives us hope.

I believe people especially turn to Nostradamus because his prophecies have been examined more than any other works that claim to see into the future, and he seems to have had much success in prophecy, judging from the number of quatrains that are widely believed to have come true (see the "Discovering the Truth (or Not) Behind His Prophecies" section later in the chapter).

Whew, okay, if you can swim your way out of that philosophical hole, then you won't have trouble understanding another key that keeps Nostradamus high on the list of recognized names: sheer curiosity. Television executives know that ending a TV show with unresolved issues keeps people coming back. Life, as it has gone on so far, has been one great big cliffhanger, because none of us regular people (who can't see into the future) know what's going to happen next. Nostradamus even made sure that his prophecies weren't only about his own time so that people would constantly revisit his work. His prophecies cover just over 2,000 years, which is a ton of material. Nostradamus insures that people will keep coming back, sheer genius for someone wanting to leave his mark — and a marketing plan that'd be hailed as brilliant if such things existed in his day.

Discovering the Truth (or Not) Behind His Prophecies

The one question that stands out among the debates over the topic of Nostradamus is, "Did he actually predict the future?" And I'm prepared to give you both my answer and other people's answer to that question. But first, I think a more basic question has to be considered: "Is predicting the future possible in the first place?"

Determining whether predictions are possible

For many years, scientific testing of all manners has been conducted to try to prove or disprove the idea of prediction, including testing with coin tosses, astrology, shuffled cards, and other seemingly random procedures. The arguments for and against prediction being real are pretty convincing on both sides and keep many people balanced on the fence and uncertain about their conclusions. In this section, I discuss predictions and my view on whether they're real or just fireside stories, and I examine what critics say about the truth or fiction of Nostradamus's prophecies.

Accounting for one author's view

In the end, whether or not predicting what will happen in the future is possible is a matter of personal opinion, and I definitely have an opinion. Through my own life experiences and after studying dreams, divination, and prophecy for years, I believe firmly that knowing the future is possible. I've been surrounded by the past, the present, and the desire to know the future all my life. It's one of my compelling passions, which is why I'm bringing my ideas about Nostradamus and prophecy to you.

4786230

I also believe that predicting the future can be accomplished in countless ways — divine insight, tarot card readings, astrology, dreams, or other methods (see Chapter 5 for in-depth explanations of these ways). Whether associated with a culture or religion, types of divination have existed as long as mankind has, and for me, that says a lot. Surely people would've put down divination and left it to rot if it wasn't working for them. But every year, people continue to try to view the future, most especially when there's trouble in the world. Major events like terrorist attacks (I explore these quatrains in Chapter 15) and earthquakes (these quatrains are in Chapters 18 and 19) create a flurry of interest in prediction because people want to know how to prepare, how to adjust, and how to react to the changes.

One important distinction you may notice as you read this book is that I believe in predicting the future, but I don't believe that the future is set in stone. I look at it this way: The future that's seen in visions is simply the pattern of life's tapestry as it's currently being woven together, and we still have the ability to make changes to the tapestry as it's woven. You and I have free will to move about in the world and make our own decisions. After all, in my view, we're part of the system on Earth and aren't separate.

Counting on critics

The modern age has brought with it a fascination of all things scientific and provable. Critics of prediction insist that people are merely listening to the parts of a prediction that they want to hear and conveniently tying them to facets of their lives that seem to match. This kind of convenient matching is the key for critics who say we're just filling in the blanks, but I believe that an outline of events can be in place with the details (even ones that don't match) changeable as time moves forward, and we weave changes into the tapestry of life.

For example, imagine that a fortuneteller predicts that a dog will come into your life in the next three days, and the event will be important to your future happiness. Because you're probably like most people and want to be happy, you'll probably be on the lookout for a dog. Two days later, you happen to see an attractive person walking a dog and smiling at you. Events happen, you manage to meet and fall in love, and the fairy-tale ending of your choice follows in due time. Was it the fortuneteller's prediction coming true or just events that were going to happen?

Critics insist that the prediction isn't necessarily true just because a dog was involved in this event. The happiness could just as easily have come from a sudden inheritance of money from a dog-lover than it did from falling in love with the dog-walker. The point is that you're suddenly trying to match the circumstances to the prediction and are in effect making events match the prediction. Unlike the critics, I believe the fortuneteller saw a general pattern, and tipping you off to it is a way of helping you to recognize the potential of that smiling dog-walker rather than ignore it.

It's a dog eat prophecy world, and the critics can continue to debate over whether predictions are scientifically possible, but I prefer to look at prediction with a wider perspective than just the scientific. I give the doubting critics some credit, but I believe that quite possibly the fortune teller's prediction (even if it's imaginary) was a valid way to look at likely patterns ahead. Determining what to do with the prediction is the individual's decision, but the prediction of what's likely to happen is still real.

Turning the attention to Nostradamus

Nostradamus's prophecies keep the average person interested, because people are curious and have a need for hope. Scholars and critics are a tougher crowd to keep hooked, but Nostradamus even managed this feat, because everyone sees something different when he or she reads the quatrains, and the argument over who is right and who has missed a clue within the twisting words of the quatrains makes for an interesting academic study. Beyond academics, though, everyone wants to know what's hidden in the prophecies to know what events are going to happen in the future.

Ever hear the story about the five blind men who all touched the same object? Each one described what he experienced, but every description was different. They were each touching a different part of an elephant, and the tusks, feet, trunk, tail, and skin are all very different when described individually. Both scholars and critics of Nostradamus are like the blind men, seeing only a small piece of the elephant-sized picture. I believe that if you listen to everyone and don't discount everything, eventually the truth will find an outline, and you can recognize the whole elephant (true meanings and messages from Nostradamus) among the quatrains.

Critics of Nostradamus

Not everyone agrees that Nostradamus was the best of the best when it came to slinging prophecy and creating astrological charts. Even astrologers who shared the same night skies doubted the man they referred to as an amateur. The list of evidence to support their claims that Nostradamus was an amateur astrologer included inaccurate planet positions in his charts, missed calculations, including two suns in an astrology chart, sloppy conclusions, and inaccurate predictions that were almost completely opposite of what actually happened. These objections arose mainly from the yearly almanacs but were applied to the *The Prophecies* after they were published.

In modern times, objections to Nostradamus aren't based on his astrology but on his choice of words (namely, that they're obscure) and the fact that all the predictions seem to be recognized in the clarity of hindsight. Critics tend to discount foretelling if there isn't enough information to actually recognize the event *before* it happens.

If you look at the prophecies after an event and say, "Hey, Nostradamus predicted this," you run the risk of using _selective agreement,_ which is a lot like selective hearing: You pick out the parts of a quatrain that agree with what you want to see (like the details of an event) and then ignore everything else that might contradict that point of view. The unusual symbols and vague references within the quatrains make Nostradamus's prophecies a playground for those people who want to interpret his words to suit a particular need (especially political). Nostradamus's critics frequently remind everyone that the reliability of the prophecies is just about average, statistically speaking.

Supporters of Nostradamus

The people who avidly read and study Nostradamus's works tend to think that critics are overly harsh on the man who was trying to save his own neck from persecution. They say it's not Nostradamus's fault if the real meaning in the quatrains remains hidden until after a predicted event has happened. It's possible that Nostradamus intended the real meaning to be discovered afterward as a record of events that couldn't be changed but that he foresaw. Later seers like Jeane Dixon even divided their predictions of the future into two categories — those that could be changed and those that would happen regardless of anything else.

I believe that Nostradamus thought it was important to have a background of valid quatrains (those that were identified _after_ the event as being right) to provide the rest of his prophecies with a foundation of legitimacy. He was building a reputation, you see. This kind of record would support the idea that the other predictions were true, if only the meaning could be deciphered. Knowing that some quatrains have been identified as real prophecies (predictions that have come true) makes looking at the other quatrains more interesting and worthwhile. People want to keep reading his work, meaning Nostradamus succeeded in his goal of leaving a record for mankind.

This book reveals that by and large, I believe Nostradamus had a pretty strong knack for this kind of work. I also believe that he was human, and people make mistakes, which would explain why some of his prophecies seem like gibberish and some of the prophecies are just wrong. Either that, or the way we understand the individual quatrains is faulty, which is always a possibility.

But the interpretations within this text, as with any text on Nostradamus, are just that — an individual's thoughts on what Nostradamus might've meant. My thoughts about the power of prediction and prophecy (that they're real and interesting areas of study) have influenced my interpretations of the quatrains. Keep this in mind as you read through _Nostradamus For Dummies_ and develop your own opinions.

Throughout the book, I give you tips and guidelines for coming to your own conclusions about Nostradamus's meaning so that you're not stuck listening to me. I'm just here as a guide and to provide you with the right tools, so you can get your own idea of where you want to go to do your own exploring.

Hearing from Nostradamus himself

Although Nostradamus didn't have a publicist to make sure that press releases contradicted bad reputation or rumor, the prophecies themselves became a tool for him to rebuff critics. In the *Preface* to *The Prophecies,* written to his son, César, Nostradamus admitted that his prophecies weren't going to be easy to decipher. Apparently, the real meanings are only going to become clear when a new age appears, and ignorance becomes a thing of the past. I guess that time is now, because here I am with the power of technology and worldwide publishing, writing *Nostradamus For Dummies.*

Nostradamus admitted in the *Preface* to *The Prophecies* that he clouded the meaning of the quatrains intentionally, and he made no apologies for being difficult to understand. Most people who study Nostradamus believe he clouded the meanings to prevent the ignorant (who might misuse the information) and the vengeful (who might kill him) from figuring out what was going to happen in the future.

In The *Epistle to Henry II* (another writing by Nostradamus that contains prophecy), Nostradamus noted that his critics may find him hard to understand. But Nostradamus made no attempt to explain why he insisted on writing this way, other than to say that only wise people (whom he described as people who studied the same mystical traditions he did) would be able to understand his prophecies.

Chapter 2

Winds of Change: Renaissance Life

In This Chapter

▶ Walking a mile in Renaissance shoes

▶ Trying to improve Medieval medicine

▶ Working on alchemy and astrology

▶ Paying homage to the Mother Church

▶ Changing minds in art and thought

▶ Being wary of the political scene

This chapter takes you on a stroll through the streets of Nostradamus's world. The bonus is that this is a *For Dummies* stroll, so I've tried to limit the amount of muck you get on your shoes.

Limited amount of muck aside, you may wonder how it could possibly matter to you what Nostradamus's world looked like. It matters plenty. The filth in the gutters (Renaissance sewage system, rats included) helped spread the plague and provided an opportunity to increase the healing reputation of one Michel de Nostredame (now forever known as Nostradamus). In addition, the superstitions of the common people and the power of the Catholic Church were everyday concerns for Nostradamus. The events and controversy that surrounded him became common themes in the prophecies that made him famous. So crawling into his world is like crawling into his mind a bit, and doing so can help you understand how and why he chose some of the topics for his prophecies.

I'll warn you upfront that The Renaissance Ride was one of the wildest rides history ever conceived. Art, money, and deep thinking — all the things that make life worth living — spread like wildfire (along with disease). The fuel for those radical changes came from some uncommon sources. If you feel a little dizzy and confused bouncing between the Church, businesses, and governments of the time, don't worry too much. Walking in the Renaissance is like walking on shifting sands of thought.

What Was Rocking the Renaissance World

After the gray and depressing plagues and wars of Medieval times, the *Renaissance,* or "rebirth" from the Middle Ages, turned the attention of many in Europe toward the bright, shiny lights of humanism (which valued human thought, creativity, and beauty), personal advancement, discovery, learning, and financial rewards. Music, nonreligious paintings, and debates about the purpose of mankind were the new artistic pursuits of the day. And business was good: New banking and manufacturing methods helped increased trade. It was, in a way, the European Spring.

In addition to all its forward-looking attributes, the Renaissance also took a long look back at the past. Scholars and other bookish types returned to the works of the thinkers and philosophers of ancient Greece and Rome for insight. The likes of Aristotle and Plato were again discussed in the parlor rooms of the elite throughout Europe. (Nostradamus was a young and very eager student of these new ideas and ancient texts, and you can find references to many Renaissance concepts in his writings.)

Historians usually place the beginning of the Renaissance at the end of the 14th century in Italy. From Italy, the spirit spread across Europe, gaining a toehold in different countries at different times, and lasting through the late 16th century. These dates are a bit imprecise, because the period we know as "the Renaissance" wasn't defined and labeled until after the fact. It's not like everyone woke up across Europe one morning and decided in unison, "Hey, what we have here is the Renaissance." The Renaissance began to bloom fully in Nostradamus's France under the rule of the first Renaissance king, Francis I, who ruled from 1515 to 1547, just as Nostradamus was getting his education and establishing his career (see Chapter 3).

Of course, not everything changed during the Renaissance. The Catholic Church saw to that (see "The commanding presence of the Catholic Church," later in this chapter). And although science and medicine began to make advances, there was still room for future innovation. For example, people still generally agreed that the sun revolved around the Earth, and illness was caused by badness in the soul.

Even though the Renaissance kept some of its medieval flavoring of faith and superstition, I still say the Renaissance folks took a large step toward changing into the scientifically oriented people of today. Renaissance people asked questions and sought answers about science, philosophy, and observation — a shocking notion that the Church disliked. In some ways, the elaborate clothing and display of wealth during this period was a rebellion against the Establishment. If this notion sounds familiar, think tie-dye and "returning to nature."

It's all there in black and white

In an era without indoor plumbing or paperback fiction, one of the most astounding changes seen during the Renaissance began in 1455, when Johann Gutenberg perfected a *movable-type printing machine* that quickly printed multiple copies of a single manuscript. Immediately (well, almost immediately) following Gutenberg's accomplishment, the first printed Bible was produced (for a bit of trivia regarding this Gutenberg Bible, see the "Name that Bible" sidebar in this chapter).

Although reading and writing had been around for as long as anyone could remember, the common man (peasants who made up about 95 percent of the population) didn't have access or need for the written word, especially because they couldn't read. The nobility and upper classes were the real bookworms. Until the late 15th century, Joe Medieval learned everything he needed from standing next to his master craftsman and from on-the-job experience. He received any spiritual training he needed from church sermons. Printing, instead of the painfully slow process of hand copying manuscripts, allowed for the quick and cheap distribution of information. Anyone who has done public relations or even a yard sale can understand the impact this kind of quick paperwork has.

The printing press was for the Renaissance what the Internet has been for the 20th century: a highway of ideas — some good, some bad, some just downright controversial. The printed Bible, in particular, would provide people with greater access to spiritual texts — and even those texts not controlled by the Christian Church (gasp!). People began to read about and understand for themselves the faith they'd only heard about from priests.

You may not be surprised to find out that the Church had strong objections to the new printing techniques. Officially, the Church objected that the speed of the layout created errors and made the printed texts lower quality than earlier texts. (Of course, the Church *never* made errors in its publications.) But unofficially, under the Church's campaign of "win friends and influence people," the idea was that if you control what people know or read, you can control them. The Church knew that if it lost the monopoly on information, it could lose most of its power and political influence. Imagine, if you will, the Christian Church skating on thin ice.

Looking back at humanism's foundation

The *humanist movement* was a literary and nonreligious movement that began in Italy in the late 14th century and moved onto other European countries — including France in the late 15th century. It celebrated everything that was beautiful, creative, or powerful about humanity, especially if the individual found dignity through reason and logic. In addition to new endeavors, the movement emphasized the deeply contemplative teachings of ancient Greece and Rome. (Humanism had a strong influence on Nostradamus's education; see Chapter 4.)

The printed word's particular super-power during the Renaissance was that people began to think on their own and study the literature of the ancient civilizations. Printers and writers dug up the thoughts of the Greek and Roman writers, the classics from the pagan and Christian traditions, and even some fictional prose. The antique theories of life and its purpose found in this literature began to emerge in print all over Europe, influencing everyone's ideas — again! And know this: The Renaissance thinker deserves your respect because he typically took the time to read and study theories both in the original Greek and in translation. Pretty impressive, eh?

Taking a look at some of the common theories discussed and published during the Renaissance can give you further insight into the depths of the humanist movement:

- **Neoplatonism:** Platonius, the founder of this school of thought, stated (around the 3rd century A.D.) that the universe was an expression of a universal God or One, and that man was a down-line part of that One. Man's soul, however, could choose to express itself in perfection through learning or spiritual growth or fall off the bandwagon and indulge in the sensual and corrupt worldly experience. Salvation for such lost souls could be found through ecstatic experience and personal choice to return to life before corruption occurred. This school of thought was revived by the Renaissance and became part of Nostradamus's education.

- **Aristotle:** A prolific Greek mathematician, writer, philosopher, and statesman, Aristotle was a great friend of scientific thought and deductive reasoning (moving from general knowledge to more specific). Although Aristotle died in 322 B.C., his works were translated and reprinted widely during the Renaissance.

- **Docta pietas (learned piety):** This 12th-century concept suggested that one of the true ways to achieve a pure religion was to study secular languages, natural sciences, and law. These studies sharpened the mind and prepared people to read and comprehend deeply (as opposed to just nodding their heads in agreement during church).

- **As above, so below:** This concept, although originally part of the ancient alchemy tradition, suggested that the beauty and glory of God didn't have to wait until a person died. The natural world, including (and especially) people, was part of a beautiful reflection of the divine. (If you don't know what alchemy is, don't fret. Just divert thine eyes to the section "Much ado about alchemy," later in this chapter.)

Name that Bible

The now-famous Gutenberg Bible wasn't actually published by Johann Gutenberg, but by Johannes Fust. It seems that after spending his time and investors' money on expenses to create the first movable-type printing machine, Johann Gutenberg couldn't pay his bills. Johannes Fust, one of the investors who "pressed" to be repaid, took over Gutenberg's equipment in lieu of payment. Fust hired other printers to complete the publication of the famous Bible, but history remembers Gutenberg as the father of the Bible. After losing his shop, Gutenberg continued to work in other small print shops.

Take heed: Summarizing theories that have taken thousands of years to explore and express can be very dangerous. Such ideas don't take well to shrinking. For a more complete idea of what the various philosophies contained, go to the original texts.

Okay, people, settle down into classes

In a strange similarity to high school, the Renaissance had its cliques. The "in" people were easy to spot. They were the nobles with the fancy clothes, the right manners, and the money for leisure activities that made the Renaissance famous (or in high school made the local papers). The average folks were the people who didn't break any records but lived fairly decent lives as clerics, merchants, and professional people.

But here's the twist: The in crowd and the average folks comprised a very small part of the population. Below these classes were the commoners, or peasants, and their existence wasn't easy. A social structure based on *feudalism* reigned, where a lord owned the land that the peasants worked on. Peasants paid a percentage of their harvest to the lord for his protection and were tied to the land in an almost slave like bond. In Europe, approximately 95 to 97 percent of the population belonged to this struggling third class. The bright and shiny lights of the Renaissance definitely didn't fall upon everyone equally.

Oddly enough, the social classes that divided society during this age slowly began to break apart (like high school cliques after a year of college). Merchants started earning enough to walk the talk of the noblemen, and peasants left the land for cities that promised more money and an increase in social status. These changes happened slowly over many years, but the plague's heavy toll on the population helped kick start this shift in the classes.

Oh, behave!

The Middle Ages were a time of very strict expectations for how everyone should behave, and the changes of the Renaissance didn't alter the social ideas of the day very much on the surface. Arranged marriages were the standard operating procedure during the Renaissance. Wealthy families were so eager to show off their success that they'd bankrupt themselves for the ceremony and dowry. In addition to extravagant marriages, the nobility made a point of living the high life for all to see. Great weekend hunts were held, along with sumptuous dances and balls, with famous artists (Leonardo DaVinci even) creating the decorations.

Know too that folks had to be careful about how they acted on the streets. Laws weren't in place to protect the people but rather to punish those who offended society. Crimes considered the worst included murder, treason, heresy, witchcraft, counterfeiting, arson, rape (unless the offender was married), homosexuality, and failed suicide attempts. These capital crimes were sure to send the accused to the town square. Almost any time folks walked into a city, they'd find the latest criminals hanging around the town square — by the throat. Of course, the lucky ones (mostly nobles and gentlemen) were beheaded, because this way of dying was supposed to be the least painful.

Putting on the Ritz

From the soles of their raised shoes or *pattens* (worn to keep "above it all" in the filthy streets) to the tight hose on men's legs, the Renaissance was definitely a time for the well off to flaunt their stuff. Women's dresses were stiffened to stand out with wires to hold up the heavy brocade, and even men's shirts were inset with furs and richly woven cloth. People knew the power and prestige of others by how much new Venetian lace or how many precious stones were sewn to their clothing and hair. Jewels, lace, and formality were the brand names that everyone who was anyone showed off. Take a look at the nobility in Chapters 7 and 8 for an idea of how the upper crust lived.

The government in most cities imposed limits on what different people could wear (a woman married many years couldn't wear pearls, for example), and some people — like lepers and former prisoners — were even required to wear certain colors as a warning to others. Even doctors like Nostradamus were expected to wear long robes with a particular three-sectioned hat. (Interestingly, doctors also typically wore multicolored coats, which were supposed to protect them from disease — a strong superstition — but Nostradamus kept to his scholar's robes and physician's hat.) Like the teen who's told he can't do something, though, some of the up-and-coming merchants thumbed their noses (metaphorically of course) at the restrictions and sewed jewels to their robes and outfits.

Scratching the itch to explore

Like strict parents, the Christian Church told the world that the only thing to explore was one's own heart. But the Renaissance brought with it the christening of a new urge to explore. Navigators dusted off old maps of the world and began to look at them like treasure maps. And at that point, they were. New areas of the world were opening up to trade routes that could make countries very rich very quickly. Monarchs and countries reached out their greedy hands for the wealth and prestige of discovering new countries and new resources. It seems everyone had his eye on the prize, and crews set off in record numbers from ports in England, France, the Netherlands, Africa, and Portugal.

Enter Christopher Columbus. Beyond having an itch for the financial rewards of expanding territory, this Italian explorer wanted to continue spreading the Christian faith far and wide. However, Columbus didn't have great piles of money, and his strange ideas (like that the world was round) gave him trouble when he tried to find financing. Finally in 1492, with the cash provided by King Ferdinand and Queen Isabella of Spain for his expedition, Columbus reached the Americas, and the world hasn't been the same since.

This age of exploration gave Nostradamus a broadened sense of where people fit in the world and how large the world really is. Instead of focusing entirely on France, or even Europe, Nostradamus included in his prophecies the people and lands that were only just then being discovered.

Main Ideas in Medicine

I bet just the mention of Medieval medical practices gives you images of darkened rooms and torturous procedures. The Renaissance tried to improve on some medical practices, but between the plague, superstition, and doctors doing everything from spreading lies to making false accusations about other doctors, making any headway was truly hard.

Most of the common medical knowledge, including what Nostradamus was taught at school, seems laughable today. For instance, people believed that

- **Heavenly bodies controlled human bodies.** Renaissance doctors often consulted the position of the stars before performing any treatment. They believed that certain positions of the stars and moon were more favorable to cures. (Some healers still today prefer to work under a full moon because of its gravitational effects on the Earth.)

- **The costlier the cure, the more successful it was.** Because trade and wealth ruled the day, the more something cost, the more likely people found it useful as a cure. Resources used for cures included spices from India (nutmeg for colds) and gold (taken internally for leprosy).

✔ **The body was made of four elements called *humors*.** The elements of the body were earth, air, fire, and water, and they were associated with four by-products of the human body — blood, phlegm, yellow bile, and black bile. Doctors believed the relative colors (or discolors) of these humors indicated such ailments as depression or a tendency to catch a cold.

✔ **Boiled toad helped the heart.** As wild as it sounds, boiled toad is exactly what doctors prescribed for heart disease. Much later in history, scientists discovered that the skin of some toads contains digitalis, which is a common heart drug today.

A plague on all your houses

Large outbreaks of the *Black Plague* — a nasty virus that spread via fleas on rats (although a variant also became transmittable through the air and saliva) — occurred throughout Europe for generations, from the middle of the 14th century until the late 17th century. Although the exact origins weren't clear, most scholars believe the epidemic began either in Asia or India and arrived via port cities (they were the first to succumb to this disease). The plague was also called the Black Death because of the black oozing spots (blood and infection under the skin) that appeared on victims' skin. In a little under a week, nearly 75 percent of victims died. The government and Church officials offered little help during the Black Plague outbreaks and other epidemics.

Sometimes thought to be the punishment for a bad soul, the plague soon came to be recognized as an equal opportunity killer of nearly one-quarter of the European population. The epidemic created fear and mistrust, and infected people were shunned and abandoned.

Did any good come out of the plague? Consider the job market: Workers were needed in every craft and guild as manufacturing and trade increased. With that much opportunity (and fewer people to enforce the feudal system), peasants left their lands to become free workers in cities.

The plague, along with childbirth and smallpox, presented the most challenges to the doctors of the Renaissance. The desire to search out and eradicate plague was one of the factors that motivated Nostradamus and other educated men to look to nature (herbs) and science for answers. Still, the most common method of treatment was to *bleed out* a patient of the ill humors that were in her blood system. In other words, doctors cut on the body or used leeches to remove the bad blood from the patient. Interestingly, Nostradamus generally refused to engage in this practice, despite its noble history dating back to the days of early Egyptians.

Cross your fingers and swallow this

Nostradamus started practicing medicine just as the medical profession truly began to get organized. Before the 1500s, the Church governed the practice of medicine, because people commonly believed that most illnesses originated with the curse of God.

In Nostradamus's time, though, schools for physicians were established in the large cities of Europe. With the start of medical schools came the idea of limiting medical practice to licensed and qualified people. After all, folks didn't want an unlicensed doctor bleeding them (see preceding section).

Medicine relied on guesses and knowledge from prior generations to explain the workings of the human body until Andreas Vesalius (1514–1564) began dissecting the human body. The Church forbade God-fearing bodies to be used, so the bodies of criminals were used for scientific research. Vesalius contributed to the study of anatomy by requiring detailed drawings of the dissected parts.

In 1488, the first official *apotheke* (or *apothecary* — the 15th century version of a pharmacy/herbal shop) was created in Berlin. With the spread of natural remedies and a new scientific approach to medicine, the number of apothecary shops increased. I wonder whether Nostradamus could've predicted that 500 years later mankind would once again turn to herbal remedies for modern ailments.

Checking In with the "Other" Arts

Alchemy and astrology, along with magic, were collectively called the *hermetic arts* of the Renaissance, and they were precariously seated at the edge of the Catholic Church's tolerance. The reason? People who studied such ideas were often viewed as working with the devil or, worse, playing God. Nostradamus, though, attempted to use his knowledge of alchemy and astrology to further his connection with the divine (which I discuss in Chapter 6).

Much ado about alchemy

You can trace the cornerstone of alchemy back to Egyptian metal workers who tinted metals a warm, golden yellow to please pharaohs and wealthy patrons. From these sweaty and humble beginnings came the study of *alchemy,* which is basically the science (and I use that term loosely) of using secret knowledge and strange chemistry secrets to change regular old metal into the shiniest of goals — gold. But Nostradamus didn't pay attention to alchemy for the gold — he wanted the philosopher's stone.

Harry Potter may have found (and then lost) the famed philosopher's stone, but guess what? It's been missing for ages. Okay, I know J.K. Rowling's book is entitled *Harry Potter and the Sorcerer's Stone* (Scholastic), but we're talking about the same stone here. Trust me.

Depending on whom you listen to, most people believe the stone was never real to begin with, but practitioners of the art of alchemy pursued this powerful stone for thousands of years, and with the Renaissance revival of the Greek and Roman philosophers, alchemy gained a renewed following. These pseudo-scientists studied chemistry, philosophy, and just about any other "ology" they could find in an effort to obtain the allusive philosopher's stone that would turn easily acquired metals into gold — a leprechaun's dream if ever there was one. (There's no record that alchemists ever successfully turned base metals into gold.)

The philosopher's stone (if it really existed) was also supposed to provide immortal life, cure disease, and raise one's mind and soul to be in harmony with God, a goal Nostradamus could really get involved in. True alchemists went beyond the quest for money to search for the other wealth that could be obtained through the process of studying alchemy. The process of refining metals toward a golden end can be (and was) compared to the process of removing the impurities from a man's soul and forming him in a new mold. Although the metaphor of the change sounds harsh, the men who mixed their religious and philosophical beliefs side-by-side with their powders found the process to be very empowering. Through careful study and application of the mind, an alchemist could find a pure heart that connected him to God.

Physicians like Nostradamus became interested in alchemy because the elusive philosopher's stone promised health cures and immortal life — always-attractive skills for the practicing doctor.

The art and science of stargazing

Every known society has developed some belief about the roles and meanings of the stars and their heavenly positions. Renaissance Europe was certainly no different. Physicians consulted the moon to find out when to treat the plague, and everyone requested horoscopes from the noble and well-known Nostradamus.

Astrologers of the time believed that all events — good, bad, past, present, future — were written in the movement and placement of the stars. Following the theory that God lay his plan out for the looking and that the stars were the keys, the Renaissance astrologer could then know the plan of God, and interpreting the stars would put him dangerously close to stating what God had preordained. The Church wasn't too keen on that notion. Another issue was that the Renaissance astrologer's belief system ran afoul of the Church's belief that man had free will. The Church knew that getting people to accept its free will teachings would be difficult if people believed their actions were already written above them each night.

Theory discussions aside, you may wonder how 16th century astronomers actually astrologized. Well, one thing to consider is that Nostradamus and his fellow astrologers drew all the star charts by hand. The stars themselves were observed with the naked eye and placed on the charts. The angles between constellations, the horizon, and everything else were calculated by careful math and a collection of charts containing many angles and reference numbers (the astrologer's cheat sheet).

In addition to having charts and a strong head for math, the Renaissance astrologer owned a brass *astrolabe* to assist in his calculations. An astrolabe is a model of the celestial world formed by overlapping several brass discs (which were frequently highly decorated) to form a picture of the heavens. An astrolabe allowed astrologers to accurately tell time, determine where planets were in the skies, and even determine latitude (perhaps the very first Global Positioning System used in the exploration of the world).

Although observation and science increased in popularity during the Renaissance, you can't underestimate the power of fear and superstition during that age. For example, Haley's comet makes a pass by the Earth approximately every 75 to 78 years, and it stirred up trouble every time it streamed across the night sky during Nostradamus's time. The superstition was so strong that the crowned heads of Europe — and even the pope — held off on big decisions until the comet passed. Seriously. (Check out the "Charming superstitions" sidebar in this chapter for a few more superstitious situations.)

Astrology wasn't just a once-in-a-lifetime event where you got your chart made; it was a way of life. At the birth of a royal or noble child, the parents frequently requested an astrologer to read the stars and tell them about the child's future.

Charming superstitions

Here are a few other superstition tidbits from the Renaissance era:

- Children getting christened wore religious images, medals of saints, and rosaries to protect themselves from being bewitched.

- People believed that cutting a child's fingernails caused her to become light-fingered (a thief).

- A child born with a deformity or a peculiar birthmark was the sign that the crops for that region would be unsuccessful.

- Burning toe nail clippings, especially during the full moon, would bring good luck.

- A powerful witch could change the weather, cripple a horse, and make a woman barren.

O Father, Where Art Thou?

Lost souls knew just where to look for salvation, education, and guidance on marriage and death: the local church. The Medieval Age left a legacy of faith in the Church as correct in all things religious, but the people of the Renaissance started drawing lines that actually separated the Church from other parts of life.

The commanding presence of the Catholic Church

After Emperor Constantine I legalized Christianity in 313 A.D., Christian beliefs changed how the world worked. Instead of many paths to many gods, now only one path to salvation existed, and it was through the Catholic Church. Outside the connection between God and salvation was an intolerance of other beliefs that ran deeper as time went on. With the Roman Empire supporting Christianity's claim, this exclusive religion found itself in a very powerful position — and liked it.

Being the big religion on campus wasn't always easy, however, and the Church had its faults. While the Black Plague made the common man wonder about the wrath of God, the rest of the Church suffered from an identity crisis. Some of the priests, with their large houses and elaborate robes, apparently thought money was close to godliness, because it brought them close to nobility. To find power, they were even willing to sell indulgences, which was a way people could pay for extra forgiveness. By controlling and influencing the rulers in Europe with its power to grant official permission to rule (kings often ruled by *divine right* or by the selection of God, something the Church could help sanctify), the Church was meddling in affairs of state rather than affairs of the spirit and came to resemble an earthly political power rather than a spiritual center.

The power and pain of the Inquisition

You've probably heard of the Spanish Inquisition, but did you know it was only partly Spanish? The French also participated in this grand house cleaning. The Inquisition began as a way to clear out the troublesome Moors (a Muslim sect living in Spain during the 15th century) and developed into a tool for the Spanish, French, and Italian governments to handle the affairs of state under the holy banner of religious uniformity. Christopher Columbus even took some of the Inquisition with him on his voyages, and one version of the Inquisition held fast to Mexico until Mexico gained independence from Spain.

During the reign of the Inquisition (a leftover of the Middle Ages that gained new power in Spain around 1492), Jews were forced to convert or leave the countries of France and Spain. And even the people who accepted Christianity were under a cloud of suspicion because the government figured they may be wearing the mask of Christianity while still having Jewish or Moorish hearts.

Frequently, the people brought under scrutiny by the Inquisition weren't the traditional witches of song and story; they were intelligent statesmen who flaunted the restrictions of the Church. Even Nostradamus himself was under scrutiny.

On the road to purifying the Church, which was one of the Inquisition's overall religious goals during the Renaissance (for other goals, look toward Chapter 4), the Inquisitors made a few personal stops. People who had quarreled with the local priest or said something uncomplimentary about the leading Inquisitor were likely to find themselves answering sticky questions or facing death.

The men who shook it all up

So a guy walked into a church in 1517, and then he walked out again and nailed 95 statements to the church door of the castle in Wittenburg. This guy, Martin Luther, started a reform process that led to the formation of separate branches of Christianity called Protestantism and Lutheranism and the idea that the inner heart of a man and his faith will find him a place with God. Overall, this theory sounded pretty good to the Renaissance people, who were well acquainted by now with the idea of using reason, logic, and one's own experiences to define an experience. At first glance, the problem with that way of thinking was that it removed the need for priests, because people began to consider religion for themselves. If man could find his way to God with just a pure heart, what purpose did the priest serve? The priests felt like they were being downsized. After people could commune with God on their own, there'd be no real need for priests as the intermediary to talk with God for the people.

Martin Luther's action of nailing his thoughts to the castle church door wasn't actually an act of vandalism like you may suspect. In the days before quick copies, placing important announcements where everyone could read them was common.

Perspective is an amazing thing. The glass is either half-full or half-empty. The reason I bring this notion up is that following closely on the heels of Martin Luther was the somewhat more zealous John Calvin, who was either a coura- geous man or a heretic, depending on who was asked during the Renaissance. Calvin, who wrote and published his first book on theology in 1536 when he was only 26, learned from Martin Luther but took his ideas further by declaring that individuals didn't need priests to rule their lives and that the power of

Church officials was limited, including the power of the pope. Calvin believed that every man's life was destined by God to happen in a particular way (known as *predestination*). In other words, God has a plan, and nothing you do or say changes it.

Those Who Gave Form to Ideas

The ancient thinkers and philosophers started the fire of change in the Renaissance, but the people who truly made the Renaissance stand out were the Renaissance men who learned to love art and beauty for the sole purpose of appreciating the art, a concept that was part of the humanist movement discussed above.

Big names in the art of, well, art

Perhaps you've never taken in an art gallery or a museum, but I bet you've been to the movie theater and seen the latest from Hollywood. Movies today are like the paintings and ideas of the Renaissance. Both are technically well developed and try to push the edge of what's been done before.

Because Renaissance artists, influenced by the ideas of humanism and the love of humanity's power to create (for more on humanism, look at the section, "Looking back at humanism's foundation," earlier in this chapter), were no longer restricted to just church paintings, they experimented and expressed their own ideas. Wealthy folks spent huge sums of money to decorate their world, particularly with images of themselves. People became bored with the idea that just because the world wasn't perfect, it had to be ugly or, well, boring. People wanted their surroundings to be beautiful and inspiring.

Squint at the lower corners of Renaissance paintings, and you see some very familiar names, of which I can only name a few:

- **Leonardo da Vinci (1452–1519):** In addition to creating the *Mona Lisa* and *The Last Supper,* Leonardo completed an intensive study of philosophy and anatomy. This man of many talents believed that painting was more powerful than science because it involved study and creation. (If you want to know more about him, check out *Da Vinci For Dummies,* published by Wiley.)

- **Michelangelo (1475–1564):** Each of Michelangelo's projects became more elaborate than the last. He was ultimately responsible for painting the Last Judgement on the wall of the Sistine Chapel, painting the rest of the Sistine Chapel (a blend of man and God in harmony), and creating the famous sculpture of David.

✔ **Raphael (1483–1520):** A student of Leonardo, Raphael quickly produced fine paintings (largely with commissions from the Church) that accented arrangement of figures and visual imagery.

Through these accomplished artists and their peers, the human body was unwrapped again (do I see shades of Greek sculpture there?) and honored as a thing of beauty. Man was a part of nature, and both were beautiful. The art reflected life, and both were worth celebrating. These artists brought the idea of the human form and true-to-life details alive, but their methods were unconventional — specifically, their topics strayed away from the strictly religious figures encouraged before the Renaissance. Don't get me wrong, the Church with its wealthy patrons and large buildings was still a major client for these artists, but the Church wasn't the end all and be all of art anymore. While Nostradamus prepared to see across the centuries, these artists provided the Renaissance with a sense of scale and perspective on everyday life that was equally as impressive.

Big names in the art of changing the way people thought

Looking through the ages, you may not be able to separate out the daring people who sparked the beginnings of humanism or the people that started the economic and scientific changes of the Renaissance, because so very many people were involved in this societal movement. Although a number of shining stars certainly gleamed in the Renaissance night, I only have space to briefly mention a few. My apologies to the rest who must sit aside:

✔ **Desiderius Erasmus (1466–1536):** A Christian humanist, this deeply thoughtful man of the Renaissance wrote widely and disliked anything extreme in religion. He preferred tolerance and some flexibility in religious practice. He greatly influenced Nostradamus.

✔ **Niccolo Machiavelli (1469–1527):** A political writer from the heart of the Italian Renaissance (just before the French Renaissance), this man believed that the ends justified the means of establishing and defending a state. He based his ideas less on Christianity and more on the idea that rulers aren't ruled by the same morals as the rest of the people. Many of his ideas are similar to later ideas that underpin the French Revolution (more details on that are in Chapter 9).

✔ **Giovanni Boccaccio (1313–1375):** A humanist writer from the early part of the Renaissance, Boccaccio's most famous work was the telling of 100 stories that reflected his views on society. He was a friend and supporter of Francesco Petrarch, one of the men considered to be the founders of the Renaissance.

> ✔ **Marsilio Ficino (1433–1499):** A priest who learned astrology, this gentleman translated many of the ancient texts. He saw no conflict between the work of astrology and Christian thought and was highly admired by Nostradamus, who struggled with many of the same philosophical issues about mixing astrology and religion.
>
> ✔ **Nicolaus Copernicus (1473–1543):** A Polish astronomer, mathematician, and economist (this guy could do it all), Copernicus probably turned Nostradamus's world inside out more than any other man with his theory that the Earth moved around the sun.

The Hot Political Climate

I mainly consider the Renaissance a social revolution, but the changes in people's thoughts were echoed in the changes of the leadership in countries all over Europe. During the early Renaissance, the Church and rulers struggled over who would be king of the hill, and Nostradamus witnessed some of this struggling during his lifetime. I limit my discussion to the struggles that would've been most familiar to the prophet.

What was up with France and England

France and England found a kind of unsettled and temporary cease-fire after the Hundred Years War (which lasted 116 years, from 1337 to 1453), and they were both worn out from the war that lasted almost half of the Renaissance (and at least five French kings from the Valois family line; see Chapter 8 for more on this group).

In addition to the battles between the governments, the people of both countries endured endless territory struggles among the nobles of the city-states. The middle classes of these countries, and their counterparts in Spain, supported the rulers as they took control back from the corrupt common law courts, the bickering nobility, and the power-hungry Church. The average person was tired of the wars and paid the heaviest price when the soldiers living off the land invaded, especially in France where the majority of the campaigns, minor struggles, and conflicts of the Hundred Years War took place. (Troops who traveled great distances often took the food they needed from the villages surrounding the battles instead of waiting on supplies from back home.) By the end of King Louis XI's reign in 1483, the individual city-states of France learned to get along, and that type of peace followed in England a few years later under Henry VII's rule from 1485 to 1509.

Although the countries themselves began to settle down, France and England didn't necessarily get along with each other any better than they had before the Hundred Years War. The issue of trade and religion continued to plague their relationship, and after a short rest, the countries were soon fighting again. Although times of peace existed, the two countries never found a true equilibrium.

The treacherous English throne

Being associated with royalty was especially dangerous in England during the Renaissance. Contenders for the throne were often assassinated (Edward Stafford, the duke of Buckingham, for example was accused of treason and killed), and queens married to Henry VIII were notorious for losing their heads. In his lifetime stretching from 1491 to 1547, the English King Henry VIII managed to marry six wives — something the Catholic Church just didn't want to allow. But not a man to be stopped, Henry set up his own Church of England and very quickly came to be the head of his own church. (Talk about a swelled head.)

Of Henry's six wives, only the last, Catherine Parr, survived him. As for the rest, two wives were executed after being held in the Tower of London (adultery wasn't cool in the 15th century either), and one wife died during childbirth. In addition, one marriage was simply annulled. In the middle of his marital maneuvers, however, King Henry VIII found time to become king of Ireland and head of the Irish Church.

The Holy Roman Empire and the German throne

At the end of the 15th century, Germany as the central portion of the Holy Roman Empire, found itself surrounded by conflict on every side. But it was still a considerable power.

The states within the Empire operated independently and with much confusion and jockeying for position while political control issues had the king of Germany and the Church playing tug-of-war. One thing remained constant at least: The Hapsburg family remained firmly seated in the Holy Roman Empire's throne (thanks to a ruling by the imperial electors in 1338 that stated that the German king automatically became the emperor of the Empire, so being the German king made you the Roman Emperor, a nice double feature).

As kings/emperors went, first came Frederick III (made king of Germany in 1440 and ruled as Emperor 1452–1486), second came Maximilian I (became the first elected Holy Roman Emperor in 1486), and then came Charles V (1519–1558) with a cross and a basket. Charles V gathered an impressive collection of countries (during Nostradamus's lifetime) but was unable to create the unified Christian empire he wanted. It seems our friend Martin Luther with his gang of German Protestants (who supported religious freedom) battling against the French was too much for Charles to overcome.

The conquering quests of the great bear

In the time leading up to the Renaissance, Russia found its Czars. Ivan III and then Vasili III ruled over the entirety of the Russian lands, and in 1533, Ivan IV (known as Ivan the Terrible) came to power at the tender age of three. The Russian Empire was constantly stretching its borders and taking the Renaissance idea of absolute monarchy seriously. Siberia, Lithuania, and Poland all found themselves invaded, conquered, or at war with the *great bear,* Russia's nickname because of its association with the constellation Ursa Major (known as The Great Bear).

Interestingly, in 1547, when Ivan IV was crowned as the Czar of Russia, Moscow was almost entirely destroyed by fire. Such an epic event could be attributed to the close buildings and danger of fire in that century, but who's to say that the event wasn't a warning of Ivan's natural tendency to be a troublemaker? Huh? Huh?

Chapter 3

The Man Behind the Legend

*P*erhaps the only thing more debated than the meaning of Nostradamus's prophecies is how he came to be the visionary, prophet, healer, and all-around good guy that you've heard about. Many biographies of Nostradamus have been written and revised, but precious little in the way of verifiable information (first-hand recorded information and not just stories told over and over) about his day-to-day life can be found.

Most of the information about life during the Renaissance and for Nostradamus comes from scholars looking at old paper notes and leftover accounting registers. There obviously isn't any home video of Nostradamus writing, so his life story has been pieced together from town hall records, letters to friends, and the kind of notebooks and journals that are kept in attic trunks and discovered later on. Scholars peek at these pieces of paper and like sleuths, discover information hidden among the seemingly useless writings. But the key point is that these are actual pieces of paper from that time period

Nostradamus was a product of his time, yet he was also ahead of his time. He was a man who felt the transforming energy of the Renaissance and the struggle to survive the Black Death. Through examining his life's story, you can start to uncover the ideas and concerns that were of special interest to him — and you begin to see why he wrote the prophecies that he did. In this chapter, I take you on a whirlwind tour of the personal life, professional triumphs, and writings of Nostradamus, walking you through the events that helped him form the most talked about predictions ever written. I tiptoe lightly over some of the less documented areas of his life and focus instead on the aspects that made him famous in his own time and on into ours.

The Early Years: Safe at Home

The birth of Nostradamus was celebrated by parents Jacques de Nostredame and his wife, Reyniere de Saint-Rémy, on December 14, 1503. The last part of Mom Nostredame's name, *de Saint-Rémy,* was a way of saying that she was from Saint Rémy in Provençe, France, where Nostradamus was born. The proud parents called their son by his given name, but you know Michel de Nostredame by the Latin version of his surname, Nostradamus.

Many folks believe he changed his name for his writings and predictions, but the exact reason he made the change isn't clear — though it could've been for religions reasons (in case he needed to hide or deny his identity from the powerful Church, which wasn't very positive toward prophecy) or because taking Latinized names was the fad of the day.

Growing up in southern France

Early in his life, Nostradamus developed quite the reputation as a doctor (see the "Taking his healing prowess on the road" section later in the chapter), and when trying to figure out why he excelled in this line of work, you don't have to look any further than the landscape of Provençe for your answer. Provençe, a region in southern France known for abundant orchards, olive groves, and flowers, was a perfect backdrop for the young Nostradamus. There, he was constantly exposed to a variety of plant life that would make any decent natural conservatory jealous. Plants became a resource for Nostradamus as he began to study medicine and the apothecary arts. (During Nostradamus's time, *apothecary* was a title for someone who prepared, mixed, and sold "medicines," which were largely made of herbs and oils.) He used his innate knowledge of the local plants to develop treatments and cures for the plague.

Oh brothers, where art thou?

Nostradamus had four brothers, but history has left only a few bits and pieces about them. One interesting tidbit is that Jean, the youngest son, showed a flair for writing like his brother, but instead of predictions or poetry, Jean wrote songs and commentaries. In addition to dabbling in the arts, Jean de Nostredame became the Procureur of the Parliament of Provençe (public prosecutor for the region). Having a lawyer in the family who was also a government official was probably very handy for someone as controversial as Nostradamus.

~~bbbb~~ glasses
yoga mat
taxes
photos
cellar
bleach ~~teeth~~
porch steps
garage door
Barn roof
Chimney
Jack basement

Provence also provided Nostradamus with a poetic language to use in his prophecies. Despite changing French rulers and invading armies, the people of the region steadfastly maintained their own unique qualities, including a dialect of French (virtually a language of its own) well suited to poetry. Nostradamus wrote most of his prophecies in the French of his day, but he used the subtleties of his native Provençal dialect to increase the meanings and depth of his poetry. (See "The Prophecies," later in this chapter to discover more on this topic.)

Forging family ties

The shadow Nostradamus cast clouded the details of the people and events that made up the rest of the Nostredame family. Historians do know that his family tree included doctors, merchants, public officials, and scholars. With encouragement from his family to learn and to achieve great things, Nostradamus's home life must have helped spark his intellect and fuel his search for answers to life's burning questions. By taking advantage of the money and education available to the eldest son, Nostradamus was able to show his true colors as a doctor, astrologer, and humanitarian.

After Nostradamus began his formal education, little information was documented about his immediate family members or their interaction in his life. Historians do know, though, that like other youngsters from professional families, he probably traveled around (to broaden his education) and stayed with his grandfathers, cousins, aunts, and other family members during his childhood and early teenage years while learning much from the formal and informal schools of the age. Although Nostradamus was naturally inclined to examine the world around him (he was a true Renaissance man, after all), the family's nurturing of Nostradamus and their early recognition of his quick mind can be credited for a great deal of his confidence.

The School Years: Soaking Up Knowledge

In a world without TV and video games to distract a young man, brightly colored St. Rémy kept the curious Nostradamus occupied. In my school days, he would've been called precocious. But in his day — and coming from what you and I would classify as an upper-middle-class family of scholarly people — people regarded him as bright. His parents knew that Nostradamus's quick thinking and vivid memory weren't skills to be ignored, so they began his schooling early. And he took to schooling like a sponge takes to water. Apparently the "early to learn, early to rise to fame" idea worked, because Nostradamus pursued information, answers, and ideas the rest of his life.

Spending time with great-grandpa

In 1512, at age 9 (the equivalent of a fourth grader), Nostradamus's education was handed over to his maternal great-grandfather, Jean de Saint-Rémy. If ever a man had an impact on Nostradamus's prophecies, it was great-grandfather Jean. Although other people and life experiences were important to Nostradamus (I tell you more about that in Chapter 4), if you look at Jean and Nostradamus, the resemblance was remarkable — both were doctors and astrologers, both studied Hebrew and the Judaic mystic tradition of the Kabbalah, and both sensed the importance of power and position.

Some of Jean's lessons were part of a curriculum also taught in public schools, though certainly not at the one-on-one level of Jean's class. Jean's curriculum included Latin, the language used for formal lectures at schools and universities and used at court. He taught Nostradamus the Greek classics (in their original Greek), which gave Nostradamus a firm grasp of the ideas and theories that underpinned 16th-century Renaissance Europe. Hebrew and Mathematics rounded out the basics of Jean's instruction. Other lessons were informal but still influential. Beyond the basics, Jean shared his interest in Jewish mysticism and the occult (see Chapter 4), celestial science and alchemy (see Chapter 6), and medicine. These topics sparked the young boy's interest and eventually grew to become his lifelong passions.

Unfortunately, Jean passed away while Nostradamus was still an adolescent. Called home after this sad death, the teenage Nostradamus was again sent away to be educated — this time to his paternal grandfather, Peyrot (Pierre) de Nostredame, and the schools in Avignon.

Attending school in Avignon

The town of Avignon, a strong center of Christianity and the focus of Renaissance thought at the time (a Provençal Ivy-League town), had a powerful influence on Nostradamus during his teenage years. In this town, Nostradamus first began to gain notoriety — both good and bad — for his ideas about astrology and the universe.

The good notoriety came from the quick memory and astute insight that Nostradamus demonstrated almost the minute he began his studies. He amazed his teachers by memorizing and reciting long sections of text in Latin that kept his classmates struggling. This talent served him well in the classroom, in his own private studies, and during the strenuous oral exams to become a physician, which I discuss in the following section.

The things that caused Nostradamus some trouble can still, in certain circles, raise an eyebrow or two. In the vast libraries of the academic town, he continued studying astrology, which he began studying with great-grandpa Jean (see the preceding section). Astrology was considered a scandalous topic because the powerful Catholic Church viewed it as heresy, and it was a killing offense for those people not on good terms with the Inquisition folks and local church officials (see Chapter 2 for more on the Inquisition).

In addition to astrology, Nostradamus took interest in Copernicus's crackpot theories (like the Earth moving around the Sun). Those theories were fascinating but not very popular at the time, and Nostradamus was viewed as slightly odd because he was both brilliant and still believed those theories.

Studying medicine at the university

After studying at Avignon, Nostradamus went to the well-respected University at Montpellier in 1522 to become a doctor. I suspect that due to the powerful interest he had in the questionable celestial sciences (which he studied independently for nearly eight years at both schools), his family pushed him to do something "respectable" with his life.

A determined mind can take any situation and fulfill his or her destiny. I believe that for Nostradamus, destiny meant that he was going to be writing the prophecies that would influence people for years. But to get to that point, he needed a career to support himself while he grew into his role as prophet. The study of medicine would provide just such a career. Going into medicine wasn't a far stretch for Nostradamus, because some of his family members had been doctors and because physicians were taught astrology — partly for the math involved (which would've left me behind) and partly because of the Renaissance belief that the stars controlled parts of the body.

At Montpellier, Nostradamus was no frat boy. He was a fabulously quick study, as in serious geek. (Do you hear that Hogwarts theme music in the background?) In addition to attending formal classes, Nostradamus learned as much from his classmates as he did from his professors. His classmates included some heavy-hitters in the intellectual world, including Sylvius (Jaques Dubois), a leader in the field of anatomy, and François Rabelais, a humanist, physician, and writer of a humorous and scandalous series of books depicting the adventures of two giants (Gargantua and Pantagruel).

Nostradamus earned the equivalent of his bachelor's degree from the University at Montpellier in 1525. His postgraduate education to gain the Renaissance equivalent of a doctorate was interrupted by outbreaks of the Black Death, which forced the school to close and the faculty and students (some very unprepared) to go out and treat the victims. So Nostradamus put on his scholar's cap and robes (traditional physician attire of the time) and struck out into the world (see the "Taking his heading prowess on the road" section later in this chapter for more on this as well as his post-doctorate trip).

Although students didn't normally treat patients, Nostradamus had a great deal of confidence and strode out to treat plague victims in the countryside. In many ways, it was a homecoming for him — a return to natural surroundings. His treatments were so successful that he returned to Montpellier with a strong reputation (and maybe a chip on his shoulder) concerning his unique techniques and abilities, but I save that discussion for later in this chapter when I get to his particular healing methods.

Shortly after reentering the University at Montpellier in 1529, Nostradamus earned his doctorate, despite disagreements with the faculty about his strange treatments. The university professors were men of their age, stuck on old medical practices, and believed that "what's good enough for our grandfathers is good enough for us." In addition, any advances made by one doctor were kept secret because they represented a corner on the market of cures. The idea of healing as a generally charitable institution hadn't fully developed, and sharing just wasn't a skill they'd developed yet.

Nostradamus, who didn't follow the old school and willingly shared his new ideas with the students he met, created quite a scandal for the established professors. Despite a lack of records from the university, some biographers claim that Nostradamus spent a short time teaching at the University at Montpellier after his successful treatments in the countryside. At a college today, his degree would be called a Doctorate of Philosophy, and his office would be placed at the end of the hall away from the "serious" professors.

Taking his healing prowess on the road

During his time in college and in the years that followed, Nostradamus twice took his mind, cures, and scholar's hat and traveled the countryside to treat the population that was dying from plague. Here are the approximate dates and cities of his tours (and the map in Figure 3-1 shows you just how much travel was involved — most of which was by foot or horse):

- **1525–1529:** Nostradamus stepped out into the world at the ripe ol' age of 22 and began to make quite a name for himself during his first trip while he was still a student. He went to Narbonne, Carcassonne, Toulouse, Bourdeax, back to Avignon where he began his early education, and finally returned to Montpellier in 1529.

- **1531–1534:** Another outbreak of the plague (and a disagreement with the staff; see Chapter 4) was incentive enough for Nostradamus to wander again after earning his degree, this time through Bordeaux, La Rochelle, and Toulouse, before ending up in Agen (see the "Life in Agen: Good, Bad, and Ugly" section later in the chapter).

As he wandered, Nostradamus had other things than just the plague on his mind. The variety of plants in the surrounding countryside gave Nostradamus's inner apothecary a little gleeful grin. He sought out local apothecaries and made notes on both the good and bad methods he encountered, and he later used this information to publish a small book on methods, recipes, and the general state of the apothecary trade. In the *Traité de fardemens et confitures,* Nostradamus listed those apothecaries whose methods he approved of and even those who were questionable in his eyes. I discuss the general trend of Nostradamus's publishing later in this chapter.

Figure 3-1:
At home in France with Nostradamus.

Although some people called Nostradamus a quack, most of the population called him quick. His radical cures seemed to do the trick on the plague, and even in a time of very slow travel, the fame of Nostradamus's treatments spread — something that was true from the first time he began wandering through his settled time in Agen (which I get to in the following section) until the end of his doctoring days. Here are a few of his cutting-edge cures:

- Nostradamus recommended running water and fresh air for patients. His approach was the opposite of that used by most doctors at the time, who recommended shutting away the sick to contain the disease.

- While most doctors were *bleeding out* patients (cutting their bodies or using leeches to remove the evil and other bad stuff), Nostradamus made a stir by refusing to bleed his patients (although in one publication he admitted to bleeding patients without any success in treatment).

- Nostradamus insisted that patients constantly suck on lozenges he prepared from rose petals and that healthy people use them as a preventative. Because of the vitamin C in the roses, this treatment was probably helpful to his patients. Many people felt the lozenges were a cure for the plague and that Nostradamus was unbelievably fabulous.

So much was he appreciated that one town gave him a stipend of money every year for the rest of his life. (Oh, to have such gratitude!) But at the same time, other doctors claimed that he danced dangerously close to the edge of being irresponsible (not to mention what the owner of the local Leech Emporium likely thought of him as sales tanked).

Life in Agen: Good, Bad, and Ugly

Even wanderers need to rest, and Lady Luck had an opportunity ready for Nostradamus in 1534. Through reputation alone, the philosopher Julius-César Scalinger heard of Nostradamus and wanted to meet with the man behind the stories. Nostradamus obliged and traveled to Agen, where Scalinger lived.

As mentors go, César Scalinger was a fine feather in Nostradamus's hat. In addition to being a very opinionated humanist, Scalinger attempted an organized evaluation of poetry and literary criticism. Scalinger was also a doctor, but his skills weren't in healing the plague. He focused on improving the study of botany (the study and classification of plants), an area where Scalinger did not stir up as much trouble as he did elsewhere in his life.

Nostradamus and Scalinger only enjoyed each other's company for three or four years until they had a quarrel. No one is really sure what the quarrel was about, and it's water under the bridge of time at this point. (Check out Chapter 4 for more on Scalinger's influence on Nostradamus.)

Upon moving to Agen, Nostradamus found love, marriage, and happiness. But as happens sometimes, Lady Luck can turn sour. After a while, awful events interrupted the pleasant times and changed Nostradamus's life forever.

First comes love, then comes marriage

Life in Agen, at least for a while, was pleasant enough for Nostradamus. He even found love in a young lady and married Henriette d'Encausse around 1534, although there's some debate as to the name of his wife. Everything seemed to be coming up roses for Nostradamus. A healthy physician's practice, a wife, and two children (whose names aren't known) completed the picture of happiness for Nostradamus and kept him settled for a while. A short time passed, however, before the plague struck a blow close to home.

An outbreak of the deadly Black Death sprung up in Agen, and the prosperous doctor was kept busy healing the afflicted. During the plague outbreak, his wife and children fell ill, though no clear records state whether it was the plague or another illness. Sadly, Nostradamus's cures failed him in his hour of need, and his wife and children died.

His wife's family was so upset by this event that they sued Nostradamus for the return of her dowry. Not only was his personal life in shambles, but his professional life also took a serious nosedive. No one wanted to hire a physician who let his own family die. The effects of the deaths and bitter accusations on Nostradamus were disastrous. Agen became less and less a place of rest for the wandering man.

What — me? Heresy?

Just when Nostradamus thought life couldn't get any worse, it did. A year or so before the plague hit Agen and killed his family, Nostradamus walked by a man constructing a statue of the Virgin Mary. Nostradamus made a passing comment that the man was casting devils (by making such unattractive images of the Holy Virgin). Nostradamus didn't bother to explain himself to the workman and likely didn't think any more of the matter.

The artisan must have thought — and talked — a bit more about the matter, because some folks got offended. After the deaths of his family, the Inquisitors asked him to come to Toulouse to explain the now year-old comment and to defend himself against a charge of *heresy* (opinions, ideas, or actions that were against — or believed to be against — the teachings of the Catholic Church). Nostradamus decided that going to Toulouse and explaining his comment to the Inquisitors wasn't in his best interest. So, because Agen wasn't the only place in Europe suffering from the latest plague outbreak, he picked up his doctor's bag and headed out the door. Fast.

Nostradamus left the city where his reputation was destroyed and headed out into the countryside to restore his confidence and livelihood. During this time, the first rumors of his prophetic powers surfaced (see the following section). Nostradamus didn't write down his insights at this point in his life, though, so rumors of these prophecies are all that have survived (check out Chapter 7 to hear about them for yourself).

The actual moment during Nostradamus's life when he began having prophetic visions remains a mystery. If Nostradamus had visions before the mid-1530s, there aren't any records from his early schooling or travels to prove it. But there isn't a guarantee that these papers would've survived nearly 500 years either.

Time in Salon: Looking into the Future

For six years, Nostradamus criss-crossed France and parts of Italy, treating victims of the plague in cities and villages along the way. From his home in Agen, he went to the Lorraine region in eastern France and then to Venice and Sicily. After this journey, Nostradamus returned to France — to Marseilles — and settled for a while. The plague rang, though, and he answered the need for assistance in Aix in Provençe and Lyon.

When the plague started to decline in 1547, Nostradamus went to the beautiful walled city of Salon, France. He intended to settle down to his work as an astrologer, apothecary, and prophet. Medicine didn't make Nostradamus famous in the long run, and he placed it squarely on the backburner for the remainder of his life. Maybe he was worn out from serving as a doctor to the ill and dying and felt the time had come to take care of himself.

Overall, Nostradamus's life included more than just prophecy during his time in Salon. He made cosmetics, read and wrote on many topics, drew up astrological charts and made individual predictions for people based on the stars, and helped finance and build a canal. Nostradamus was even a model and devout Roman Catholic at this time and attended mass and confession on a regular basis. Salon was a time for Nostradamus to show his true colors, and in the end, prophecy (whatever color that might be) colored everything he did from this time forward.

Life in Salon

Almost immediately upon moving to Salon, Nostradamus met and married Anne Ponsard Gemelle, but for nearly three years he still occasionally followed the call of the plague, traveling to cities that needed his expertise. Anne had two things going for her: She was rich, and she was a widow. Doctoring had been mildly profitable for Nostradamus, but a little extra cash never hurt. Anne's age and experience as a widow gave her a fair understanding and acceptance of the eccentric Nostradamus. Together these things made her a good match for the determined prophet.

Nostradamus changed the top floor of their home (actually, it was just one large room) within the walled confines of Salon into a retreat for himself where he could pursue his private studies in alchemy, Kabbalah, and astrology. This attic study in Salon is the place where Nostradamus saw his nightly visions and wrote *The Prophecies*. (You can find the details of how he accomplished these tasks in Chapter 5.) He didn't, however, remain hidden in his attic, and he managed to have six children with Anne.

While living in Salon, Nostradamus went from doctoring people to doctoring their cosmetics and facial creams. His medical practice became more of an apothecary practice for the local wealthy clients. In 1552, Nostradamus published his knowledge of this trade in *Traicté des fardemens et des confitures,* or in plain English, *Treatise on Cosmetics and Conserves.* (Well, almost plain English.)

Unfortunately, the lower classes didn't take as kindly to the strange new doctor as the wealthy did. Their distrust existed for a couple reasons: Nostradamus was a Jew who converted to Christianity (religious beliefs can stir up emotions quickly), and he was also an astrologer, which wasn't a respectable occupation among the common people.

Turning out his most famous works

While in Salon, Nostradamus seemed to have lived a fairly peaceful existence — if you call staying awake in the night to write down prophetic insights peaceful. He didn't find a reason to wander too far from home during the last few years of his life. He did, however, travel far and wide in the adventures of his mind and began to record his thoughts and publish them.

Why did he start to write down prophecies at the time he did — and not earlier or later? Perhaps his confidence had returned from his travels through Europe. Perhaps his mind was overflowing with the knowledge and information he'd gathered as he traveled. Or, and this is my theory, perhaps he was distressed by the unhappy political situations and religious fighting in France and the surrounding lands. The possibilities for why he wrote are as wide open for discussion as the enigmatic writings he created are.

The most famous of Nostradamus's publications are those that contain his predictions for the future — also known as *prophecy*. Nostradamus started with small-scale predictions (floods, civil unrest) and then moved on to the heavy stuff (world wars and antichrists). This book covers the whole gamut.

The almanacs and prognostications

In 1550, Nostradamus started off with a small project — a yearly publication that contained information about the upcoming year's weather and events, along with quatrains that predicted events for months in the coming year (not all the months had quatrains for them, however). Originally, he called the small publications *almanacs* because they contained traditional almanac kinds of information — weather, astrological information, and so on. Nostradamus began including in the title the term *prognostications* — which means foretelling events in the future — after the success of the first couple almanacs generated interest in his quatrain predictions.

Nostradamus published these yearly (and sometimes twice yearly) almanacs or prognostications until 1566 or so. Even though many of the almanacs were lost to time — like the sale paper for the local grocery store might be tossed out today — many of the predictions were collected by Nostradamus's assistant, a man named Jean Aymes de Chavigny, and included in a work called the *Presages*.

The predictions in these yearly almanacs were only occasionally accurate, but his supporters never wavered, and his sales were brisk enough to be encouraging. The information published even contained some very glaring errors, but some Nostradamus interpreters believe that the inaccurate information was intentional — a way of drawing attention to the date specifically because the date predicted was wrong. Only those people who were in the know of all things mystical or who knew astrology noticed the mistake and thus paid attention to the date. His "mistakes" were like coded messages that only those with secret decoder rings could see.

The Epistle to Henry II

During the publication of the almanacs, Nostradamus occasionally paused and printed other items of interest. One of those items was an open letter to King Henry II of France, which dedicated the second edition of *The Prophecies* to the king. This letter was called, oddly enough, the *Epistle to Henry II*. In this letter, Nostradamus addressed the king in very glowing terms but proceeded to predict gloom and doom for the entirety of Europe (see Chapter 11 for one such prediction). *The Epistle of Henry II* was a strange way to honor Henry, but Nostradamus saw his dedication of the prophecies as an offering at the feet of the great king. See the section, "Friends in high places," later in the chapter for more on ol' Henry and his queen, Catherine.

The Prophecies

While Nostradamus continued to produce his almanacs, he also produced *The Prophecies of Michel Nostradamus,* which became his most impressive work and covered events through the end of the world (see Figure 3-2). *The Prophecies* became his big kahuna — the granddaddy project that took much of Nostradamus's time and energy. The topics covered in *The Prophecies* weren't limited by the upcoming year (like the almanacs); they stretched far and wide into the future and around the world to touch every shore.

Nostradamus divided his prophecies into groups, called *centuries,* and each individual prophecy within the group was written as a four-line poem, called a *quatrain.* The first set of prophecies was published in an incomplete form in 1555 and contained only the first three centuries (300 verses of predictions) and an incomplete fourth century. A second incomplete publication (this time of 642 quatrains) was published in 1557, but some scholars have suggested that this is a forged copy of *The Prophecies.* The complete text of his prophecies were published after his death (he died in 1566) and contained ten centuries, one of which was incomplete (see "The publication of his prophecies posthumously" section later in the chapter). For more on the prophecies and the mechanics behind writing them, see Chapter 5.

Other works of interest

Although I mainly focus on the quatrains in *The Prophecies* and a bit on the *Epistle to King Henry II* in this book, those works aren't the only ones that come to mind when discussing Nostradamus. The first publication of *The Prophecies* had a dedication to Nostradamus's son, César, and is commonly called the *Preface to César* — no mystery there. In this dedication, he tells the world (and his son) that he's writing so the world might be a better place one day, and he tosses in a few prophecies for good measure.

Another work that seems to arise during Nostradamus discussions is something referred to as the *Sixains* — sets of prophecies written in six-line poetic form rather than the four-line quatrain Nostradamus mostly used. These predictions were published in 1605 along with a reprint of *The Prophecies*. However, there's no real way to determine whether these are truly lost predictions of Nostradamus, the work of an imposter, or simply the overly helpful hand of Chavigny (Nostradamus's assistant; see the "A devotee" section later in the chapter), who could've taken Nostradamus's notes and created his own predictions. Chavigny wasn't known as an impersonator, though, so I doubt he's the author of these predictions.

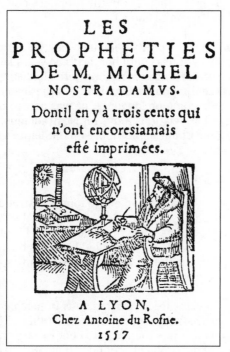

Figure 3-2:
An early copy of *The Prophecies*.

Meeting his best supporters

Many of today's most successful superstars will tell you that their family members are their biggest supporters. Nostradamus's situation was no different — his wife and family were behind him through everything. But they weren't the only people who stuck by Nostradamus through good times and bad.

Friends in high places

After the publication of the partial prophecies of Nostradamus, France expressed mixed emotions about the work. People who read in the quatrains success for themselves were delighted; others (especially people in Paris at the royal court) who saw themselves slighted or found unhappy endings weren't so quick to declare *The Prophecies* a grand success.

The rumors at court were so intense that Nostradamus came to the attention of Queen Catherine de Medici, wife to King Henry II of France, and she summoned him to Paris for some one-on-one questioning — particularly about a prophecy concerning the king's death that appeared in the 1555 edition of *The Prophecies.* (Chapter 7 gives specifics about the prophecy concerning the death of King Henry II, if you're dying to know.)

Nostradamus must've provided some pretty good answers. Catherine continued to consult with him (or his writings) until her death 34 years later in 1589. Her children, including future kings of Frances were often subjects of Nostradamus's prophecies (see Chapter 8). Eventually, Catherine named him Physician in Ordinary, or in common language, he was named the royal doctor in service — a great public relations move for Nostradamus, even if the title was only honorary. (See Chapter 4 for more on Catherine's influence on Nostradamus's life and work.)

A devotee

The extremely wealthy weren't the only people who found Nostradamus's prophecies interesting, and a man by the name of Jean Aymes de Chavigny made quite an impact on Nostradamus when he came into his life around 1554. Chavigny, as his biographers and friends called him, was the mayor in Beaune, France, but gave up his position to study astrology and astronomy with the famous Nostradamus in Salon.

A student of Nostradamus, Chavigny freed Nostradamus from many of the mundane tasks associated with astrology and prophetic writing, like copying and translating texts. Nostradamus was then able to concentrate on the business of writing the nearly 1,000 quatrains of prophecy that later made him famous. Chavigny is responsible for keeping records of many of the prophetic quatrains that were part of the yearly almanacs, few of which have survived the ravages of time. Chavigny's most important role, however, was probably as an editor (along with Nostradamus's widow) of the full prophecies upon their publication after Nostradamus's death.

But, I'm not too quick to thank Chavigny, because I have some doubts about his ability as an editor. The records Nostradamus left behind don't indicate that Chavigny was a very favored student, but Chavigny tells a different story — one where he's the favorite companion to the prophet. If Chavigny's tale of day-to-day life varies from other records and he overestimated his own importance with Nostradamus, I think Chavigny very possibly overestimated his power to understand and edit the prophecies as well and could have made changes that didn't reflect Nostradamus's intentions

Ladies and Gentlemen, Nostradamus Has Left the Building

Although nothing lasts forever, the legend of Nostradamus has lasted longer than most things. He managed to last 63 years on Earth and died in 1566 in his own home. Nostradamus has managed to make his publications and reputation last nearly 500 years.

A prediction of his own death

Biographers are conflicted about the exact details of the last hours before Nostradamus crossed over (to where, I'm not quite certain). Nostradamus's death created the strongest of all his controversies (surprise, surprise), and it has been talked about for years among historians, biographers, and the general rumor mill.

- Nostradamus is *rumored* to have predicted his death verbally to his secretary, Chavigny, but no proof exists — just Chavigny's word, and he was known to exaggerate on Nostradamus's behalf.

- Nostradamus was buried, and then his grave was robbed during the French Revolution, which I believe he did accurately predict. No evidence exists, however, that a mystical medallion around his neck revealed the date his body would be disturbed as some legends have suggested, although it makes a great ghost story.

- Nostradamus did predict his own demise in *The Almanac* written for the year 1566, but he missed the date either intentionally or on accident. Presage 141 (the name generally given to the prophecies in the almanacs he produced) is associated with November of 1567 and not July 1566 when Nostradamus actually died.

- Nostradamus was buried standing upright, supposedly to prevent people from walking on him, although no solid evidence exists that proves he worried about such a trivial matter.

The publication of his prophecies posthumously

A writer's life can be tough (editors, slim payments, and the critique of the entire world), but Nostradamus was a writer and a prophet, which made life even more complex. He faced all the dangers a radical writer would expect to face in the Renaissance, as well as trouble from imposters who wanted to use his name for their own purpose. It ain't easy being Nostradamus.

Keeping it real

Most writers are eager and even pushy about having their works published right away. After the wandering trips settled down a bit, Nostradamus began publishing bits and pieces on medicine, the apothecary trade, and even some translations of other people's works. Although Nostradamus was very regular about publishing his almanacs and prognostications, he was hesitant about finally publishing the entire collection of prophecies.

His hesitation was probably caused by a fair sense of self-preservation. Not everything he predicted was tea and cookies for everyone, and the upper classes and royalty seemed to have the hardest time overall in his prophecies. Keeping the prophecies quiet until after his death meant that the accusing eye and wary look that turned on him after he predicted King Henry II's death (see Chapter 7 for the details that got him in trouble) wouldn't have any effect on him personally. After all, he'd be dead.

Nostradamus's widow and his assistant, Chavigny, arranged to have the entire collection of prophecies published in 1568. In all, they allowed 26 valid editions of the quatrains to be published.

Forgery is the finest form of flattery

As the almanacs and prophecies gained in fame, the temptation to use the notoriety of Nostradamus for nefarious purposes became too much for some individuals. The printing of *The Prophecies* spawned at least four specific forgeries that are known, recorded, and in some cases still exist in a few rare book collections. For example, one 1649 reprint of Nostradamus's prophetic works contains forged quatrains about Jules Mazarin, the chief minister of France at the time. Mazarin's enemies probably used the quatrains to encourage public doubt and lower his image within France. Other false editions have been printed so that a publisher could claim to have found new material in order to increase sales. (Some of the forgeries even came from the same printing presses as the authentic almanacs.)

The trend of bending prophecies to fit the needs of a person or situation has continued through the ages (like the forged quatrains that circulated after the September 11 terrorist attacks, which I discuss in Chapter 16) and, in a way, is a tribute to the power of Nostradamus. The endurance of Nostradamus's prophecies makes him one of the most imitated writers in history, and I'm sure he would be both frustrated and proud all at the same time.

Part II
The Big Influences on Nostradamus

The 5th Wave   By Rich Tennant

NOSTRADAMUS' EDITOR

"War, famine, plague...Pretty grim stuff, Michel.
How about a dating tip prophecy? Or one about
vacation spots, or what to do with leftovers,
just to round out the book?"

In this part . . .

Part II offers insight into how events and people influenced Nostradamus and his writings. You meet the teachers, family, friends, and members of royalty that touched his life and, thus, influenced his works. Then I dive straight into the depths of prophecy and how it works, because Nostradamus's motivations and methods were, in part, based on and built from what others knew at the time. You explore basic methods for seeing into the future, discover the specific methods Nostradamus used to make his predictions, and look at various techniques he used to add layers — and obscurity — to his writing that make his predictions a challenge to interpret. I also provide you with some tools to help you start peeking around *The Prophecies* on your own.

Chapter 4

People, Events, and Institutions that Shaped Nostradamus's Prophecies

Great men stand on the shoulders of the people, beliefs, and events that come before them, and Nostradamus had a very good foothold. He stood at various times on the shoulders of his family, his friends, his religious faith, and the events of his life. Each person and experience molded him in such a way that he became the man we know as Nostradamus. By getting your hands on the original bricks that helped build Nostradamus, you can more easily understand why he focused his prophecies on religion, war, certain people, and affairs of state. You can understand why he didn't write prophecies about fashion trends.

Being aware of who and what influenced Nostradamus can also help you keep his prophecies in focus. For example, you may read too much into the fact that he concentrated on French royalty unless you know that one of his biggest supporters was Queen Catherine de Medici of France. You have to understand what was important to him to begin piecing together meaning from the prophecies. Such is the stuff of this chapter — the people and events that shaped Nostradamus and his predictions.

Men and Women who Shaped the Man

Imagine if you could step back in time and interview Nostradamus about the influences in his life. My guess is he'd stop after talking about his faith and the inspiration of God as the source of his personal strength (which I discuss in "The Catholic Church and Competing Beliefs," later in this chapter). In other words, he'd leave out the *many* people who inspired him along the way. Not because he was ungrateful, though. Nostradamus was just a very enthusiastic Catholic who wanted to make sure to keep his head firmly attached and prevent any trouble with the Inquisition. In this section, I intend to share who he has left out.

Learning from great-grandpa

"It takes a village to raise a child" is a saying with a lot of merit — especially when it comes to Nostradamus. His early childhood was spent at home with his siblings, but his parents noticed his quick mind and sent him to study with his great-grandfather. (I discuss his home life in more detail in Chapter 3.) During the time Nostradamus spent with great-grandfather Jean — the doctor and town treasurer — Nostradamus learned skills and concepts that he later used and incorporated into his prophecies.

A physician's focus

Great-grandfather Jean was a physician, and he influenced Nostradamus to enter into the same profession. Nostradamus's work as a physician greatly impacted his prophecies. I wish I could put the preceding statement in neon lights to emphasize how much impact this one fact had on his prophecies — but instead I attached that handy Remember icon to this paragraph. Think about the characteristics you associate with doctors. They're people who care for and look after others. Whether Nostradamus was caring and thus became a doctor, or the egg came before the chicken, it isn't a point that needs much attention.

Nostradamus was motivated to write his prophecies and almanacs by a need to share information and help his fellow human beings. In addition, throughout the prophecies, he maintained a focus on how the events he was detailing would affect people — not just people nearby, but people far away, too. Jean was also a man who was involved in helping run the town, and Nostradamus certainly learned that events can have pretty far reaching effects, and things you do should be undertaken with care. Although no one can be certain where each of Nostradamus's traits originated, great-grandfather Jean's influence on Nostradamus to become a physician and the resulting qualities Nostradamus adapted from his profession certainly affected his prophecies.

More than reading, writing, and arithmetic

Nostradamus's great-grandfather Jean considered the *celestial sciences,* a mix of astronomy (study of stars and planets) and astrology (using patterns from the sky to predict what's going to happen), to be just as valid as math or Latin. He presented celestial science to Nostradamus as part of his regular education. Most people in the Renaissance trusted that a connection existed between the stars and individuals, so Nostradamus wasn't breaking new ground there, but the strong emphasis that Nostradamus placed on the power of the stars set him apart from his fellow students and thinkers.

For the curious child who learned that the mysterious in life wasn't to be feared, the door was open for later study of the mystic traditions in religion, as well as the study of alchemy. (Turn to Chapters 2 and 6 for the scoop about the science — loosely speaking — of alchemy.)

Jean's lessons in languages gave Nostradamus the key to the ancient texts, which form the basis for Judaism and Christianity. These texts were written in Latin, Greek, or Hebrew at the time. Translators were slow and hard to come by, so being able to read the texts in the original language definitely gave Nostradamus a corner on the ideas and a leap ahead of most people. (For a short lesson in comparative beliefs check out the section, "The Catholic Church and Competing Beliefs," later in this chapter.)

Experiencing the power of the people

The wandering Nostradamus made quite a reputation for himself in the role of physician, and news of the doctor with a difference spread, well, like the plague. But at medical school in Montpellier, he was a point of distress for the instructors, because he refused to follow the traditional, tried and true treatments. Departing from the agreed-on prescriptions became a successful trademark for Nostradamus, however, because his services were in demand from Aix to Venice, where people everywhere suffered from the plague. (For details on his cures, see Chapter 3.) Whether or not he actually cured people of the plague didn't matter. People believed he was a great healer, and as a result, his services grew more valuable. Nostradamus later used this popularity to give his new career of telling the future a boost.

While wandering the countryside on his second great tour at the ripe age of about 28 (the first tour was after an outbreak of the Black Plague — see Chapter 3 for the details), rumors of his unnatural ability to tell what the future held became known to the people around him. This skill fascinated people, partly because it was unusual, but also because he was a healer *and* a seer. Two for one is hard to resist, and people demanded Nostradamus's skills as healer and seer.

Superstition was a strong force among the common folk of Renaissance Europe. Nostradamus saw this interest in his predictions as encouragement and thought that it could only be a sign from above that he should follow his intuition and become a man of prophecy. If it weren't for the fascination of the common people, who ironically shunned him later in life, Nostradamus may never have tried his hand at full-time prophecy. Their interest and his spreading reputation combined to help establish him later on in Salon as a man of learning and astrology.

Studying with a mentor

During his adult life, Nostradamus was enamored with Julius-César Scalinger, a man of many talents. Scalinger's credits included physician, zoologist, philosopher, and literary critic. And he also knew how to stir up trouble. Scalinger was a man who let his passions rule his mind, and he took to calling Desiderius Erasmus names and writing several published papers trying to get Erasmus to respond and argue. (Erasmus was a Christian humanist who wrote widely and disliked anything extreme in religion.) In addition, Scalinger spent some time in front of the Inquisition, possibly due to his interest in alchemy and other occult arts, but having low friends in high places gave him the break he needed to escape a heresy charge. (See Chapter 2 for more on Erasmus and the Inquisition.)

Scalinger loved debate and learning, and he was a fabulous mental gym for Nostradamus. Scalinger was a fiend about details. You may not have heard of this volatile critic, but Scalinger's influence on Nostradamus was great. Scalinger's influence can be seen in two areas:

- **Critical evaluation skills:** Scalinger excelled at finding form and order in Latin grammar, ancient philosophy, and even in the qualities of plants that made them distinct from one another. This ability to distinguish and classify items was very helpful for Scalinger and was an amazing boon to Nostradamus. In addition to studying the benefits of herbs and their healing properties, Nostradamus refined the art of critical evaluation within himself. He used his talent with plants to improve his plague remedies and used his skills in critical evaluation as he interpreted the midnight visions (the meditation process that gave him the information he used to write the majority of the prophecies; check out Chapter 6) into full-fledged prophecies.

- **Awareness of public perceptions:** One of the best gifts from Scalinger may have been that he inadvertently showed Nostradamus how *not* to act. While staying near Scalinger in Agen, Nostradamus no doubt watched firsthand the negative backlash of having a difficult personality. If Nostradamus wanted his words heard, he needed to find a way to placate and please those around him. Although the prophet didn't hide his negative prophecies, he learned to phrase them carefully to prevent upsetting the powerful people around him.

Gaining royal admiration

After moving to Salon, France during the latter years of his life, Nostradamus worked quietly on his prophecies and began publishing a yearly almanac, but he didn't hide in obscurity or rest on his laurels. People purchased his almanacs (well, those who could read), and many regarded them quite highly. His readers were mostly the local nobility, but Nostradamus began to move up in the world with the first publication of his prophecies in 1555. This great work, *The Prophecies,* included the first three complete *centuries* (groups of prophecies) and one partial century. It became the talk of the royal court and caught the interest of a very powerful lady, Queen Catherine de Medici.

Married to King Henry II, Queen Catherine de Medici, as she was known at the time Nostradamus published his first prophecies, was unpopular with the French royal court because she was neither French nor royal (she was actually an Italian orphan). She also wasn't the admired and accepted mistress of King Henry II. That honor went to Diane de Poitiers. Catherine had some habits that Henry II's court considered odd. In addition to keeping a large staff of chefs to make delicacies from her homeland, the superstitious Catherine studied *tarot* (cards with symbolic pictures that are used for prediction of the future) and consulted questionable Renaissance characters — astrologers and alchemists. As Nostradamus gained a reputation for prophecy, Catherine continued to struggle with her reputation among the French people. As a result, she was concerned about the fate of herself, her children, and France.

When Nostradamus's prediction of Henry II's death came true exactly as predicted, the queen took careful notice of the rest of Nostradamus's predictions. The queen demanded that he predict the fates of her children (see Figure 4-1), which he did with careful wording that seemed to satisfy her. (In Chapter 7, I discuss the details of Henry's gruesome joust with death. Chapter 8 covers the predicted fates of the royal children.)

The relationship between Nostradamus and Catherine de Medici influenced his writing in a number of ways:

✔ **Popularity boost:** Visits to the royal court at the request of the queen, even if she was unpopular, were wonderful lifts for Nostradamus's popularity as both an astrologer and a man of prophecy. While at court, many of the famous and well-to-do visited him and had their astrological charts prepared by the queen's astrologer.

The queen eventually gave Nostradamus the title of Physician-in-Ordinary, earning him an even greater reputation. As Physician-in-Ordinary (the title for a common doctor currently working for the crown) to the queen, Nostradamus was associated with the royal court, giving him a bit of a shine he hadn't had before. This popularity was helpful while Nostradamus was alive, but it was very influential after his death. When the remaining quatrains were published, excitement was high. After all the publicity and talk about the accurate prophecies for the queen, everyone was curious about prophecies that might have personal meaning. The same curiosity holds true to this day.

- ✔ **A bit of cash:** Nostradamus's initial meetings with Catherine seem to have inflated his reputation more than his pocketbook, but later visits with the queen yielded a better paycheck.

- ✔ **Subject matter:** During Catherine's reign, Nostradamus wrote a large number of the quatrains about her and the Valois family (the royal line). The quatrains about the royal family were prolific and maybe not as exact as they may have been if he hadn't been so close to the queen. Nostradamus pleased Queen Catherine with his quatrains at the possible expense of honesty.

  Also, without the queen's patronage, the quatrains may have contained less political focus. Today, you can be grateful to Catherine that her influence on Nostradamus kept the political within his sight, because you're left with quite a number of prophecies that could relate to current political situations.

- ✔ **Timing of publication:** Fear of displeasing the queen and quite possibly meeting an uneasy ending paralyzed Nostradamus and caused him to hold publication of the remaining quatrains. The entire prophecies were published two years after he died when he was beyond the queen's authority (obviously!).

Figure 4-1:
Nostrada-
mus at court
with
Catherine
de Medici.

Snark / Art Resource, NY

Struggles That Strengthened Nostradamus

A blacksmith can forge one single piece of iron into a thousand different shapes, but two things must happen: The iron must be softened and open to change, and the hammer must be heavy. Between weighty political events and personal tragedies, Nostradamus withstood quite a bit of struggle and "forging" to become a man who stood up and not only held his own ideas, but published them out loud for the world to see.

Troubling times in school

If your experience in school was typical, then just mentioning peer pressure can cause flashbacks that conjure up feelings of embarrassment, the need to conform, the need to be accepted, and a fear of being ostracized. Unfortunately, some things haven't changed in 500 years, and you can understand how Nostradamus probably felt at secondary school in Avignon, France, when other students didn't understand his intense focus on astrology or even his radical stance that Copernicus had it right — the Sun stood still and the Earth moved. Even the teachers at the University at Montpellier, where he studied medicine, were harsh on Nostradamus when his healing methods conflicted with their own.

As a man of strong beliefs, Nostradamus wasn't one to bend to peer pressure easily. Still, keeping one's own ideas isn't always easy, and Nostradamus stayed somewhat apart from his fellow students by diving into his studies and reading ancient texts. Much of the intense study during Nostradamus's formative years was the result of crossed ideas and stubborn teachers, and it gave him a more in-depth knowledge than he might otherwise have gotten.

The more he studied astrology and alchemy, the more Nostradamus came to incorporate these ideas and blend them together with his religious training. Nostradamus's formal education' combined with his interactions with people' taught him about human nature, the value of thought (a humanist idea about focusing on people), and the interconnected nature of the universe. These themes are reflected heavily in his quatrains.

Although uncomfortable at the time, the struggles in school made Nostradamus's departure in 1525 for plague-infested towns (to help treat victims) an easier decision. He didn't feel extremely connected to the school, and he knew that the friction there concerning his different way of thinking would certainly be lessened if he went elsewhere. Not to mention the fact that by some historical accounts, the school actually closed its doors in order to free up the faculty and students to treat plague victims. This testing ground for Nostradamus gave him time to develop a firm confidence in himself that he carried throughout his life.

Dealing with the death of his family

The first part of Nostradamus's life contained only a little struggle, and for the most part, he followed the path toward becoming an educated man and a physician. The path that led to the calm future of a country doctor, however, wasn't the one he stayed on, and he spent the later years of his life focusing instead on prophecy and astrology.

What makes such radical changes in a person? If anything can try someone's soul, it's the death of a family member (or, in Nostradamus's case, several family members). After moving to Agen in 1534, Nostradamus married and began a family, but he quickly lost his family to a mysterious illness, likely the Black Plague.

In addition to suffering from the sadness of losing his family to a mysterious illness, likely the plague, Nostradamus was affected by the fact that he couldn't save them. The loss made people question his skills as a physician, and his career tanked in Agen. With doubt surrounding him, Nostradamus had to leave Agen, and he wandered around as he tried to find a new pathway.

Before Nostradamus lost his family, there were no rumors or stories of prophecy about him. But during the wandering time that followed, tales surfaced about how the prophet could hear voices and make on-the-spot prophecies. (I go into these stories of greatness in Chapter 7.) Without this tragic episode, the young physician may never have found the inspiration or the need to write to the world about the future.

The Catholic Church and Competing Beliefs

Asking experts about Nostradamus's religious heritage and how it influenced his prophecies is like asking army brats where they're from. The answer is guaranteed not to be simple or boring. Every step this traveling healer took introduced him to new experiences, new people, and a variety of religious beliefs.

Although the most influential religions Nostradamus studied and used for symbols and references in his prophecies were organized schools of thought and belief, like the Jewish ancestry with its mystical traditions or the teachings of the Catholic Church, a wider and more general religion among the peasant people also influenced his writings. This background religion was a blurry backdrop of superstition and leftover pagan practices from invaders long since gone.

These practices were strongly related to the seasons and the forces of nature, which could easily be seen to influence the survival of humans. One of the main themes in this group of folk beliefs is that everything has a season, and things come and go in a natural order. The larger picture of the prophecies Nostradamus wrote contains this idea that there's a time for everything: destruction, growth, and then rebirth in a new way (after the antichrist, whom I talk about in Chapter 13).

Scholars can debate for hours the details of Nostradamus's life, and some of these individuals can spend quite a bit of time on whether Nostradamus was raised Jewish and then converted to Christianity or whether he was simply Christian at birth. I advise you to skip such debates (and leave the scholars with their dusty books) unless you have a time machine and can actually get to the 16th century. For purposes of gaining a general understanding of the man and the quatrains, don't worry about this controversy.

For the sake of clarity, my take on Nostradamus's religious experience is that he converted to Christianity at a young age but kept his Jewish mystical heritage close at hand. I use this assumption in my discussions throughout this book. Sorry — I couldn't help myself.

The central role of the Church

Nostradamus, by all accounts available, observed the practices of Catholicism on a nearly fanatical level and could easily be counted as a devout Catholic. While living in Salon, France, during the latter years of his life, he was seen walking to church almost daily. (The provisions of his will at the time of his death also demonstrate strong ties to the Church in Chapter 20.)

This devotion to church attendance wasn't enough to remove skepticism that he was just putting on a pretty face, however, and many critics during Nostradamus's time accused him of being a pagan and practicing the arts of witchcraft. (Astrology and spells counted among these evil arts.) But the critics obviously never read through any of Nostradamus's prophecies, or they wouldn't have bothered to accuse him at all. In all of Nostradamus's publications, he gave a courteous bow to his inspiration — God.

Nostradamus was a Catholic at a time when about 90 percent of France belonged to the Catholic Church. He was also part of a world where people were forced to convert from one faith to another (see the following section), and the rising interest in Lutheranism (a religion started by Martin Luther) brought many tempers to the boiling point. Nostradamus felt as though the religious mantle spread over Europe was suddenly being crumpled and ripped into pieces by Martin Luther's hands. And as a devout Catholic who believed that the Catholic Church was the only way to salvation, Nostradamus worried about this struggle.

Nostradamus voiced his concern for the people of the Renaissance by writing prophecies about religious challenges and the great struggle with evil forces. Catholic symbolism and the struggle against the devil, for example, are themes that run throughout the prophecies. And many of the negative quatrains begin with a ruler or country turning away from Christianity. He even included a traditional Christian bad guy — the antichrist. In the quatrains, some evidence shows that the biggest threat to the Church wasn't an antichrist person but a pattern of non-belief, which would've been just as destructive in Nostradamus's eyes. (I talk more about the antichrist references in Chapter 13.)

In today's world, Nostradamus's warnings of religious trouble still ring true, so understanding what Nostradamus said is important. On the daily news channel, you see fighting and wars in the name of religious causes that have killed hundreds of thousands of people. Nostradamus's warnings and prophecies about this terrible modern activity grew out of the struggle that surrounded him in the Renaissance.

Jewish roots, Jewish mysticism

According to biographers (and none of them agree on everything), Nostradamus probably came from a line of Jewish merchants and doctors who settled in southern France. The central role of Judaism in Nostradamus's upbringing can be teased out of the past with a bit of detective work: Education was very important in Nostradamus's time, and his family didn't make decisions about his learning without serious thought (and probably some heated debates). Hebrew was basically off limits at the time, as France harbored strong anti-Jewish feelings. Yet great-grandfather Jean taught Hebrew to Nostradamus. Hebrew (and the Jewish concepts that are part of the language) must've been a fairly important concept if Nostradamus's family insisted on risking their fortune by teaching off-limits material. Latin and Greek were the languages of formal education, so the purpose of teaching Nostradamus Hebrew could only have been for reading the Torah and Talmud (sacred text) and for instruction in Jewish concepts.

During the early 15th century, the Catholic Church in both France and Spain began forcing Jews to convert to Christianity or leave the country. Those who converted weren't out of danger completely, though, because the Church and its officials were suspicious that their conversion wasn't a true conversion. In other words, the Church thought the Jews were just going through the motions and that they could secretly be hiding their old religious ways. The Catholic Church wasn't satisfied and began the *Inquisition* (famous for its strength and brutality in Spain particularly) to hunt down those who weren't true believers or who had committed the crime of *heresy* (speaking against the Church).

According to some of the family trees, Nostradamus came from a long line of seers, prophets, and astrologers, and he may have inherited this the gift of insight. The Issachar tribe of Israel, from whom Nostradamus could've claimed lineage in less threatening times, had been a family of prophets for hundreds of years, so maybe it isn't shocking that Nostradamus displayed a talent for prophecy — it was in his blood and certainly in his studies.

Basic Jewish religious teachings were part of Nostradamus's instruction, but those teachings were covered up or packed away in a closet when Nostradamus converted wholeheartedly to Christianity. But covering up is a tricky business, and he missed (intentionally?) packing away some of the more subtle mystic teachings.

The Kabbalah

Nostradamus's great-grandfather and the sacred texts presented him with stories and teachings about changes in the world using hidden knowledge, which appears to the onlooker as magic. This *Jewish mysticism* is frequently referred to by the name *Kabbalah* and has been outlined roughly into something known as the *Tree of Life*. In a nutshell, because the essence of the divine can't be described directly in the Jewish belief (believers don't even write down the true name of the divine), the Tree of Life is used to describe how the energy of the divine is connected to and interacts with humans — like a manual for enlightenment. By studying the Kabbalistic Tree of Life and its ideas, Jewish mystics hope to climb up the tree in a very carefully balanced manner to bring themselves back into their rightful place in relation to God. (And, no, it's not recommended to bring a swing.)

There are 42 different paths along the Tree of Life, which is rooted in the divine (up in the sky) and extends into a physical manifestation here on Earth. So the climb isn't up the tree so much as it is down toward the source of the universe and back toward the purist expression of God. Nostradamus's knowledge of the Tree of Life helped him to understand that through each obstacle (war, famine, plague, and other horrors), people overcome obstacles and move along the Tree of Life to a more enlightened place.

By giving prophecies of the future, Nostradamus was trying to guide our paths, warn us of the trouble ahead, and let us know that many paths can be taken and some can be skipped (which explains why some quatrains are valid and others miss their mark as we take an alternate route).

The Tree of Life includes ten areas called Sefirot that describe ten aspects of deity, including wisdom, intuition, mercy, greatness, strength, glory, greatness, majesty, sovereignty, and the pure expression of divine energy. These aspects are usually represented as interconnected circles, and the pattern of the Tree of Life contains a balance of energy and ideas. The bottom of the tree represents the entirely physical side of life, and the top represents the entirely spiritual/divine side, and then there's everything in between.

Symbolism

In addition to the Kabbalah, the Jewish mystic tradition includes the use of letter and number symbolism, along with *anagrams* (rearranging letters in a word to make another word, such as changing "life" to "file"). Nostradamus used these techniques and symbolism in all of his prophecies to add complexity and disguise his meaning. The complex symbolism of the Kabbalah was part of the teaching Nostradamus received at home. Not only did he have beginner's classes at his great-grandfather Jean's knees, but he also probably sought out Jewish Rabbis or mystic lecturers as he wandered from city to city. However, his home region of Provençe was more tolerant of Jews and was a great Jewish mysticism resource for him.

Christian mysticism

Christian mysticism is described as an ecstatic one-on-one bonding with God, in which literally every moment of every day an overflowing sense of happiness and joy is present. It's the kind of eye rolling, overwhelming sensation of happiness and perfection you get when you eat something very delicious (like chocolate) — only the feeling is spiritual and is much bigger.

Nostradamus studied Christian mysticism with the idea that he could use it along with the other techniques from Judaism and alchemy to gain a clear connection to God. A strong Catholic faith with its personal connection through prayer to God and the new humanism idea that people were capable of guiding their own personal growth through personal experience of events, like visions, laid a firm groundwork for Nostradamus that he could and did communicate with God on his own to receive the prophecies.

Early mystics — before the Catholic Church existed — stated that by abandoning the idea of self and letting go of the physical world, anyone can reach an ecstatic state (which was linked occasionally to prophecy). Trying to reach this state of ecstatic union with God became the focus of the Christian mystic's life. Enlightened mystics prayed, performed rituals to call on angels, and applied their own intuition to find a direct line to God. In other words, they *felt* the presence if their hearts were pure and their intentions correct. They studied methods and strange rituals to achieve this ultimate goal.

This idea went very well with the Renaissance idea that experience shows the true nature of something, but as theories went, it tended to give the Catholic Church an upset stomach. Many of the activities associated with mysticism were banned as witchcraft and heresy.

The occult

Occult studies and Nostradamus walked arm in arm down the prophecy path, and the connection between them is undeniable.

The term *occult* can have several meanings, but be careful not to make assumptions or add connotations to the definition. The occult can mean that something is *supernatural,* meaning simply that it's beyond what you and I know of the world, or that it's simply a type of hidden knowledge. Just as the unknown boogieman scares children, the strange and mysterious stir up fear in people. But unknown or hidden knowledge shouldn't seem scary.

Here are some occult techniques used by Nostradamus and his contemporaries:

- **Astrology:** The study of the planets, stars, and heavenly bodies with the belief that tracking their courses could influence (and predict) human events.

- **Astral projection:** The ability to send a person's soul (without dressing it up in a body) out into the world to find answers to questions.

- **Palmistry:** The study of the lines on the hand as a method for telling someone's future.

- **Scrying:** The act of unfocusing the everyday mind and instead watching a flame, water surface, or even clouds with the intention of freeing the spiritual or higher self and enabling it to seek a goal — whether the goal is to prophesize or to find out whether, say, one's husband is cheating.

- **Sacred geometry:** The study of sacred patterns and shapes and the repeating patterns of those shapes in the universe as a method to find meaning.

Nostradamus read many occult books that inspired him. They provided *divination* (prediction) methods, ways to prepare his mind and thoughts for the sacred act of prophecy, and techniques for disguising his works, because many of the occult texts included complex plays on words, and their meanings were hidden behind symbolism. It was even the fashion of the day to use word games to hide information in sensitive government documents. Nostradamus even quoted from a known occult book, *De Mysteriis Aegyptorum (Concerning the Mysteries of Egypt),* which was in print while he studied and wrote (see the sidebar, "Snuggling up with a good book").

Astrology for the sake of telling the future was considered to be a part of the occult, because the methods (meditation, trance visions, and all that jazz) and the idea of people knowing God's intentions resembled witchcraft in the Church's eyes. Using texts from long before Jesus didn't help the Church's opinions much either.

Snuggling up with a good book

Nostradamus was known to use quotes in his prophecies almost directly from *De Mysteriis Aegyptorum (Concerning the Mysteries of Egypt),* an occult book that was probably available in Avignon, France, where Nostradamus did much of his study. The book was attributed to Jamblinchus in the 4th century and supposedly described the ancient Babylonian mysteries of prophecy, rituals in a priest's magic work, as well as more detailed information on the power of numbers and symbolism. These mysteries revealed the rituals and methods (like an alchemist's recipe card) for relieving the soul of its fated life (and that pesky body) and reaching a connection to the ultimate divine. Unfortunately, copies of this text are lost to the ravages of time and a book burning of immense proportions.

The influence of astrology on Nostradamus was enormous. For each stage of writing, Nostradamus reflected on the heavens and cast an *astrological chart* (a listing of planets and their positions, which told when certain activities were favorable and which activities to avoid). Nostradamus made a regular habit of selecting nights when the positions of the stars were favorable for his late-night prophecy sessions. After finishing his meditation and prophecy (see Chapter 5 for a description of Nostradamus's methods), Nostradamus often used astrological references (which have a tendency to confuse the average reader) for obscuring the dates on some events and mentioning rare moments in planetary alignments to clearly state the dates for other events.

Chapter 5

The Motivations and Methods of Nostradamus

*N*ostradamus wasn't a shawl-draped gypsy who waved his gnarled hands over a crystal ball. He wasn't even prone to dark alleys and requests that someone cross his palm with silver before telling her future. The stereotypes about fortune-tellers don't apply, but predicting the future was definitely his gig. What exactly was Nostradamus doing in the upstairs room of his house in Salon, France? Knowing how Nostradamus created his famous quatrains can help you understand his goals. He didn't work for money; he worked toward a higher purpose. (The queen of France, Catherine de Medici, did provide him with a little bit of gold — after all, a guy's gotta make a living.)

In this chapter, I begin to unravel the tangled web of prophecy left by Nostradamus. I walk you through the mechanics by explaining the actual form the prophecies took and giving you a few tools to work through quatrains on your own. And I explore exactly how Nostradamus came up with his predictions.

A Briefus Historius on Prophecy

To understand Nostradamus, you have to understand that although he has been influential in his own time and ours, he wasn't the first person to attempt to predict the future. In fact, the history of predicting the future is a long one. Entire civilizations, great rulers, and the average Joe (and average Joan) have sought to know what tomorrow holds, and they've used a surprisingly wide variety of techniques to discover that information. From looking at patterns in sand to the order of cards in a *tarot deck* (set of cards with intricate meanings and symbols), techniques for predicting the future have become increasingly complex as society and people have developed.

If you look at all the basic fortune-telling techniques, they begin to form a pattern: A culture, person, or group gives symbols specific meanings; these symbols are arranged randomly (by throwing them, drawing out each one, and the like), but the pattern they form is interpreted to have meaning. For example, one person may interpret the patterns of sand in a way that predicts the movements of weather, and another may use the turn of tarot cards to discover the best way to win an upcoming political election.

Prophecy through the millennia

Here's a list that outlines the development of prophecy. Don't worry if you've never heard of the people and places. They're not the focus here, and neither are the dates, which are approximations. My aim is to show you that the development and practice of prophecy have been around for a long, *long* time:

- ✓ **4000 BC:** Babylonian astrologers (whose address would be in present-day Iraq) began tracing the movements of the stars.

- ✓ **3100 BC:** A collection of ancient tribes built Stonehenge in England and possibly used it to predict the seasons, events for the year, and especially astrological events.

- ✓ **2953 BC:** Chinese Emperor Fu His began writing the system of divination known as I Ching.

- ✓ **1000 BC:** The Shang Dynasty in China began using tortoise shells and their pattern of cracks for divination.

- ✓ **624–518 BC:** Nebuchadenezzar of Babylonia sought divinatory council for his actions in the same way leaders from 4000 BC in his town sought out astrologers.

- ✓ **6th century BC:** Priestesses in Etruscan temples (which crumbled in the landscape you'd recognize as Italy) recorded prophetic readings.

- ✓ **3rd century BC:** Runes dated to this period have been discovered that showed divination in the colder climates of Iceland.

- ✓ **165 BC:** The Book of Daniel from the Bible prophesied the coming of an end to the present suffering and divine release. Other books within the Bible contained dreams and divine revelations of God's will.

- ✓ **Late 4th century AD:** The scrolls of ancient knowledge and prophecy were burned in the great library at Alexandria.

- ✓ **AD 1440:** This year marks the first record of the tarot deck being used as a game for nobles in Italy.

From this time in the history of prediction and prophecy until more modern times, the details of how people predicted the future become conflicted. The rise of a single, powerful Church put an end to much public use of prophecy. Wars and political struggles, while definitely a topic for prophecy, kept people busy enough that developing new systems or spreading the knowledge of the old systems was sometimes more trouble than it was worth.

Prophecy and the occult in Nostradamus's time

Oh, what a tangled web — prophecy, the *occult* (hidden or secret knowledge, often viewed as outside of Christianity; see Chapter 4), the Catholic Church, and the curious Renaissance nobility. Both prophecy and the occult were considered heresies that the Catholic Church condemned. But prophecy occupied special objectionable ground, because knowing the future was claiming a god-like power for a human (a sin for sure), plus it involved a connection with God that wasn't through the Church — definitely a no-no. The Church took the stance that all these activities distracted a person from the true purpose of life — finding salvation through acceptance of Christ.

Here's the twist: Nostradamus indulged in the study of the occult and prophecy, but he specifically studied occult techniques so that he might increase his connection with Christ and God. The typical tools and techniques of these practices (and there are more specifics about them in Chapter 6) were meant to open a person's mind to what was just beyond human sight. This is where Nostradamus walked a fine line with trouble. The Church didn't teach or approve of the techniques of meditation and water gazing, but Nostradamus believed his prophecies came from the Christian God, and that made every-thing okay. Unfortunately, the Church believed other influences (like the devil) could easily weigh in when an individual tried to connect with God directly (through meditation).

But what the people of the age believed was entirely different from the Church's stance. No matter how loudly the Church protested the concepts associated with the occult, the devout continued to participate in occult practices. For example, monks (who were holy men, but individuals with their own ideas on how things worked) were known to sell finger bones from saints and other holy people with the idea that the bones held some of the person's holy powers. This practice was very close to the occult idea that individual items could reflect the larger energy of the universe. Some of the finger bones were even used by monks in the art of *cleromancy,* or drawing lots to answer a divination question. I think the monks ignored the occult connection in such practices to find out the future (a natural human curiosity), because they figured that using holy items made the whole thing okay.

The nobility, with their renewed enthusiasm for learning (see Chapter 2), openly spurned pagan rituals of prediction like the belief that a crow was a sign of a person's death. But if you look a bit more closely, you can see that many nobles practiced these rituals in new ways. For example, young ladies often used a tarot deck to figure out whom they'd marry. Tarot predictions were considered to be on the edges of the occult — a dangerous place to play according to the Church. These predictions were done in fun (although secretly believed to be true), but they didn't have the divine influence necessary to make them prophecy. The divine seal on predicted things (like the monks might claim) tended to give predictions more believability.

And just beyond the door of the nobility stood the commoners who cooked, cared for the children, and otherwise made life easier for the nobility. Thanks to them, many of the old superstitions, habits, and wives tales survived as nursery rhymes and traditions. Looking at reflected light on water, for example, is a folk and occult method of viewing one's future and resembles the description Nostradamus gave of his prophecy methods (see the "In His Own Words: Nostradamus's Methods" section later in the chapter). I think he used the limited scope of the water gazing with his own prayers as a Christian twist to get more than a local view of what was to happen.

In the end, the people of the Renaissance (especially the Church) officially despised the occult and prophecy, but those in charge were nearly helpless to stop the practices entirely, because they became nanny's games and legends told as bedtime stories. These games and stories were part of the general culture of his times, and Nostradamus was bound to absorb some of the ideas — especially the idea that the individual could see into the future without the aid of someone else, something Christianity didn't offer to Nostradamus.

Divination 101

Any discussion of prophecy — Nostradamus's main claim to fame — is bound to bring up questions of how it works. As I discuss in Chapter 1, *prophecy* is answering questions about the future, through divination, with some added power and guidance from a divine source (the Christian God in Nostradamus's case) to produce a divine prediction. To get a grip on this concept, you need to understand a bit about what divination is, when divination is most often used, and why you should particularly care. Generally, *divination* is a method for finding answers that aren't usually accessible to human knowledge (beyond the senses), and it most often involves finding out what's going to happen in the future.

Nostradamus used divination as a practical tool to find answers to his questions, and then he wrote down the answers — his prophecies — so that people could use the knowledge for the betterment of mankind. One distinction between the average divination and Nostradamus's version is the intent. Generally, people ask very specific questions related to personal issues, such as a relationship or finances. Nostradamus, however, didn't look for answers about tomorrow, and only occasionally did he look for answers about next year. His main focus was the larger future, and for that kind of info, he certainly didn't ask narrow-minded questions.

Ultimately, the purpose of divination is to provide guidance and advice, something Nostradamus wanted from God to write his prophecies. Using divination is a lot like asking your friends for their opinions on a situation, though the powers that work through divination can be more universal and perhaps more divinely inspired. For Nostradamus this was exactly what he needed. Like any advice, you're responsible for what you do with it.

Counting the components of divination

In my experience, divination works not by one mechanism alone but through a combination of things that I list here. Heavy stuff, you bet:

- ✔ **Belief in divination:** You have to trust that the system you're using will give you important and relevant answers. If you doubt that divination works or believe that you're just shuffling cards, then you probably won't get anything meaningful from the experience. Nostradamus fully believed in what he was doing. The Renaissance idea of reviving ancient ideas and writings (which revived some of the divination techniques) lent some credibility to his work. He took his work seriously and considered it a way of listening to the voice of the divine.

- ✔ **Intent:** Divination provides a larger perspective on a question or problem, so if your goal is to truly solve a problem, you'll likely get helpful information or guidance. For Nostradamus, his intent was narrow when he wrote *The Almanacs* (weather, small changes), but it got broader when he started working on *The Prophecies*.

- ✔ **Connection to the universe:** In Renaissance Europe, many people believed that the *macrocosm* (the large universe beyond human comprehension) inspired and was reflected in the *microcosm* (the natural world). If you follow that line of thinking, a flower has the same perfect intention and form as the greater universe — or God — that created it. By studying the flower or other patterns in nature, you can find a reflection of God's pattern and study God's world. In other words, you can use a smaller picture to find your answer from the larger universe.

You can take a small set of items and throw them out into the world (shuffle cards, stir tealeaves, throw sticks into the air), and the pattern of the bigger universe will influence how those items that you moved form patterns in the smaller universe. The patterns you find can be interpreted to reveal events or answers that already exist in the universe. In Nostradamus's time, the most important reflection of the greater universe was in the stars and their movements. By knowing the movements of the planets, Nostradamus could talk about someone's future.

✔ **Intuition:** The hardest aspect of divination to define, *intuition* is that little feeling that tells you not to go out with someone on a date or that sudden urge you feel to call someone. It's the process of knowing something or "intuiting" it from the world around you without an explanation. Divination uses intuition to help pick out the patterns in the objects or images of a vision. Nostradamus believed that God guided his insights and intuition. When a person doing a divination sees a coin, for instance, intuition determines how to read that sign. Intuition may tell the person that she'll find a rare coin, pay too much money for something, or find herself down to her last dime. The right interpretation is the one that the person doing the divining sees first and strongest.

✔ **Language:** For divination, language is a series of symbols and patterns. Divination is a lot like reading poetry. Everyone sees the words (or the tarot cards, stones, and so on), but not everyone agrees on the meaning. Everyone has an independent set of associations for words and ideas that makes communicating unique to that person. Nostradamus used his own associations with words to write down his prophecies.

People and the Church got cross-wise about divination because of the ideas of free will and predestination. The Church believed that using divination, reading God's plan, and revealing what the future holds remove a person's ability to make an independent choice (free will) to accept Jesus Christ and the teachings of the Church as the only way to salvation. But losing free will isn't necessarily a given. Divination traditionally only reveals the answer to one question or identifies one possible outcome. The system reflects the current state of affairs in the big ol' cosmos, and that state can change. So just about every divinatory reading should end with the phrase "Your mileage may vary." (See the section, "That sticky subject of free will," later in the chapter for more on the subject.)

Defining the ways of divining

In divination, just about any system of seemingly random items or symbols can be used. These divination forms include but aren't limited to

✔ **Astrology:** Studying the patterns and movements of the stars

✔ **Augury:** Interpreting signs and omens

✔ **Cartomancy:** Using cards (especially tarot cards)

- ✔ **Catoptromancy:** Gazing into mirrors

- ✔ **Hepatascopy:** Examining the liver of an animal (rare in Nostradamus's time)

- ✔ **Ornithomancy:** Studying the flights of birds

- ✔ **Scrying:** Gazing into any surface until images appear (Nostradamus's favorite technique)

- ✔ **Tasseomancy:** Finding patterns in tealeaves

One of the most common forms of divination is called *cleromancy,* or drawing lots. In ancient Greece, oracles used this system, and people continue to use it even today. In this system, beans, marbles, or uniformly shaped items are placed into a container. Some of the items are one color and represent the answer "no," and the rest are another color and represent the answer "yes" (like black for no, white for yes). The person divining asks a yes-or-no question and then selects a piece from the bag to get the answer. I've never "black balled" someone, but this is where the phrase comes from.

At court during the Renaissance, the biggest fads were having your astrological chart read — part science, part divination — and working with tarot decks. *Tarot* cards actually came into favor in the upper classes a century before Nostradamus. Originally, tarot was a parlor game that entertained the nobility, but the cards were soon used to tell the future in answer to a question. Note that Catherine de Medici, queen of France and client of Nostradamus, was very fond of her decks of cards. Nowadays, you still don't have to look too hard to find these decks. They're the granddaddy of the regular playing cards my husband uses for poker.

During the Renaissance, divination systems seemed to require less in the way of tools and more in the way of intuition. People were busy fighting the plague and trying to survive, so they didn't have much time for making special tools to find out about the future. Instead, people like Nostradamus learned to listen to the inner voice that told them to look here or there at a particular moment, what you may call a sixth sense about things. When looking for visions of the future, it was probably his intuition that told Nostradamus which of his visions to record and which ones to ignore.

That sticky subject of free will

One of the sticky problems with knowing about the future is the possibility that the prediction will interfere with someone's *free will,* which is the ability of individuals to make independent decisions about their lives for their own good without being affected by the opinions, ideas, and influences of other people, even if Nostradamus is one of those people. But the thing is, a statement about a future event, read by you in the present, *can* affect your decisions and *can* remove your free will by influencing you to do one thing or another.

Here's an example: Suppose you like candles and tend to light them each night to relax after a hard day of work. Now say that a person writes down a statement that there will be a fire in your house on Monday. If you read that prediction, you may be influenced by the idea and change your decision about lighting candles on Monday. That choice wouldn't be entirely yours.

A prediction can act as a kind of control over your actions. The idea of being controlled by other people, or ideas, doesn't sit well with certain schools of thought, and those who advocate individual freedom just can't stand prediction. Unfortunately, though, you're influenced by everything and anything you experience — from coffee making you nervous to newspaper reports giving you ideas of the boogieman in every corner. I consider predictions to be just another piece of information, just like the rest of the information your brain processes. Ultimately, making a decision about something is still your choice, and you can use the prediction information as you wish, which is an act of free will anyway.

Why Nostradamus Moved from Normal City to Prophecy Central

People do the strangest things, and trying to understand why they do them can be a struggle. Post-Nostradamus commentators can't be certain what provoked him to try to look into the future and write *The Prophecies* without traveling through time and asking Nostradamus directly. So, in this section, I only give you the briefest suggestions for why I believe Nostradamus wrote commentary on the future. Hints of Nostradamus's motivation to write his prophecies can occasionally be found in his writings:

- ✔ *Epistle to Henry II:* Nostradamus claimed to blend divine inspiration with the emotional inspiration of his ancestors, so maybe the voices of his ancestors egged him on to write. (I discuss the Jewish ancestral aspect of his history, and the *Epistle to Henry II,* in Chapter 3.)

- ✔ **The preface to *The Prophecies*:** Nostradamus addressed the preface to his son, César. He cited the need to be memorialized by his own words and the need to leave his son a legacy of inspired writings, which Nostradamus created as a sort of divine gift with astrological wrappings. But the final phrase of the address to César provides a grander rationale: Nostradamus suggested that he left the writings as a legacy meant to help all of mankind.

Those two motivations aside, what made an intelligent and precocious young doctor take a walk on the wild side and start spouting prophecy? Several factors came into play, including

✔ **His profession and caring nature:** Nostradamus's concern for the plague-ridden souls of France and the reports of his kindness during these episodes support the idea that he genuinely cared about people. Nostradamus's basic caring nature is probably what prompted him to leave the prophecies, as he indicated in the preface to them, for the benefit of mankind.

✔ **Hardships:** The death of Nostradamus's family in Agen, which was certainly a life-altering event (see Chapter 3), sparked a depression in Nostradamus and probably fueled a need to answer the age-old question of why certain things happen. Losing his family opened him up to a quest for knowledge, and that quest took him deep into his spiritual connections (which were ripe with mystical meanings).

✔ **Devout nature and relationship with the Church:** The power of faith for Nostradamus was impressive, and while traveling the countryside after his family's death, he began to have flashes of insight that came true (for stories of his early prophecies, see Chapter 7). The strength of his Christian connection probably influenced his belief that the visions (images of what the future would look like as if it were a painting) were from God — the only person who could legitimately know the future — and they were given to him to share with and help humanity.

Between Nostradamus's desire to know and his religious convictions, his visions were a way of answering his needs. God was dialing his number and answering his prayers — and with the heart of a caring man, Nostradamus kindly recorded the process for posterity.

The Shape of Things to Come: Breaking Down the Predictions

Nostradamus didn't start out with the intention to write a book of poetry. Instead, he spent his nights in the attic in his home in Salon. This attic became the retreat where he studied his favorite topics, read, and pursued his interest in astrology. It was also here that Nostradamus began using meditation techniques and a prayerful attitude to ask for visions of what the future might be. He wrote notes and even made sketches of the visions he saw (for more on these nightly trips to his study, see the section, "In His Own Words: Nostradamus's Methods," later in the chapter). He then transformed the notes into the poetry form that exists today as his prophecies. (For more on the poetics of Nostradamus's work, see the "Of rhyme and reason" section later in the chapter.)

A quick lesson on quatrains

You may remember the term *quatrain* from high school English class. If not, don't sweat it, because I have the facts right here. Simply put, a *quatrain* is four lines of poetry that are grouped together. Sometimes these lines are set apart by spacing and sometimes because they all rhyme. The quatrain your teacher taught you as part of an English lesson is the same structure Nostradamus used as a lesson on life for the rest of mankind in *The Prophecies.*

Each quatrain Nostradamus wrote is a separate piece and not part of one long poem; so don't sweat it if you look at things that seem to be out of order, because they're not (in order that is). The quatrains were meant to stand alone. Rhyme, while not a requirement, seems to have been one of Nostradamus's elements. Most of his quatrains contain rhymes between the first and third lines and the second and fourth lines. This kind of weaving together of rhyme makes poetic lines feel like they're built strongly to stay together.

Nostradamus probably wrote the quatrains in a rough form of Latin, and then he translated them into a mix of French, Provençal, Italian, Latin, and made-up words that suited his purposes. Each one of these four-line wonders spoke of at least one future event and sometimes several that could be related.

When a century isn't 100 years

Nostradamus arranged his prophetic quatrains into ten groups of 100 (well, almost — Century 7 only has about half its quatrains, and no one has figured out why Nostradamus shorted this century). These ten groups are called *centuries,* but don't get derailed into thinking that these grouped prophecies covered 100 years. Here, centuries have nothing to do with years and everything to do with keeping 942 prophecies organized somehow.

In terms of Nostradamus's prophecies, *century* simply refers to the 100 quatrains into which most of the prophecies were divided. Nostradamus didn't pull this format out of a hat. His knowledge of numerology and the power of numbers gave him a distinct form for his message. I talk about the importance of numbers, and especially 100, in Chapter 6.

The most common way to note which of the 942 quatrains is being referenced is to identify them by both the century and the quatrain number. Century numbers are typically in Roman numerals, and the quatrain number follows after a dash. For example, C II – 45 refers to Century II (2) and Quatrain 45.

An exception to every rule

Just when you think you have quatrains and centuries all sorted out, I have to throw a wrench in the works. Nostradamus wasn't a great poet. The overall form of his poetry would've given his mentor and noted critic of poetry, César Scalinger (see Chapter 4), quite a fit. Frankly, the rhymes were rough.

Without making this discussion too complex, consider the idea that a poem normally has a beginning, middle, and an end. You'd expect a poem (if the collection of quatrains in *The Prophecies* is considered together to be one piece) that covers many years to at least have a regular sort of timeline, but Nostradamus didn't give readers that comfort. The quatrains appear in a seemingly random order that certainly isn't guided by time, and topics are spread throughout the entire collection in quatrains that are separated instead of being collected in nice, neat bundles where all the quatrains in one section talk about a specific time or a specific topic. But even the exception has an exception, and in several instances, a prophecy continues from one quatrain to another in a series.

In His Own Words: Nostradamus's Methods

We don't have to speculate on the methods Nostradamus used for divination. Because Nostradamus left his prophecies for all of mankind to read, he kindly left descriptions of how he got his prophetic information and how he prepared for his divination sessions.

In his first two quatrains of Century I, Nostradamus described his methods (see Table 5-1). Those methods add to the mystery of it all with their solitude and mysterious practices, and you can almost hear the spooky music playing when you look at a picture of Nostradamus. Although no one can confirm or deny that he actually read *De Mysteriis Egyptorum*, a book on occult practices, much of the divination process Nostradamus used in writing *The Prophecies* and described in these first quatrains sounds familiar — almost like it came directly from that book (see Chapter 4 for more information).

For example, the techniques he describes in C I – 1 and C I – 2 are very much like the typical occult techniques for quieting the mind, clearing thoughts, and focusing on the purpose at hand. Being alone is pretty standard stuff in the occult if you want to keep yourself focused, and a single candle also helps keep down the distractions by limiting what you can see to what's directly in front of you — in his case a brass tripod and water. Nostradamus approached the act of acquiring the prophecies as a very serious and profound moment. As he prepared for his prophecies, he had a strong flavor of religious reverence in his attitude.

Table 5-1		Century I, Quatrains 1 and 2
Line	*Original Text*	*Translation*
1	Étant assis de nuit secret étude,	Being seated by night in secret study,
2	Seul reposé sur la selle d'airain:	Alone resting on the brass stool [tripod]:
3	Flamme exiguë sortant de solitude,	A slight flame coming forth from the solitude,
4	Fait prospérer qui n'est à croire vain.	That which is not believed in vain is made to succeed.
5	La verge en main mise au milieu des BRANCHES,	The rod in hand set in the midst of branches.
6	De l'onde il moulle et le limbe et le pied:	With water he wets both limb and foot:
7	Un peur et voix frémissant par les maches:	Fearful voice trembling through his sleeves:
8	Splendeur divine. Le divin près s'assied.	Divine splendor; the divine sits nearby.

The translation of the quatrains in Table 5-1 is kind of cryptic. Don't fret, though; I'm here to help. For starters, the individual lines are a lot like the pieces of a jigsaw puzzle. Look at the individual pieces until the shapes and colors seem to form a pattern, and then place the corresponding pieces next to each other until you have a complete picture. For the quatrains, that means looking at the people, places, and events described and then seeing if they're related and can fit next to each other to form a prophecy that makes sense.

In the following sections, I use this technique to give you my interpretation of Century I – 1, 2 and the methods Nostradamus used. Reading Century I – 1, 2, you get a picture of Nostradamus sitting in an attic, alone at night with his books and his thoughts. He was away from the world and set daily worries aside to focus on the greater worry of what would happen in the world down the road. His goals were lofty, coming as they did from a sense of religious duty, and he used all the tools he had at hand to create a space that felt sacred. He received and interpreted the visions of the future from his trance-like state in this sanctuary. He used the divine presence to guide and inspire him.

The recipe to make prophecy, then, becomes one part man (Nostradamus), one part divine, and two parts mystery and universe. Somewhere in there is a dash of your own understanding as well.

Of rhyme and reason

In Table 5-1, look at the lines of poetry in the quatrains. In the English trans-lations, understanding that Nostradamus wrote in rhyme is very difficult. The lines are rhymed in pairs with the first and third lines rhyming, and the second and fourth lines paired up. This kind of rhyme (which is clear if you could read it in French) tends to give a feeling that the lines flow from one to another and that they're tied together very closely.

Nostradamus used this structure and regular rhyme to give his questionable endeavor of telling the future some validity by placing the prophecies in a very formal setting. If he'd simply written the messages down in unconnected sen-tences, they might seem more haphazard and less valid. Structured poetry gets some of its strength (and some of its social acceptability) because it follows rules. The importance of the quatrains ultimately comes from the message rather than the poetry, however — especially because the actual poetic aspect of the quatrains leaves quite a bit to be desired.

Because Nostradamus wrote and then rewrote his prophecies to make sure they were exactly as he intended, the wording is important. You can bet that his word selection wasn't random, and he included ideas to give information rather than to fill space.

Description of methods in Century 1 – 1

To help you understand the description of methods in Century I – 1, I've ana-lyzed each line of the quatrain as presented in Table 5-1. Together, the pieces of the first quatrain's puzzle show a man alone, using his quietness to reach into the emptiness — the quiet place where information and knowledge from the divine might fill in the blank spaces in his understanding of his visions and the future. He was using his study of secretive matters to enrich his prophecy. In nearly every way, this image fits the stereotype of a man working on some-thing unexplainable and mysterious.

Line 1

Nostradamus noted that he was by himself in *secret study.* Being alone allows for prayer, meditation, and an amazing ability to concentrate, which all would've been useful for receiving and writing down notes on his prophesies. His family knew his secret study, so he wasn't talking about a secret in the sense of an unknown place. Perhaps he was referring to the idea that the study of ideas (his books) was secretive. He was definitely not on the bright and shiny path of daily living.

Line 2

Nostradamus referred to a *brass stool,* or tripod, that's the topic of much debate and discussion these days. This tripod was the one specific tool that Nostradamus mentioned, and the tripod probably supported a bowl of water for gazing. *Scrying* (gazing into water until images appear) was a technique used in divination described by the occult book *De Mysteriis Egyptorum.*

Line 3

The *flame* mentioned could've been a real candle flame used to illuminate Nostradamus's work. But more likely, Nostradamus was referring to the flame of inspiration. This flame would've come from the emptiness of his mind after he removed cluttering thoughts about money, worries, and other daily details. Either symbolically or in reality, the flame may have reflected off the water's surface to become the source of his visions. The uneven flicker of a candle would've given many variations and reflections to the water's surface, and Nostradamus's intuition (or inspiration) would've interpreted those variations into images with more form. In this kind of divination, the situation and the person doing the divining blend together to help create the visions. Nostradamus added to the flickering images created by the flame and his own intuition the influence of God, shown in the second quatrain.

Line 4

This line is a continuation of the third line about the flame. Part of the reason the flame is most likely inspiration rather than a candle is that the flame was responsible for the success of his exercises, and Nostradamus likely wouldn't have given credit to a candle. The flame of inspiration, then, helped him to succeed with something that *is not believed in vain.* Nostradamus wanted people to see his activities (and his prophecies) as worthwhile and as having a purpose. He certainly didn't want people to think that his process was fruitless or unsuccessful. Nostradamus was saying, hey — trust me.

Description of methods in Century 1-2

At the beginning of Century I – 2 (see Table 5-1), Nostradamus seemed to be speaking about events in his own clear voice. Near the end of the quatrain, however, he began to use short, disjointed phrases that suggest a change in what was happening. At this point, he was using inspiration rather than intellect to create, and he let the reader know by changing his writing style. He also shifted to talking very distinctly about "he," as if the person doing these actions was separate from himself.

In the act of meditating, the person often feels separated from the body by a small distance — like the person is watching himself perform an action, for example. Nostradamus most likely experienced this feeling, and he recorded it for the reader. The fact that Nostradamus wasn't in control of his prophecies (he was distanced from himself and influenced from outside) gave him a way to step out from under some of the responsibility for what he said.

Three ideas of the second quatrain are especially important, and I describe each of them line-by-line in this section. (Although I usually refer to a quatrain by Lines 1 through 4, in this section I describe Lines 5 through 8 instead because they're presented as such in Table 5-1.)

Lines 5 and 6

The first important idea in Century I – 2 involves an action performed with a *rod* (wand) and the sprinkling of water. The wand is *set in the midst of branches,* which was most likely the depth of the water bowl held be the tripod. Symbolically, Nostradamus was touching the depth of knowledge (as far as he'd be able to see) and the joining of forces (the point of convergence for the tripod). Taking that water and anointing his robes and feet *(With water he wets both limb and foot)* were ways for Nostradamus to connect with these symbolic forces from the tripod. By anointing his robe, he blessed himself, and by anointing his feet, he imbued that blessing and guidance on his path (which he'd walk, naturally and symbolically, with his feet). This concept may remind you of a Catholic priest giving blessings with holy water, and certainly it would've given Nostradamus a similar feeling.

Nostradamus was aware that he needed to separate himself from the world of regular daily thought into a new way of thinking. Using a ritual set of actions like anointing his robes is like putting on a name tag or badge at work; it's something you do that triggers you to think more about work than home, and for Nostradamus, it made him think more about visions than his family. Ritual is used in nearly every religious tradition to mark the change between the regular world and the slightly out of focus spiritual world. Dressing in special clothing like Nostradamus's robes or using a sacred language during religious services reminds people that they're in a different space for a very spiritual purpose. Nostradamus was setting the stage for a connection beyond the everyday, and he used tricks and signals to tell his mind to let go of logical thought and start using the other, more intuitive parts of himself.

Some interpreters consider "BRANCHES" from Nostradamus's original text a reference to the *oracles* (priests and priestesses) of Branchus, an ancient Greek god who gained divine powers of prophecy. This tidbit of history adds emphasis to the notion that Nostradamus sought prophecy.

Line 7

The second piece of Century I – 2 that draws attention is Line 7, where Nostradamus talked of a voice and fear. Although he didn't identify the voice, the next line gives a fair clue that the voice he was hearing was probably divine. Nostradamus expressed fear and described trembling as a result of the voice's presence. The trembling could've been from the anticipation of finding out what was going to happen in the future, from the idea of dealing with the divine force directly, or from the simple strangeness of the new experience. I believe that the powerful importance of the work he was beginning and the connection with God would've been nearly overwhelming for the serious and devout man.

Line 8

Line 8 draws immediate attention because you can see that Nostradamus felt a divine presence near him as he worked on the prophecies. He described the divine presence using *splendor* — a word that suggests a bit of awe and wonder, which is why I think the fear in line 7 was from an overwhelming sense of connection to something greater than himself. I know I'd be a bit overwhelmed by connecting to the entire universe.

Lines 7 and 8 provide a clear peek into Nostradamus's view of his visions and the idea that the power of the divine, while necessary for his work, wasn't something that he was always comfortable with. The importance of the connection with God is emphasized by the fact that Nostradamus used everything he knew to build up to this point where he was in touch with something larger than himself. His prophecies get an extra bit of emphasis because they weren't just his own words, so they're just that much more special than everyone else's regular predictions (those without the divine hand of guidance). For him, this connection is the punch line.

Chapter 6

Peeling Back the Layers of the Prophecies

In This Chapter

▶ Discovering the whys and hows of Nostradamus's obscurity

▶ Connecting astrology and the prophecies

▶ Bringing alchemy into the mix

▶ Counting the reasons why numbers were important to Nostradamus

▶ Deciphering the symbols in the prophecies

▶ Looking at language

*P*eople around the world have always searched for signs and omens that tell what the future brings, and they've looked just about everywhere. Since 1555 or so, people have looked to Nostradamus's writings to see if they could shed some light on events. But *The Prophecies* aren't a quick reference, and Nostradamus wasn't a simple writer. Divination is always steeped in symbols and meaning, but Nostradamus brought things to a whole new level.

If you wonder why he felt the need to make his quatrains so complex, you're in good company. If I had to pick one aspect of *The Prophecies* that led to Nostradamus's stardom, I'd credit his obscurity. In 942 quatrains, there are enough strange lines, vague references, and possible interpretations to keep theorists coming back for more than hundreds of years.

The many elements of his life and learning are all mixed into the quatrains for layers of meaning. And everything that he put into the mix added something (even if it was a layer to keep people confused). So in this chapter, I share some of the tools he used to add layers of meaning to *The Prophecies,* how to sort them out, and why there are so many layers in the first place.

Revealing the Reasons for All the Obscurity

The Renaissance was a time when a quick word from the people in power could cost a person his life — a very real problem for anyone who seemed too much out of sync with the norm. And Nostradamus was certainly walking on the edge. Some of his quatrains could've been interpreted (and misinterpreted) as very dangerous stuff. So to protect himself, Nostradamus took great care with the wording of his predictions. In the following sections, I explore the reasons for his obscurity in greater detail.

Dodging the wrath of the Church and God

Here's a puzzle for you: A man sits alone at night and predicts (with a little divine help) the death of a king or two. No one is around, the door is locked, and the books on the table are all related to the occult. The king dies. Who's responsible? The Church considered prediction a matter of witchcraft and astrology an offense, so it found the methods Nostradamus used (created by those heathen mystics, no less) offensive. The Church was offended mostly by the threat to its power. But by claiming that God was the originator of his visions, Nostradamus avoided the majority of the Church's official scrutiny. To make sure he stayed on the safe side of the fence, Nostradamus layered his prophecies about the Church, its foes, and the antichrists (see Chapter 13 for more on these villains) with confusing symbolism and vague details. That way, he could easily deny his real meaning if he were questioned.

But for Nostradamus, how to present his predictions was a life or death question in more ways than just the physical. He believed that ultimately he would answer to a power mightier than the men of his age, and he and his prophecies would be subject to God's judgment. I know that would keep me up more than a few nights if I predicted the range of tragedies found in *The Prophecies*. The weight of so many negative images could also affect my mental state.

Keeping tight with the queen

Nostradamus didn't want to upset anyone's apple cart, especially the royal cart of Queen Catherine de Medici of France, who helped him toward fame (see Chapter 4 for more on their relationship). So when writing prophecies about the Medici family, Nostradamus used vague enough language to tell Catherine what she wanted to hear. He conveniently left out the messy details of how events would happen, using the theory that what she didn't know wouldn't hurt her.

Avoiding the blame

Another reason Nostradamus avoided writing down future events in plain English was that after developing a reputation as a man of prophecy, he ran the risk of being blamed for predicting bad events. The door swung both ways: When he was correct on good predictions, people applauded him, but when he accurately predicted a death or bad season, he took some blame for helping to cause it (see Chapter 7 for more on the predictions he made for events during his lifetime). On the flip side, who's responsible when prophecies *don't* come true? In Nostradamus's case, people either blamed him, the occult books he used, his Jewish mystical training, or astrology, which wasn't quite a science.

Preventing panic while helping humanity

Besides worrying about the people who'd point fingers at him for right and wrong prophecies (seems you can't please anyone), Nostradamus probably struggled with the responsibility of having what he believed to be deeply powerful information. Revealing too much information could harm people and cause panic; revealing too little would be like denying the divine gift he believed he received in his visions. In addition, Nostradamus considered his knowledge of occult secret teachings and mystical intuition to be very powerful. That kind of information was to be kept secret and out of the hands of the average person. After all, you never know where the guy next to you will point a prophecy.

So he kept his messages under the lock and key of hidden meanings and symbolism so that only people who knew all the mysteries involved — people of Nostradamus's level of learning — could truly understand the prophecies. Presumably, their training gave them insight on how to handle such important information, and they wouldn't run out into the street screaming that the sky was falling.

Nostradamus's obscure references made interpreting his prophecies difficult, so his quatrains weren't poems the everyday man could understand. But they were intended to help the everyday man. In other words, Nostradamus was concerned about the greater good of mankind, and he published prophecies to help mankind. Ironically, he left them in complex puzzles so that the helpfulness was limited.

Seeing Stars: Astrology in the Prophecies

The most substantial element of Nostradamus's prophecies is the astrological connection. *Astrology,* during Nostradamus's time, was the study of how the movement of the planets and stars influences people's lives. Nostradamus approached nearly everything through his study of the stars. From his early education until his death, he used the angles and movements of the heavens to predict the events that would be significant to himself, France, and the world.

Nostradamus was an astrologer first and a physician second. Although astrology was part of the typical doctor's diagnostic kit (docs might see whether the moon was in the right phase to be favorable for treatment), Nostradamus went above and beyond in his study and use of the stars. His skills as a doctor earned him a living early on, but his skills as an astrologer played an integral part in verifying his visions and dating the events in his prophecies. Astrology became a major part of his life in Salon and was a key element in his fame.

Charting a clear path

An *astrological chart* is a record of the planets and stars and is used by astrologers like Nostradamus to look at which of these celestial bodies could influence an individual. These charts are based on where the stars were in the sky when a person was born, so birthdays (including the exact time) come in handy. When Nostradamus needed to know which stars would influence a future event or required that information to predict events, he did everything by hand — from drawing the actual chart of the stars to calculating the angles and degrees in the sky. (The Renaissance didn't have quick computer programs to analyze the placement of the stars at a particular moment in time.)

Nostradamus's visions probably weren't crystal clear and easy to understand when he saw them, and astrological charts allowed him to clarify the direction of a vision. If, for instance, he saw the death of a monarch, he may have drawn up the astrological chart for the reigning monarchs of several countries or regions and their children using birth dates, the dates the countries came into existence, or significant dates in the future. By doing so, Nostradamus may have seen that the king of France, and not the king of Germany, would be the one to find his death on a field of battle. This method helped him narrow the information in his visions and double-check his accuracy. Plus Queen Catherine de Medici called upon Nostradamus to cast charts for her and her family, and Nostradamus likely used these charts later to enhance his prophecies of the French royal family (see Chapter 8).

Some astrologers (both then and now) have taken a dim view of Nostradamus's ability to correctly calculate a chart, which may seem like grounds upon which to doubt his prophecies (which were heavily influenced by his astrological calculations). But it's possible that he sometimes simply made an error in one of his measurements or forgot to carry a number when doing the math.

I give him the benefit of the doubt and credit him for doing all the laborious work of the charts to add layers of meaning and the backing of the celestial scheme to his prophecies — even if they weren't perfect.

Dialing in the Zodiac

Astrology, as Nostradamus used it, also included the *Zodiac,* a way of representing the stars that are visible to the Earth throughout an entire year. These stars are identified in 12 groupings, called *constellations,* and are assigned names and attributes. The 12 constellations are called the *signs of the Zodiac,* and they divide the year into equal portions, with each sign influencing a certain portion of the year more than its counterparts. (This whole Zodiac setup didn't happen all at once. The process began with the people in Mesopotamia — the hotbed of civilization way back when — and grew over time.)

To help you chart out the influence of astrology, consider this example. Each sign of the Zodiac has a ruling planet (you can see these in Table 6-1) — a planet that lends its influence over anyone born during that Zodiac sign. A person born under the section of the year controlled by Cancer (June 23–July 23) has an astrological chart that's influenced heavily by the moon's motions.

Nostradamus would've known that important events happen in this person's life during full moons (completed tasks, end of journey), during the dark of the moon (heartache, secrets), or even during an eclipse (tragedy, strange events). This information, plus the typical attributes of those people born under the sign of Cancer, would be combined with Nostradamus's visions to help identify people or date the event in the prophecy. Your knowledge of these astrological traits may allow you to recognize hints in the prophecies indicating that a moon-guided person is a Cancer.

Nostradamus used astrological references and Zodiac times in his prophecies so that the reader could get a complete understanding of an event. For example, instead of saying that something would happen on Tuesday in a particular year — which is exact but isn't particularly informative — he'd state that the event would occur when three planets aligned or when two planets were connected by a particular angle in the sky. In this way, he could date the events using the planets (cryptically) and also provide further clues about the events. For example, if Saturn is involved, hold on for great changes. But if the moon is influential, then the event will stir up emotions — something that's commonly associated with the moon's different phases.

Nostradamus inserted these astrological influences into the prophecies in symbolic language so that the reader who's really in tune to astrology will see the hints and get more out of the prophecy. A true astrologer with years of study may understand all the slight tweaks and shades of meaning Nostradamus used. But for now, use a good resource text to identify any astrological references within the prophecies (see Chapter 22 for a list of these resources).

Table 6-1 lists specific information about the signs of the Zodiac. For each sign, the ruling planet is listed, as is the sign's various meanings and associations. The four aspects of the body during the Renaissance were understood as earth, air, fire, and water, so I've included these in the table as well. As you read through the quatrains in this book, or other quatrains on your own, you can use this chart as a general reference point for understanding why, for example, Nostradamus mentioned Saturn in a quatrain about war or Capricorn in a quatrain about leaders (both typical traits of the planet Saturn and the Zodiac sign of Capricorn). You can find a clue about what point Nostradamus may have been trying to make.

Table 6-1		Signs and Significance of the Zodiac
Zodiac Sign	*Ruling Planet*	*Some Meanings and Associations*
Aries	Mars	Fire element; urge to survive, to do; sometimes associated with the ancient god of war, Aries
Taurus	Venus	Earth element; appreciation of love and beauty; artistic; the spiritual over the mundane; determination
Gemini	Mercury	Air element; commerce; travel (Mercury was the messenger god for the Greeks); expressive
Cancer	Moon	Water element; emotional and instinctual; nurturing; patient
Leo	Sun	Fire element; represents ego; conscious will; the essential being
Virgo	Mercury	Earth element; expression; travel; methodical; industrious
Libra	Venus	Air element; socially correct; likeable and attractive qualities; balance
Scorpio	Pluto	Water element; spiritual changes; political power; purifying and intense energy; ability to determine the truth of things
Sagittarius	Jupiter	Fire element; optimism; freedom; generosity
Capricorn	Saturn	Earth element; restrictions and obstacles; patience; endurance
Aquarius	Uranus	Air element; rebirth of consciousness through experiences; humanitarian
Pisces	Neptune	Water element; deep and mysterious; idealism; oneness with the universe

Alchemy's Role in Guiding the Prophet

As I explain in Chapter 2, *alchemy* is the secretive study of how to turn base metals into gold, a process called *transmutation,* along with the search for the source of immortality. A key goal of alchemy was to improve one's personal growth, because a person of pure heart was more likely to achieve the transmutation of metal into gold.

Nostradamus imagined himself as part of the greater universe (an idea), and as part of that universe, he began to understand what might come next as time and events progressed. He began to see part of the larger pattern of the universe — the macrocosm. Alchemists expressed this concept in the phrase "as above, so below." They were talking about being part of the stars, the greater cosmos, the universe, and, well, everything.

Throughout his life, Nostradamus displayed a keen interest in alchemy, and its influence can be seen both directly and indirectly within *The Prophecies.* At the everyday level, several alchemy practices help guide the process through which Nostradamus received and recorded his visions:

- **Meditation:** Nostradamus learned how the meditation and ritual of his alchemy studies could help provide the one thing he desired most— a direct line to God. The techniques he used to meditate and look for visions of the future in a bowl of water were ones the alchemists used to increase their insight and knowledge.

- **Focus and concentration:** The alchemist's need for study and concentration helped Nostradamus as he wrote his prophecies, because they trained him to remain focused on both the basic level (getting visions and details along with the astrological charts he later created) and keeping the spiritual side of things in mind. Nostradamus mentally walked through a special process of solitude, prayer, and focused attention (described in more detail in Chapter 5) in his mind's eye and shortened the distance between himself and the divine.

- **Timing:** During the Renaissance, alchemy emphasized astrological connections with celestial bodies. For example, certain processes in the laboratory were done during a full moon or when Venus was low on the horizon. Nostradamus used these kinds of ideas to choose the dates and times that were most favorable for an opening with the divine. With the knowledge Nostradamus gained by studying alchemy and astrology, Nostradamus planned his work schedule to ensure he had the best chance of connecting with his divine inspiration and creating his prophecies.

Besides guiding his sit-down time with the divine, alchemy played a number of other roles in shaping *The Prophecies,* which I explore in the following sections.

Predicting humanity's ultimate fate

Although the everyday alchemist tried to get rich quickly by turning base metals into gold, the alchemist who was truly worth his weight (in gold) was on the path to spiritual enlightenment. Alchemists were constantly seeking perfection in their techniques and their understanding of the world around them. These perfectionists also sought something called the philosopher's stone — a stone or metal that could impart immortality — but this stone was only available to someone who had improved his soul so that it was nearing a pure state. Nostradamus was the second kind of alchemist, and he definitely worked hard to achieve enlightenment.

This view of enlightenment also directly affected *The Prophecies.* Reaching an ideal state — connected to all the riches (both material wealth and spiritual wealth; Nostradamus valued both) — is where Nostradamus predicted humanity would find itself after all the bloodshed and wars, through which humanity is made pure, and faults are removed (see the "Looking on the bright side" sidebar in this chapter).

Some alchemists followed just the pathway to material riches, but many alchemists — like Nostradamus — were also philosophers who sought to clear up the illnesses of the human heart through use of the philosopher's stone.

Encouraging imagination

Alchemists encouraged the use of a new and wondrous tool that very few people during the Renaissance considered useful — the imagination. The ability to create concepts, which were only described using symbols and analogies (which is as close as the alchemists got to a formula), and make them real processes in the laboratory required imagination. The concepts, symbols, and analogies meant very little without it. For Nostradamus, the tools of alchemy and its symbols were very useful to confuse some of his readers while enlightening those who knew this secret language of symbols.

Nostradamus counted on the initiated people who could interpret his meanings to use their imagination. Imagination wasn't limited to alchemists, but in Nostradamus's mind, they were clearly the group of people that encouraged it. As an alchemist, Nostradamus knew that using imagination to picture the formulas could help bring the far-off (and slightly unreal) goal of immortality closer.

Nostradamus used the concept of imagining something until it becomes a reality as an underlying theme in his quatrains. There's struggle (similar to the struggles that alchemists go through to be purified) throughout the quatrains, but in the end, there's a reward for those who persevere (the goal of divine connection and immortality). By describing this process, Nostradamus gave us the formula for the gold in the future — for the divine connection that I think he saw lacking in the years that followed his own.

Counting on Numerology

Stuffed suits and nitpicker scholars agree on very little that relates to Nostradamus. But one of the few things most agree on is that numerology was an important piece of Nostradamus's puzzle. The meanings of and connections between numbers (which can vary) were major elements of the mysticism and alchemy that Nostradamus studied (see "Alchemy's Role in Guiding the Prophet," earlier in the chapter). Numerologists see the number of people in a story or the number of books in a sacred text as pieces of information intentionally placed by the divine as extra insight. Nostradamus intentionally used sacred numbers to add yet another layer to his prophecies. Understanding the meaning of the numbers, like those in Table 6-2, is one way for you to clear up one of Nostradamus's intentional layers of mystery in the quatrains. (For an example of a number having an impact on a quatrain, check out Chapter 18.)

The power of numbers

Numerology is the study of the relationship between each item, person, place, or event and the significant numbers associated with it. When numbers are associated with something, they can reveal information about that person, that text, or even a specific prophecy. The number is like a secret decoder ring to find the hidden message. Without knowing that the numbers are important, you may miss some of the meaning. For example, if a quatrain discusses drastic changes, you may not know whether Nostradamus is talking about death or intellectual changes of thought, unless you recognize that the quatrain is in Century III. In alchemy, three is the number of growth and blessings, and it could mean a positive change for the event in the quatrain.

Unfortunately, the meaning of a number varied for Nostradamus, because he used several numerology systems. Nostradamus most likely used a system of numbers and meanings that integrated part of the Jewish mystical tradition of Kabbalah (which I discuss in Chapter 3), alchemy, and astrology.

Most numerologists recognize the sacred numbers as 1 through 9, and sometimes 11 and 22. To find these numbers, which are contained in sacred texts, they add the individual numbers in a date, or they add pre-assigned numerical values of letters in a name. To add another layer of complexity, the values for a name in English are different than one in Hebrew, and the system for French is different still.

Resources on each of these languages can give you an idea of the number value for each letter. In English, the letters are often matched with numbers 1 through 9, and you start over when you get to 9. Nostradamus used numerology within the names and placement of the quatrains (certain lines within a numbered century or as a certain numbered quatrain) to add another layer of meaning to his work that would be available only to those people familiar with numerology.

If the power of numbers has really piqued your curiosity, take a look at Table 6-2, which lists the basic sacred numbers and some of the meanings associated with them (but certainly not all of the meanings). These numbers are a good starting guideline as you begin to explore the quatrains I discuss in other chapters or if you try to interpret a quatrain on your own.

Table 6-2   Sacred Numbers and Some Associated Meanings

	Christian Mystic Meanings	*Jewish Mystic Meanings*	*Alchemical or Occult Meanings*
1	God-Creator	Power	Ambition; independent; self-sufficient; lucky
2	Duality; divine having two aspects — man and God	Attention; wisdom and self-consciousness	Supportive; diplomatic; analytical; double or symmetry; opposites that finally resolve into one (sulfur/quicksilver)
3	Trinity (God, Christ, Holy Ghost)	Memory	Enthusiastic; optimistic; fun-loving; growth or alive; triple blessing on those who study alchemy
4	Thought	Imagination; four worlds of Kabbalah	Practical; traditional; serious; death
5	Love	Reason; strength and severity; in Kabbalah — fear	Adventurous; mercurial; sensual; balance; five petal flower and star reflecting quintessence
6	Mastery; days of creation	Intuition; meditation; beauty	Responsible; careful domestic; wealth

	Christian Mystic Meanings	Jewish Mystic Meanings	Alchemical or Occult Meanings
7	Transition; seven deadly sins; sacraments	Discrimination; occult intelligence	Spiritual; eccentric; loner; 7 metals as part of the work of alchemy; 7 stars in Great Bear
8	Infinity	Receptivity; perfect intelligence; number of the true name of God	Money-oriented; decisive; stern; fertility
9	Completion	Suggestion; truth; foundation in the Kabalah	Multitalented; compassionate; global; long life
11	Interior fight, rebellion; a reflected meaning of 1; victory in the end with knowledge	Not a sacred number as this is considered unlucky	Enlightened; intense; high-strung
22	Movement; diversity; infinity	Not a sacred number	Goal-oriented; global planner; inspired

Nostradamus's use of numbers is key to many interpretations of individual quatrains (including many of the interpretations I provide throughout this book), and the importance he placed on numbers and their associated layers of meaning can be seen at the macro level as well. For example, he selected 100 as the number of quatrains in each grouping, because within the occult tradition, 100 is the number of perfection. And within Christian mysticism, 100 represents the ultimate in happiness — a celestial connection to all that exists. In addition, the Kabbalistic meaning of 100 is organization, and the number is associated with the moon, which was a constant companion to Nostradamus as he developed his prophecies. A pretty solid number to be associated with, for sure.

How he determined specific dates

Nostradamus used two separate systems for dating events within the prophecies. The first was the traditional Gregorian calendar dates (yep, those are numbers), and the second was a calendar he created, based entirely on Christian events. In the *Epistle to Henry II*, Nostradamus explained part of his Christian calendar, but some of his "facts" don't match the biblical and scientific dates available for when the floods and famines of the Bible occurred. So his dating system was a bit off, but he even said that it might be, so at least he covered all the bases.

I believe he used his own system of dating events as a way to incorporate more of the numbers he saw as important signs for future interpreters. Nostradamus combined his ability to choose his words carefully with his knowledge of numerology to provide the people who are in the know with clues. For example, one of the antichrists (I get to them in Chapter 13) is mentioned along with the name *Mabus,* which in numerology adds up to 11 — a sign of struggle in which knowledge and enlightenment are victorious in the end. For this quatrain, then, it's important that the interpreter understands that the horrible changes brought by the antichrist *Mabus* may have positive outcomes.

Some would-be commentators say that the placement of a prophecy at a particular point in a century indicates the year that the prophecy was/is supposed to occur. But so far, that theory hasn't had a lot of success in predicting event dates, so I put it in my file of unsubstantiated rumors. You may want to do the same. But, first, check out Chapter 10 for more information on the issue, along with some examples.

Unlocking the Secrets of Symbolism

People have been developing complex symbol systems as a way of communicating since the dawn of time. *Symbols* are simply an alternative way of representing an idea or thought. And they aren't just pictures; words can stand in for another thing as well. Like an artist's sketch of your face, however, symbols can lose something in the translation, so interpreting them is an art, and it isn't exact.

Although some symbols change with time, others remain the same. The longer a symbol is used, the more likely its meaning stays the same. For example, most of the symbols that bring the Catholic Church to mind haven't changed over hundreds of years. You're likely to associate the rosary with the Catholic Church, for instance. Add in the meanings for the rosary — prayer, reverence, and holy actions — and the symbol is suddenly very useful for saying a lot with very few words.

Nostradamus worked with both mysticism and religion, and these two systems of thought probably use more symbols than just about any other system created by man. So you shouldn't be surprised that the prophecies are chock full of symbols. Every quatrain is thick with item upon item of deeply meaningful references to people, events, places, and ideas.

The prophecies are an entanglement of symbols and ideas, but they aren't so bad if you take a deep breath and approach them with some semblance of order. I'm here to help, but before I turn over the keys, keep the following points in mind:

✔ Don't assume that just because Nostradamus mentioned a tree in a quatrain that he was talking about an actual tree — or even the Kabbalistic Tree of Life (see Chapter 4). Look at the other pieces of the quatrain and other possibilities before selecting a meaning.

✔ Symbols used in one quatrain may or may not have the same importance in a different quatrain, and the neighborhood of the symbol is important. Take a good look at the entire picture presented by the quatrain before assigning meaning to a particular symbol. The symbol may take on a special meaning if the topic of the prophecy is sensitive or if Nostradamus added one layer of meaning over another.

✔ Keep in mind the many influences of religion, people, and the Renaissance on Nostradamus, and check out any meaning of a quatrain's symbols in light of these different influences. Modern interpretations of symbols may not give you his intended meaning.

Tune into important topics

The first key to unlocking the meaning behind the symbolism in the prophecies is to know which topics were important to Nostradamus. The topics that made up the majority of the known (understood) prophecies — the topics that mattered most to Nostradamus — concerned France, Italy, the Catholic Church, and Napoleon. Nostradamus used imagery associated with each of these topics as well as astrological, medical, and mystical symbols.

Look for signs of the times

The second key to unlocking the meaning behind the symbolism of Nostradamus is to be aware of the culture of the time. His language of symbols reflected the world around him (see Chapter 2 for a look at Renaissance life). Nostradamus may have used the shepherd's crook and papal hat of the pope, for example, to symbolize an individual pope or the entire line of Church rulers.

Explore universal themes

The third key to unlocking the meaning behind the symbolism is to remember that Nostradamus was concerned with certain universal ideas. Survival, struggle, a place to belong in the Universe, and even a place of rest for the soul are concepts that have been discussed in literature for as long as writing has been around — and they ran throughout Nostradamus's prophecies.

The conflicts that concern people can be broken down into three simple categories. Sometimes it's helpful to look at the symbols and see which category they may fit in. Doing so can give you a starting point for determining the symbol's associated meaning. Here are the three basic categories and some examples that fall under each category:

- **Person versus Person:** Assassinations, feuds, and power struggles (includes the battle against self to discover identity and personal strengths)
- **Person versus Nature:** Pestilence, flood, earthquake, and famine
- **Person versus God:** Spiritual struggles and enlightenment

Talking the Talk: Language

Obscurity is fine if you're a government witness in hiding, but it's time to bring Nostradamus's language skills to light so you can better appreciate the related layers they add to *The Prophecies*. The first tactic Nostradamus used to obscure his meanings was to talk about a topic indirectly. Instead of talking openly about the people or the action, he'd use a *metaphor* (a word or phrase that represents something other than itself) and/or an *anagram* (a rearrangement of the letters in a name) to mask the exact meaning of his quatrains. Also, instead of calling a city by its current name, Nostradamus used an older name or a reference to a trait that made the city stand out.

A *double entendre* (when one word can take on another meaning) is one of the tools Nostradamus used to confound his interpreters. You can trace some of Nostradamus's French words back to Latin, where they mean one thing, or back to an older version of the French language, where they mean something entirely different. Not only did he use words that could be traced to several places, but he also rearranged, abbreviated, and otherwise altered words to suit his own prophetic purposes — talk about adding layers of languages. So, even though he may have originally written a quatrain in Latin (in his notes), it may not look that way after he finished working his magic. Scholars and critics have even accused Nostradamus of making up his own language, which isn't far from the truth considering all the changes he made to existing words.

Looking on the bright side

Some critics say that Nostradamus saw humans as basically evil and that his quatrains reflected that belief. Baloney. I have to step in here and defend Nostradamus for just a minute. Yes, a lot of his predictions sound pretty bad, but he wasn't a depressed chicken little. If you can look past the surface, you can see a more positive attitude. Beyond the doom and gloom of natural disasters, deaths, and overthrown governments, some quatrains suggest a happier, more peaceful future. Frequently in his writings, Nostradamus expressed a hope for mankind's overall future as one of peace and learning. And in the *Preface to César,* he said that his words would be understood when ignorance dies down, which sounds like the world will make great strides toward understanding and peace. But it's not easy to reconcile the idea that he saw *all* these things — doom and gloom, as well as peace and happiness.

To resolve the seeming contradictions that run throughout the prophecies, some critics would like for you to believe that Nostradamus didn't know what to say, so he said it all — doom, gloom, and peace to boot. But this idea doesn't fly for me — remember that Nostradamus didn't include the weather or petty events in the quatrains. He focused on the events that were important on a larger scale as revealed by his visions.

I'd like you to consider a different option to reconcile the contradictions. Think about good ol' Dr. Sigmund Freud (a controversial figure in psychoanalysis). He viewed items as *symbolic* of other items, and I think Dr. Freud would've gotten along with Nostradamus just fine. If you look at the overall pattern of the quatrains from beginning to end, you see a great deal of pestilence where the strong survive, events where evils are removed, and a constant reference to the influence of faith on the process being described. I actually see the larger picture painted by the quatrains as a rather overly exuberant extended metaphor, where ridding the word of illnesses and problems brings a happier age. Perhaps Nostradamus saw the human race as children who have to learn lessons the hard way before they can grow into better selves. Like a parent, he set about instructing us with his prophecies, and it wasn't (and still isn't) easy for the children to hear.

As you read through the prophecies that move forward from Nostradamus's time to your own and then beyond, keep in mind that sometimes a pestilence isn't a pestilence. Bad ways of thinking or maybe the habits of addiction are what plague society.

Nostradamus used a wide mixture of languages to write the prophecies, so being certain of a word's origin is extremely difficult. Obscure is definitely a word you can easily use when talking about Nostradamus. Overall, looking at the entire quatrain and trying the meaning of one translation over another is the best method. Often, one translation simply sounds more correct than another one. Although not a very scientific way of working through the quatrains, this method seems to work more often than not.

Part III
The Prophecies From Nostradamus's Time to Napoleon

The 5th Wave   By Rich Tennant

©RICHTENNANT

Bernice takes advantage of Harold's lack of Nostradamus knowledge.

"No. It says right here, 'And the idle man will rise, shortening the grass will be his destiny'."

In this part . . .

Part III begins the really good stuff — exploring Nostradamus's actual visions of the future. This part concentrates specifically on the prophecies that made Nostradamus famous during his own lifetime and then turns its attention to later matters, through the reign of Napoleon.

Throughout this part, I take you step-by-step through the process of figuring out the meanings of the symbols in the quatrains and how they relate to events of Nostradamus's day and today. I also look at stories about Nostradamus's earliest predictions that circulated during his lifetime and helped build his reputation.

I then show how Nostradamus stretched his vision beyond the shortsighted arena of his own lifetime to make prophecies about the late 18th and early 19th centuries. Nostradamus predicted events surrounding the French Revolution and Napoleon, and in this part, I walk you through a few of his visions for the future France, which are unmistakably studded with villains, horror, and blood loss. I keep these quatrains about the French Revolution and Napoleon's reign together to reflect the focused concern Nostradamus had for his homeland. During the process of looking at these visions, I help you view them from a more modern perspective, which isn't quite as scary. I also give you a taste of Nostradamus's broader view of the world at large.

Chapter 7

Predictions that Created a Legendary Beginning

*1*f you've skipped to this chapter to get to the meat of Nostradamus's prophecies, you've *almost* made it. Consider these prophecies to be the appetizer to a full-course menu of his work. This chapter covers the first of Nostradamus's prophecies to come true and traces the growth of the legend of Nostradamus even before his death. Each of the predictions I discuss in this chapter adds color to the portrait of Nostradamus as a prophet of the times.

Most great people aren't truly appreciated until after their time, but Nostradamus began building a reputation for prophetic tendencies when he predicted some everyday events while traveling the countryside and when some of the early quatrain prophecies came true while he was still alive. Particularly interesting in these early prophecies are some royal stars — a guaranteed way to get your name in the papers — and the military maneuvers around the strategically important Isle of Malta. Predicting dangerous events for your country isn't always good for one's health (especially with the Inquisition around), but Nostradamus phrased his words delicately.

Telling Two Tales of Early Predictions

Rumors and urban legends surround the histories and early careers of famous people, even the moderately famous. Most of the records of Nostradamus's early predictions come from second- and third-hand oral stories from the time before his inspired pen was put to paper. The first story in this section describes one of Nostradamus's simple predictions of the immediate future that helped to build his reputation as a person with uncanny knowledge and helped him to develop the self-confidence to stand behind what he believed. I put the other story in the box of divinely inspired prophecy.

Picking pigs for dinner

Like a great urban legend, this story doesn't have a lot of background information validating it, but it could be true. This tale is one of the first about Nostradamus's powers for prediction, and it marks the beginning of his mystical reputation among the country people in France. Nostradamus didn't write predictions at this point in his life (between 1543 and 1545). Instead, he traveled as a doctor curing the Black Plague. During his travels, Nostradamus stayed with many people, such as Seigneur de Florinville — a learned doctor from western France who very much doubted any of the so-called prophetic arts.

Three little pigs . . . No, wait, wrong story.

While staying at the home of Seignior Florinville, Nostradamus told his benevolent host that he had the gift of prophecy, and the Seignior decided to test the young man's ability. As they were taking a walk, Seignior Florinville asked what would happen to the two pigs they saw, and Nostradamus replied that he and Seignior Florinville would eat the white pig, and a wolf would eat the black pig. (The names have been changed to protect the eaten.)

Well, get this: The Seigneur secretly arranged to have the *black* pig served for dinner. Turns out, though, that a tame kitchen wolf ate the men's dinner, and the cook, who didn't know about the prediction, prepared the white pig so his master wouldn't get upset. They discovered the switch during dinner, and Nostradamus's reputation for prediction quickly spread, because he proved himself to a man with great doubts about the power of future telling.

During this time of relative freedom without ties to a home, his medical/apothecary practice, wealthy patrons, or church, Nostradamus began to feel less constrained by the expectations of his world, especially the Church, which didn't approve of his occult studies. This was a time when he didn't answer to anyone and began to express his own voice.

Identifying a future pope

You don't expect monks to gossip about such things as prophecy, but they were the only witnesses to this example of Nostradamus's visions. As the urban legend goes (if you consider the countryside in 16th-century France to be urban), Nostradamus was walking down a lane one day when he met a group of monks. He stepped aside out of respect for their position, and as one of the order approached, Nostradamus fell to his knees. He explained his action by commenting that he fell down before "his Holiness." The pope Nostradamus was referring to was Brother Felice Peretti, a one-time pig farmer turned monk who would become Pope Sixtus V in 1585.

Although the prediction took a while to come true, the holy men remembered it and viewed it as a vision from God because it dealt with the Christian pope. The legend of this prediction coming true (just after Nostradamus's death) increased Nostradamus's reputation and helped keep his works in print.

Detailing the Death of King Henry II

I present to you the most notorious story surrounding Nostradamus's prophecies — his prediction of the death of King Henry II of France, who reigned during Nostradamus's lifetime (you can check out the live version of Henry II in Figure 7-1). Up front, you need to know that in Nostradamus's centuries and quatrains (see Chapter 5 for the mechanics of *The Prophecies*), he mostly concentrated on events that would occur in a far-off time from his own, and few predictions came to be during his lifetime that would gain him attention or wealth. All that changed, however, when he predicted the king's death in Quatrain 35 of Century I.

After the 1555 publication of this quatrain, Catherine de Medici (see Figure 7-2), wife of King Henry II (for more on the de Medici and royal Valois family, stroll through Chapter 8), called Nostradamus to Paris to answer some questions. Rumors at court had brought the dangerous quatrain to her attention, and she demanded to know what the doctor and astrologer meant by these words:

> The young lion will overcome the old one
>
> On the field of battle in single combat:
>
> He will put out his eyes in a cage of gold:
>
> Two fleets [wounds] one, then to die a cruel death. (C I – 35)

Figure 7-1:
Hanging
out with
Henry II.

Réunion des Musées Nationaux / Art Resource, NY

This quatrain drew nearly everyone's attention and caused people to worry about King Henry II's health, because the standard symbol on his shields and banners included a lion. No one knows what Nostradamus said to Catherine about this quatrain when they met in person, but she seemed satisfied (because Nostradamus continued to live) and even consulted him about other events.

Events in 1559 brought a startling new interest in Nostradamus, because nearly every detail of the prophecy matched the unfolding of King Henry's death during a *jousting tournament,* a mock battle with long sticks used to knock one's opponent off his horse. Henry's opponent (the leader of the Scottish guard who also used a *lion* on his shield) missed his aim at the king's chest, and the lance splintered and went through Henry's gold helmet *(cage of gold)* and throat. Apprehension filled the air for ten days while Henry lay in agony from his wounds *(two* of them), after which King Henry II died his *cruel death* as predicted.

People at court looked at Nostradamus's prediction and his previous meeting with the queen and suggested that they planned the death. After many discussions, meetings, and consultations with wise advisors, though, the general feeling of the court softened, and the incident faded from memory — though it wasn't completely forgotten. For more on Nostradamus's ongoing relationship with the queen, see Chapter 8.

Figure 7-2:
Catherine
de Medici.

Scala / Art Resource, NY

Viewing Visions of the Siege of Malta

Based on the first batch of quatrains Nostradamus published in 1555, events happened that seemed to further prove his gift of prophecy. The general buzz about his prophetic powers was loud and a little bit angry sounding, so Nostradamus decided to withhold publishing the rest of his prophecies to divert the wary eyes of the Church and the royal court.

Even though the rest of his prophecies were withheld, people continued to read his published prophecies and *The Almanacs.* And amazingly, he continued to be right about the most important events, including the Siege of Malta in 1565, which happened just before Nostradamus's death in 1566. This prophecy was one of the last ones to come true during Nostradamus's lifetime, and it was important because Nostradamus proved he could predict beyond the borders of his native France. In Quatrain 9 of Century I, he predicted the fates of nations and entire regions:

> From the Orient will come the Punic heart
>
> To vex Adria [Hadrie] and the heirs of Romulus
>
> Accompanied by the Libyan fleet
>
> Malta trembling [temples at Malta] and the neighboring isles empty. (C I – 9)

Understanding C I – 9 requires knowledge of history, geography, and most especially languages. If those subjects aren't your forte, don't fret. I get you up to speed in this section.

The siege according to history books

The facts about the Siege of Malta — the topic surrounding the prophecy in C I – 9 — are pretty clear. A Turkish force from the Ottoman Empire began bombarding and laying siege to the island of Malta in 1565. The Knights of the Order of St. John, leftover from the era of religious Christian crusades, lived on the island home that the king of Spain and Pope Clement V gave them as a place to retire after their escapades and their expulsion from Rhodes. Malta was a strategic place to be given to this band of knights (for Spain and most of Europe) because it was at the bottom tip of Italy and could help control the flow of traffic from East to West in the Mediterranean.

An overwhelming number of Ottoman forces (mainly Turks) pounded on Malta, but the battle wasn't just one of location or ownership, because both sides viewed the battle as one of religions — Christian faith (knights) versus Islamic faith (Ottoman forces) — and the determination of the smaller Christian troops was impressive. After a force of Italian troops along with Spanish reinforcements joined the knights on Malta, the Ottoman invaders lost any chance of taking the island before winter set in, so they returned home in defeat.

The words may vary

Nostradamus used several techniques to blur and hide his meanings, and he was a master craftsman at this job. Know that there are several interpretations of the words Nostradamus wrote. Each one of the lines of C I – 9 varies slightly, and we can begin the game of discovering the meaning somewhere in the middle of these interpretations. Let's begin by looking at some of the different translations and how the slight differences in words can alter the quatrain's meaning.

- ✔ **Orient/Africa versus East/Punic heart:** You can translate the first line as I've done with specific references to the Orient and Punic heart where *Punic* is an old slang term for treachery, so it ends up being a treacherous heart that comes from the Orient. But in other translations, the first line simply says, *From the East will come an African heart.* This translation takes the original term *Punique* from the quatrain and associates it with the Punic people and their wars. The vicious wars of Carthage (located in northern Africa on the Bay of Tunis) were well known to Nostradamus. The variation in translating these words can give you two different concepts of where the threat originates and what kind of threat it is, but the difference is simply in how you translate the word. Overall, the idea of treachery still applies.

Although others suggest that the threat *From the East* was simply the invading Turks, I see a layer of meaning beyond the actual siege, in which Nostradamus incorporates the conflict of world beliefs as represented by the competing sides in this siege. Despite the differences in interpretation, both interpretations could refer to the challenge of ideas that came along with the Ottoman invasion. The Turks, after all, were motivated by money, land, and the conversion of other people to their Islamic faith. Both Christianity and Islam believe that it's their duty to convert people to the one right way — Christianity if you're a Christian and Islam if you're a Muslim. One of the beliefs of Islam is that the revelations from God to Muhammad supercede those rules revealed to Jesus, and the Islamic ideas are meant to override the Christian ideas. Another difference between the Islamic and Christian faiths is that although the Muslims claim to worship the same god, they see god as one deity rather than as part of the Holy Trinity of Father, Son (Jesus), and Holy Ghost acknowledged by the Christians.

✔ **Adria [Hadrie]:** The second line has alternately been assigned to a prophecy for King Henry III or the Adriatic Sea, depending on whether the interpreter views the word *Hadrie* (the original word used by Nostradamus) as a *cryptogram* (a word written in code) for Adriatic or as an *anagram* (a word made by rearranging the letters of another word) with a letter changed (as Nostradamus liked to do) for Henry. Nostradamus occasionally used leaders to stand for countries, and in this case, I believe his reference to King Henry III represented France (during his reign, the differences between the Protestants and the Catholics would be very public and violent). France would face more religious struggles from outside and inside its borders after Nostradamus's time, and I believe this quatrain compares the religious troubles in France with the religious struggle around the siege of Malta.

Stepping back from the prophecies to see the big picture can often help you select a meaning when more than one option is available. Remember that Nostradamus wrote about what he knew best — France — and in several other places in the prophecies, he used Hadrie to refer to Henry. I use that bit of information to assign the Hadrie reference to Henry.

✔ **Heirs of Romulus:** And as for the rest of line 2, *the heirs of Romulus* can refer to Rome and Italy if you look through mythological history books to find that Romulus killed Remus (they were twin brothers) and then built the city of Rome, the home of the Catholic Church.

You can be fairly certain about applying the last two lines to the Siege of Malta by the Ottoman Turks. Ally ships from the Libyan region supported the Turks, so at least here Nostradamus didn't mince many of his words.

The prophecy in focus

The history references and details in Nostradamus's prophecies may seem overwhelming, but by picking the major pieces from each prophecy and deciphering how they relate to one another, you can begin to resolve the prophecy.

In the case of C I – 9, the major pieces are

- ✔ A threat
- ✔ The Libyan fleet
- ✔ Malta

Here's my take on the quatrain:

> *From the Orient/East will come something (with help from Africa) threatening to Henry (stand-in for France) and Italy. The island of Malta will be abandoned.*

Although the Ottomans threatened, attacked, and thoroughly ran down the island of Malta and its inhabitants (even though they went home in defeat, they still did lots of damage), the threat that probably most concerned Nostradamus was the larger battle of religions. The invading Turks brought with them a belief in the Koran and the faith of Islam. In many cases, these men crusaded on behalf of Islam and used conquering as a technique for converting people (something they ironically learned from the Christian crusades) — a very clear religious threat from the East against Rome (home of the pope and the Roman Catholic Church).

I see a double meaning in the final line of the quatrain, which speaks about the abandonment of the temples of Malta. Nostradamus could've been referring to the Turks as they retreated home. But Nostradamus also could've been referring to the Knights of the Order of St. John, the religious order that settled the island. These religious warriors also took up commerce (and occasionally pirate activities against pirates in the area) to support themselves and their temples. Through the eyes of Nostradamus, such activities would've been a way of deserting the temples — or turning their focus away from religion. I believe that Nostradamus was leaving a reminder for future generations that this event was a pattern for mankind, and a dangerous one for the Christian faith.

A Forewarning to the French

Nostradamus had many loves, and France was certainly one of them. The others were religion, study, prophecy, and astrology — in no particular order. I bring this tidbit up because I think Nostradamus's great love for his country and his religion were the intertwining motivations for the warnings of struggle to come that he wrote in C I – 5:

> They will be driven away without much fighting,
>
> They will be very much harried in the country:
>
> Town and city will have a greater debate:
>
> Carcassonne and Narbonne will have their hearts tried. (C I – 5)

In the following sections, I dissect the meaning behind these vague, vague words.

Facing the Wars of Religion

No specific details stand out in C I – 5, and in fact, the first three lines generally describe a troubled land that could be just about anywhere. But Nostradamus gave the last line enough details (the city names of *Carcassonne* and *Narbonne*) for the quatrain's meaning to return to France. The details are vague, though, so looking at what those cities may have symbolized for Nostradamus is the key to unlocking this quatrain's meaning.

Carcassonne and Narbonne are cities in southwest France, and during the middle 1500s, these cities were the scene of a fair share of religious struggles between the Protestants and the Catholics. Nostradamus was familiar with both towns because they were on his walking tours to heal the victims of the Black Plague (see Chapter 3).

Both cities were host to massacres motivated by religious fervor. In addition, Carcassonne became a town divided after officials decided that the town would join the Catholic League. This league was organized by the Guise family, one of the powerful French families who tried to control the throne and ultimately helped start the French Wars of Religion. Angered by the decision, the Protestants took part of Carcassonne hostage. I think that in Nostradamus's eyes, Carcassonne represented France and described the split personality of the religious situation. France really was in a crisis of faith. (Check out Chapter 8 for more on the Guise family and the Catholic League.)

Revealing personal concerns

Quatrain C I – 5 was certainly a warning about religious dissent that the French should've heeded, but the religious wars that washed over France shortly before and after Nostradamus's death in 1566 were almost unavoidable. Nostradamus didn't forget his Jewish heritage and the forced conversion of his family. In the same way that the young Nostradamus watched the rising tensions between Jews and Christians, the older man watched the beginning of the struggle for religious power between Christians and Huguenots (as the Protestant followers were called). If you want some details about this other religious faith, check out Martin Luther in Chapter 2.

Nostradamus wrote down his quatrains out of order in terms of date, but they weren't *completely* randomized in their placement. He published this quatrain, with its warning of religious unrest, in the first batch of prophecies — the batch published before he died — and in my opinion, he put it there on purpose. I believe he thought it would do more good at that point than later on in the religious struggle. The fact that he tried to make the religious dissent known before the religious wars were out of hand shows his deep concern for the people.

Quatrain C I – 5 doesn't have the same powerful imagery that other quatrains have. I believe the reason is that this was a prophecy inspired by Nostradamus's own concerns for his country rather than a prophecy for mankind that he felt was divinely inspired. The fact that the quatrain was an average, run-of-the-mill prediction doesn't mean that it wasn't accurate. The wars and the struggles concerning religion happened very similarly to how Nostradamus described them.

This quatrain reveals an important piece of information: Nostradamus didn't feel that he was always divinely inspired. Sometimes he made predictions out of his own concerns. It's a mark in his favor that he seems to have gotten these regular predictions accurate as well.

Chapter 8

Foreseeing Royally Good (and Dangerous) Times

··

In This Chapter

▶ Foretelling the lives of the fabulous de Medici line

▶ Finding fault with Henry III in *The Prophecies*

▶ Predicting the end of days for two royals

▶ Seeing London's future falling down

··

*N*ostradamus wasn't of royal blood, but it's clear by the amount of references he made to the royalty of the time that the topic occupied his visions. This preoccupation with royalty wasn't completely strange for the Renaissance. Many details of the royal court and its goings-on were reported and rumored, much like the details of celebrities' lives are reported on sensational news channels today. With all the intrigue, murder, romance, emotions, and struggle for power and prestige (all while dressed to the nines), you can think of the royal houses as the reality shows of the Renaissance.

After publishing some of his quatrains in the first installment of *The Prophecies* in 1555, Nostradamus went to Paris to answer Queen Catherine de Medici's questions about C I – 35, which foretold the death of King Henry II (see Chapter 7). The meeting would mark the beginning of a long-lasting relationship with the queen. Queen Catherine de Medici and her children were one of Nostradamus's favorite topics because Catherine gave him a great deal of encouragement and notoriety (see Chapter 4 for more on this relationship).

Nostradamus wasn't exactly taking Sunday strolls on the street when he first predicted the death of Henry II. He walked into some questionable territory. Predicting the rise and fall of the kings of France was a dicey business that had to be handled carefully. Nostradamus knew he had to be careful, but he continued to write prophecies about the entire Medici clan — effectively foretelling major events throughout the final 30-year stretch of the family's time on the throne.

In this chapter, I explain some of the quatrains relating specifically to the queen and her children. Although some of these were published officially after Nostradamus's death, he was known to circulate advance copies of his prophecies among those most important to him, which included the queen. But, Nostradamus's royal visions for his time weren't limited to Catherine and family. As his visions broadened, so did the topics his prophecies covered. So, I also look past the French shores in this chapter, examining some of the more spectacular examples of prophecies that occurred near his lifetime like the London fire in 1566, fleeing queens, and all around devilish doings in the royal houses of Europe.

Keeping It in the Family: The Medici Prophecies

Catherine de Medici was a quiet and unobtrusive queen during the rule of her husband, King Henry II from 1547 to 1559, but when her sons took the throne and were too sickly (Francis II) or too young (Charles IX) she acted as *regent* (someone who rules until the true ruler can fill the role). She also acted as an unofficial regent and tried to maintain her decision-making role when one son (Henry III) was too weak in spirit to rule on his own. Of Catherine's ten children, Louis, Victoire, and Jeanne died in infancy, the women faired poorly, and three of the men served as kings of France. Not a bad legacy for the daughter of a merchant.

Catherine de Medici's sons had a pretty difficult time sitting still in the throne. And, if you're going to keep track of the prophecies about this family, you have to have a handle on the boys and their tenure in office:

- **Francis II (1559 to 1560):** Francis II (the first-born son) came to the throne as a child in 1559, and Catherine ruled for him until his death at age 16 in 1560.

- **Charles IX (1560 to 1574):** Next came Charles IX, who was crowned at the tender age of 11, but he lasted only 13 years until his death in 1574.

- **Henry III (1574 to 1589):** The death of Charles brought Henry III to the throne in 1574. He ruled until 1589.

Hercules Francois, Duke of Anjou and Catherine's favorite, never made it to the throne after dying in 1584 during the reign of his older brother Henry III.

Although the sons play a prominent role in the quatrains, the daughters were only barely alluded to in one or two (grouped as part of the Valois children). But I'll put them out in front now:

✔ **Elizabeth** (second by birth) married Phillip II of Spain and died during childbirth at 23.

✔ **Claude** (third by birth) was hunchbacked and also died during childbirth. She was married to the Duke of Lorraine.

✔ **Marguerite** (sixth by birth) lived the longest (1615) after remaining in a convent the majority of her days. She married the king of Navarre, who later became King Henry IV of France (who does show up in Nostradamus's quatrains).

Witnessing a widow renewed

Take a look at C VI – 63, which tells the tale of a grieving widow who lived on as a strong leader for her country:

> The lady left alone in the realm
>
> By the unique one [spouse] extinguished first on the bed of honor:
>
> Seven years will she be weeping in grief,
>
> Then with great good fortune for the realm long life. (C VI – 63)

Catherine did in fact stop mourning seven years after the death of her husband, but she was a superstitious woman who believed very strongly in Nostradamus's writings. She may have stopped mourning formally after seven years (by changing her dress, appearance, some of her demeanor, and how much she appeared in public) because the number seven was significant to her or because it would fulfill Nostradamus's prophecy.

Nostradamus used his powers of prophecy here but wasn't stretching himself too far. I believe this is a feel-good quatrain that could've applied to Catherine no matter when her husband passed. Nostradamus saw very positive results in France and Catherine's future from the queen's long life, (increasing France's political connections through the marriage of her children with the rulers of Spain and England, for example).

This type of feel-good quatrain was important during Nostradamus's lifetime because it kept the attention of important people who knew Nostradamus (no one wants to keep a negative prophet around) and enabled him to keep his name circulating at court (the more contacts, the better for business).

Now fast-forward about 450 years. For the modern understanding of this prophecy, note that Nostradamus wrote quatrains that weren't always filled with the violence of war and natural disasters. (I talk about these horrible-sounding events in later chapters of this book.) The ending line of hope for the kingdom here is a reminder to look at the overall goal for humanity rather than to concentrate on the individual's suffering or personal goals.

Revealing the regency

The trick to understanding many prophecies is to keep an open mind about how the lines within a quatrain are connected. Life's a breeze when each line of a quatrain is related in meaning to the next line in a nice, even flow. But sometimes, lines are separate thoughts and may not be related chronologically or discuss the same subject. Poetically, Nostradamus chopped up his lines so the reader has to do some problem-solving to unwind the twists and turns.

For example, C II – 14 discusses the general regency of Catherine de Medici — or her *Highness*. But don't assume that the same person performs all the actions or that the events in all four lines happen at the same time:

> At Tours, Gien, guarded, eyes will be searching,
>
> Discovering from afar her serene Highness:
>
> She and her suite will enter the port,
>
> Combat, thrust, sovereign power. (C II – 14)

To resolve this prophecy, you need to break this quatrain down by the large puzzle pieces in each line:

- ✔ *Tours* and *Gien* are towns that touch the Loire River, a large and important river for the French. I think Nostradamus used the rivers here to represent the whole of France, from one end to the other (from sea to shining sea is the American equivalent).

- ✔ *Enter the port* is a phrase that could literally mean a port with boats and water, or a safe harbor in a storm. Nostradamus likely used a double meaning here to refer to the 1564 journey by King Charles IX and Catherine de Medici (who wasn't popular with her French subjects because she was from Italy, France's long-time enemy) across the countryside in an attempt to increase her popularity and into the safe haven of Salon, Nostradamus's hometown.

- ✔ *Combat, thrust,* and *sovereign power* are in the final line. *Combat* and *thrust* could refer to physical or political combat, but combined with the phrase *sovereign power* and the other lines focusing on political power, I place the idea of combat into the political realm. Near the end of Catherine's reign as regent, she struggled to maintain control over the throne and her children who ruled France; in addition, the religious wars were in full swing. (You can find quatrains about the religious wars in Chapter 7 and uncover additional background on the subject in the "Oh Henry: The End of the Valois Line" section later in the chapter.)

After you lay out the key pieces, you can begin to put them together and find meaning. I believe that Nostradamus envisioned a time when Catherine de Medici (described elegantly as *serene Highness*) would watch over all of France, tour to a safe place, and then find that her efforts to keep peace were mostly fruitless. In the end, that's exactly what happened, but her influence prevented France from growing weaker under the rule of her weak children. Nostradamus predicted the general flavor of his patron's later years of ruling.

C II – 14 was published in 1555, and it would've been available to the queen. If her faith wavered during this time period, this quatrain reaffirmed her belief in Nostradamus's abilities to prophesy, and it couldn't have hurt his reputation that he was predicting Catherine's long reign. Catherine ended up running France from behind her children (as an influence) or beside them (as an official regent) for nearly 30 years.

Foreseeing the end

Although Catherine's patronage was important to Nostradamus, Quatrain C I – 10 reminds you that his nighttime visions weren't all laced with flowery verse for the queen and France. This prophecy was placed in the first set of published quatrains, but it didn't have the same promises for a productive rule for Catherine. Nostradamus could've ascribed the prophecy to the fact that nearly all astrologers and predictors of the future saw death eventually in their work. That said, read on:

> The serpent conveyed in the iron cage
>
> Where the seven children of the King are taken:
>
> Their progenitors will come out from their underworld below,
>
> Before dying seeing of their offspring death and cries. (C I – 10)

Whether this quatrain gives the details of the passing of King Henry II or Catherine de Medici (more likely), Nostradamus stated clearly that the royal family line would end. My take (my paraphrase) on the quatrain is that seven royal children will already be in the *iron cage* (representing a crypt or vault) when the *serpent* (a symbol Catherine added to the family crest, and represents one of that family in this line) is taken, and the *progenitors* (ancestors) will weep. Note that throughout *The Prophecies,* Nostradamus used seven as a symbol for the children of Henry II and Catherine de Medici (even though ten children were born, only seven lived to adulthood).

Nostradamus probably wrote the quatrains as he interpreted his visions and then scattered the quatrains relating to the same topic to better hide them within the larger work of the ten centuries. For a complete picture on a topic, try looking through a good index of topics and quatrains (available in many of the complete interpretations of Nostradamus) and reading all the quatrains that have your topic as their focus.

In the original language of C I – 10, the first line reads "Serpens transmis." You can trace *serpens* back to origins in Greek for *shroud,* but some translators suggest it can be traced to the French form of the word and is a reference to a *snake* or *serpent*. With that piece of info in your pocket, know that after King Henry II's unfortunate run-in with fate, Catherine changed her *heraldic emblem* (the symbol of her house and its power — think coat of arms) to contain a snake holding its tail with its mouth. This symbol is typically used in the occult (mysterious studies) and by alchemists (those who sought to refine metal to gold and fine immortality along the way) to reflect the circular nature of things and the delicate balance between keeping things going and biting your tail off to spite your fate.

Francis II: The Conspiracy

Each and every president of the United States expects threats to life and limb, and for the crowned heads of Europe during the Renaissance, it wasn't much different. Take a look at C I – 13:

> The exiles because of anger and intestine hatred
>
> Will bring a great conspiracy to bear against the King:
>
> Secretly they will place enemies as a threat,
>
> And his own old ones against them sedition. (C I – 13)

This quatrain tells the story of powerful people, political intrigue, conflict, high emotions, and a king in danger. Like a really good spy novel, this quatrain doesn't tell who the people were, but I think the hints are clear enough for a reasonable guess. Because this quatrain was published in 1555, it's possible that, along with the other Medici family quatrains, the events were to happen during Nostradamus's time — and it appears that they did.

The best-fitting scenario for this quatrain surrounds the time period when Francis II ruled France with the help of his mother, Catherine. The conspiracy of Amboise, as it came to be known, occurred in 1560. It revolved around advisors and spies, and Nostradamus was very accurate in predicting this kind of trouble. He wanted to warn his friend Catherine de Medici of events that would threaten the throne. But, of course, with a royal house, you can pretty much assume that a conspiracy happens on an almost constant basis.

Francis was sickly, and the other royal houses in France, namely the Bourbon and Montmorency families, wanted a chance at the throne. To "save France," Huguenots (Protestants) developed a plot to seize Francis II at the Château in Amboise (the city where the conspiracy gets its name) and imprison his advisers François, Duke of Guise (older brother to Henri Duke of Guise, but I tell his story along with the other Guise cardinal's story in the next section) and Charles de Guise, cardinal of Lorriane. The plot, which was never really about France's betterment at all, was revealed secretly, and the traitors were treated to ill hospitality and some rather strict punishment — death.

The Duke of Guise wasn't royal and didn't expect to take the throne, but he could've made a bid to take over as regent from Catherine de Medici if he could get her out of the picture. Add to that the fact that the family was strongly Catholic, and you have clear reasons for the Protestants to conspire to keep them away from the throne.

This quatrain was one of several that were especially memorable for people of the time. The events of the conspiracy came to pass just five years after the quatrain was published, and interest in what else Nostradamus had to say increased. Instead of simply reading his prophecies as a pastime, many people from the French court began scanning the quatrains for references to themselves or current situations. Some very motivated individuals even circulated forgeries of the prophecies with slightly changed quatrains that "predicted" certain changes in power or wealth for the person.

Oh Henry: The End of the Valois Line

Before I get to the details, it's off to the history books to find out what was going on with King Henry III of France, the topic of these quatrains (see Figure 8-1). Henry, the last of Queen Catherine de Medici's children to rule in France, was active in government service before he became king in 1574 and participated in the French Wars of Religion (mid-16th century to 1598) against the Protestants and helped in the St. Bartholomew's Day Massacre (mob violence on the part of the Catholics beginning with assassinations on St. Bartholomew's day in 1574 which lasted for months) where thousands of Huguenots (Protestants) were killed.

This pattern of religious struggle between Catholicism and Protestantism continued throughout Henry's reign. One of the major players in this game was Duke Henry de Guise, a member of the House of Guise, a real power in the government of France and the French Catholic Church. Henry de Guise, the pope, and in a show of support for both parties even Catherine de Medici (who had reverted to her pattern of compromise between the groups) joined what became known as the Catholic League, a group designed to defend (with military action if necessary) the Catholic religion in France.

Royal families were often grouped together in categories called *houses,* and everyone of a particular bloodline was considered part of that house. Although most kings and queens were called solely by their first names, they were always known to be part of the house that currently held power — for example, the House of Tudor for Queen Mary in England or the House of Valois for King Henry III in France. Members of the ruling family were considered to have privileges because, well, they were related to the king, and life just didn't get any better than being related to the guy in charge.

Figure 8-1:
Henry III.

Erich Lessing / Art Resource, NY

Taking the reigns of power

Check out the vision in C VI – 29:

> The saintly widow hearing the news,
>
> Of her offspring placed in perplexity and trouble:
>
> He who will be instructed to appease the quarrels,
>
> He will pile them up by his pursuit of the shaven heads. (C VI – 29)

Although some people argue that Catherine manipulated France through her children, Nostradamus called her the *saintly widow* anyway. My take is that this quatrain says her children are struggling and dying while she tries to maintain control over France.

I think that this quatrain accurately predicted the situation of struggle for Catherine, who was forced to send for Henry III to return from Poland and take the throne after the death of Charles IX. This was a move to restore peace to France, and I think Henry III was the *he* who was supposed to *appease the quarrels* between the Protestants, Catholics, royalists, and anti-royalists who were fighting for power. Henry III had that power because he was the king, and a firm hand in leadership could've helped the situation, but Henry III was firmly on the Catholic side of the fence.

Henry III fulfilled one version of the final line's prophecy by ordering the death of Henri de Guise (the third duke of Guise) and his brother, Louis the Cardinal de Guise in 1588. *Shaven heads* referred to priests because many monks chose to shave their heads as a sign that they were not vain or worldly, and Cardinal de Guise was indeed a priest, much like the priest and possible lover of the Henry III who ultimately killed the king in his bedroom. Here are some additional tidbits from my analysis:

- ✔ Nostradamus gave details of the events in fairly clear order — years before the struggle for the throne began — but it was important to the popularity of *The Prophecies* that he didn't just come out and say that the situation was hopeless.

- ✔ He maintained some dignity surrounding the bisexuality issue when he could've made a very open statement.

- ✔ Nostradamus may have left this particular quatrain as a warning to Catherine to leave Henry in Poland or to prepare her for the fact that she (and not her sons) would have to be the strong leading force. Even in this quatrain, she was the one who guided Henry III.

The king commits murder

Together, the following two quatrains predict death for the de Guise at Henry's order and reveal a very accurate prophecy about the beginning of the end of the house of Valois in the hands of King Henry III, king of France.

Citing the city

Take a look at Quatrain C III – 51. In this quatrain, each of the cities is a symbol for something or someone else involved in one of the most notorious French murder plots ever concocted. In the tradition of great detectives, and with a nod to the fictional detective Sherlock Holmes, I want to look at the pieces first before putting them together in this story of power and death.

> Paris conspires to commit a great murder
>
> Blois will cause it to be fully carried out:
>
> Those of Orléans will want to replace their chief,
>
> Angers, Troyes, Langres will commit a misdeed against them. (C III – 51)

Here's my interpretation of what the cities symbolize:

- ✔ **Paris:** As the seat of the French government, Nostradamus often used Paris as a symbol for the king. Nostradamus was unlikely to know the exact names of all the future kings of France, so this method saved some work on his part. The king here was most likely King Henry III. (Read on for my reasoning as to why it was probably him.)

- ✔ **Blois:** This was a large house near Paris where the assassination of the Henri Duke de Guise occurred in 1588. Blois possibly also had a double meaning, referring to Henri de Guise himself.

- ✔ **Orléans:** Everyone was choosing sides, even the towns. Henri, the Duke of Guise was also the governor of Orléans, but King Henry III replaced him with D'Entraques, a man who wasn't part of the Catholic League. Orléans was a refuge during the War of Religions (as this struggle came to be known) for the Protestants. Nostradamus would've seen this town's change of power as a miniature version of the struggle for religious power between King Henry III, who had granted minor concessions to Protestantism, and the strongly Catholic Henri, Duke of Guise, who wanted to make France a Catholic nation.

- ✔ **Angers, Troyes, and Langres:** Like pieces on a chessboard, these towns lined up on one side (or was it the other?) of the battle between King Henry III and Henri Duke de Guise.

If you paraphrase the quatrain using the symbolism from the cities, you begin to see a clear picture:

The king plots murder and makes sure that it happens, and then there is a revolt in Orléans and other cities.

Unfortunately for Nostradamus, his vision must have blurred near the end, because the information about whether all three cities joined the Catholic League and were disloyal to *them* is unclear from the history records. For that matter, the vague reference to *them* weakens the final line in the overall strong prophecy of the murderous events.

Carrying out the act

Nostradamus continued his commentary on King Henry III with another quatrain but placed this one in a different century (book-wise, not time-wise). Separating the prophecies helped hide meanings, and sometimes the harder Nostradamus worked to hide the meanings, the more significant the prophecy was to the overall history of mankind. In the case of Henry III, the historical impact was large. The trouble with Henry III and the French Wars of Religion effectively ended the French rule by the Valois line, and France took a tour under the Bourbon kings (for more on the prophecy foretelling the rise to power of this house, famous for their Louis's, see the "Growing Up Bourbon" section later in the chapter; and for prophecy on the death of another Bourbon monarch, Louis XIII, see Chapter 9). Take a look at C I – 85:

Because of the lady's reply, the King troubled:

Ambassadors will take their lives in their hands:

The great one doubly will imitate his brothers,

Two who will die through anger, hatred and envy. (C I – 85)

This quatrain requires some bottom-up thinking. The last line talks about *two who will die* and is the closest link to C III – 51. Although deaths surrounded the royal houses during other times in history, the pairing of two Guise murders stands out — the murders of the Duke de Guise (Henri) and Cardinal de Guise (Louis) by Henry III in 1588. The murders deeply affected the people of France, with whom the Duke de Guise was popular, and set them against King Henry III.

The third line says *The great one doubly will imitate his brothers*. Note that other translations say that the brother *doubly disguise(s)*. Either translation most likely refers to the brother of the de Guise men — the Duke de Mayenne. The Duke did in fact imitate his brothers by taking control of the Catholic League after their deaths and rising up against King Henry III in favor of the Bourbon family as the rulers of France.

The first two lines involve some fairly high officials in France. Assuming that the lines still refer to 1588, when the brothers were murdered, the *Ambassadors* were most probably the men sent by King Henry III (his minions) to perform the killings, and the *lady* was my favorite strong mama — Catherine de Medici. Catherine was Queen Mother at this point and was attempting to control Henry's actions. She wasn't succeeding and was upset by Henry's plot, because she believed it would create more trouble than good.

Despite Nostradamus's warnings, the murder of the de Guise brothers occurred in 1588, and history has never been the same. For the most part, Nostradamus accurately described the story of how King Henry III plotted to murder two brothers (Henri Duke de Guise and Louis Cardinal de Guise). The actual murders took place at the Château of Blois (which housed King Henry's supporters), and the people in the cities mentioned in C III – 51 were troubled by these actions. *Voilá!* — how's that for hitting the nail on the head?

The men weren't the only ones with issues, though, and in C I – 85 the Queen Mother, Catherine de Medici, was mentioned as having her own problems regarding her son's behavior. The historical truth (and what bothered the royal mom) was that the de Guise brothers held a ton of political power, whether Henry liked it or not. Catherine had intended on using their power to keep other contenders for the throne away, so she preferred to deal with them rather than just killing them. The assassins were severely chastised by the courts, and Henry III lost a great deal of support from the people of France.

A dream come true: The death of Henry III

Now flex your interpretation muscles with Quatrain C I – 97:

> That which fire and sword did not know how to accomplish,
>
> The smooth tongue in council will come to achieve:
>
> Through repose, a dream, the King will be made to meditate,
>
> The enemy more in fire and military blood. (C I – 97)

Because the imagery of this quatrain is fairly general, the interpretations of its meaning tends to fan out like a magician's hand of cards, and you can be tempted to pick a card, any card. Before making your choice, try looking at the major images first and picking out the keys to the quatrain.

One interpretation isolates the first two lines as a prophecy separate from the third and fourth lines. Some interpreters assign this first pair of lines as a prophecy for modern times — for the United Nations *(council)*, because neither weapon nor flame has relieved the struggles of the world community. Of course, you can also put most modern marriages into this pair of lines with their imagery of battle, possibly fiery tempers, and a resolution with soft words in marriage counseling. I tend to file this interpretation in the "not really so valid" category.

The more common understanding of this quatrain hinges on the combination of a king, a dream, and then some sort of resolution in a council. If you look backward through time, the most likely scenario to fit these details occurred in 1589 when King Henry III of France was assassinated. To see the match, you need to check the basic facts about the situation against the quatrain.

The central figure in this quatrain is a king who has a dream about the enemy. Many accounts exist of King Henry III having just such a dream about his death. Note that other kings have dreamed sporadically about their deaths, but they haven't been connected to a resolution in council, which was the case with King Henry III. (More on what that resolution was in a minute.)

Moving on, the quatrain says there's something that *fire and sword did not know how to accomplish.* I think that particular something was the decadent lifestyle and violent rule King Henry III had over France (including the murder of the de Guise brothers; see "The king commits murder," earlier in the chapter). About that *fire* reference, I don't think Nostradamus was talking about burning down the town to stop the problem. In this situation, I think he used the Christian symbol of fire to represent the destination of hell for the sinner, the troubled king.

The quatrain also says that something must be resolved by *smooth tongue in council.* But rather than use the term resolve, which may suggest paperwork or a legal act as if you were resolving a dispute among countries with a treaty,

Nostradamus used the word *achieve,* which suggests something more like an end in itself. Death, perhaps? Maybe, but I'm getting ahead of myself.

Now consider the *smooth tongue* reference about the council. I think it's a poetic phrase for the generally gentle-minded and soft-spoken monks of the time. Why? Because a monk did in fact meet with King Henry III and bring messages to council him. His name was Jacques Clément, and he stabbed Henry while delivering a whispered message. Ultimately, the solution offered or *achieve(d)* by the monk was surprising and final — death.

Last but not least, the quatrain says that the enemy is *more in fire and military blood* — and odd way to identify the enemy. Nostradamus avoided telling straight out who the enemy was (or giving identifying clues) and insisted, instead, on saying what surrounds the enemy. My take is that Nostradamus most likely did this dance around the facts of his vision because the culprit who committed the murder was a fanatical monk, probably driven by the general feeling against the king who had killed the Duke de Guise. In some interpretations line 4 says that the *enemy is not in war or military blood,* which sounds a little closer to the real meaning of the line and the quatrain since the sword (representing military power) has already been discarded and the situation has moved on to other forms of negotiation in *council.* And the tie-in to this interpretation of line 4? A monk is neither military nor at war and neither is a general population which feels the king has behaved badly.

So based on historical facts, I think this prophecy was indeed about King Henry III and that Nostradamus predicted the events surrounding Henry III's assassination accurately. Interestingly, the early quatrains — this one included — were published well before King Henry III's death in 1589. At the time this quatrain was published, I doubt it had much impact. But when King Henry had a dream about his royal robes being trampled by the feet of the monks and the French people (which is the version of his dream that he gave), it should've sparked the connection to this quatrain and been a warning to the king. Perhaps the king did know about the warning, and it isn't recorded in the journals from the period. Because this death was predicted twice — by Nostradamus and in King Henry's dreams — it has the feeling of an event that would've happened regardless of any warnings.

Growing up Bourbon: The rise of Henry IV

Nostradamus must've had a chart to keep all the Kings and intrigue straight, or else he was simply brilliant because many of his quatrains trace the development of the French throne, like this one about the follow-up to King Henry III, King Henry IV (originally king of Navarre). Check out C II – 88:

The circuit of the great ruinous deed,

The seventh name of the fifth will be:

Of a third greater the stranger warlike:

Sheep [Aries], Paris, Aix will not guarantee. (C II – 88)

If you unravel the spaghetti of references, you discover that Nostradamus was harping on his favorite topic of politics. Here's a line-by-line breakdown:

- ✔ **Line 1:** It's difficult to say which of the things that threatened France in the 16th century Nostradamus would've considered a *ruinous deed.* Maybe it was the great religious schism that threatened religious war at every turn, the fight for the throne, Henry III's bisexuality, or the St. Bartholomew's Massacre that Henry III ordered at Catherine de Medici's urging. That last event — a massacre of Protestants — was possibly the cruelest of actions and may have been what Nostradamus meant. Honestly, though, if you're talking about Europe during the Renaissance, Line 1 can be applied in any number of ways.

- ✔ **Line 2:** If the *seventh name of the fifth will be,* then there's just one name, but whose name is it? Here's my take: Nostradamus frequently used seven to refer to the seven children of Henry II and Catherine. In this case, he saw how the pieces of the royal line would fall into place in France when the fifth child would become King Henry III (part of the seventh) and the last of the royal Valois (surname) family line.

- ✔ **Line 3:** This line says that the third (as in Henry III) finds a greater person, a *stranger warlike* which in other translations comes out as a warmonger. Well, know that Catherine's daughter Marguerite married the king of Navarre (not part of France at the time), and he became King Henry IV of France. As for the *stranger warlike* reference, there's a connection to King Henry IV, too. Read on.

- ✔ **Line 4:** The first three lines of this quatrain are very vague and could refer to various situations, but the fourth line seems to anchor this prophecy to King Henry IV, a member of the Bourbon family, who marked the end of the line for the Valois rule of France. France disliked the idea of being ruled by a foreigner, and Henry IV, a definite foreigner from Poland, used force to take Paris before the French finally accepted him — not the last act of war by this pushy king.

In line 4, Nostradamus used astrology to give supporting details to his prophecies. Instead of placing a specific date, he used *Mouton* in the original text, which can translate as *sheep* (which is a little far fetched and doesn't make any sense) or to the wool-processing centers of France, especially Reims. I believe that the reference is to an astrological Zodiac sign of Aries (symbolized by the ram), which covers the months of March and April. This was the time period when Henry IV took over Paris. And just for the record, Aix is a reference to Aix-en-Provençe.

For what it's worth, although this is one of the quatrains that many authors point out to prove that Nostradamus was a prophet with great powers, I think it isn't one of his best examples of detail work. The reference to Aries is a bit difficult to get to without several translations, and the unaware reader may trip easily and miss the prophecy. My main problem with this quatrain is that the first three lines are vague and don't seem to lead anywhere in particular.

Nowhere to Hide: A Queen on the Run

Although you and I may need a chart to keep up with who was killing whom and who was next in line to the throne of certain countries, the people of the time generally knew this information as a matter of public record. Nostradamus sometimes foresaw events regarding these very topics.

When one symbol is changed for another, you can lose meaning or even introduce confusion (like describing a picture with words — it isn't going to be exactly right). This trouble in interpreting visions may account for some of the discrepancies in the following quatrain.

For your reading and mulling pleasure, here's Quatrain C I – 86:

> The great Queen when she shall see herself vanquished
>
> Will act with an excess of masculine courage:
>
> On horseback, she will pass over the river entirely naked,
>
> Pursued by the sword: it will mark an outrage to faith. (C I – 86)

There are many stories about fleeing queens, but I believe Nostradamus gave enough detail here to accurately identify the flight of Mary Stuart, queen of Scots, in 1568 (not to be confused with Bloody Mary I, queen of England who lived at the same time). This was the second country Mary had fled, the first being France after her husband, Francis II of France, passed away and her relatives tried to take the power of Scotland from her. Nostradamus probably called her *The great Queen* because he saw the beginning of her reign in Scotland, in which a peaceful country and strong advisors kept things on an even keel (or maybe it was unavoidable to call a 5 foot, 11 inch woman *great*). The rest of the quatrain describes her loss of power and flight from Scotland to England. The *excess of masculine courage* isn't a slight against women but rather a prevailing attitude by men in earlier times that women were more timid and less aggressive when confronted with difficult issues.

For a little historical background, know that Mary's half-brother, James Stuart, the Earl of Moray, and many of the common people in Scotland objected to her second marriage and even suspected her of killing her first husband (Francis II, who died in 1559; see the discussion of the de Medici family line earlier in this chapter). Mary faced defeat after a battle with forces led by her half-brother, and rather than die or be captured (for the second time in her life, but that's another story) she fled Scotland. The last two lines of the quatrain accurately describe in strong detail the events surrounding Mary's sudden departure from Scotland for the court of Queen Elizabeth I (her cousin) of England. Blood is thicker than water, but not in this case. Mary didn't receive a very warm welcome at the court and was imprisoned.

Okay, so Mary wasn't naked during her horseback ride, and some critics of Nostradamus point this fact out as a failure in the prophecy. But most of Nostradamus's descriptions weren't literally true, and enough of the details were specific to this event that the prophecy is still amazingly accurate. I think that if Mary wasn't naked in body, then she was naked in spirit. The people of her country abandoned her due to the troubles of her second marriage, and this lack of support left her exposed (some might say *naked*) to foul play and criticism.

Swords have always been a symbol with many meanings, and Nostradamus probably used this image in line 4 for that reason. On a very literal level, the sword of the conquering army would've certainly chased her from her country. Symbolically, the sword could mean many things.

If you want a prime example of Nostradamus's powerful use of symbols, look no further than Quatrain C I – 86. Rather than rambling on about the events of Mary's life and her influence, Nostradamus simply included the sword with its multiple meanings to drive home his point.

- **Justice:** Determining right or wrong in a moral situation, especially because Queen Mary remarried three months after her first husband's death to a man suspected of being responsible for the murder.

- **Separation:** Cutting things apart, like a queen and her country.

- **An active force of will:** Acting as the result of a decisive choice rather than reacting on emotion, similar to Mary's choice to flee to England despite the advice of her friends.

- **Military power:** Representing all the troops that defeated Mary.

- **Crucifixion of Christ:** A sword turned with the handle up looks like a cross, and Mary's actions (she was implicated in an affair and the death of her second husband) weren't approved by her Catholic faith, which would've pursued her from within her heart and drove her away from any place of righteousness. She'd be unable to feel at peace with herself over her actions. She eventually ran to England where she was imprisoned and later executed wearing red and confirming her Catholic faith.

> ✔ **Will of God:** Performing an action because God wants the hand of man to accomplish the task. This piece of symbolism was a clear judgment by Nostradamus against the actions he saw within his visions of Mary's affair, the possible murder of her husband, and the many rumored plots against Queen Elizabeth I of England, her cousin.

I think Nostradamus used the symbolic layers of the sword to give a lot of depth to the description of Mary's flight from Scotland. I also think that Nostradamus would've preferred the sword to be interpreted as a symbol for justice, military power, and probably the Christian faith and the crucifixion.

A Frightening Forecast for London

The world was wide open for a man of the Renaissance to explore, especially because Christopher Columbus had opened up entirely new places during Nostradamus's lifetime. New ideas and new places were overwhelmingly the talk of the day, but for Nostradamus, the centers of learning and historical importance stood out in his visions. He was concerned first for his own country, but he was also concerned with the other major European countries locations — like England's capital, London. Quatrain C II – 51, for example, mentions London by name:

> The blood of the just will commit a fault at London,
>
> Burnt through lightning of twenty threes the six:
>
> The ancient lady will fall from her high place,
>
> Several of the same sect will be killed. (C II – 51)

This section dissects two interpretations for this quatrain — one that places the event 100 years after Nostradamus died and one that places the event within his own lifetime. In addition, this section takes a look at another quatrain that's tied to this one.

A city on fire

I don't think there's much doubt about the meaning of Quatrain C II – 51. Overall, it seems to speak about an event in London that would kill and burn a great number of people. Exactly who would fall is a bit more difficult to pick out, but the *blood of the just* suggests people who certainly weren't dying because they'd done something wrong. If the deaths are interpreted literally, this quatrain refers to the great fire that raged through London in 1666.

The date, *twenty threes the six,* is of particular interest because Nostradamus broke it up into pieces that individually have meaning but are greater than their sum and accurately date the fire in London when put together. If you have twenty threes, you have sixty, plus the six on the end makes this number 66, so the last two digits of the year for this event are '66. Here's my interpretation of the three numbers that make up the date:

- ✔ **Three:** I believe this number represented the holy Christian Trinity and was Nostradamus's reminder that the struggles that would dominate would be religious.

- ✔ **Twenty:** Most numerologists recognize the sacred numbers as one through nine (see Chapter 6 for a discussion on Nostradamus and sacred numbers). Within a multi-digit number, like twenty, you can find the sacred number by adding the individual digits. In this case, add two and zero to get the sacred number two. I believe that for Nostradamus, two represented two forces in opposition, two forms of the divine in man and God, and according to alchemy, the idea that two things struggle and eventually resolve into one. The use of two in this quatrain probably represented the struggle between the factions of Christianity.

- ✔ **Six:** In Christian numerology, the number six represents the number of days it took to create the world before God rested. I believe that for Nostradamus, six represented the idea of working hard before resting and creating something beautiful out of a muddled mess.

The pieces each have meaning, but bringing them together paints a complex picture that includes a two-part problem from the number twenty: In the years leading up to the London fire, there was a religious struggle (between the Catholic Church and the Church of England) and opposing sides (the English Civil War was in 1660 when the monarchy was abolished and then later reinstated) — a definite reflection of troublesome events. The troubles before the fire and after the fire could be the hard work represented by six. The number twenty (with its opposing sides in a struggle) represents the religious issues that were paled by the fire. It's also worth noting that Nostradamus could have been using the numbers to refer to a time of sin, or 666.

The one piece of this quatrain that remains vague, after you figure out the overall event and the date, is the *ancient lady* who'd fall as a result of these events. Prior to 1666, critics and interpreters made several suggestions about the woman they believed Nostradamus was referring to, but a better answer may be found in a metaphorical female match. The Church was sometimes viewed as female, and so were particular church buildings, especially because they were dressed up with lacy moldings and elaborate *spires* (raised pointed roofs that resembled the large headdresses of the Renaissance).

During the London fire, the Cathedral of St. Paul was destroyed along with many other Catholic churches, a concrete example. He also could've been referring to either the buildings or the many people (especially those who were Catholic) who fled to the churches for safety and died within them as the buildings collapsed or exploded from the heat of the fire. Metaphorically, Nostradamus could've been describing the fall of the Roman Catholic Church to the issues and demands of the Protestant religions and the Church of England. Nostradamus would've viewed both of these groups as causing the fall of the *ancient lady,* Catholicism. In either interpretation, you find one of Nostradamus's common themes — the threatened toppling of the faith that meant so much to him. A hundred years after his own life, Nostradamus was warning of harmful situations developing within religion.

Interpretation of poetry, especially when it's translated from one language to another, can be a very personal process, and it isn't actually a question with a right or wrong answer. Sometimes the writer doesn't even understand completely what or why he's writing. Nostradamus believed he was divinely inspired and may not have been able to explain all his prophecies.

Bemoaning Bloody Mary

Occasionally, an alternative explanation for a quatrain makes sense. Quatrain C II – 51 may reveal the struggles between the Catholics and the Protestants in a much different way. Rather than the *blood of the just* referring to the people who died during the fire of London, the word *blood* could've been a code name for Queen Mary I of England, who was also known as Bloody Mary for her persecution of the Protestant faithful during her reign from 1553–1558. In this view of the quatrain, the fire becomes the torturous blazes where heretics against the Church were burned at the stake — all on Queen Mary's orders. These heretics were all of Protestant faith, which fits with the last line of the quatrain *(several of the same sect will be killed).*

Plaguing problems

Two phrases connect the next quatrain to C II – 51's London fire and Queen Mary interpretations: the *just blood* and the *lady.* If you try to put all the like quatrains together, these little hints probably place C II –51 and C II – 53 together and C II – 53 becomes the next major event for the city. That said, take a look at C II – 53:

> The great plague of the maritime city
>
> Will not cease until there be avenged the death
>
> Of the just blood, condemned for a price without crime,
>
> Of the great lady unwronged by pretense. (C II – 53)

Nostradamus wrote here of using very harsh forms of punishment (general plague and misery) as well as killing a man who apparently did nothing wrong (or was *condemned for a price without crime*) as revenge for *the just blood* of people who had died years earlier. Linking this quatrain to C II – 51 — and to the Bloody Mary interpretation — helps give you a timeframe for the events. You're looking at unfair killing in the 1560s, which coincides with the deaths caused by Bloody Mary's (as the queen was called) persecution of the Protestants.

Until there be avenged the death — someone dies — *who is condemned for a price without crime* is a description which fits the death of King Charles I of England, Ireland, and Scotland and a man who favored Catholicism like Queen Mary I. He was tried for high treason and then executed in 1649. Technically Charles was *without crime* because the king represents the state, and Charles was essentially accused of being disloyal to himself. If this quatrain is discussing King Charles I's death, then it's the death of the king which avenges the *death of the just* (those killed by Bloody Mary).

The final line could refer to two great ladies: Lady Jane Grey or the Church:

✔ Lady Grey was appointed queen of England in 1553 (just before "Bloody" Mary became queen) on the questionable reasoning that she was a cousin to past King Edward VI, and his final wish was for her to take the throne. (In addition, she was Protestant and Mary was a devout and zealous Catholic who threatened to return England to Catholicism.) Mary was the daughter of Henry VIII, but when King Henry had his marriage to Mary's mother annulled, Mary became illegitimate and dropped out of the official line to inherit the throne. Lady Grey wanted no part of the intrigue (and after she realized his power lust she refused to name her husband king). But her rule was brief (less than two weeks), she was executed, and Mary I became queen of England.

✔ The Church could be the lady. After the plague ravaged London, Protestantism rose significantly, which was certain to upset the Church.

However you slice quatrains C II – 51 and 53, London was bound to have trouble related to religion. Certainly the creation of a new Church of England during the 1500s (in addition to the Protestants) would've been a vision of considerable sadness for the Catholic Nostradamus. Who knows which lives may have been saved if the events in the quatrains had been recognized by people during this time.

Today, it's important to acknowledge that the details of the quatrains are frequently a little slippery, but the overall themes in a quatrain (in this case, religious trouble and unjust killings) aren't lost in symbolism and double talk.

Chapter 9

Royal Betrayal and the French Revolution

In This Chapter

▶ Dealing with death and deception among the great

▶ Looking at the people and events involved in the French Revolution

▶ Bringing God into it: The state of the Church during the French Revolution

I know Nostradamus didn't watch TV, and I'm certain he wasn't into video games, so most modern theories about why someone focuses on violence and death don't work to explain why the prophecies are so chock full of trouble and violence. You need to keep in mind that Nostradamus was trying to discover (with some help from God if he could get it) the events that would become important points in human history. He was hoping to point out the error of our ways.

All in all, I think Nostradamus may have been a little near-sighted with his predictions. The predictions he made for hundreds of years after his death include details and elements that are difficult to understand and then match up with events so that you have a prophecy match-up with an event. However, the predictions of events that occurred during his lifetime and for the couple hundred years afterward (including the ones in this chapter) were amazingly accurate. And Nostradamus gave some impressive details about events that influenced the path of his beloved France.

This chapter takes a look at some quatrains from the mid-1640s to the late 1700s. Many of them discuss the struggle for power in France, and all of them, in one way or another, relate to the events of the French Revolution. Take heed: They aren't for the weak of heart.

The Death of a Cardinal and His King

I want you to notice just how often the ideas of religion and politics are mixed up and served as one throughout the Nostradamus prophecies — and especially in Quatrain C VIII – 68. It's no accident, and you can't avoid it.

The power of the Christian Church (later called the Catholic Church) was inseparable from the king and his rule of the nation, mostly because of the *divine right of kings* — a concept stating that certain kings ruled because God selected them especially for that role in his universe. The kings who ruled by divine right were also only divinely wrong when God judged them. In other words, these kings didn't answer to anyone in the physical world and tended to do just as they pleased. I believe the events predicted by Quatrain C VIII – 68 involve this divine right of kings and more than a little bit of intrigue:

> The old Cardinal deceived by the young one,
>
> He will find himself out of his dignity disarmed:
>
> Arles do not show that the duplicate is perceived,
>
> Both "Liqueduct" and the Prince embalmed. (C VIII – 68)

Quatrain C VIII – 68 tells a detailed story about Cardinal Richelieu, his struggle for power, and his death in 17th century France. But there's more for you to get out of it.

Understanding Quatrain C VIII – 68 can help you find meaning in other quatrains that *haven't* revealed their secrets yet. Only by taking all the pieces of the quatrain puzzle together as a whole can you get the entire picture and an accurate prophecy. You may find an old cardinal and a prince embalmed in many events throughout history, but those situations weren't the ones Nostradamus was talking about. The difference is in the details. The quatrain presents a *whole* picture for a reason. Keep that in mind when searching out the secrets of the prophecies.

To get a handle on whom in history Quatrain C VIII – 68 is about, first try outlining the major pieces. Every outline you wrote in high school started with big ideas and then included the smaller ones. So what are the big pieces?

- *Old Cardinal*
- *Young one*
- *Out of his dignity*
- *Arles*
- *"Liqueduct"*
- *Prince embalmed*

Four lines of prophecy, six major elements, no problem — trust me. The next step is to look at the elements together and see whether any events in history contain all or most of the items predicted. Looking for just one or two of the pieces will send you off on a wild goose chase.

Quatrain C VIII – 68 happens to be an almost exact match for a situation that happened in Nostradamus's beloved France, involving Cardinal Richelieu (infamous for his brutal use of force, political maneuvers, and his role in *The Three Musketeers* as the power-seeking cardinal) and coming to a peak in 1642. If you look at the time near the end of Richelieu's life, the elements of the prophecy click into place, and you can solve the prophecy puzzle.

Picking out the people

The people involved in this quatrain were

- Cardinal Richelieu *(The old Cardinal)*
- Henri Coiffier de Ruzé, The Marquis of Cinq-Mars, who was 22 at the time of the events in question *(the young one)*
- King Louis XIII of France *(the Prince)*

Here's the story: In 1617, Louis XIII of France turned 16 and took control of France from his mother, Marie de Médici, who'd been ruling on his behalf. Yes, that's right. A 16-year-old was in charge of one of the most powerful countries in Europe. He ruled France (although some questioned his ability to do so effectively) until his death in 1643.

While Marie de Médici was in charge, she named a young but important man as one of the key advisors to the king — Armand Jean du Plessis de Richelieu (he took the name de Richelieu from his family's home). He was a learned man, and in addition to being a key advisor to the king, he was also a cardinal, a military and political leader, and a man who worked to strengthen the power of the monasteries. He walked with one foot on the religious path and the other on the political path, a very delicate balance. But late in his career, Richelieu finally swayed onto the path that firmly favored politics.

Richelieu became an advocate of the divine rule of kings; the taxation of everyone, including the clergy; the removal of the power of the nobles; and even the use of spies. All these tactics were intended to support the power of King Louis XIII, who was controlled largely by the cardinal's advice and opinions. Anyone who opposed Cardinal Richelieu was exiled (in the case of the king's mother and brother) or simply killed. It seems that Richelieu was a very firm believer in the idea that the end justifies the means, and he was willing to plot secretly to achieve his goals, tax the poor, kill, and even make alliances with Protestant nations against another Catholic country, Spain, for the sake of centralizing French power.

At one point, after the death of a friend, Richelieu was given custody of a young man named Henri Coiffier de Ruzé, the Marquis of Cinq-Mars. This man, who folks simply call Cinq-Mars, became Richelieu's protégé. Richelieu introduced Cinq-Mars to King Louis (whose friends and advisors were young, attractive, and male), hoping that the king would take him as a lover.

Cardinal Richelieu believed that Cinq-Mars would be an easy person for him to control, and he hoped to influence King Louis through the young man. Cardinal Richelieu was wrong, and Cinq-Mars turned out to be trouble for everyone. Cinq-Mars tried to convince the king to execute Cardinal Richelieu, and he signed a secret treaty in 1642 (a year before Louis's death) with Spain, an enemy of France, in the name of the king's brother.

So there you have it — an old cardinal, a young man, and a king (which, granted, isn't a *prince,* but bear with me). You can add these three pieces together and still not find any meaning in the prophecy, however. So you need to keep searching history for the other major pieces.

Pinpointing the places

Okay, Nostradamus only referred to one *real* place in Quatrain C VIII – 68, but he also referred to one metaphorical place. The real place is the city of Arles, which is in France near the Rhône River. Cardinal Richelieu frequently visited Arles, which was also where he discovered that Cinq-Mars double-crossed him and signed a secret treaty. Arles, according to the quatrain, *do(es) not show that the duplicate is perceived.* That line almost sounds like Arles was hiding something, and in fact, Richelieu saw *(perceived)* a copy *(duplicate)* of the secret treaty at Arles. In fact, Richelieu hid the fact that he knew about the treaty *(do not show)* from Cinq-Mars until the cardinal could reveal the trouble to King Louis. Cardinal Richelieu then had Cinq-Mars imprisoned and executed, something that didn't sit well with King Louis, who never seemed to quite forgive Richelieu for this act.

The metaphorical place is tied to line 2. It contains a reference to the old cardinal being *out of his dignity.* In this case, his dignity came from his position as cardinal and advisor to the king, which he lost after he was replaced in his role as advisor to the king by Cinq-Mars (who took away Richelieu's powers slowly as the cardinal aged and became distracted). It wasn't a real, physical place, but for the cardinal, the position of advisor gave him real power. In Nostradamus's vision, the distinction between a real place and a place of power wouldn't necessarily be pointed out.

Putting the other pieces together

One piece of the puzzle has been difficult for just about anyone who's ever tried to decipher Quatrain C VIII – 68. The term *"Liqueduct"* isn't a word in French. It's a word that Nostradamus made up. If you take the word apart, though, "lique" means water and "duct" means to provide passage for something. Together, the word stands for something or someone traveling by water. This piece of the puzzle fits very neatly with the end of the story and the resolution of the difference in opinions between King Louis XIII and Cardinal Richelieu (over the cardinal's brutality, especially regarding Cinq-Mars' death). The king called the elderly cardinal to Paris, and he traveled there while lying on a bed on a barge because he was very ill.

On the surface, one piece of the quatrain seems unattached to the events and intrigue surrounding Louis XIII and Cardinal Richelieu, but a connection exists. The last word of line 2 says that the cardinal will find himself *disarmed*. *Disarm* can have two meanings: to remove a person's ability to defend or attack (with weapons or armaments) or to remove a person's doubt and suspicion to keep him from worrying or interfering. Both meanings of the phrase work here. Richelieu was disarmed because Cinq-Mars had managed to steal away much of the power and control over the military. He was also disarmed because Cinq-Mars kept him in the dark about important matters, and Richelieu didn't suspect that the man he trusted and placed near King Louis XIII would double-cross him and eventually try to have him executed.

The last line of the quatrain says that both the cardinal and the prince (King Louis) will be embalmed. This prediction wasn't a great insight, because embalming the nobility of Europe was a well-known practice. Still, Nostradamus linked the two people and their embalming, which suggested that they'd be closely linked in other ways. The history books support this connection, because the king died less than a year after the cardinal.

Translating Nostradamus's prophecies is a lot like trying to hold marbles in a stable formation. Meanings are going to shift here and there, no matter how hard translators try to grab and hold onto the one true interpretation. Several of the words in Quatrain C VIII – 68 give translators fits and shift the meaning of the quatrain just a little, yet not enough to change the prophecy's accuracy. In the original quatrain, Nostradamus used the word "double" in the third line. This word has alternately been interpreted to mean *double* (as in double-crossed, referring to Cinq-Mars) or to mean *duplicate* (as in a copy of the treaty that the cardinal saw — the interpretation I use). In either interpretation, the accuracy of the quatrain doesn't change, which makes this an astounding piece of work. It's a rare talent to be able to get your point across through language translation, years of history, and interpretation.

Witnessing the French Revolution

One of my all-time favorite musicals is *Les Misérable,* which depicts the human side of what became an inhuman struggle for freedom, a struggle that has been repeated throughout the world on many levels. The classes within 18th century France (especially the poorer classes) were tired of the rich getting richer and the poor getting less than nothing — a scenario that's recognizable in America, even today. The story is a familiar one of inspirational leaders, righteous causes, bloodshed, and ultimately a heavy price for the right to do what you want.

I doubt Nostradamus wanted to predict these kinds of world-changing events, but with the possibility of divine inspiration, he probably went with what he saw. The French Revolution was a large piece of what was revealed to Nostradamus during his nighttime studies, and it turned out to be a major shift in how people thought about power and politics in Europe and throughout the remainder of the world. It stood out as a very large sign on the roadmap of possible turning points in the events of mankind, because France went from a centuries old monarchy to a republic. Not surprisingly, then, many of Nostradamus's quatrains predicted the events of the French Revolution.

Major events on the path to independence

In Quatrain C VI – 23, Nostradamus recorded a vision of events that would stand out along the pathway to French independence. But before trying to interpret this quatrain, you need a little lead-in history about the state of France just prior to the Revolution.

On July 14, 1789, the citizens of Paris used all the resources they could find and barricaded the city after destroying the Bastille (a prison that for the populace of Paris represented the horrible treatment and general dismissive attitude of the monarchy; acquiring the weapons inside the Bastille was another reason for charging the prison). Throughout the country, troublesome mobs caused all sorts of danger. (Side scoop here: The wheat crops had failed, and the winter was the harshest ever. There's nothing worse than an angry *and* hungry mob.) The storming of the Bastille, along with widespread riots, started the downward spiral into the full-fledged French Revolution that occupies so many of today's heavy history books.

With that snippet of history in your back pocket, take a look at Quatrain C VI – 23. It wasn't a prophecy for a specific event, like the troubles of Cardinal Richelieu (see "The Death of a Cardinal and His King," earlier in this chapter). Instead, it was a prophecy about the overall elements that would combine to form the explosive revolution:

Coins depreciated [The defenses undermined] by the spirit of the realm,

And people will be stirred up against their King:

New peace made [Peace a new saint], holy laws become worse,

Paris was never in so very severe an array. (C VI – 23)

Breaking it down

The style Nostradamus used to present this quatrain is different from most others in a couple of ways:

- ✔ The pieces are more interconnected, which means it's hard to separate one from another and look at them individually before you put them back together. You have to examine the whole quatrain at once.

- ✔ It has more of a sentence-like flow to it. Most of Nostradamus's quatrains are choppy, with many different images in one place, and I believe the difference in style here is because Nostradamus was in a more poetically inspired mood when he wrote these lines.

Quatrain C VI – 23 tells the story of France, especially Paris, in a serious state of distress. Like every good story, there's a beginning, a middle, and an end. Let's start at the beginning of the story: The *coins depreciated* tells of a downward spiral in the finances of the country, possibly because of the overwhelming taxes that came largely from the poor. An alternate translation of this phrase in line 1, *the defenses undermined,* gives a similar picture of the situation, where what was once stable has become unstable in some way. Both translations provide an accurate view, just from slightly different angles.

These changes, Nostradamus goes on to tell us in line 2, are due to people's moods *(people will be stirred up)* and a rebellion *(against their king).* Line 3 continues the story with a twist in the plot where there's a *new peace* and problems with religious laws *(holy laws become worse).* The final piece of the story in line 4 tells of overwhelming problems for Paris *(in so very severe an array).* Granted, the pieces in the quatrain have individually been happening in various places throughout history (and will probably happen in the future if we don't listen to Nostradamus's words), but the one certain cornerstone is Paris, which tells you for sure that Nostradamus was talking about France.

The quatrain appears to say that each piece adds weight to the situation, which then quickly spirals downward. In other words, if you take the volatile mix of the fall of money due to people's moods and rebellion (lines 1 and 2) and add new peace and religious troubles (line 3), you're bound to have chaos and confusion in the city (line 4). A failing economy and low spirit of the populace certainly don't help any situation. And bad finances and depression almost certainly cause people to turn against their leader.

Interpreters have debated whether the third line actually means *new peace, new saints, peace a new saint,* or even *peace being made.* I think Nostradamus's skill shows through here and he meant not one but all of these interpretations together. I can look at the events of the French Revolution and the political struggles of Paris and recognize that all of these events:

✔ **New peace.** New constitutions and peace treaties were signed with and without the king's approval.

✔ **New saints.** The revolution produced many new heroes who hadn't yet had a chance to shine. Some were philosophers, and some were military men (including Napoleon, but I tell you all about him in Chapter 10).

✔ **Peace a new saint.** With the creation of a new republic that represented the people, there was a new saint in the form of personal liberty.

✔ **Peace being made.** The people of France carved out their own kind of peace by taking events into their own hands. They, in effect, carved out peace within their hearts by doing all they could to get rid of the system and people they believed to be harmful and to create a peaceful world that supported their needs.

Throughout *The Prophecies,* Nostradamus used the word *Rapis,* and most translators simply replace this word with Paris. It's true that Nostradamus frequently used Rapis as an anagram for Paris (just switch the letters around), but even translators take liberties in getting to the heart of the quatrains. Whenever possible, be careful to look at the original text first and then the translated text. If the quatrain is important for you to unravel, you don't want to lose anything to translator errors.

Building it up

The general description of Quatrain C VI – 23 is just as important today as the accurate identification of people and dated events in specific quatrains is. Maybe even more important. Overall trends of a situation (the general parts) can sometimes be spotted more quickly than specific events. Over time, Nostradamus watched his homeland of France in his nightly visions, and he knew the French people and France well enough to recognize that the events in his vision would combine into something horrible. For example, on a smaller scale, you can watch a person over time and know that she will struggle with, say, money problems or relationship problems, simply because of the pattern of events in her life in the past. That same strategy can be used on a larger scale with groups of people and nations.

Nostradamus was general, yes, but that doesn't mean he missed the mark. Accuracy doesn't require dates and names; it's about being able to match an overall pattern. Oh, dates and names are nice to have, but they're not a requirement. In Quatrain C VI – 23, Nostradamus pointed out the overall events of the French Revolution in the correct order: failing money, falling spirits, rebellion against the established government, and then general chaos as people tried to figure out how to survive without the structure they hated. That's a pretty good prophecy for a man sitting in the dark.

The riots of Paris and the fall of the king were symbols for Nostradamus of a change in the French tide. For our generation, the quatrains that mark these changes are symbols of the possible changes in modern tides. If you recognize that processes stir up and agitate the present way of life and then allow the less desirable elements of society/politics/ideas to fall away, then the harder stuff can be easier to handle. In other words, you know there's a light at the end of the tunnel. Dr. Nostradamus's prescription for healing the future can still be helpful, even if the events of the prophecy have already happened.

Louis and Marie meet Madame Guillotine

Nostradamus gained a personal connection to the French throne through his patroness, Catherine de Medici (you can find more information about her in Chapter 4 and a whole bunch of quatrains that focus on her and her family in Chapter 8), but he also focused on the royal power because it was a very strong force in his universe. Whatever happened to the people on the throne affected the people of France in every way, and Nostradamus wanted to share this insight into the future with the people it most concerned. Nostradamus used Quatrain C IV – 85 to do just that. Take a look:

> The white coal will be chased by the black one,
>
> Made prisoner led to the dung cart,
>
> Moor [Black or Vigorous] Camel on twisted feet,
>
> Then the younger one will blind the hobby falcon. (C IV – 85)

Some quatrains are easy to figure out, some are hard, and some qualify for the puzzle book for geniuses. This quatrain happens to be one of the genius puzzles, but don't worry. With a little help, you'll be puzzling like a pro.

Although Nostradamus used symbols and description together here, he didn't skimp on shoveling out the deep meanings. You need to look at the individual pieces and what they typically mean. Then look at the deeper meanings and Nostradamus's play on words. Bring the pieces together and you can see that Quatrain C IV – 85 was a prophecy for King Louis XVI (and family).

King Louis XVI (at 16) married Marie Antoinette in 1770 and ruled France from 1774 to 1792. It's a long story, so I'll sum it up for you. Louis was probably an honest guy trying to do a difficult job of running a monarchy, but he came to the throne as the troubles within France began to boil over, but his indecisive and conservative nature made him a scapegoat for the Revolutionaries. He was guillotined on January 21, 1793.

The typical meanings of the words

To figure out this prophecy, the first step is to look at the typical meanings of some key individual pieces:

- **White coal/black coal.** White is a color of purity, especially religious or sacred, and it's opposite is black, the color of darkness and the unknown (think superstition). Louis XVI and the rest of the Bourbon family of kings used white as part of their banner.

- **Prisoner.** This reference was probably to a literal prisoner, but Nostradamus also could've been referring to someone trapped by a situation, decision, or idea — like Louis XVI was trapped within the stereotype of a monarch.

- **Dung cart.** I think this was definitely a reference to a real item, because dung carts were used to haul people to the guillotine during the French Revolution (and Marie Antoinette, Louis's wife, rode to her death in one). Beneath the literal level, however, the cart could symbolize hauling off something that's no longer of use or using the refuse to fertilize new growth. (Look at Figure 9-1 for an example of Madame Guillotine, as the machinery was called.)

- **Hobby falcon.** No, this isn't a falcon that knits or collects coins. During the French Revolution, the nobility prized the falcon because it could be trained to hunt. In fact, a well-trained falcon would hunt on the command of the owner only. The bird was kept as a symbol of prestige.

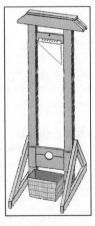

Figure 9-1:
The guillotine was used to kill opposing forces during the French Revolution.

Nostradamus's play on words

You may be wondering about the reference to the *Moor camel on twisted feet.* Is it a key piece of the puzzle? Yep. Thing is, this line gets translated differently by just about everyone who has ever interpreted *The Prophecies.* The words and their order differ slightly in each translation. But when it comes down to the basic meaning, I think Nostradamus simply used a figure of speech that doesn't make the translation jump from French to English.

By *camel,* he just meant a scoundrel. (Think in terms of calling someone a dog in the United States to suggest that he's unattractive.) By *Moor,* he meant a scary, mischievous person you'd call a thief or a "dog of the night." And by *twisted feet,* he meant tied up. So, after all that digging, the phrase tells you that a scoundrel might be tied, which is very possible if this is the same person from line 2, who's riding in a dung cart on the way to the guillotine. It's a figure of speech. What can you do?

Not only do you need to figure out the camel joke, but you also need to know that the French word *noir* can be translated as *black Moor* and as a near anagram for the French *roi,* which means king. This tidbit changes the first line from *a white coal being chased by a black coal* to a *white coal being chased by a king.*

But wait, there's more. Although the original French word *Charbon* in the quatrain translates to *coal,* we're not really dealing with coal you'd burn in a stove. Nostradamus used the same part-anagram part-rhyme throughout *The Prophecies* for the name Bourbon (as in the ruling family of France). *Charbon* and Bourbon sound very similar with a French accent. So the original word *Charbon* shouldn't be translated at all. The letters should be substituted so that the *Ch* is switched to a *b* to form Barbon, and from there, it's only a small step to Bourbon. This tidbit changes the first line to *a Bourbon king being chased out by another king,* which makes a lot more sense.

If that isn't enough, it's also very helpful to know that the original French word Nostradamus used is *l'aubereau* which is translated as *hobby falcon* but isn't really a falcon or a hobby. It's a slang term in French for a squire (a person who learns the skills of a knight by assisting him in his duties) or someone working closely under the direction of another.

Matching the words with history

If you take the information about the symbols from the preceding section and read back over Quatrain C IV – 85, you get something like this:

> *The Bourbon king will be chased out by another king, trapped and led without dignity to the guillotine, tied up like a thief, a young person will blind the squire.*

Okay, so it's not completely making sense yet. Some interpreters have washed their hands of this quatrain, but I think you can begin to identify events that match up with the details. In fact, I think this quatrain specifically predicts the fall and death of Louis XVI and his family during the French Revolution.

The story goes like this: Louis XVI (who was a Bourbon and used white as one of his symbols) wasn't having a very good time ruling France in the late 1780s, and some troubles with his ministers, finances, awful harvests, and wars just wouldn't let him gain control of the unsettled nation. The poor didn't have enough of anything, and the upper classes were fighting against being taxed to support Louis and his wars (including the help France gave to the American Revolution in 1776). At first, French revolutionaries weren't ready to have the king totally out of the picture, so they went to Versailles, his home outside of Paris, in 1789 and forced him to return to Paris, where he was kept on a very short leash and watched closely by the people.

In June 1791, King Louis XVI and his wife — you may know about Marie Antoinette, at least by reputation — attempted to flee Paris using disguises (an action I'd expect from a thief rather than a king), but they were discovered and brought back to Tuileries Palace, where guards watched them even while asleep. King Louis XVI reluctantly signed a constitution in September 1791 that limited his power significantly (and no doubt his dignity), but he was still confined to the palace. Paris was dangerous at this time, and mobs with extreme revolutionary ideas ruled the Paris streets.

The royal family (Louis, Marie, and a young son) were imprisoned late in 1792, and King Louis XVI was put on trial in December. In January 1793, King Louis XVI was taken to the guillotine and beheaded for treason and crimes against the people. He was chased out of office by the new "king" of ideas — liberty. Marie Antoinette was taken to her meeting with the guillotine in a dung cart (as recorded in Nostradamus's quatrain), and the young son was never seen again. Rumors and suspicions have suggested that he was taken to a man in the prison, who tortured and killed the only true heir to the throne. After the royal deaths, a period of confusion ensued known as the Reign of Terror (I get to the bloody details of that time period later in this chapter), because no monarch and no real system of government existed.

Nostradamus probably noted this event rather than other events in his visions because in the big scheme of things, the deaths of the king and his family showed a rising conflict between nobility and commoners that would affect people far into the future. Nostradamus used the entire episode in France as a metaphor for the fall of monarchy (a system where one ruled many) and a distinct shift toward the individual's thoughts being part of determining how people's lives are ruled. It was a shift toward a republic that would continue to influence European countries and the world long after everyone forgot the details of the French Revolution.

Nostradamus predicted the death of King Louis XVI in strong words, and I don't believe he thought this event could be changed, because this quatrain's point isn't wishy-washy. The point was that the struggles between the government and the people, noble classes and commoners, and poor and rich are important enough that they can bring a country to its knees if the warnings of certain prophets aren't heeded.

Despite the liberty won in the French Revolution, a very high price was paid in human life, and a very sick side to human nature was revealed through the Revolution's brutal acts. Nostradamus recorded the events he foresaw, even though I think they were unchangeable, as a warning to be aware that people have a darker side. Forewarned is forearmed, as some say.

The Noyades at Nantes

The images suggested in Quatrain C V – 33 are of civil fighting, a strong and violent struggle for personal freedoms (which has brought about war in nearly every nation of the world), and the gruesome deaths of innocent people. Certainly Nostradamus recorded these images in his prophecy to warn about and prevent the horrible events that he saw. Take a look for yourself:

> Of the principal ones of the city in rebellion
>
> Who will strive mightily to recover their liberty:
>
> The males cut up, unhappy fray [mixture],
>
> Cries, groans at Nantes pitiful to see. (C V – 33)

Unlocking the mystery with a key from history

The clues for meaning in Quatrain C V – 33 remain somewhat vague until the last line mentions *Nantes,* a city in France on the Loire River. This city is the key to unlocking the meaning Nostradamus wove into the quatrain, because it gives you a starting point for discovering the events being discussed.

A little research on Nantes reveals that the city has been contested over the years by religious and political factions, but two events made Nantes stand out in French history and for Nostradamus:

- ✔ The first event was the Edict of Nantes signed in 1598 that ended the war between the Catholics and Protestants (for a time) and gave the groups equal rights to worship peacefully.

- ✔ The second event was the terrible Noyades at Nantes in 1793, a large-scale murder of townspeople which was done at the direction of the National Convention (the revolutionary government's ruling body) during the Reign of Terror portion of the French Revolution. Some of the townspeople participated in a rebellion against the new government of France (supporting the king) while some were completely innocent. This revolt was one of many struggles in towns across France between the supporters of the monarchy (Royalists) and the supporters of the revolution and the National Convention.

Looking at the clues in the quatrain and the choice of words, I'm certain Nostradamus was talking about the Noyades at Nantes, because the peace treaty didn't involve blood and guts.

After you recognize that the quatrain is connected with the Noyades (a general term for drowning that came to be used specifically for the events in Nantes), it becomes a very graphic picture of what happened in the city and a warning to future generations. Nostradamus accurately noted that even *the principal ones* of the city (leaders like the mayor) wouldn't be immune to the fake trials and mass shootings that would happen at the hands of the Republicans to quell the Royalist rebellion in the city of Nantes. His description even included details that the people would be struggling for their independence (in the French Revolution) and that the method of death for the men would mostly be via the guillotine. The sharp blade fell swiftly and *cut up* the men who were unlucky enough to be within the prisons of Nantes.

The final line of the quatrain gives you a clear picture in graphic terms of the daily horrors in the port city of Nantes, beginning in October 1793. The whole city heard or felt the influence of the *Cries, groans at Nantes,* which were the screams of the dying people, those suspected of being Royalists, as the Republicans followed the orders of the French Revolutionary government to squash uprisings. Approximately 1,000 to 2,000 people died in a period of less than four months. Many of the deaths were brutal and considered torture.

Looking at the "unhappy" factor

The last part of line 3 in Quatrain C V – 33 — *unhappy fray* — seems a little odd. This phrase has also been recorded in various translations as *unhappy confusion, unhappy mixture,* or even *unhappy quarrels.* With each translation, the line takes on a slightly different meaning:

- **Unhappy fray.** This translation refers to the distressing battles between the Royalists and the Republicans. *Fray* generally means a struggle or brawl of some kind.

- **Unhappy mixture.** This translation refers to the mixture of the political world and the religious world. During the monarchy, the king was viewed as a religious figure, connecting the power of the throne with the power of the Church. Two meanings are possible:

  - During the French Revolution, religion and politics were still closely entwined, a mixture that Nostradamus saw as unhealthy. The king could play favorites depending on whether he was Catholic or Protestant. France was Catholic, but leading up to the French Revolution, the Protestants had gotten certain rights from supportive monarchs.

- At the Noyades, women and priests were stripped naked, tied facing each other, and then thrown into the Loire River to drown. Part of the purpose of this exercise was to increase the discomfort of the victims, a clearly unhappy mix of people.

✔ **Unhappy confusion.** This translation refers to the confusion between what's right and what's wrong and that two wrongs don't make a right. It was probably very apparent to Nostradamus that killing for liberties wasn't right anymore than killing for the divine right of kings. Both sides of the French struggle went to horrific extremes.

✔ **Unhappy quarrels.** This translation refers to the clash between the Royalists and the Revolutionaries. But if Nostradamus really meant these words as a reference to the differences between these two groups, then he was making perhaps the biggest understatement of all time.

I prefer the translation *unhappy mixture,* because that phrase seems to flow with the rest of the description Nostradamus gave of the events in Nantes. He tended to keep description and commentary separate, which rules out the *unhappy confusion* and the *unhappy quarrels* interpretations. Besides, *unhappy quarrels* represents a huge understatement, and I don't think understatement would've been one of Nostradamus's tools if he were trying to make a point about what can happen if you go by the mindset of "whatever it takes to get the job done." Sometimes, whatever you do to reach your goal is *not* okay, even if the end goal is a good one.

Taking a look at the big picture

Looking at and studying the horrible possibilities of human nature can be very depressing, but I don't think Nostradamus brought these images to light to put a damper on the mood. I think he was playing on the emotional link to connect with the people of his future. In other words, the images carried a very strong emotional connection, and he hoped to trigger someone to act to prevent such events, even if on a small scale. The emotion of the heart is something that truly identifies mankind as unique among the species of the world (particularly our ability to sympathize with other people), but unfortunately, it was completely lost at times in the French Revolution by people who were driven to create change.

In today's world, understanding Nostradamus's purpose with Quatrain C V – 33 is important. Massacre has unfortunately always been part of the history of people. It almost always occurs when emotions run high and people lose control of the emotion of their hearts and forget to see others as individuals.

A persecutor pursued

After the monarchy (meaning the king) had released many of its powers in a new constitution signed in 1791, the revolutionaries confined the entire royal family to the palace in Paris. With the king sufficiently out of the way, the energy of the revolution picked up speed. One of the major movers and shakers during the French Revolution was a man named Maximilien François Marie Isidore de Robespierre, or just Robespierre for short (thank goodness). This gentleman was placed in charge of the Committee of Public Safety (responsible for repressing enemies of the country) in 1792, which sounds like he should've been one of the good guys. In fact, he was one of the people who contributed to the Reign of Terror, as the mass executions, chaos, and military rule of the revolutionary days were called.

This period of violence began in June 1793 when the Committee for Public Safety began to use executions, including events like the Noyades at Nantes in 1793 (see preceding section), to silence anyone who might be an enemy of the newly forming republic of France. The wholesale use of the guillotine for eliminating the competition continued past the January 1794 death of King Louis XVI and on into the summer of 1794 when Robespierre was killed.

Quatrain C II – 42 discusses the frightening picture of life during this time and points out Robespierre as one of the leaders:

> Cock, dogs and cats will be satiated with blood
>
> And from the wound of the tyrant found dead,
>
> At the bed of another legs and arms broken,
>
> He who was not afraid to die a cruel death. (C II – 42)

Pick a symbol, any symbol

This quatrain would be impossible to understand if you tried to read everything literally. So free your mind, in a sense, and do some free associating when it comes to the symbols Nostradamus used. In this quatrain, he used both symbolism and poetic license to describe the events:

- ✔ **Cock:** One of the emblems used to represent the royal throne of France has been the cockerel or rooster.

- ✔ **Dogs and cats:** As common household pets, they represent the commoner and peasant class.

- ✔ **Bed of another:** This phrase can mean a strange bed, or in this case, it can be a very unusual description of a hotel bed — a bed that's strange to the people who stay there.

Okay, so now that you know the quatrain isn't about a barnyard, you can begin to place it within the proper place — the French Revolution, where tyrants were everywhere and death was a daily event. I can rephrase the quatrain with just this little bit of information:

> *The monarchy, commoners, and everyone else are tired of the bloodshed; one of the people who helped cause all the deaths is found dead in a strange bed with his appendages broken. He wasn't afraid of death, and his own death was cruel.*

Now you begin to get a better picture, but it's still not clear. If this quatrain were a TV, you'd call the cable company to see about better reception. Instead, you have to dig further for clues to what Nostradamus saw.

The tyrant from the Reign of Terror

Although a lot of the revolutionaries responsible for the Reign of Terror (the *tyrants* from Quatrain C II – 42) were ultimately found dead, not all of them were found in a strange bed with their arms and legs broken. In fact, only one of the revolutionaries, Robespierre, was found dead in a strange bed.

The trouble with this prophecy is that it seems Nostradamus wasn't quite right about the kind of wound that would kill the man. Robespierre was shot in the jaw; he didn't get his arms and legs broken. In fact, he escaped custody after being arrested by the very group he used to support but was recaptured and shot. Apparently, Robespierre became a criminal after he had the audacity to think that the actions of the revolution had gone too far and should stop.

If you look at this quatrain as a piece of poetic description, you see that Nostradamus wasn't far off. Without literal connections, the strange bed may symbolize Robespierre's switch from the customary place as leader and mouthpiece of the National Convention to the new and strange place of trying to call a halt to the out-of-control murders at the guillotine. As a metaphor (a figure of speech comparing two unlike things), the strange bed would be the strange (meaning new or different) side of the argument concerning what to do about the revolution and France — namely, to end the Reign of Terror.

I'm going to keep going with this metaphor (I believe it adds meaning to the quatrain) and suggest that Nostradamus was right when he said that the tyrant was wounded in the arms and legs — metaphorically. Robespierre wasn't a soldier who used his body to do his job or to make changes. He used his mouth to motivate people, make elaborate speeches, and argue with the other leaders of the National Convention. His mouth became the tool he used to participate in the revolution, and it was his jaw that was wounded. A wound to the jaw for many people wouldn't be critical to their job, but for a man who made his living talking, it was definitely a harsh blow and was comparable to a wound to the arms and legs of someone who did manual labor. The tyrant died the next day in 1794 at the guillotine he was trying to stop.

And the moral is?

Methinks Nostradamus nailed it again with Quatrain C II – 42, in which the French Revolution looks its worst. Even the tyrants began switching sides and pointing out that the Reign of Terror had gone too far. Robespierre started out as a statesman motivated to make changes in France for the betterment of all, but he found that the passions of men are overwhelming, and people can sometimes get swept away in their own hot air balloon of pursuits.

I believe Nostradamus included Quatrain C II – 42 for two reasons. First, he wanted to point out that no one, not even the nobility or the leaders of the revolution, would be immune from the horrors. Second, he wanted to leave a reminder that "mob mind" (that urge to follow the way everyone else is going when large groups of people get together) can be very dangerous. These warnings still apply today, even if the event of the prophecy is long past.

The fate of faith and the Church

Religion has been a motivating factor for people everywhere for as long as they've had a vague notion that there's something bigger than the self — so basically since the beginning of humanity. Churches, religions, and faiths of all kinds have come and gone through human history, but there's been a consistent feeling that religious sites should be untouched by physical wars.

A devoutly religious man, Nostradamus held a deep-seated concern for the future of the Church and religious faith in general. Evidence of his concern is revealed in *The Prophecies* by the frequent reference to both the clergy and the Church itself.

Many quatrains address the troubles of the Christian faith and specifically focus on two main themes: the battle between the sacred Church and those people opposed to it and the sacrifice the clergy make when changes to the Church and the world occur in the future.

In this section, I want to touch very briefly on two quatrains that address the troubles of the Christian faith during the time of the French Revolution.

Difficult times and a high price to pay

A perfect example of Nostradamus's concern for the future of the Church is Quatrain C I – 44:

> In short sacrifices will be resumed,
>
> Transgressors will be put to martyrdom:
>
> No longer will there be monks, abbots or novices:
>
> Honey will be much more expensive than wax. (C I – 44)

Sacrifices is a reference to the revival of ancient pagan religions, whose followers were known to make sacrificial offerings (bread, wine, meats, and even the blood of an animal in desperate times) to the various gods and goddesses they worshipped. Nostradamus would've seen the rise in interest in the ancient religions as a threat to Christianity. He believed that everyone must go through Jesus Christ to be closer to God, and certainly the pagans didn't do that. In this quatrain, Nostradamus may have provided a general description of the rise of other religions in the changing future of mankind.

Alternatively, he may have been describing the difficult times the Church would experience during the French Revolution. As a result of the revolution (and the Age of Reason, where thought was more important than faith or passion), the Catholic Church was removed as the official church of the government of France.

Maybe Nostradamus's vision of the Church as separate from the monarchy was something completely alien and disturbing to his understanding of how the world worked. For Nostradamus, the king was also the head of the Church in France, and the Age of Reason was probably a terrible force that might wear away at the foundation of the Church. I can certainly understand why that would get him fired up and talking loudly.

The last line of this quatrain mentions *honey,* a reference to bees, which were sometimes used as an emblem for the king of France because of their persistence and endurance. It also mentions *wax,* a reference to candles (possibly Church lights) and a by-product of bees. Within Nostradamus's worldview, honey and wax occurred naturally together, just like the monarchy and the Church went together naturally. During the French Revolution, however, the churches extinguished their candles, because the price of candles grew very high. But even Nostradamus noted that the price of *honey* (the price the king would pay with his life and the loss of the monarchy) would be more than the price of *wax* (what would happen to the Church). So, although he knew the Church would go through troubles, he seemed to feel that its fate wouldn't be as bad as the fate of the monarchy.

A warning about the dangers ahead

Perhaps the most clearly stated warning about the dangers to the Church comes from Quatrain C VIII – 98:

> The blood of the Church people will be poured out,
>
> In as great abundance as water:
>
> And for a long time it will not be stopped,
>
> Woe, woe for the clergy ruin and wailing. (C VIII – 98)

Quatrain C VIII – 98 contains nothing that really ties the prophecy to a particular time. It's reasonable to think that Nostradamus was talking about a trend rather than a specific event and that the vision he received was one that he found very frightening. If Nostradamus had looked at the path of the Church from his own time to now, he would've seen many trials and travails. But the imagery of the vicious French Revolution, including the wholesale deaths of the clergy (because they were associated with the king and the established order of society under the monarchy) and the defacing of the holy churches (the decorations in the churches symbolized for the revolutionaries the wealth of the few while many were too poor to eat), probably would've set his teeth on edge more than anything else. The biggest blow against the power of the Church was just as Nostradamus predicted in C I – 44 — the separation of the Church from the power of the king.

If you want to take a sideways perspective on Quatrain C VIII – 98, look closely at the idea of *blood*. Instead of referring to the literal red stuff flowing out of dying priests, Nostradamus could've been talking about the life-blood of the Church — the faith and the money being eroded by the Age of Reason and the taxes of the new French republic. I think Nostradamus was perfectly capable of including faith and money in the same quatrain without feeling the least bit of conflict. After all, the devout man knew that the world ran on more than just a good word. Loss of income and the dangers of a rational and skeptical approach to religion would certainly have caused the Church to lose some of the source of its power — the faith and emotional connection of the congregation with the Divine.

The point of it all

Humans are a stubborn lot, and we rarely listen to warnings that we're doing something dangerous. Such was the case with the warnings put forth by Nostradamus about the dangers ahead to faith and the Church.

I don't think his message was a complete waste of paper, though. His quatrains about the dangers to the Church and the clergy can stand as a reminder that he was one man with a particular point of view. For many people from the modern, scientific viewpoint, reason isn't a terrible thing. But if you were standing in Nostradamus's shoes, the logical and unemotional Age of Reason would be disturbing to you. Think about the ideas that are terrifying to the beliefs you hold dear. Your point of view, just like his, may limit your understanding of the world around you. Nostradamus predicted in the *Epistle to Henry II* that a time would come when ignorance would no longer be the ruling force, and people would understand his predictions. Maybe that time is now, and you're the one to understand.

Chapter 10

Suffering from a Napoleon Complex

In This Chapter

▶ Prophesying Napoleon Bonaparte's rise to power

▶ Examining the details of Napoleon's life as seen by Nostradamus

▶ Predicting Napoleon III's unsuccessful reign

*I*f you could have lunch with anyone in the world, I doubt you'd think about Napoleon Bonaparte, but maybe you should. Nostradamus certainly spent a good deal of time considering how this young upstart would impact the future of France. Napoleon's control in France and throughout Europe from 1799 until 1814 wasn't only the talk of the town but was also downright shocking because he was an outsider from Corsica, not France (although the island of Corsica was sold to France in 1769, the year before Napoleon's birth).

Nostradamus didn't just predict the identity of the star of the show. He also described events that would sweep Napoleon to power, Napoleon's reign, and the cause of his downfall. A ton of quatrains describe the life and times of Napoleon, and they're very much out of order in *The Prophecies,* but with a little combing and selecting, I've brought together some of the more startling ones in this chapter.

Predicting Napoleon's Reign

Politicians and philosophers who observed the French Revolution up close and personal predicted that the entire bloody struggle would end in a dictatorship — or something equally unpleasant for the freedom-seeking masses. And one look at Nostradamus's writings would've confirmed their feelings. He predicted Napoleon's rise 200 years or so before the events. (In Chapter 9, I provide some background info on the French Revolution, if you're interested in the gory details.)

Some quatrains in every part of *The Prophecies* reference Napoleon Bonaparte. The topics include specific battles, the kinds of fashion that Napoleon would bring to the scene (specifically the wig), troubles with the Church and priests, and even the exact length of time Napoleon would rule.

Here's a quick piece of a quatrain regarding that latter point: In Quatrain C VII – 13, the final line says, *For fourteen years he will hold the tyranny.* Nostradamus must've been counting by the stars very exactly on the night he wrote this prophecy, because Napoleon ruled from 1799 when he became First Consular of France to 1814 when he lost his battle for France and went into exile on the island of Elba (with 600 of his closest soldiers). Yes, that's slightly over 14 years, but if you count from the months that these events happened, it's 14 years. Trust me.

A bit of trivia for you: Napoleon's influence on Europe was striking, but he may not have been what you'd call a striking figure of a man. A long-held assumption has been that Napoleon was short. But, depending on how his height is converted from French to English measurements, he may have been as tall as 5 feet, 6 inches, about average height for a man of the times, instead of 5 feet, 2 inches as has been widely reported. Check out the painting of Napoleon in Figure 10-1.

Figure 10-1:
Riding with
Napoleon
Bonaparte.

Erich Lessing / Art Resource, NY

Spelling out his identity

Imagine trying to identify one individual from the future from the countless billions that would walk the Earth at one point or another. It's a pretty tall order. And Nostradamus must have known that he ran the distinct risk of having the quatrains misinterpreted and the people he described misidentified. So when it really mattered, he included plenty of clues to help readers identify the right people.

In Quatrain C VIII – 1, for example, the very first line is

"PAU, NAY, LORON will be more fire than of blood."

The first three words of the line are an anagram — a word that forms a new word — in this case, two words — when the letters are rearranged. Switch the letters around, and these words become NAPAULON ROY (*roi* is the French word for king), or Napoleon the king. After you figure out the anagram, the line reads

"Napoleon the king will be more fire than of blood."

Because the future emperor wasn't born of royal blood and came to the throne through the fire of guns and cannons, I applaud Nostradamus for placing to rest any doubts about the identity of this man whose influence would be felt throughout Europe and the world.

But with that little detail out of the way, Nostradamus wasn't always as transparent in his other 40 or so quatrains about Napoleon, though the clues are still certainly there, as you'll see in Quatrain C VIII – 57:

From simple soldier he will attain to empire,

From short robe he will attain to the long:

Valiant in arms in the Church the very worst,

To vex the priests as water does the sponge. (C VIII – 57)

To restate in general terms, this quatrain talks about a brave soldier who'll be in charge of an empire and be a problem for the Church. But stick with me, it gets better.

Will the real subject of the quatrain please stand up?

Although the majority of interpreters believe this quatrain is intended for Napoleon, others argue there's another match for the quatrain in the history of England. Oliver Cromwell is his name, and religious fervor was his game. In Table 10-1, I compare the pieces of this quatrain and their relationships to both Napoleon and Cromwell.

Table 10-1	Match the Man with C VIII – 57	
Quote	Napoleon Bonaparte (1769-1821)	Oliver Cromwell (1599-1658)
Simple soldier	Born to the lower aristocracy, he attended military schools, fought as a soldier for Corsica's freedom, and then served in the Franco-Corsican administration.	Not quite noble, not quite common, he was made a minor cavalry commander.
Attain to empire	Through military and political maneuvers, Napoleon became emperor over much of Europe in 1804.	Put down rebellions harshly in Ireland and Scotland in 1649 and then overthrew the monarch, taking control of England as well.
Short robe (symbol of the politician)	After military victories, he was in the right place at the right time when France needed leadership and was appointed First Consul in 1799.	Served in House of Parliament in 1628 and again later as part of the temporary parliament after the death of King Charles I in 1649.
Long robe (symbol of the royal robes)	A powerful personality and decisive vision enabled him to become sole ruler of the empire, uniting France.	After forcibly dissolving the temporary parliament, he proclaimed himself Lord Protector (never king or emperor) with a council.
Valiant in arms	Quick wit and a lifetime of military experience made his battles epic.	Swift and firm action guided his direction of cavalry troops and then entire armies.
In the Church the very worst way	Had no use for the Church. At his coronation as emperor, he took the crown from the pope instead of having the pope place it on his head. He granted freedom of religion to conquered areas, which had been Catholic.	Opposed the religious intolerance of Presbyterians.
To vex the priests	Imprisoned the pope for refusing to give the Papal State (Italian lands controlled by the Church) to Napoleon's empire.	Ruled as a radical Puritan with strict laws of behavior and religious observance.
As water does a sponge (water very thoroughly invades a sponge)	Everything he did concerning the Church, including abolition of the priesthood and attempts to move the center of the Church to Paris, caused the priests and popes great distress.	Ruled with strict concern for all aspects of life, including the religious and social facets.

By looking at Table 10-1, you see that for each of the major pieces within Quatrain C VIII – 57, Napoleon is a very good match. I believe he was the object of the prophecy. Granted, the quatrain's lines do match some of the details for Oliver Cromwell, but I have several problems with Cromwell as the object of this quatrain:

- ✔ Cromwell went insane and converted to Puritan beliefs around 1630. (The two aren't linked exactly, but they happened around the same time.) It would make sense for Nostradamus to mention something important like a religious conversion and an attack of mental illness, especially because Nostradamus was a doctor, and he watched health closely.

- ✔ Cromwell was troublesome to religious groups but not especially to priests. As a deeply religious man, Cromwell wanted to help create a God-ordered realm and wanted all the different church groups to help. But fighting over petty issues and power struggles made this kind of joint work impossible, so it's almost like the different religious groups vexed him more than he vexed them in some ways.

- ✔ Cromwell started out as a businessman — and a failed one at that — before inheritance and luck placed him in a military position. He didn't start life as a simple soldier and thus doesn't really match the first line of the quatrain. Even when he gained a military position, it was as the head of a small cavalry unit, not as a simple soldier.

Sorry, Cromwell, you have to go. This isn't the quatrain for you. Napoleon simply makes a better match. And beyond that, Napoleon seems to have had a larger impact on the world in general. Between his conquering techniques, his centralization of the French government, and the Napoleonic Code (a system of unified laws that became the basis for French common law and law within many of the countries Napoleon conquered), I have no doubt that Napoleon's impact has been felt from his own time to the present.

Where have all the good men gone?

Nostradamus wrote prophecy for the entire world to see and read, but I think he wrote Quatrain C VIII – 57 mostly for the greedy people — with the warning that power and prestige are very fickle company. History shows that Napoleon was on top of the world as long as he continued to win military campaigns and keep peace at home, which wasn't always simple because some groups opposed his rule. Those things kept people distracted from his more aggressive (and some may say brutal) policies. But eventually his harsh tactics and cowardly moves (like lying about a victory and leaving his troops on the battlefield) earned him exile and a total loss of power (as I cover in the "Escaping Elba" section later in the chapter).

Perhaps Nostradamus was highlighting Napoleon's inability (or even Cromwell's, for those people who insist it was him) to rule because he wasn't born to do so (he wasn't of royal blood). Nostradamus favored the monarchy, and this kind of drastic, upside-down cake of a ruler certainly would've made him cringe. Whether he liked what he saw or not, though, Nostradamus was right in identifying Napoleon as an important figure in the world's history. So looking through the quatrains for other important people may help prepare today's world for future movers and shakers.

Examining the quality of his rule

I'm glad Nostradamus didn't predict *my* career. Most of the quatrains Nostradamus wrote about Napoleon focused on his failure in campaigns and the disappointment to the people of France. But don't let these topics fool you. Nostradamus wrote prophecies about this man because of his wide-ranging impact on the world.

At least some of Nostradamus's focus on Napoleon (like on his losses in war rather than on his long-lasting improvements to the law code) come from the prophet's own personal agendas, like religion and politics. (I talk about these troublesome issues for Nostradamus in Chapters 4 and 5 if you want more detail.) If you were able to look at Napoleon through the eyes of 16th-century Nostradamus, the drastic changes may look like catastrophic failure to you as a religious and generally peaceful man, but even from today's perspective, Napoleon was no minor character.

The details on the length and quality of Nostradamus's rule are spelled out in Quatrain C I – 4:

> In the world there will be one Monarch
>
> Who will not long be in peace or alive:
>
> Then the fishing bark will be lost,
>
> It will be ruled to its greater detriment. (C I – 4)

The *one Monarch* (Napoleon) wouldn't rule very long, and his peace wouldn't be very lasting, so said Nostradamus. You can double-check the prophecy in history books, but I can tell you that his vision held true. Although peace was part of Napoleon's world, he wasn't truly happy unless he was conquering something or someone, so he was constantly at war. Note that another interpretation for *will not long be in peace* is that Napoleon was restless and kept looking for new conquests.

Whether or not Napoleon ruled for the detriment of all is still a matter of debate. Napoleon encouraged the arts, brought prosperity to France, helped centralize the government, and established a common code of law that's still widely used as the basis for law in several places around the world. He was definitely a man who left his mark. But Nostradamus's perspective from a time of a friendly French monarchy saw only trouble and mayhem.

From his viewpoint, the *fishing bark* (a reference to the biblical Peter and the fisherman of men — Christ) would find dark times during Napoleon's reign. The lack of Napoleon's religious drive probably showed up in Nostradamus's visions, and if someone wasn't for the Church, then he was against it in Nostradamus's opinion. The Nostradamus that found inspiration and peace in his spiritual life could only view the decline of religion (which worsened during Napoleon's reign but didn't start there) as an overall problem, and if you add in the military struggles with their pain and death, Nostradamus didn't see a pretty picture.

Hindsight is 20/20, so the saying goes, and in some cases, the view isn't nearly as bad after the fact. Nostradamus frequently saw events that were life altering and world shattering *for him.* Whether those events maintain their shock value now for you is another thing entirely.

Humans are an adaptable group that manage (generally with an adjustment period) to continue making progress with the events at hand. I believe Nostradamus saw the events of the future and the changes that Napoleon would bring, but perhaps he couldn't always see the reactions and the impact of these events very clearly — either that or he underestimated the power of people to take a bad situation (of which he saw plenty) and learn from it. One of my theories about Nostradamus is that he used very impressive examples like Napoleon to make you sit up and take notice.

Cataloging the Events

During my study and research, I've maintained some skeptical thoughts about all this prophecy business, but then I ran across amazingly detailed descriptions I think truly apply to only one situation, and I have to give a nod to old Nostradamus. He really did himself proud on predicting the events of Napoleon's reign. This section provides some snippets about a few quatrains that are big on the details.

Capturing Milan

Napoleon wasn't the end all and be all of a military commander when he started leading the French troops at the Battle of Toulon in France (1793) near the Italian border (Toulon was a center of resistance to the Revolution, and Napoleon was in charge of gaining control of the area), but he had qualities that most great leaders have — skills and the gift of gab. His skills at Toulon were noticed, and Napoleon was put in charge of the army campaigning in

Italy. But Nostradamus heard Napoleon long before the troops heard him speak before the attack on Milan in May 1796. Look at Quatrain C III – 37 for the 16th century sneak preview of Napoleon's ability to lead:

> The speech delivered before the attack,
>
> Milan taken by the eagle through deceptive ambushes:
>
> Ancient wall driven in by cannons,
>
> Through fire and blood few given quarter. (C III – 37)

Nostradamus may have missed his calling as a news reporter, because this quatrain is so accurate. Taking charge of the Army of Italy (a French army aimed at the Italian lands), Napoleon had a rag-a-muffin group on his hands that had been battling the Italians for months with little support from France, because the revolution required many of the resources that would normally support an army in the field.

Underfed and exhausted, the troops had nothing going for them. But in a rousing speech, Napoleon promised that by taking Milan, they'd gain the riches, food, better clothing, and prestige they desired. In other words, he pointed out the self-interest in the campaign, and for the first time, a European army was fighting for its own benefit. This inspiring speech apparently worked, and after defeating the opposing army at Milan, the army went on to conquer and loot a fair portion of the countries around France, including a return trip to Milan to carry off art and wealth from the city that started it all.

To Nostradamus, the attitude of self-interest from these future armies couldn't have been high on his list of respectable goals. As a healer and prophet, Nostradamus was concerned about the greater good of the human race rather than the benefit of the individual. As I discuss in the "Examining the quality of his rule" section earlier in the chapter, I believe that at times, Nostradamus had many personal issues that tainted the prophecies he wrote, but everybody is human, and you can't escape bias when humans are involved. Napoleon isn't the only person who shows up in the quatrains as a poor example in Nostradamus's opinion, but he's one of the clearest examples of instances when I believe Nostradamus put his own spin on his visions in order to express his opinions on religion and politics as some of the truly troublesome issues the future would face.

Walking on shifting sands in Egypt

Not all of Napoleon's adventures were successful, and Quatrain C II – 86 describes a situation that Napoleon went so far as to cover up:

Wreck for the fleet near the Adriatic Sea:

The land trembles stirred up on the air placed on land:

Egypt trembles Mahometan increase,

The Herald surrendering himself is appointed to cry out. (C II – 86)

Before assuming control of the entire French military in 1799, Napoleon was in charge of the Army of Italy (see the preceding section) and then the French army, which he took into Egypt in 1798 to cut off England's trade routes. Here's a line-by-line break-down of Quatrain C II – 86:

- ✔ **Line 1:** *The fleet near the Adriatic* waters is the English navy, led by Admiral Horatio Nelson, which had been chasing Napoleon since he escaped a blockade against the City of Toulon, France, early in 1798. The English navy chased Napoleon down the coast of Italy through the Mediterranean Sea (which is near the Adriatic Sea of line 1).

- ✔ **Line 2:** The second line may refer to French soldiers who went ashore in Egypt and were disheartened after hearing that their ships (which were their rides home and their backup from the sea) had been blown up; the pieces were flung up on the shore *(land trembles).*

- ✔ **Line 3:** This line refers to events on shore as Napoleon battled the Turks (who were kindly helping out their friends, the British) and found that they were very determined. Alternatively, the plague or an illness similar to it swept through Napoleon's troops while they were in Egypt, and this could fit the bill of an earth-shaking development for Napoleon.

- ✔ **Line 4:** *The Herald* and his *surrendering* in line 4 refer to the city of Acre, which Napoleon offered terms of peace to. But Napoleon's offer wasn't accepted, and he was forced to siege the city.

Napoleon's battles in Egypt were mostly successful on land (the opposing armies retreated to regroup), but the destruction of the navy and the unsuccessful siege of the city of Acre were very costly. Nostradamus predicted these defeats, and I believe the *Herald* who cries out in the last line is the messenger Napoleon sent ahead back to France. The messenger carried news of Napoleon's successful campaign in Egypt to cover up his defeats so that he hopefully retained enough influence to take power on his return to Paris.

Dancing in Spain

Napoleon was an all-around conquering kind of guy, and he managed to occupy Spain and Portugal from 1808 to 1814. Quatrain C V – 14 ties the struggles during the Napoleonic wars to control Spain to the earlier time period of the Siege of Malta (a separate siege from the one in 1565; for more on that, check out Chapter 7) during the early part of Napoleon's career.

This quatrain is an example of astrological dating that gives strength to Nostradamus's prophecy. Like many quatrains that deal with war, the lines read like a war story all chopped up:

> Saturn and Mars in Leo Spain captive,
>
> By the African chief trapped in the conflict,
>
> Near Malta, "Herodde" taken alive,
>
> And the Roman sceptre will be struck down by the Cock. (C V – 14)

Looking at what was written in the stars

To begin unraveling this quatrain, look at the ideas that seem to jump out of it:

- Spain is held captive.
- It's kept captive by an *African chief*.
- The island of Malta is involved.
- The mysterious "Herodde" combines with a fall of power to the cock (which, by the way, is a bird symbol for France).

At first, the mix of pieces seems like too many cooks in the kitchen — a certain way to ruin a good prophecy. Finding a foothold is important, so I suggest starting with the first line and the stars that date the events.

First things first, a bit about the movement of Saturn and Mars. These two planets move around the sun at different speeds, so they rarely cross each other's paths and line up in the sky as Nostradamus describes, but they were close to this alignment (which covers nearly five years when it does happen) when Napoleon was busy conquering Malta. Nostradamus used his astrological charts and planetary knowledge to allude to 1798 without directly stating the date.

Napoleon set out to get his hands on the island of Malta in 1798 (a strategic strongpoint) beginning on June 9. His victorious quest continued through the time when Saturn and Mars were within the Leo time of the year — July 23 to August 22. This is a perfect example of how Nostradamus used astrology to obscure some of the details in his prophecies like dates, because anyone unacquainted with the movement of the planets would be bewildered.

In 1807 and well after the official five-year window of astrological influence would support him, Napoleon began the Peninsular Wars (fought along the Iberian Peninsula in Southwest Europe), which included the conquering of Spain and Portugal. With the slow fade of astrological support from Saturn and Mars, Napoleon would find that he wouldn't be able to keep Spain. History confirms the situation: In 1808, as the influence of the planets was truly gone, Napoleon convinced King Charles IV of Spain to step down in favor of Joseph Bonaparte (Napoleon's brother), but the people of Spain revolted at having a French ruler. The tide turned against Napoleon's conquering ways.

In 1814, Arthur Wellington (the same duke of Wellington who would defeat Napoleon later at Waterloo) helped the Spanish in a civil revolt to force the French forces to leave. (To find out more about alternative ways some folks try to date quatrains, including this one, check out the sidebar, "A different system for dating the quatrains," in this chapter.)

In addition to dating the quatrain, Nostradamus also used his knowledge of astrology to enhance the details. When Saturn (which represents hard work and tests) and Mars (which represents a person's will to do something) get together, there's sure to be plenty of action and determination, two terms that describe Napoleon's approach to war and conquering very well. Together these two planets in Leo (an astrological sign associated with pride and arrogance) are used by Nostradamus to suggest that the actions of Napoleon are motivated at least in part by his own desires rather than those of his country.

It's important to note that if Nostradamus had just given us the date of the siege of Malta, we would've missed the commentary on Napoleon's overall attitude, as well as the hint that after the siege (because Spain is listed separately), there'd be trouble to come for the dictator. By including astrology, Nostradamus added layers of meaning, commentary, and depth to the prophecies.

Understanding the symbols

The final line of the quatrain gives the impression that the cock (France and its ruler, Napoleon) will force parts of Rome to fall or give up its power, symbolized by the sceptre (a staff or baton used by the ruler to represent his authority). In 1801, Napoleon managed to wear down the pope into signing a Concordat (agreement between the pope and a ruler on religious matters), where the Church gave up claims to lands that had been confiscated during the French Revolution, and Napoleon admitted that most of the French population was Catholic. In addition, the Church maintained its ability to select bishops, but they were required to swear allegiance to the French government.

Although the agreement released tensions between the Catholic Church and France, the Church was required to give up much of its claims in France, thus symbolically laying down the sceptre of power by the force of *the cock,* used to represent France. Nostradamus closed this quatrain with commentary on how the power of the Church influenced politics, and he seems to have been fairly accurate. Both religion and politics were near to Nostradamus's heart, which is why I believe he inserted these comments on the Church, even when the majority of the quatrain discusses war.

Two other symbols in this quatrain remain unexplained, but I can help with that confusion. Kind of. *Herodde* in Line 3 is one of those words that makes every Nostradamus scholar wish for a nice vacation, because there's no clear answer for what it means. Some say that by rearranging the letters in the anagram, you find the word *Rhodes,* which can be a reference to the Knights of Rhodes who occupied Malta when Napoleon captured it. This interpretation fits nicely with the astrological dating in line 1.

Other interpreters insist this is a reference to King Herod, the ancient enemy of Christ who had all male children born near Jesus's time killed in order to prevent the prophesied child from living. Herod can be interpreted as a place (Judea, the home of King Herod) or as a more general reference to all the enemies of the Christian faith — those people who weren't full believers in the Church.

Line 2 also contains a symbol that's confusing even to scholars — *the African chief.* This reference to Africa may not make sense without a history lesson. To prove himself worthy (before taking control of France entirely), Napoleon went to Egypt and fought the North *African chief* (the ruling British and their supporters). Unfortunately for Napoleon, he was *by the African chief trapped in the conflict,* or in other words, he was unsuccessful in his battles and then trapped (or nearly so) in Egypt when the navy — his support and ride home — was sunk.

Deserting the troops in Russia

I tend to think of Napoleon in terms of the grand portraits that were painted of him (like the one in Figure 10-1), and I imagine that's what comes to your mind as well. Trouble is, we frequently forget that the history makers have always been people with real lives and faults, so they tend to seem a little grander than life and bigger than you and me. Quatrain C IV – 75 records one of the not-so-brilliant moves made by Napoleon during his career and reminds us that he was very human:

> Ready to fight one will desert [faint or disappear],
>
> The chief adversary will obtain the victory:
>
> The rear guard will make a defense,
>
> The faltering ones dead in the white territory. (C IV – 75)

Although this quatrain doesn't provide a lot of concrete details, there's a fairly reasonable chance that Nostradamus foresaw the march of Napoleon and his half-million troops (approximately) into Russia in 1812 to invade and fight the Russians. If this is the event in the quatrain, then the symbols are as follows:

- **The one who deserts:** Napoleon left his troops, found a disguise and a ride back to Paris, and left his men to die in the harsh winter.

- **The chief adversary:** Russia's Czar, Alexander I, placed Marshal Kutuzov in charge of the smaller Russian military.

- **The defensive rear guard:** The defensive strategy of the Russian army was to destroy the land and resources as they retreated, essentially leaving Napoleon's invading army with nothing to eat or to repair their materials.

> ✔ **The faltering ones:** These French soldiers who faltered and fell behind were the unfortunate men who were sick and disheartened that Napoleon deserted them in the "white country" of a Russian winter to freeze or starve to death while he returned to France to keep his position of power.

The symbols in Quatrain C IV – 75 match up closely with the events of Napoleon's invasion of Russia and the fact that Napoleon's original half-million army struggled back to France with fewer than 40,000 soldiers. I think Nostradamus wrote this prophecy about the brutal destruction of human life as a reminder for future generations that admirable leaders may make pricey mistakes. Napoleon abandoned the men who protected him, reminding you that no matter how many glossy speeches you hear (and Napoleon was great at this art), you should also judge someone by how he acts.

For what it's worth, I figure that the healer in Nostradamus probably saw the bloodshed and the human price for the military glory that Napoleon gained and was disgusted by it. The description of the Russian campaign could've been done without emotional words like *faltering* or *desert,* but Nostradamus used them specifically to express his opinion of this future Frenchman. Although accurate with the prophecy, Nostradamus just couldn't resist a few moral overtones in the writing of the prophecy.

Escaping Elba

Napoleon was a very persistent man to say the least, and I'm sure that on the nights Nostradamus saw these visions, he wondered whether Napoleon's influence would ever end. Certainly, Quatrains C X – 24 and C II – 66 were a warning from Nostradamus to the future that Napoleon wouldn't go quietly into the good night. I know these two quatrains are linked, because they share too many details to be talking about separate events. They share a captive, an escape, a military struggle, and the draining effects of power on everyone:

> The captive prince conquered in Italy
>
> Will pass Genoa by sea as far as Marseilles:
>
> Through great exertion by the foreigners overcome,
>
> Safe from gunshot, barrel of bee's liquor. (C X – 24)

> Through great dangers the captive escaped:
>
> In a short time great his fortune changed.
>
> In the palace the people are trapped,
>
> Through good omen the city besieged. (C II – 66)

Nostradamus began Quatrain C X – 24 by labeling Napoleon a *captive prince*. History tells us that in 1814 he was just in exile (which means he had to leave France) at the insistence of the armies of Britain, Russia, Prussia, and Austria who had joined forces to defeat Napoleon and occupy France. His exile was on the island of Elba, and he was never a prince. Even if you consider kings who are kicked off the throne or dead to be princes (because they can't take the title with them), Napoleon doesn't qualify. He was never the king.

The dating game

The complex arrangement of quatrains within the ten centuries has given many a graduate student a headache. The trouble is figuring out the order of the quatrains and whether their placement has any significance. Some scholars suggest that the way Nostradamus ordered each quatrain — the specific number he gave each quatrain and century — provided clues to the actual date of the event at hand. Using Quatrain C V – 14 as an example, the quatrain number (14) becomes the last two digits of a year, and the century number (5) becomes the month for an event in the future (alternately, it can be used as the century indicator for the year).

Because Nostradamus could calculate the astrological connection for events if he had a starting point for the charts (like using France's Constitution Day as its birthday), he could place quatrains in the appropriate locations to reveal the dates of the events predicted. You can identify Quatrain C V – 14 as referring to an event in a year ending in 14, so that's the year the event would be predicted to occur. Combine this knowledge with the images of Napoleon's wars, and it appears that you should look at Napoleon's life for a match in the 1800s — specifically 1814. 1814 was the last year Napoleon ruled over France, except for a brief 100-day stint in 1815 when he forced his way back to power.

If the century number is included as the month of a particular event (in this case, Roman numeral V or 5), then you're looking at May in 1814. This would be a close, but not quite a hit for a very important event in Napoleon's life — his abdication in April 1814 (just a few weeks before May).

Yet another system uses the century number within the year, making Century 5 Quatrain 14 into the year 1514, which makes this quatrain into a retrospective look at the past rather than a prediction, because Nostradamus wrote in 1554. Another alternative dating system suggests that everything is moved forward, and you should add the century number to the hundreds place in the date, so the dating is 2014, and the prediction has yet to be fulfilled. Other experts theorize that the quatrain could apply to 2514, which is well after the time of Napoleon but still a possibility for a prophecy of a future event, because Nostradamus had visions and made prophecies for events through the year 3757, according to information in the *Preface to César*.

This system of dating the quatrains by their organizational placement is only occasionally accurate and seems to be more chance than real prophecy. If I were placing bets, I'd still rely on the symbols and hints in the quatrains to tell me a time for an event. Besides, after a while, all the numbers that easily correspond to events would be taken, and the neutral numbers within the quatrains would have to be used.

Don't get me wrong, though. I think Nostradamus was accurate in this prophecy, but his point of view made him select words in odd ways sometimes. Nostradamus identified Napoleon as an emperor in other quatrains, so this term was definitely a switch to a lesser title, and it wasn't a mistake or slip of the pen. Nostradamus used the term *prince* to let readers know that he saw Napoleon's decline, even though the prediction concerned Napoleon's return from the island of Elba to a place of power.

The path Nostradamus traced in line 2 for Napoleon's 1815 escape from Elba past Genoa to Marseilles is mostly correct, but Napoleon actually stopped short in his trip westward along the shore and landed in Cannes, a city just to the east and north of Marseilles by about 100 miles. Either Nostradamus missed the detail on the landing site, or he was confused by the fact that Napoleon hugged the coast for the last part of his sea trip. Nostradamus then went on to talk about Napoleon's defeat later at the battle of Waterloo (see the next section) by the Prussians and the English — the foreigners he labeled in line 3.

Note that Nostradamus described this same rise to power and quick fall as *fortune changed* in Quatrain C II – 66. A decent writer typically tries not to repeat material, but I think Nostradamus repeated himself deliberately to link these two quatrains together after he spread them out in *The Prophecies*.

Back to Quatrain C X – 24, the escape from Elba earned Napoleon safety (at least from *gunshot* in line 4), as well as the power to regain control of his troops because he was the king bee. The bee (a symbol of the monarchy, where one person rules and others follow, that's frequently used as a symbol for Napoleon) produces sweet honey, but in this case, Nostradamus referred to bee's liquor — something that's intoxicating. I believe Nostradamus was commenting on the fact that Napoleon would let the effects of ruling the country go to his head.

In Quatrain C II – 66, the third line takes up the idea of power gone bad and points out that *In the palace the people are trapped.* Nostradamus wasn't talking literally. He was pointing out that the lives and fortunes of the population are tied to the events surrounding the people who rule the country, thus trapping the people with the same fate of the country's leadership.

For you, Quatrains C X – 24 and C II – 66 carry a warning about the dangers of political power and of controlling other people in any form. Controlling others is bad manners, but it's also bad governing. Knowing that you can move big pieces of the world puzzle around may sound like fun, and it may be tempting to do. Like in the case of Napoleon, though, just because you can do something, doesn't mean you should.

Battling it out at Waterloo

All good things must come to an end, and even Napoleon's reign over most of Europe had to end eventually (whether you think it was a good thing or not). Nostradamus saw Napoleon as a terror who would challenge many of the standing ideas of the time. But Napoleon was tougher than people of his time imagined, and the man was put into exile not once, but twice. Just before his final exile and eventual death, he returned to France, gathered supporters, and went out to fight one last battle.

One last hurrah

After the idea of a military dictator (or emperor as Napoleon called himself) was clear to Nostradamus, the question to be answered was how long the newly ascended person would rule. Nostradamus wrote that answer in Quatrain C I – 23, which marks the rising and setting of the Napoleonic sun:

> In the third month the Sun rising,
>
> The Boar and Leopard on the field of Mars to fight:
>
> The tired Leopard raises its eye to the heavens,
>
> Sees an Eagle playing around the Sun. (C I – 23)

If you're telling time in an astrologer's world, you must be using the stars. And that's exactly what Nostradamus did. He was telling time in line 1 of Quatrain C I – 23 when he wrote that the sun (a common symbol used for emperors in general and Napoleon specifically) will be rising in three months. Based on that line, I think Nostradamus was dating from the Spring Equinox (where light and day are equal). Here's my reasoning:

- ✔ The beginning of the astrological year (and the charts of influence from the stars) begins with the equinox in March — sometime around the 20th.

- ✔ From the equinox forward in the calendar, there's more sunshine than darkness for three months. But after the crest of sunlight, everything's downhill to a matching equinox in the fall.

Based on those deductions, "In the third month the Sun rising" places the event in June, and wouldn't you know it, Napoleon's glory was all downhill after his greatest loss in the battle at Waterloo, which occurred on June 18, 1815.

Understanding the intended prophecy for a quatrain is easier if you begin with one piece and start to unravel from there. Select a person, place, or thing within the quatrain, and see whether the item can be placed in time or space along Nostradamus's favorite topics of France, religion, the Medici family, the unknown 21st century, or whatever. After you start researching and studying the original piece, you may find references to something else in the quatrain. Don't forget — some of the quatrains are for the future and are much harder to figure out.

After you figure out the date when Nostradamus predicted events would occur, figuring out the rest of the symbols in a quatrain and making sense of the prophecy is easier. Although Nostradamus left the exact year for this particular prophecy a little blank, he got the action on the nose. During the Battle of Waterloo, Napoleon was up against English troops led by the duke of Wellington (represented by the lion on the English coat of arms and sometimes called a leopard). The English weren't hoping for too much in the way of victory, because the Prussian army (led by a man named Blücher who had avoided Napoleon's forces) was defeated in a battle just before Waterloo and wasn't going to be able to join the English for the last round with Napoleon's army. But Blücher managed to come in at the last possible moment to help out, and Napoleon was defeated.

Past the basic details, however, this quatrain becomes bogged down with a myriad of possible misinterpretation. Two pieces of symbolism — the sun and the eagle — provide hours of entertainment for Nostradamus's academic friends. But beyond their dusty desks, the symbols may seem a bit too much, so I boil them down to just the major combinations. I believe Nostradamus used the sun and the eagle for these layers of meaning:

- ✔ The sun was an alchemy symbol for life (which was running out for Napoleon), and Napoleon and his Empire were combined into the eagle symbol, circling dangerously close to the sun like Osiris. (Osiris was an Egyptian god who made wings of feathers and wax and then flew too close to the sun. When the wax melted, he plunged to his death.)

- ✔ The sun was a symbol for the Empire of France, which Napoleon (the eagle) circled. He returned from exile and was trying to come full circle to regain his empire. Nostradamus used the circling imagery to suggest that the eagle never manages to reach the goal. Napoleon's attempts to reach his former glory followed the same unsuccessful pattern.

- ✔ The sun was Napoleon's career, rising in the first line of the quatrain and circled as if being stalked by the eagle in the fourth line (possibly the white eagle Prussia used on state seals during the time Napoleon became Emperor).

The layers of meaning work together without contradicting each other, and they replay the theme that the conquering hero, Napoleon, was destined to meet a troublesome fate. I think Nostradamus intended to have multiple layers of meaning to increase the chances that the educated person would be able to pick out one piece and then discover the prophecy. Nostradamus tried to give as many clues as possible without giving the information completely away, because the Church and/or royal family could have him killed if they believed the prophecies were aimed at them.

Sunset at Waterloo

Quatrain C I – 23, discussed earlier in this chapter, begins a prophecy about Napoleon that's completed in Quatrain C I – 38. I believe both quatrains refer to the Battle of Waterloo in 1815, which has been immortalized in history as one of the bloodiest battles ever recorded. Take a look at the lines that complete the prophecy:

> The Sun and the Eagle will appear as victor,
>
> The vanquished is reassured with a vain reply:
>
> With hue and cry they will not cease arming,
>
> Revenge, because of death peace made right on schedule. (C I – 38)

Quatrain I – 38 begins with the *Sun* and the *Eagle* from Quatrain C I – 23, which for Nostradamus were symbols of Napoleon and the empire he ruled. I believe that using the same imagery in related quatrains was one of Nostradamus's tricks he used to assist interpreters who would later attempt to understand the quatrains.

The victor in line 1 of Quatrain C I – 38 is a reference to Prussia and the English troops that defeated Napoleon. Line 2 refers to a false message *(vain reply),* which was an interesting touch by Nostradamus. He was predicting false reassurances that Napoleon would send to his troops saying that the soldiers on the left and right were French troops and not those of the enemy. The *vain reply* also refers to the double-dealing of the leader himself, who would send such a message and then abandon his troops, where they would in vain wait for some reply from their leader.

In nearly every situation, Napoleon managed to find some way to protect himself, and at the Battle of Waterloo, the false message left him just enough time to escape being captured. The French troops realized they were surrounded and started to run in a full retreat, but the advancing enemy killed many of the French empirical soldiers, and the Eagle of Napoleon fell for the last time.

The last line of this quatrain was Nostradamus's attempt to bring meaning to the deaths of thousands of soldiers in this battle. After Waterloo, Europe experienced a time of peace and liberty under the rulers Napoleon named (he placed many of his family members as rulers of the countries he conquered) and the code of law he instituted in all the countries he controlled.

Sometimes it's a toss-up

Nostradamus had a lot of things on his mind. I think sometimes he had a clear idea of his own visions but had some trouble getting it down on paper. Quatrain C II – 70 is frequently listed as one of the quatrains describing Napoleon's final battle at Waterloo, but it isn't the most straightforward prediction Nostradamus ever made. I think one of two things happened with this quatrain:

- He was so overwhelmed by the strength of both Napoleon and the battles that Nostradamus just kinda rambled about how the event would look.

- The rumors of his divine inspiration were true, and the Divine One didn't speak plain English (or French as it was).

Take a look at the vague Quatrain C II – 70:

> The dart from the sky will make its extension,
>
> Deaths in speaking: great execution.
>
> The stone in the tree, the proud nation restored [surrendered],
>
> Noise, human monster, purge expiation. (C II – 70)

If you look at this quatrain as a metaphor (where one thing represents another), it could apply to Napoleon's last days:

- The first line, if you view the dart from the sky as God's lightning judgment on Napoleon, reflects Nostradamus's strong religious views.

- The quatrain continues the metaphor with a brief but bloody description in line 2 of the vast carnage as a result of the *speaking*, a possible reference to a false message Napoleon sent to his troops to reassure them of a victory and keep them in line, only to be mowed down by the Prussian army.

- Lines 3 and 4 describe the felling of the empirical tree of Napoleon's empire (and goals) with the earthly reality of so many casualties. Or, to put it another way, Nostradamus saw the death of Napoleon's rule as something that had to happen as a result of how he ran his life and country.

The trouble with this quatrain is that there's very little in the way of firm cornerstone pieces to anchor this prophecy to any time period or place. With a metaphor this broad, the prophecy could be anytime and any place that involves death, nations, great change, and some really dark imagery. I wouldn't give Nostradamus any awards for this as a verifiable prophecy.

Prophecy doesn't always have to be about dates and places. Those kinds of predictions get more attention in the press because we're from a scientific era that needs facts to hold onto before we believe in something. The era that produced and educated Nostradamus placed great importance on faith and would've hated the Age of Reason that produced Napoleon. The vague Quatrain C II – 70 and some of the other general quatrains weren't intended as event-specific prophecies in my opinion. I think they were in a special category of their own where Nostradamus wasn't telling *what* would happen to mankind but *how* and *why* things would happen to mankind.

I believe that sometimes Nostradamus predicted events in the future that we should pay attention to. I think he believed that the power of a spiritual aspect in life can combine with individual decisions to create the world we'll live in during the future. For Napoleon, a lack of faith and respect for the Church combined with poor choices (according to Nostradamus) for some truly terrible effects. But Nostradamus believed that if religion and faith are combined with the right action, however, the negative and destructive patterns can be avoided.

Reaching the end on St. Helena

No matter how great the monarch, he or she eventually reaches the end. Death may be a great equalizer on some levels, but for kings, queens, and emperors, the details of death are more important because the how and when can change the fate of nations. Nostradamus understandably focused on the end of Napoleon's time, because the end of his days meant more changes for France (and the world).

Although Nostradamus made Napoleon's path appear to be a hideous walk through war-torn Europe, he didn't present the end using terms quite that strong. Here are some interesting lines from two of the many Napoleon quatrains that deal with the end of his reign:

- ✔ **"In the middle of [a petty country] he will come to lay down his sceptre" (C I – 32).** The image of this line reminds me of a dramatic scene in a well-orchestrated movie, where Napoleon stands in a small office in St. Helena, the island he was exiled to the second time, and symbolically lies the sceptre of France in a box, and the lid closes as the credits roll.

- ✔ **"A hundred times will the inhuman tyrant die . . ." (C X – 90).** This line accurately predicts the 100 days Napoleon spent trying to regain power of France after escaping exile on the island of Elba. A subtle second layer of meaning predicts the many poisoning attempts to kill Napoleon. (A scientific test of his hair revealed loads of arsenic, but he died of stomach cancer.)

Although Quatrain C I – 32 provides a prediction for Napoleon's final exile, it has also been matched to the 1556 abdication of King Charles V from ruling the Holy Roman Empire so that he could retire to a peaceful monastery in Yuste, Spain, where he died two years later. Nostradamus printed the prophecy in the first editions in 1555, and if it applied to the situation with Charles V, it would've predicted the events by only a few months.

Foreseeing Napoleon III's Role in the World

After building a great empire, one of Napoleon's goals certainly was to leave behind an heir to take charge of the many countries he conquered. Unfortunately, as Nostradamus predicted in Quatrain C VIII – 41, Napoleon's only heir was his nephew, Napoleon III, whose rule wasn't necessarily an improvement over the original Napoleon's rule:

> A Fox will be elected without saying a word,
>
> Playing the saint in public living on barley bread,
>
> Afterwards he will very suddenly tyrannize,
>
> Putting his foot on the throats of the greatest ones. (C VIII – 41)

Line 1 of this quatrain isn't referring to Napoleon Bonaparte of the French Revolution, because he made quite a few speeches on his own behalf to help form the government he would dominate. But Nostradamus sketched a very accurate picture of Napoleon III, who did, in fact, come to be elected president of the Second Republic of France in 1848 and then emperor of the Second French Empire in 1852 without too much talking on his part. Napoleon's heir wasn't welcomed with open arms, however, and he began to have trouble with the people of France.

Monarchs with the same name were numbered consecutively — I, II, III, and so on. The fact that Napoleon III took control of the Second French Empire indicates that there was a Napoleon II (a legitimate heir from Napoleon's second wife) who never actually ruled France. In fact, Napoleon II was the king of Rome, duke of Reichstadt, and prince of Parma, but never king of France. He was kept in Austria from the time of Waterloo (1815) until his death in 1832.

This new Napoleon tried to rebuild people's faith in him by *playing the saint* (line 2) and rebuilding the city of Paris, but their trust was soon destroyed by two acts that fit the description in lines 3 and 4:

- ✔ Napoleon III helped organize a military takeover of the government that established the Second Empire and made him emperor. This act terrorized the countryside with its suddenness and effectively stepped in the way *(putting his foot on the throats)* of the other contenders for control of France.

- ✔ Napoleon III allowed himself to be drawn into and fight the grand Franco-Prussian war, which was a complete disaster. The war began at least in part because Napoleon III refused to give the Spanish throne to a German prince because he feared more political fighting. In this way, the trouble over the Spanish throne was Napoleon III putting his foot in his mouth and having to pay the price.

The language Nostradamus used to describe Napoleon III (*Fox* and *saint*) wasn't as strong as the descriptive names like *destroyer, thunderbolt,* or *great legislator* Nostradamus used to describe Napoleon the original. Naming a person by describing his actions was certainly a way for Nostradamus to comment on Napoleon III's importance — or lack thereof. Nostradamus gave just enough detail to identify Napoleon III as a successor, but his underhanded comments also suggested that the leader wouldn't be very strong.

Quatrain C VIII – 41 should remind you that every prophet is a person, and the prophet may have an issue that's touchy for him or her. Several issues were touchy for Nostradamus (religion, politics, medicine), and knowing about his concerns allows you to look at the prophecies with a bit more objectivity. When speaking about Napoleon III, for instance, Nostradamus is sensitive to the issue of how rulers are elected and how they manage their realms. I can see this as a reflection of Nostradamus's own concern for how France was being run during his own time.

Part IV
The Prophecies of the Modern Era

The 5th Wave
By Rich Tennant

© RICHTENNANT

"They say Nostradamus predicted air travel. Did he mention the removal of shoes and belts as a prerequisite for human flight?"

In this part . . .

Prepare yourself with a hardhat and thinking cap, because Part IV takes you from the 1800s to today with prophecies about wars, battles, science, religious struggles, and even more wars. Covering *three* World Wars, including the one still to come, the appearance of three antichrist figures, technology's growth by leaps and bounds (including the exploration of space), and even a shocking end to the 20th century — kind of — this part of the book brings you up to modern times and concerns with a bang. You'll be familiar with many of the topics covered in this part, and you can begin to gain a more personal understanding of Nostradamus's visions and how they relate to you in the here and now.

Chapter 11

Revealing Times of War

*N*ostradamus's prophecies can be grouped by topic — including Catherine de Medici, Napoleon, the French Revolution, natural disasters, and religious concerns — but the largest category by far is that of war. From revolutionary wars confined to one country to conflicts that engulfed the globe, armed struggles filled the nighttime sight of Nostradamus.

The idea that a healer would focus on war with its death, destruction, financial ruin, and political upheaval seems unlikely until you remember that Nostradamus was both a product of his times and an astute observer of the nature of people. He had already seen enough war and conquering in his own lifetime (including the religious wars between Catholics and Protestants that raged around him and the long-standing battle between Italy and France for territory) to know the violence wouldn't end anytime soon.

As a man of science Nostradamus also recognized that some of the greatest gains in knowledge and science resulted from war's demand for better, faster, and more efficient ways of handling the needs of the military. For example, geometry proved its worth on the battlefield by improving cannon-aiming abilities, among other applications. This opened the field of geometry and mathematics to many practical applications, including constructing sturdier buildings. Even today, the influence of military technology can be seen in our homes. Whenever you use the Internet or a cell phone, you're using by-products of the modern military need for information exchange. You and I have benefited from the great wars in some very unusual ways, and Nostradamus saw the possibilities in his visions of the future.

In this chapter, I trace the outlines of the major modern-era wars Nostradamus predicted and share some of the insight he offered. Nostradamus hoped to help people today learn from history (our past; his future) and guide us because we'll be the history that's studied 20 years from now when his predictions are probably still being debated.

Feasting on Aggression like It's Fat Tuesday

One of Nostradamus's most general predictions, and one of the most terrifying, isn't in the quatrains and centuries of *The Prophecies*. It's actually part of the *Epistle to King Henry II,* an openly published letter from Nostradamus that dedicated the first partial publication of *The Prophecies* to King Henry II (see Chapter 2).

In this letter, Nostradamus took a stab at some predictions for his own time and then broadened his perspective to include the far future — a time when the world would gorge itself in unhealthy ways. Among the unhealthy things Nostradamus saw for the future were troublesome quarrels, political struggles, natural disasters, and a terrible habit for going to war.

All the ideas in the *Epistle to King Henry II* are strung together in paragraphs, but I believe that this sentence from paragraph 16 is a strong summary of Nostradamus's view of the world's future:

> " . . . And this third one [of three brothers] will cause a great inundation of human blood, and for a long time Lent will not include March [Mars]." (*Epistle to King Henry II,* 16)

In this section, I explain the meaning behind this sentence and the way it reveals Nostradamus's frightening vision of the future. I discuss the people who aren't the cause of the bloodshed, some possible people who are, and the warnings Nostradamus provides. There's even a bit of hope here and there.

Meeting a hungry new face

The subject of this sentence is the last of three important men Nostradamus believed would make great changes in the face of European politics and who heavily influenced his vision of the future. To make sense of this statement, you need to know that the previous section of the *Epistle* describes a conquering army moving into the Pyrenees (a section of high mountains between France and Spain). History shows that only two military leaders have accomplished this feat — Hannibal, who came before Nostradamus, and Napoleon, who came after Nostradamus. So, just before paragraph 16, Nostradamus referred to the army of the Pyrenees, and that leads me to believe that he means the infamous Napoleon (the second troublesome person of the three referenced in the *Epistle*) who got a great deal of stage time in Nostradamus's predictions (see Chapter 10 for more on Napoleon). If the second one is Napoleon, then the last of the three who will cause so much bloodshed is left unidentified except by his actions.

Nostradamus described the death caused by the *third one* as an *inundation*, or an inescapable wave, of blood. His description gave nowhere to run, nowhere to hide, and no way to escape the idea that this terrible thing was going to happen. Nostradamus's description also provides a little clue to the identity of the third person who'll cause all of this crisis. To pick up on that clue, you have to examine the other clues in the quatrains (a long drawn out process) or just take a peek in Chapter 13 where I discuss three antichrists predicted by Nostradamus who are possibly the same three "brothers" mentioned here — and that's probably brothers in the sense that they are related by blood, a rather dirty pun by Nostradamus.

Nostradamus used words with loaded meanings in his prophecies. He could've described the situation as a lot of lost life, but he didn't. Nostradamus used *blood* because it immediately brings to mind the graphic images of a person bleeding and a kind of instinctual response that the situation is a crisis that must immediately be dealt with.

If a child says he's hurt, a parent generally asks about the injury, but if blood is involved, most parents act out of reflex. In his prophecies, Nostradamus chose his words carefully (like *a great inundation of human blood*) to get that kind of intense reflex action from his readers. Yes, it's a kind of manipulation, but he was trying to make a point.

Reviewing the original version

The last part of the sentence from paragraph 16 in the *Epistle* gets to the heart of Nostradamus's point and has always drawn my attention. Here, he began to tell about the present-day world — and it doesn't look too good. I had to do some detective work to figure out that it doesn't look hopeful because the original French text has two versions, and the translations are very different.

French text	Translation
. . . ne se trouvera de longtemps Mars en Carême.	. . . and for a long time Lent will not include March [Mars].
. . . ne se trouuera de long temps Mars en caresme.	. . . and [one] will not find Mars fasting for a long time.

Printing was new enough in Nostradamus's time that errors were very common, and Nostradamus didn't escape commonly misspelled words and slight changes to his text that could alter its meanings. These errors were mostly unintentional (though sometimes adding an error was the printer's way of commenting on the material), the result of quickly printing from a manuscript without letting the author review test print, or in other cases, the errors were simply made by typesetters (men who placed the letters for each page) who may have been able to read but not at a level at which they could read all of what they were working on.

Okay. Time to break this line down:

- **First translation:** This one involves the Christian period of time known as Lent (the 40 days before Easter), which is a time to refrain from excesses (like the wild acts of war) and reflect on the life of Christ. The familiar Nostradamus wordplay suggests that his use of "Mars" isn't a reference to the month of March (one possible translation) but is a double reference to Lent (which falls in March) and to the planet Mars. If, according to paragraph 16, the time of reflection and abstaining from earthly concerns *will not include Mars* (which has a war-like symbolism in the field of astrology), then Nostradamus was suggesting that even the most divinely inspired human reflection will turn a blind eye to war, thus allowing it to continue the outpouring of human blood. Ignoring war won't allow civilization to push pause on wars already in action during Lent or truly understand war to the point where we can avoid it.

- **Second translation:** This translation has more of an astrological leaning, which I feel makes it more consistent with Nostradamus and his fascination for the stars. If he was talking about the planet Mars fasting, the line doesn't make much sense until you remember that Mars in astrological terms is most often associated with aggression, war, and the red of blood. (The high iron content on the planet and the red color of the surface suggest this connection to blood.)

  If Mars (the ancient god of war) won't be fasting, then he'll be doing what many people do just before the period of fasting in Lent — feasting. Mars will feast on acts of aggression, which is kind of like the wild party and last fling of Fat Tuesday or Carnival (literally — without meat) that people celebrate before the fasting and reflection of Lent. By connecting this line with the "inundation of human blood," Nostradamus was making a clear comment on the devastation of the upcoming times.

For people of all times, the prophecy in paragraph 16 of the *Epistle to Henry II* serves as a warning that the systems they use to evaluate their actions, many of which are religious, won't be helpful if they make exceptions and leave out the careful consideration of human aggression. In addition to the benefits of personal reflection, Nostradamus pointed out that for a long time, war will be the way of life for people. He didn't attempt to inspire fear. He just recorded the situation so people know what to expect. Although not a pretty thought that this state of warfare will continue, I believe Nostradamus was ultimately trying to soothe and heal the hearts of future people by giving them a heads up on what was coming.

Two Wars that Changed the World

Just as Nostradamus started writing predictions, the world was opening up. New markets were developing, and the big European powers (mostly England and Spain) were spending a great deal of money and time finding new places to settle. The world was getting bigger (or smaller, depending on your perspective), and Nostradamus was aware of the new opportunities for growth — and for struggle. His predictions of World War I and World War II came from a study of his own times as well as the reflection in his prophetic visions. As he sat down to look into the future, he didn't just look at France (although sometimes it may seem that way); he looked beyond the shores of his homeland. I don't think he liked what he saw. Sadly, the prediction of global confrontation in the first and second world wars proved accurate.

World War 1: Battles in the sky

Oh, the irony of naming things. World War I was originally called The Great War because no one imagined that all the nations would fight at once — nevermind the idea they'd do it again later. No one imagined it, that is, except Nostradamus. He could see that kind of destruction, and he began his long-term warnings in this pair of quatrains:

> The scourges passed the world shrinks,
>
> For a long time peace and populated lands:
>
> One will travel safely by air, land, sea and wave,
>
> Then the wars stirred up anew. (C I – 63)

> They will think they have seen the Sun at night
>
> When they will see the pig half-man:
>
> Noise, song, battle, fighting in the sky perceived,
>
> And one will hear brute beasts talking. (C I – 64)

The calm before the storm

The beginning of this pair of quatrains — one of the few pairs that are presented consecutively within *The Prophecies* — doesn't seem bad. To paraphrase, the problems that have bothered people for so long *(scourges)* will pass away, and a time of peace will come. Nostradamus didn't distinguish between the scourges — physical illness, false religions, and wars. I don't think he needed to identify them because his point was that they'd all fade away as a smaller world made impressive moves toward enlightenment.

Most quatrains in *The Prophecies* are seen to be individual predictions and are not grouped by topic. Nostradamus shuffled them to hide the correct order and some of the meanings. Occasionally, though, one or two quatrains that are together will address the same topic. Nostradamus probably did this so that you wouldn't miss the connection, so always look at the quatrains around the one you're examining to see if there's more there than just one prediction.

The second and third lines of Quatrain C I – 63 paint a pretty picture of a long, calm existence without the pestilences (including the plague) that marked the times before this. Nostradamus used terms like *world shrinks* and *lands* to acknowledge that people would discover many new places and that colonization and improved travel and navigation would make connections between places more frequent, more reliable, and the distances seem like less.

Nostradamus did his best to describe the novel forms of travel between lands that he saw in his visions but ended up with only vague types of travel, including *air, land, sea and wave.* Air travel is a straightforward connection to airplane travel, and travel by land can be connected to modern cars.

Notice that the ideas used in this quatrain are calming — peace, safe travel, and civilized lands. Nostradamus apparently admired this time period because he spent three lines describing it. He may have also paused in this pleasant situation to give the reader something less threatening to hold onto before he again dived into war. It's as if he was pointing out a bright spot to encourage people between the seemingly endless wars. But Nostradamus ended his pause of peace in the final line, where he predicted that wars would start up again.

I believe the tone of this quatrain categorizes it as a general description for the overall coming of wars in the 20th century and not just World War I. Some interpreters suggest that this quatrain is more likely a prediction of the cold war between the United States and Soviet Union, with nuclear weapons as the ultimate threat. I can't quite buy the cold war theory, though, because the rest of the quatrain is so general. When Nostradamus had a specific event in mind, he tended to give enough concrete details that you can't mistake his meaning.

A flight of fancy — or not

In Quatrain C I – 63, Nostradamus set up the idea that travel by air would some day exist. That prediction was quite amazing, although I suspect he got at least a hint of the wild idea about flight from Leonardo Da Vinci. Whether he started with his own idea or that of his contemporary, Nostradamus predicted warfare by air with an amazing amount of detail in Quatrain C I – 64. (For more on Da Vinci in particular and the Renaissance era in general, check out *Da Vinci For Dummies,* by Jessica Teisch and published by Wiley.)

As usual, Nostradamus gave one fairly clear hint of his intended prophecy target by telling that fighting in the skies would occur. This modern technology of fighting by air didn't come into widespread practice until World War I when fragile *biplanes* (planes with two fixed wings, one over the other) exchanged fire and dropped bombs and huge helium airships (like the Hindenburg), gaining a bird's eye view on the movement of the enemy.

Predicting the aerial battles *(fighting in the sky)* was the key Nostradamus left in the prophecy to help interpreters unlock the rest of the quatrain's prediction. And if you look deeper, you may notice the connection between the fighting and the fact that it would occur in one of Nostradamus's favorite places — the sky. He was suggesting that the fighting might be more than just between people (maybe it was between the bigger forces of the universe) and that the plan written in the stars looked like it included these wars.

Even though you now have the key to unlocking the prophecy, identifying the other major pieces provides an understanding of the whole prophecy:

- **Sun at night.** This piece refers to a bright light, which would cut through the darkness, surely, if it was as bright as the sun. During World War I, both the searchlights and explosions at night produced bright lights.

- **Pig half-man.** Although this may be a reference to the birth of oddly shaped babies who were seen in Nostradamus's time as omens of ill fortune, I doubt that he would've mixed up his time periods that way. He was definitely in a vision of the future and attempting to describe how a man would look with what appeared to be a strange pushed up nose and the slick skull of a pig on a man's body. This was an accurate prediction (for a man who had no knowledge of why men might look this way) of the breathing masks and slick, leather headgear worn by fighter pilots during World War I.

- **Noise, song, battle.** If you've ever wondered whether Nostradamus just saw things in his visions or whether he heard things, too, then this little piece should settle that question. The fights between planes created a great deal of noise and drama in the sky, and the noise of the bombs was deafening. Across the space of around 350 years, these loud prolonged

explosions may've sounded strange to Nostradamus, or maybe he interpreted these noises (so different from the sporadic cannon fire of his
own time) as the song of battle.

✔ **Brute beasts talking.** Nostradamus tried so hard to describe what he
didn't understand. Here, his vision revealed beasts — probably the same
pig-men from earlier in the quatrain except that now they're talking. He
couldn't have known that during World War I the men would use radios
and a controller to communicate with each other. I think it's interesting
that Nostradamus shifted from pig-men to brute beasts. This choice of
words suggests that he felt that those in the midst of the battle would
no longer be men but would become something almost entirely without
thought — beasts.

Quatrains C I – 63 and C I – 64 are important because they give you a very
complete idea of how Nostradamus viewed the world. He didn't have enough
insight to be able to call the battle in the sky *aerial,* and he didn't know why
the men would look like pigs, but he certainly got the idea across to make a
very accurate prediction about how the next battles would be fought, starting with World War I.

Knowing that Nostradamus had a limited vocabulary for describing the
modern world can help you look at other quatrains and find the prophecies
for today and tomorrow that are hidden in 16th-century words. Hopefully,
you can look at other quatrains that haven't been fully explained (there are
plenty) and find descriptions that trigger your memory or remind you of
something you've seen in cutting-edge technology.

In addition to predicting World War I, these quatrains also point out that
Nostradamus didn't focus exclusively on the wars of the world. He saw
peaceful times as well, but those times were less dramatic and would've put
his readers to sleep (and probably him as he sat in his darkened attic), so he
stuck mainly to the lively bits of the future.

World War II: A grand cosmic shift

The Prophecies include many quatrains that describe the true but still unbelievable pressures, events, people, and horrors that were to become the Second
World War. I believe Nostradamus devoted more quatrains to this topic than
to the other conflicts because he used World War II as a prime example for why
humans need to improve and change before they can lose their ignorance
and understand that, according to him, faith and self-improvement toward
a relationship with God are what's most important in life. Nostradamus left
enough evidence in his quatrains to suggest that he believed humans would
achieve this state of mind eventually — and it would be at that same time his
prophecies would become clear.

Going a little deeper, the terrible time in history that marked World War II may be an important part of an astrological concept that Nostradamus believed in. According to the concept, while shifting from the Age of Pisces (300 BC to about 1950 AD), when faith was most important and people lived by unquestioning trust, to the Age of Aquarius (2050 AD to about 4300 AD), when reason, scientific explanations, and proven methods will be the most important, society needs to shed its illnesses (like cruelty, not the common cold) before any kind of grand cosmic shift can happen. So I believe that Nostradamus saw World War II as a way of shedding the illnesses that affect humanity and airing the wound of ignorance so that healing can eventually begin. (Check out Chapter 19 for all your Age of Aquarius needs.)

You may notice that a chunk of time is missing between the Age of Pisces and the Age of Aquarius. That period of time, which isn't exact, mind you, is the *transition period* where the Earth and humans move from one age to another. So, yes, the hippies from the 1960s were correct when they sang about the dawning of the Age of Aquarius. The new age is indeed just beginning. Oh, and don't take these dates as hard and fast rules. Astrologers argue that these ages can shift up to 100 years or more in either direction.

Because Nostradamus devoted so many quatrains to World War II, I devote a whole chapter to some of his predictions about the rise of Hitler and that war. For the detailed discussion, turn to Chapter 12.

The Worst World War Yet to Come

Just when you think life can't possibly get any worse, it does — or so it must have seemed to Nostradamus when he finished his first two visions for the world at war and had to move onto a third that you and I have yet to see. Sure, humans need to grow and change, and war can produce some of the most fantastic technological advances, but war is a harsh way to get things done and you'd think we'd learn an easier way, but as the saying goes, the third time's the charm. Nostradamus predicted that the human race would indeed need to endure three global conflicts to reach our growth place.

The first but vague forewarning

In Quatrain C II – 5, Nostradamus predicted that a Third World War, different from the other World Wars, would occur:

> That which is enclosed in iron and letter in a fish,
>
> Out will go one who will then make war,
>
> He will have his fleet well rowed by sea,
>
> Appearing near Latin land. (C II – 5)

Key words and phrases

This quatrain, if you can get past the tricky first line, suggests that someone will start trouble from the sea near *Latin land* — a term that can be applied to Rome because Latin was the language used almost exclusively by the Church. Nostradamus frequently used Rome as a symbol for the greater idea of Christianity (or a reference to religion in general) and within this quatrain the results of attacking religion would be far-reaching, and I'd certainly count it as a world-class war. Religion has always stirred up strong feelings and is identified elsewhere in *The Prophecies* as one of the sources for the third World War and the third antichrist (check out Chapter 13 for more on this future troublemaker).

The term can also be used as an identifier for all of Italy. I believe both layers of meaning are precisely what Nostradamus intended so that future readers would be confused if they were focused on the past (and France's wars and struggles) instead of seeing the image as one representative of something larger (religion) for the future and World War III.

As for *rowed by sea,* this phrase can mean just about any kind of travel by water that's faster than sailing. To Nostradamus, the vision of a military vessel or submarine moving under its own power, which during the 16th century was manpower or rowing, may seem as if the ship were *well rowed.*

Translation trouble

I want to wrestle some sense of the first line in this quatrain for you. A literal reading suggests that *iron* (maybe guns or a general reference to weapons) and *letter* (either words or symbols of something important — a message of some kind) are contained within a *fish* (a fairly easy misinterpretation of a submarine from Nostradamus's point of view). The third line mentions a fleet going by sea, so the idea of the submarine may work, but I think that perhaps this line has a little translation trouble working against it.

The original text for the first line is *Qu'en dans poisson, fer et lettre enfermée.* Because you probably don't have the time or desire to learn the Middle French language, I'll just go ahead and tell you that the verb in this line isn't an easy one to handle, and a possibility exists that errors in the printing have complicated things. In other words, an alternative translation may be what Nostradamus was really shooting for. With a slight change in the verb translation, the first line becomes

"When iron and letter is enclosed in a fish,"

This may not make much more sense to you, but if you look at the line from the point of view of an astrologer or alchemist, you begin to see the point. Iron is one of the symbols for Mars (both in astrology and alchemy), and the letter is a trademark for the ancient god Mercury (who represents communication) and the planet that bears his name. Add in the symbol of a fish for the astrological sign of Pisces, and the first line suddenly becomes the astrological date for the next world war:

"When Mars and Mercury are conjoined in Pisces."

Some astrologers have placed that date as March 23, 1996, but no significant event in history seems to match this date. One possibility is that these two planets conjoined within the astrological chart — perhaps the astrological birth chart — of a specific person who'll be the powerful influence that begins this terrible third war.

At any rate, the timing is all wrong for this quatrain to be part of either of the first two World Wars.

The where, how, and why of it all

After the date has been found (or at least approximated), the next task is to figure out where and how the events may occur. In Quatrain C II – 5, Nostradamus presented the idea of a Third World War as a simple matter of one leader setting out and making trouble for the rest of the world, but the trouble becomes a full blown World War when it involves religion, a topic that rarely stays small. Although Nostradamus didn't give a lot of information about where this leader would come from, he did give a clear idea about how and where (Latin land or a battleground called religion) the war will happen. This quatrain hints at a third war instead of just describing the first two because it contains neither the detailed technological advances of the First World War quatrains nor the places and specific Hitler identification of the Second World War.

Quatrain C II – 5 is important because you now have some information to recognize the beginnings of real trouble, although it'd be helpful in preventing this war if Nostradamus had recorded why this leader will start it. Knowing what the conflict is about in a war can definitely help in resolving it. Although Nostradamus didn't come out and say that this war would be based on religion, he did suggest it through his choice of words.

If Nostradamus was correct with this prophecy, then he gave the world a powerful key (if people can find that astrological date and identify a leader with a religious bone to pick) to heading off an even bigger war than the ones that appear in his other quatrains. The key element is religion and the hint for the future is tolerance. This attitude is probably a direct reflection of the religious wars that plagued France in the late Renaissance.

Unfortunately, because Nostradamus didn't give specific details about why this war will occur, I'm forced to conclude that the war will be unavoidable. His purpose wasn't prevention, then, but protection and forewarning. Knowing that trouble will come, you and I can take measures to protect ourselves and even select government leaders who will help protect us.

The second forewarning, full of despair

The quatrains in *The Prophecies* were written as a work to be studied as a whole to get all the meaning and perspective Nostradamus intended, but occasionally one quatrain seems to stand up on its own and demand attention above and beyond the collected work of predictions. Quatrain C II – 46 is such a quatrain. Like Quatrain C II – 5, Quatrain C II – 46 warns of World War III, and as such, it's got a bit more to say for you and me now than the quatrains about past events:

> After great trouble for humanity, a greater one is prepared
>
> The Great Mover renews the ages:
>
> Rain, blood, milk, famine, steel and plague,
>
> In the heavens fire seen, a long spark running. (C II – 46)

Trouble for the ages

Okay, take a deep breath. The good news is that this third World War may not be any time soon. The bad news is that Nostradamus believed it'll be more horrible and terrifying than all previous wars. It's the wide scope of destruction, much broader than that predicted for World Wars I and II that leads me to believe this quatrain predicts World War III.

According to the first two lines, the more troublesome event for humanity will happen after the world has already had a *great trouble* (the other World Wars, another hint that we're dealing with a new World War) and at the time when the ages will be renewed. Nostradamus was either slyly mentioning the millennium without having to spell it out or referring to the change from the Age of Pisces (300 BC to about 1950 AD) to the Age of Aquarius (2050 AD to about 4300 AD).

In this translation of the quatrain, *The Great Mover* will make the change of the ages. For Nostradamus, that person had to be God, whom Nostradamus believed was part of his visionary experience.

A common belief during the Renaissance was that the stars contained God's plan for humanity. It wasn't a far stretch, then, for Nostradamus to imagine that God could move people from one age of changes (the Age of Pisces, an era of faith and grand religions with grand wars) to another age (the Age of Aquarius, an era of enlightenment and personal freedom).

Mixed reactions

According to Nostradamus, a great war has to happen before the new age can begin. Nostradamus used the third and fourth lines of Quatrain C II – 46 to describe this war, which may not seem so bad if it'll involve milk and rain. But understanding Nostradamus's use of these words as symbols changes the impression of this age quickly. Check out these interpretations:

- ✔ **Rain:** Part of nature and the world around us, rain can bring growth, cleansing, depression, or floods, or it can represent bombs falling from the sky.

- ✔ **Blood:** Recognized as necessary for life, blood is also a symbol of death when it's spilled in too great a quantity. Because blood is included in the list of things that will form the great trouble, it seems more frightening.

- ✔ **Milk:** For the young and the growing, this is nature's most perfect food, but because it's included with the other elements in this list, Nostradamus could've been seeing a milky rain that will be the result of the dust and debris in the air during battle.

- ✔ **Famine:** This was an easy vision for Nostradamus to recognize because crop failures and other catastrophes were common throughout history.

- ✔ **Steel:** One of the strongest materials known to man, it has been used throughout history to both protect and harm people.

- ✔ **Plague:** Nostradamus surely had a negative idea about infectious diseases, and the Black Plague would've been a very powerful negative image from his point of view. In the future, this could either be a dangerous threat to people's bodies, like a virus, the return of the Black Plague, or even the virus of damaging ideas or thoughts.

I find the shifts between potentially positive and negative elements in the third line to be very hopeful — as if Nostradamus strived to balance out the items and suggest that not everything will be completely awful. I believe the overall picture Nostradamus saw and recorded in this quatrain is a mixture of everyday changes that can be very drastic and changes that are brought about by war. But in the end, even with some slightly softer images, this quatrain still presents the possibility of a large war with many stressful events.

The last line of this prophecy talks about a fire seen in the heavens and a *long spark running,* which sounds like a description of a comet or a space shuttle to me. Some interpreters believe that the comet connection helps date the timing of the next war. But because Haley's comet (1986) and the Hale-Bopp comet (1997) both appeared without any major world wars happening, that theory falls a little flat. I believe that space travel and the re-entry of space-crafts into the atmosphere (with the friction that looks like burning on the outside of the space crafts) is what Nostradamus saw in his visions and had difficulty describing.

Using a balanced approach and considering the references Nostradamus made to the astrological ages of Pisces and Aquarius, I believe that Nostradamus saw the approaching wars, including World War III, as horrible but as part of the process of preparing humanity for healing. Nostradamus felt that pointing out this process was important so that you and I can see the larger picture. Nostradamus was concerned with the state of the human soul (that was the focus of his upper-level alchemy and religious studies), and he was trained to heal people. For Nostradamus, the wars were part of the truth of his visions, but I believe he saw them as a way of bleeding off the ills that affect humanity and airing the wound of ignorance so that healing can begin. I simply can't see him as all doom and gloom.

Other Upheavals

Beyond the big picture of World Wars, other wars and conflicts crossed the prophet's visions, and Nostradamus recorded them as well. So far, his ability to predict these conflicts has been pretty much on target, and the detailed quatrains on this topic have increased my own respect for the World War predictions and the rest of Nostradamus's prophecies in general. In this section, I walk you through a few of Nostradamus's predictions about events that have always piqued the interest of (and stricken fear in) modern society.

Judgment Day

Quatrain C X – 74 is a clear example — well, at least a prominent example — of the type of number games that Nostradamus included in his prophecies to confuse the average reader. I won't let his games stand in your way, and in this section, I unravel this quatrain before your very eyes:

> The year of the great seventh number accomplished,
>
> It will appear at the time of the games of slaughter:
>
> Not far from the great millennial age,
>
> When the buried will go out from their tombs. (C X – 74)

Setting a date

I have some ideas about the dating of this prophecy, but I should warn you that many other interpreters also have ideas about this quatrain and whether the events have already happened. The problem with numerology is that just about everyone does it slightly differently, and Nostradamus isn't around for people to ask him questions. Some schools of thought suggest that through various methods, the century and quatrain numbers can date the events predicted in the quatrain. (Check out Chapter 10, where I provide a few examples.)

I recommend taking a more relaxed approach to the quatrains and looking at the hints within them rather than just the numbers attached to the centuries and quatrains.

If you take this approach, *the year of the great seventh number* becomes the major numerological clue to the events predicted in this particular quatrain. Not that this clue necessarily gets you any closer to an answer. The year connected with the number seven could be the seventh millennium of mankind (these were like astrological ages and watched over by specific angels), which is hard to pinpoint because of the inaccuracies and confusing relationships in Nostradamus's explanation of dates. Nostradamus uses references to Biblical dates and astrological dates, but he makes errors in both and the result is a head-scratching attempt to pin the event on the calendar.

The number seven, taken just by itself, does give you some information because it was used as a sacred number by nearly every mystical system Nostradamus used and understood. For the Christians, seven was the number of the sacred sacraments, the number of spiritual perfection, and the number of the seals to be broken before the end of the world. Included among those seven seals from the book of Revelations in the Bible are some very familiar topics for those who have read even a tiny bit of Nostradamus's prophecies: religious persecution and deception, war, famine, pestilence, tribulation and martyrdom, signs in the heavens, and a variety of natural disasters.

I think Nostradamus was dating the event in this prophecy from the time period just after the end of the time described in the book of Revelations. For a devout man of the 1500s, this would've been a reasonable way to keep both religious and secular events in some kind of chronological order. Nostradamus essentially meant that there would be a time period during which these events would all occur and the event in the final line of the quatrain would happen. He didn't limit the time period to seven days, a decade, or even a century.

Nostradamus also added a layer of hope in this quatrain. No, really — trust me. Despite the doomsday connection, the number seven can also represent spiritual enlightenment and the complete set of materials for an alchemist's work, which Nostradamus believed ultimately led to spiritual perfection. (For more information on alchemy, look in Chapter 6.) Spiritual connection and enlightenment certainly count as positive things that the world may look forward to, and Nostradamus saw them coming just after the struggle.

All of the events in this quatrain are near the end of the millennium, but I believe Nostradamus wasn't talking about exact years but was again relying on the overall astrological ages to mark his time periods. In that case, this quatrain predicts events near the change of ages, which is about a 100-year spread. That's a lot of time and can't be narrowed down, so Nostradamus gets low marks on communicating his ideas of time to the future.

A terrible ending

Quatrain C X – 74 doesn't have a positive spin, and Nostradamus certainly placed the *games of slaughter* and the dead who rise out of *their tombs* in the quatrain to make you sit up and take notice. Almost every interpreter, including me, looks at the last line and remembers the dead rising from their graves as part of the biblical prediction about the end of the world. This last line tends to get this quatrain labeled as apocalyptic and terrifying, but only if you take it literally.

Nostradamus was only literal sometimes, and I think when talking about the end of the world — an important subject — he may have been a little gun-shy about getting it wrong and used word games and metaphors to record his visions, just in case he was wrong. As a metaphor (where one thing stands for another), the dead could be ideas, patience, understanding, or even religion rising from the tombs where the Age of Reason and the scientific era placed such beliefs. By using such a metaphor, if the world didn't end but certain ideas did, Nostradamus would still be right.

The short and semi-sweet of it all

Nostradamus indeed warned about the possible ending of the world as people have come to know it. He was telling people that great changes and impressive events will take place, but I think he cheated a little by using the same event indicators that the Bible used. Because he believed his vision was divinely inspired, though, the Bible link makes sense. I think Nostradamus was prophesying that after the seven seals are broken (and all the trouble they cause ends, including World War III), a kind of spiritual perfection (a meaning associated with the number seven) will change all the Earth.

Quatrain C X – 74 and the great change in humanity that will happen are important to understand because they give meaning to the otherwise horrible events Nostradamus described. For a prophet, this task is one of the most difficult. To help people see both the event and the reason is critical, because without a reason for something, mankind frequently misses the point and doesn't learn anything. If Nostradamus didn't show people that they should grow and learn from World War III, and then move forward toward Judgment Day as better people, then they'll likely simply shake their heads and go back to watching the news. Whether this spiritual perfection he described will occur while people are still on Earth or after death is up to you to decide, but the last line of Nostradamus's quatrain holds too much Christian symbolism for him to be talking about anything other than the Christian apocalypse. The end of your world or worldview (and your mileage) may vary.

The rise and fall of communism

Here again is a prophecy that begins slowly and comes together over a period of time rather than within a year or single event. Prophecies like this one reinforce the idea for me that these quatrains weren't meant to be associated with just one year, as some scholars have suggested. Quatrain C III – 95 brings the vision of Nostradamus slightly out of focus and looks toward the entire trend of the Russian states as they experience the growth and change of the ruling system in their countries.

Just a little bit of history here: Communism, found its foothold during a 1917 Russian uprising where the people initially found the equality promised by the communist system of rule very attractive. After struggling with ineffective leaders and a system that was great on paper but didn't translate well to real life, the people of the Soviet Union rose up and voted the communist party (and communism) out of power in their country in 1991.

Check out Quatrain C III – 95:

> The law of More will be seen to decline:
>
> After another much more seductive:
>
> Dnieper first will come to give way:
>
> Through gifts [pardons] and tongue another more attractive. (C III – 95)

Overall, Quatrain C III – 95 seems to suggest a succession of different, attractive items that take the place of the ones that came before. Exactly what those items are (three of them including the seductive one, the Dnieper, and the attractive one) and why they were important to Nostradamus (and are important to you now) can be discovered with a little detective work.

Nostradamus spoke his own language — one that used references and items within his own time. Some scholars suggest that he simplified his language because he knew that living languages (those we speak everyday and change because our lives change) would need to be used to translate his works. I think enough of the words were modified that he *was* aware of the changes in language to come, but I also think he could only do so much with the symbols. He simply had to use the ideas that were around at the time.

In Quatrain C III – 95, there are three main pieces to understand:

- ✔ **Law of More.** This is a fairly straightforward reference to Sir Thomas More (who wrote one of the first communist-minded statements of purpose around the time of Nostradamus) and to the ideal world More described.

- ✔ **Dnieper.** I think that this is a reference to the main river that runs through the Ukraine, a country that was formerly part of the Soviet Union. This river valley was the source of many of the minor revolts and ideas that formed a revolution in the 1990s to establish democracy.

- ✔ **Gifts.** Also translated as *pardons,* this word suggests a religious or social change.

Putting the first two pieces together in succession, the *law of More* represents the communist state that rose to rule over Russia and other countries near the Dnieper River from 1917 forward. The area of the Ukraine (and the river) gave rise to the notion that democracy might be more attractive, and the quatrain accurately predicts that this region would *give way* to another form — that it would switch systems to that of democracy.

I think that the third piece, which will eventually take the place of the other two and is *more attractive,* returns to the religious training of Nostradamus. He predicted that the third change after communism and democracy will be not a system of ruling but a system of beliefs. For Nostradamus, the connection with God and the forgiveness of sins, which were part of his Catholic upbringing, were gifts from God. Religious faith will be what replaces the others and will be a language *(tongue)* that the people of Russia will find to be *more attractive.*

Although I'm confident that my first interpretation of this quatrain is correct, at least one more piece of information seems to have some importance. The first word in the third line of Quatrain C III – 95, which in this translation appears as *Dnieper,* is written as "Boristhenes" in the original text and may be a reference to both Boris Yeltsin and the Ukraine since Boristhenes is the 16th century name for the region of the Ukraine, a double pun that would have tickled Nostradamus. Boris Yeltsin would match the first change to a more attractive situation because he was the first democratically elected president of Russia (in 1991). Even this interpretation leaves the third change open for a future event.

Crossed swords at the Middle East

If ever a region has cried out for prophecies of war and destruction, the Middle East is it. The many groups with historical and political claims to land, resources, and populations within the region make it a powder keg within the world. This crossroads of humanity hasn't learned exactly which way it's going, and until that direction is settled, war and disaster will occur.

Correctly sensing the unease and continued struggles in this region, Nostradamus prophesied in several quatrains, including C VI – 80, that the issues wouldn't be isolated and wouldn't remain within the Middle East region:

> From Fez the realm will reach those of Europe,
>
> Their city ablaze and the blade will cut:
>
> The great one of Asia by land and sea with a great troop,
>
> So that blués and perses [bluish grey/green] the cross will pursue to death. (C VI – 80)

Quatrain C VI – 80 is another annoying quatrain that doesn't have a time stamp on it to help you determine whether it has already come true. Without a date to attach to events, the scientific mind (the one that watches crime shows and detective programs) may not be willing to give such a quatrain as much credibility as the quatrains that are tied to specific events. Let me suggest to the logical mind within you that something can be true even if you can't take a picture of it.

Moved by blaze and blade

Nostradamus didn't pull any punches in the first line of this quatrain and (at last) told just how things will be, even if he didn't tell when they'd occur. He used the term *Fez* (which is both a type of hat typical of the region and a city in Morocco) to identify someone from Northern Africa or the region of the Middle East. Nostradamus said that from here *the realm* (a region under control or a specific influence) will reach for the people of Europe like a hand reaching out to grab hold and control the region. Physically reaching for something is more active than simply wanting, and someone willing to reach out (and I didn't hear a "please" or a "may I") is probably not going to take rejection lightly. The threat to the people of Europe is clear, however, and isn't one to be dismissed. Nostradamus made a point of giving this group of people a fair warning that their lives could be changed.

The second line refers to *their city ablaze,* and it's important for you to know who Nostradamus was referring to as well as which city. I believe that Nostradamus was saying that the Europeans will ultimately find their cities on fire. To be any more specific just isn't possible with the clues he gave.

The fire and the blade that cuts can be taken literally (burning down the cities and using blades of the invaders to cut into and divide the Europeans in a very aggressive manner), or they can be a metaphor for drastic change. (Alchemists frequently used fire to represent processes that were quick and intense and that burned away things not wanted or needed.) I believe that Nostradamus was using his descriptive powers rather than trying to be very literal here and that burning and cutting were intended to represent the removal of excess and waste.

Moved by force and faith

The third and fourth lines tell of an invasion by a force described with colors and a certain kind of religious fanaticism, a very general description. Perhaps Nostradamus is suggesting that the great one of Asia from the quatrain will lead these troops by land and sea, driven by the force of faith in the Christian cross conquer European lands, but Asia isn't generally associated with Christian crusades, so Nostradamus's explanation isn't overly helpful or realistic at this point in time.

Nostradamus was very familiar with the idea of Christian crusades, where populations that worshiped other gods were conquered and turned into Christians, and I think he likely was drawing a comparison in this quatrain between the invasion of the Fez or Asian leader and the crusades as both the crusades and the quatrain's invasion are religiously driven. But most of the crusades turned into money-making expeditions, and the large populations that were conquered didn't take up Christianity as their religion for long, so the outlook for this kind of invasion doesn't look hot.

Just for kicks, here's yet another meaning of the third and fourth lines. I know, I know, enough already, but trust me when I tell you that having some variation in mind is important when looking at the future. If you only have one idea of what might happen, then you may miss the mark entirely. (Say that you come across a pack of stray dogs and determine that only the white dog is a threat, so you don't pay any attention to the brown one. Your theory might come back to bite you, so to speak.) So look again at the last two lines of Quatrain C VI – 80 and consider this possibility: Instead of the soldiers being Christian and following their beliefs until they die protecting them, maybe the soldiers (who wear the colors blue and bluish grey) are in fact people of another faith who are pursuing Christianity until it dies.

Either way, you have one sect of people trying to get rid of another with religion involved, and Nostradamus pointed out this source of trouble in the quatrain. The details may be a little fuzzy, but he at least outlined the kind of dog that may bite.

Quatrain C VI – 80 stands out because it suggests that humanity may not have changed yet in terms of how people act on what they believe. Nostradamus was warning us that wars and struggles will certainly continue if people don't keep this idea of conquering for the sake of religious beliefs under control.

The war between the pure and impure

Sometimes you feel like a nut, sometimes you sound like one. Maybe Nostradamus should've stopped while he was ahead.

Quatrain C IX – 99 has been assigned to the siege of Leningrad by German soldiers, future wars in Russia, Napoleon's retreat from Russia, and just about any fort or settlement that eventually fought back to regain its independence. In this section, I briefly examine this vague quatrain so you can see how prophecy and giving appropriate hints can be a tricky business:

> The "Aquilon" Wind will cause the siege to be raised,
>
> Over the walls to throw ashes, lime and dust:
>
> Through rain afterwards, which will do them much worse,
>
> Last help against their frontier. (C IX – 99)

Searching for something tangible

The temptation in deciphering the meaning of a quatrain is to begin with the factual pieces and work forward from there, but the only pieces Nostradamus gave here are the *Aquilon Wind,* a *siege,* and a *frontier.* The rain that follows the siege (and does much harm) is possibly a modern rain of bullets, but it could also be the cold and killing rains of the Siberian regions, which is how some commentators connect this quatrain with Napoleon and his terrible visit to Russia. (If you want to know about this trip by Napoleon, check out Chapter 10.) Taking a hint from the term *siege* used in the first line, I believe that Nostradamus was more likely describing bullets and a battle of more modern structure than just wet rain falling from the sky. Another explanation, however, seems to hold more water than a literal siege on a town ready to get rid of its garbage in the rain.

From the city under siege, things are tossed over the walls, and they may not immediately make sense unless you remember that Nostradamus was an alchemist and an apothecary. *Ashes, lime, and dust* were the by-products of the processes used by alchemists when trying to find the secret to immortal life and to purify the spiritual self. Nostradamus certainly knew about these processes and was keenly interested in both the science of the chemical mixtures and the ultimate goal of cleansing the soul so that it more closely resembled the essence of the divine. This line suggests to me that Nostradamus was speaking not of a physical war between two armies but a war between the parts of the self — the pure and the impure.

Seeing the underlying meaning

If Nostradamus was predicting a siege of the soul, then the struggle is one of reason against blind faith, and the process of deciding which side will triumph will create some trouble. If you use the idea that this battle is within a person, then the *frontier* can be seen as the vast, open space of the person's potential, which will be changed forever by what occupies the space. Quite possibly the *Aquilon Wind* (Northern Wind) isn't wind at all but rather the element of air associated with thought and mental perception in several mystic traditions known to Nostradamus. The struggle begins then with the insight of thought and continues (getting rid of the impure and tossing it aside) until the rain comes.

The *rain* that causes harm could represent the element of water, which alchemists and mystics alike have associated with slow change and emotions. These two pieces of the human mind could be damaging to the process of purifying the thoughts and spirit of a person because emotions aren't easily controlled and frequently have more power than thoughts to make a person do (or not do) something.

Throughout the quatrain, the description sounds like war, looks like war, and may as well be war as far as Nostradamus was concerned. I believe he saw the struggle within the individual person to be as important as the kinds of political and military struggles that he described in other quatrains. This battle is for something that Nostradamus understood — spiritual connection and clarity of purpose. He was a man motivated and touched by his beliefs in everything he did, most especially in his prophecies for the benefit of mankind. It's reasonable to think that he would include this struggle for the soul and divine connection as one of the epic battles in the *Prophecies*.

Quatrain C IX – 99 touches today's world because the battle of the soul isn't over, and its importance hasn't faded. I think Nostradamus recorded this internal struggle as a larger and more physical struggle because he wanted mankind to take notice, and he knew that humans were likely to miss it otherwise. This internal struggle *is* important, so listen up and look at the things that are attacking your own ideas, thoughts, emotions, and even your own concept of who you are. In this quatrain, Nostradamus was telling you that enemies are present in the process of becoming peaceful and in touch with your own divine energy. And you're the one to handle the enemies within your own personal fortifications.

Chapter 12

Focusing on Hitler and World War II

. . . .

In This Chapter

▶ Meeting the young Hitler in Nostradamus's visions

▶ Hearing the sights and sounds in quatrains that predict WWII

▶ Seeing Hitler's most horrific actions in the prophecies

. . . .

The night had to be a dark and stormy one for Nostradamus's soul. The Nazis were coming, the sky was falling, and Nostradamus saw it first. Adolf Hitler and World War II were going to make dark and ugly marks on humanity. I believe Nostradamus focused on the events of World War II and Hitler because he knew they'd change the world forever and also because of his own background as a Jew who converted to Catholicism during childhood. (I discuss this impact on Nostradamus in Chapter 4.) Nostradamus wrote *many* quatrains about this horrible time in history, but this chapter focuses on just a few. The quatrains I've selected touch on the topics Nostradamus favored when describing World War II — the identity of a man of power, Hitler's iron control, the battlefields themselves, and the use of prophecy as propaganda.

Examining Hitler, World War II, and Nostradamus's insights on them can feel like a long trip — and in truth it is. Nostradamus's quatrains take you on the long and detailed exploration of this dark period of time, and not because he was a fan of horror movies. Instead, his prophecies show that he felt it was important for the people who follow him to understand exactly how much improvement mankind must make as a whole before it can progress beyond the past. I see Nostradamus speaking across centuries to implore us to be informed, respectful, and full in our understanding of the self and other people (religious-wise *and* humanity-wise).

Identifying the Infamous

The quatrains that identify Adolph Hitler (see Figure 12-1) and major aspects of World War II draw an outline for the entire scope of events. I believe the mention of Hitler's humble youth in Quatrain C III – 35 (which I cover in this section) was a clue from Nostradamus that identifying the people who create the most change in the world is very difficult. The trouble can come from just about anywhere, although the trouble frequently comes from extremes. It's important to see that even in the quatrain that begins to identify him, tears are forming — as if Nostradamus felt that sometimes no alternative exists for the path of man. Perhaps describing this man and his impact was the only way people could learn their lessons about respect and world peace.

Maybe, just maybe, Nostradamus *did* feel that mankind sometimes has an alternative path. In his quatrains, including C IV – 68 (also covered in this section), Nostradamus made sure to include keys to identifying Adolf Hitler from the beginning of his career through the end. Perhaps Nostradamus was warning that opportunities to change the path of the world will always be there if people can only recognize them in time. Multiple quatrains were his way of driving home the point that something big was coming this way. In addition, the pattern of warnings that we're headed for danger like those from Nostradamus should provide a heads up for folks in the future when they see someone gain power very quickly.

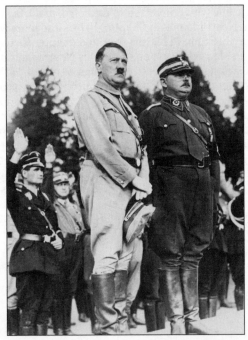

Figure 12-1:
Adolph
Hitler.

Snark / Art Resource, NY

Marking Hitler's humble beginnings

Nostradamus certainly had a lot of material to work with in discussing Hitler. I like to begin my discussion of Hitler at the beginning, with quatrain C III – 35, which predicts his birth and lasting influence in very general terms. While the remainder of this quatrain tells what Hitler did, the first two lines give him a human identity:

> From the very depths of the West of Europe,
>
> A young child will be born of poor people, . . . (C III – 35)

Western Europe is a broad area, and Nostradamus focused attention on the depths of it, meaning that the child would come from within Europe instead of being an outsider. This information is important because people are generally more forgiving (initially anyway) of one of their own. This idea helped Hitler rise to power.

The *depths of the West of Europe* is an accurate prediction for Braunau, Austria, the birthplace of Adolf Hitler, because it's surrounded on all sides by other European countries — Germany, the Czech Republic, Italy, Switzerland, Slovenia, and Hungary. In other words, Austria forms a centerpiece at the heart of Europe, which Nostradamus pointed out as *the very depths.* Although the description may fit any number of Austrian-born leaders, the quatrain goes on to connect this child to motivational speeches and military actions of a strong figure that can only be Hitler.

To paraphrase the first two lines of the quatrain, "In the deep (and possibly dark and mysterious) parts of Europe will be born a small child to parents (possibly *people* in the general sense of the population) who aren't considered to be wealthy." If Sigmund Freud (a contemporary of Hitler and fellow Austrian who studied the inner workings of the human mind) could've gotten Hitler on the therapist's couch, he may have discovered what Nostradamus predicted — that the struggle of childhood frequently shows up as a drive to achieve and to control the world.

Interestingly, the translations of Quatrain C III – 35 include the redundant phrase *young child.* Aren't all children considered young? By combining the words *young* with *child,* I think Nostradamus was leaving readers a hint about Hitler. Several things immediately come to mind when I think of Hitler and youth (my history teacher would be *so* proud of me):

- ✔ Hitler's childhood motivated him to seek power and self-improvement, especially because his father was illegitimate and his family (after the death of his father) struggled financially at times until Hitler was left to fend for himself after his mother's death in his late teens.

- ✔ Hitler sometimes showed immature *(young)* and emotional reactions to events around him.

✔ Hitler organized the young people of Germany into groups — the Hitler Youth — that concentrated on increasing the ideas of personal excellence as Aryans and the ideas of Hitler's Nazi ruling party, including discrimination. *Aryan* was a term used by Hitler and his associates to refer to non-Jewish, Caucasian people. The Nazis saw the "other people" (non-Aryans) as destroying the blond haired, blue-eyed ideal of Hitler's master race by being in Germany.

Adolf Hitler spent the first part of his life trying — and failing — to enter schools of art. He enjoyed operas and lived without much in the way of comfort. During this time, and his subsequent time in the military, Hitler became a German patriot (even though he wasn't a citizen) and developed views that the Aryan race was superior to others and that the other groups (especially the Jews) were responsible for the Germany's financial trouble.

So there you have it — the beginning identification of one of the most infamous men in history. In the first two lines of Quatrain C III – 35, Hitler doesn't sound so impressive, and his importance isn't clear, but Nostradamus made sure you'd be able to recognize this man in later quatrains.

Playing name games

Quatrain C III – 35 gives only vague clues about the identity of a person Nostradamus considered important. To discover what else Nostradamus wrote about the person's identity, you have to keep digging through the quatrains.

The quatrains linked to Hitler generally have one thing in common in the original language Nostradamus used — the word "Hiʃter". That third letter is awfully small and strange looking — it's about half *f* and half *s* — and has caused years and years of debate, which I sort out for you while looking at Quatrain C IV – 68:

> In the place very near not far from Venus
>
> The two greatest ones of Asia and of Africa,
>
> From the Rhine and "Hiʃter" [Lower Danube] they will be said to have come,
>
> Cries, tears at Malta and the Ligurian side [Genoa]. (C IV – 68)

Rivers of meaning

Most experts spend their time debating whether this quatrain discusses Hitler or the Siege of Malta in 1565 (see Chapter 7 for a detailed look at the Siege of Malta). The discussion hinges on how you interpret the word Hiʃter in the original language of line 3:

✔ **Ister:** Most Malta mavens see the term as a reference to Ister, another name for the lower portion of the Danube River. This Danube connection alludes to Hitler (he played on the river's banks), the man who ordered bombings on the island of Malta (the same island that last suffered under major attacks in 1565).

✔ **Hitler:** Most folks that lean towards the Hitler interpretation see this reference as one of Nostradamus's word games that attempts to conceal the name of the troublesome Adolf Hitler.

In my opinion, the river fans aren't giving enough credit to Nostradamus. Critics who insist on word-for-word translations (*Ister* is the name of a river rather than a word game for the name Hitler) are often tripped up by little tricks Nostradamus used in his words. Taking a dictionary to the quatrains is like reading poetry with a computer — the meaning is lost. The spirit of the words should guide translators and interpreters. Remember that Nostradamus loved to mix his language up with puns, plays on words, and other fun tricks.

But these two terms — *Ister* and *Hitler* — aren't mutually exclusive. No matter how I slice this quatrain up, it still seems to focus on Hitler, even when you read it as *Ister:*

✔ Hitler was from the general area of the Lower Danube, which runs through part of Austria.

✔ The rivers mentioned — the Danube and the Rhine — have a unique relationship. The Danube flows from west to east, and the Rhine flows from east to west — a very clear image of the German army moving from the interior of Europe outward in both directions. A two-front war was a World War II trademark and a key reason for Hitler's downfall.

✔ The treaty that ended World War I (the Treaty of Versailles) in 1919 forced Germany to give up control over the Rhineland, the area surrounding the Rhine River. This area was meant to act as a safety zone between Germany and its neighbors. Most Germans were bitter about losing Rhineland, and Hitler used the issue to fire up their emotions.

Plenty of places

Other elements in Quatrain C IV – 68 reinforce the connection to Hitler. *Venus* is a Nostradamus word clue for Venice in a number of other quatrains, which is a *synecdoche* (where one piece is used to symbolize the rest) for the whole of Italy. This Venice connection may seem strange because Hitler is connected with Germany, but Benito Mussolini was the Italian leader who worked closely with Hitler during World War II. Line 2 refers to the *greatest ones of Asia and Africa,* and suggests that Nostradamus could see how far Hitler's reach and influence would extend. Ultimately Germany and Italy, who both had a strong presence in Africa (one of the main arenas of fighting during the war), signed the Tripartite Pact with Japan (*Asia* in the quatrain). Nostradamus was seemingly able to see the major players who helped Hitler.

Nostradamus uses the places within this quatrain to identify the major players (Germany, Italy, Japan), but he identifies some of the major sites of conflict as well. The last line of the quatrain identifies two places that were also important to the events in World War II:

- ✔ **Malta:** The island of Malta is located in the middle of the Mediterranean Sea. During World War II, the British Royal Navy used Malta as a base of operations, and Hitler wanted that to change, so Malta became the location of some of the most intense attacks by Germany and the Axis powers (those countries on Germany's side in the war). In the end, the British endured and maintained control over the Mediterranean.

- ✔ **Genoa:** Genoa was one of the last cities in Italy to be taken from the German military before the entire forces within Italy surrendered and Germany gave up the war.

Think about it for a minute: Nostradamus summarized his vision to include aspects of World War II and Hitler literally from top to bottom and side to side — the focus of the war included everything from North (Germany) to South (Malta and Africa) and East (Asia) to West (*Ligurian side* of the fighting; Liguria is a region within Italy, where Genoa is located).

Fixating on the Details

As far as I'm concerned, World War II wins the prize for being the topic of the most intense and broadest range of prophecies from Nostradamus and related interpretations from those who study him. From the graphic descriptions to layers of meaning, he seems to have been totally drawn into his visions about the impact this war would have on all the future.

Hitler's rise to power

Hitler was the most prominent figure of World War II and one of the most recognizable figures of the 20th century. But hundreds of years before his birth, Nostradamus saw Hitler's overwhelming power and destruction. As a service to the future, he recorded it in Quatrain C V – 20 in the hope that people might recognize the destructive pattern:

> Liberty will not be recovered,
>
> A proud, villainous, wicked black one [wicked king] will occupy it
>
> When the matter of the pontiff will be opened [built],
>
> The republic of Venice vexed by the Danube. (C V – 29)

This quatrain covers a multitude of topics relating to Hitler's rise to power. In this section, I help you sort them all out.

So long, liberty

The first line of Quatrain C V – 29 refers to some sort of established freedom, or liberty, that would cease to exist — permanently. In very few cases do people give up their freedoms willingly, but in extreme cases they allow their freedoms to be suspended if the reason seems justified. That was the case within Germany in 1933 when Hitler, then Chancellor of the country, suspended people's civil rights (things like due process under the law and freedom from discrimination) "for their own good." The people of Germany that lost these rights never regained them during the war.

Nostradamus pointed out that liberty wouldn't return because it runs counter to what would be the consensus at the time — that Hitler would return their rights. I see this as Nostradamus's warning to the future to be wary of giving up their rights too quickly, even when a leader seems to have a good reason.

Men in black

The *wicked black man* in line 2 — now there's someone you could hate if you could just figure out who he is. You can match this and darkly clad villain with several figures within the World War II era, including Hitler (who wore dark suits); some of the high-ranking officers in Hitler's government (also fond of darker colors); and the black-shirted men of the Italian Fascist government (a very powerful and military-based government in Italy) who were directing things under Hitler's friend, Italian leader Benito Mussolini.

The only clue Nostradamus gave about this figure was at the end of the second line, where he said that the figure *will occupy it,* whatever *it* is. *It* could be one of the following:

- The space the bad man would occupy where liberty once was (from line 1)

- Something related to the matter he'd be involved in (from line 3) with the pope *(pontiff)*

I believe that reading the lines straight through without the poetic breaks at the ends gives the answer for what *it* is. Although relating lines 2 and 3 is a nifty idea for finding what *it* stands for, I think line 3 simply gives a time period for when the man in black would be active in the void left by the falling freedoms in line 1. Germany was the main country to suspend liberties completely, so my bets are placed on Germany as the liberty-lite country and Hitler as the man in black.

The role of Church and State

Nostradamus clearly laid out the time period for these events, and history shows that it was, in fact, a fertile time for the dominating power of Hitler and Mussolini to grow.

Line 3 contains a very familiar Nostradamus trait — a pun. In the original version of Quatrain C V – 29, the word *pontiff* was written as *pont,* which can be translated into English as *bridge.* But I think Nostradamus most likely used an *apocope* (pronounced *uh-PAH-kuh-pee,* in case you care), a word from which the last syllable or sound is dropped, generally from laziness on the part of the speaker. As a result, I think *pont* has lost the last syllable and means *pontife* — the pope.

I believe that Nostradamus used this technique partially because he was doing the secret quatrain thing (so as not to upset the Church; see Chapter 6) and partially because he wanted to use a play on words so the ideas of *bridge* and the *pope* could be tied up with each other to reflect his vision — that the pope would act as a form of connection between two pieces of the puzzle.

To help you see the connections I think Nostradamus was developing, here's some background info: Mussolini and the Fascist government negotiated an agreement in 1929 with Pope Pius XI that gave the pope control over most of Rome and separated it from Italy. Hitler negotiated an agreement in 1933 with the Vatican representative who would later become Pope Pius XII that protected the churches within Germany from destruction.

By negotiating with the Fascist and Nazi parties, the Church gave Mussolini and Hitler (both came to power through some very questionable means) additional legitimacy. Think of it this way: Just like you have to be of sound mind and body to sign a legal document, you have to be the rightful ruler to make agreements with other important actors on the world's stage.

So the bridge angle in line 3 is the connection between Italy and Germany through the Catholic Church. Note, though, that Pope Pius XI ultimately objected (at least formally) to Fascist party (Italy) and Nazi party (German) policies, but with no real luck because neither the Germans nor the Italians changed anything they were doing to please the pope. Regardless, by negotiating with Mussolini and Hitler in the first place, the Catholic Church provided them with legitimacy despite their practices that the Church disliked, which brings me to line 4 and the *Republic of Venice vexed.*

Nostradamus carefully referred only to the republic (by mentioning *Venice* as a symbol for Italy) and not to the Fascist government of Italy. The Nazi and Fascist parties' agreements with the pope helped keep them in control of the two countries, which would be troublesome (or vexing) for any republic based on civil liberties and freedom. Nostradamus was predicting that the liberty-loving states of both Germany and Italy would struggle through this time and that the Church wouldn't have the answers.

Some social commentary

I can't imagine that Nostradamus enjoyed relating the position of the Church in this situation, and it probably posed quite an internal struggle for him. As he foresaw in his visions, the Church would make agreements with governments that would cause massive destruction to human life.

I believe that Nostradamus recorded the failings of the Catholic Church and during Hitler's rise to power to point out that even established religions can make mistakes. A number of people in Germany, Italy, and within the Church objected to these agreements, but the leaders pushed on to meet their own goals. Hitler believed the agreement with the Church supported his right to get rid of the Jews in Germany — which is scary but true. The pope thought he was just protecting the rights of the Catholic Church to achieve its own goals within Germany and disagreed with Hitler's statements about the Jews (which were made after the agreement), but the damage was already done.

A buffet of battlefield quatrains

What's a war without exotic places, loud bangs, and heroes that walk out of the dust? Well, it's a war that Nostradamus didn't foresee. Looking at the details in the quatrains predicting World War II, you'd think Nostradamus watched the old war movies from late night TV. This section walks you through two quatrains that are vivid with those kinds of details.

From beginning to end

Look at Quatrain C II – 16 if you want an idea of how exacting Nostradamus could be:

> Naples, Palermo, Sicily, Syracuse,
>
> New tyrants, celestial lighting fires:
>
> Force from London, Ghent, Brussels and Susa,
>
> Great slaughter, triumph leads to festivities. (C II – 16)

Like many of the more-detailed quatrains (which I believe are the quatrains that are more inspired than most), this one gives a long list of places and ideas that need to be identified. Although Nostradamus is eloquent in some places, I believe he gets very stilted and provides very densely meaningful text when he's in touch with his divine source. (Check out the discussion of Nostradamus's methods in Chapter 5 for a bit more on that.)

Instead of walking you through the long process of determining the time period in history for this quatrain, I just sum it up by telling you that the places mentioned all had major events occur in a short period of time only once in history — during World War II. That said, take a quick look at the quatrain's pieces:

- ✔ *Naples, Palermo, Sicily, Syracuse:* During WWII, these towns in and around Italy felt the combined forces of the Allies attack on a single day. (The *Allied countries* opposed Germany and the *Axis powers,* including Italy, were the countries on Germany's side in the war.)

- ✔ *New tyrants:* Mussolini and Hitler are the obvious choices for tyrants in this area, but you can also use the metaphor of war acting as a tyrant in countries all over Europe. The second option doesn't change the overall meaning, so I select the two leaders of the Axis powers as the tyrants Nostradamus meant and move on.

- ✔ *Celestial lighting fires:* I think that Nostradamus's description here has a double meaning. It refers to the bombs and rockets in the skies that became the trademark of World War II and to the quick and intense actions used by the Germans to break through enemy lines. This German tactic was called *blitzkrieg,* which translates as "lightning war" and matches nicely with line 2.

- ✔ *Force from London:* London, used to represent the whole of Britain, was the source of the Allied troops, some of whom were volunteers from Belgium (*Ghent* and *Brussels*), who invaded France and tipped the tide of the war.

- ✔ *Great slaughter:* Although the invasion of Normandy and France was deemed a success in the overall view of the war, massive deaths were part of the cost of this invasion.

- ✔ *Triumph leads to festivities:* The victories of the Allied forces were marked by two separate holidays. Nostradamus accurately noted that there'd be multiple celebrations and multiple holidays. The victory over Europe (VE Day) was celebrated on May 8, 1945, and the victory over Japan (VJ Day) — a country located in a totally separate location from Europe but still fighting on the side of the German Axis — was celebrated on August 15, 1945.

Lines 1 and 2 of Quatrain C II – 16 predict the situation during the war with towns under a new kind of lightning war that Nostradamus could've barely imagined he was seeing. I think Nostradamus listed the towns one right after another to emphasize the vast number of cities impacted by the war, and I believe Nostradamus wanted to point out the sheer size of these battles. One entire war in Nostradamus's time was fought with the same number of men that were in any one of the single battles of World War II. So staggering was the size that I think Nostradamus was a little overwhelmed.

Line 3 leaves you to guess which kind force is used. I've always used military force here. Perhaps Nostradamus saw that no matter how far Germany spread, London (representing England) wouldn't be taken by Germany and would be the source of a grand attack.

In lines 3 and 4, Nostradamus predicted in grand style an attack that would lead to the death of many people. He left an open ending with the phrase *Great slaughter,* which suggests that he was referring also to the other casualties from World War II and not just to those on this one big push. I think the final two lines accurately describe the day in history that Allied forces began the invasion of Normandy, the many casualties suffered, and the celebration of the victories on formal holidays.

One alternate interpretation of the last line is possible if you look at the metaphorical side of Nostradamus. The *Great slaughter* could also refer to the ideas and conflicting concepts that started the war as well as to the men who died on the battlefield. If this interpretation is true, then the *triumphs* (victories) still lead to *festivities,* which some translators record as *holidays* — a time of relaxation and happiness. Nostradamus added a little note with this subtle word play, suggesting that after the struggles, a time of resting — a holiday (as the British call it) or a vacation (as the Americans call it) — would take place.

To you and me, Quatrain C II – 16 may seem like a simple rehashing of events that have long since passed from importance, but that isn't true. Nostradamus gave this quatrain to the future with the idea that you and I would find hope in the outcome of the war. To me, he was saying, "Yes, it's terrible, but there's something beyond the horror for you to aspire to reach." Nostradamus finished this quatrain on a positive and upbeat note (that's how I perceive *festivities* anyway), offering a guide to get past the more difficult struggles people face as individuals and as nations.

Making and breaking promises

Whether in life, in love, or in the fates of countries in Europe, a certain amount of struggle always seems to be part of accomplishing things. Nostradamus certainly didn't promise that life after World War II would be a rose garden, but that was exactly what Hitler promised the people of Germany — a kind of happily ever after. I think Nostradamus saw the thorns, as described in Quatrain C IX – 90:

> A captain of Great Germany
>
> Will come to deliver through false help
>
> To the King of Kings the support of Pannonia
>
> So that his revolt will cause a great flow of blood. (C IX – 90)

Nostradamus found that the events and epic changes of the massive war were overflowing his quatrains, so he summarized the war and gave it a final curtain call.

Line 1 calls your attention to *Great Germany,* which was one of the names Hitler (the *captain*) chose to call the country he was building. But he brought this powerful German state into being *through false help* — by doing and creating things that were advertised as positive measures but were harmful at the root, such as waging war to revive the economy, creating camps to remove the "riff-raff" and "unfit people," and so on. The economy did revive for a while, but an economy based on wartime items like building tanks, military supplies, and providing military food can only last as long as the war — sometimes not even that long. And the removal camps witnessed an inhumane treatment of a very human population that was mostly Jewish.

So here came this kingly guy, Hitler, charging in with great ideas and great solutions who was going to create a wonderful place to live, or so he said. Take heed ye in the modern world: In Quatrain C IX – 90, Nostradamus warned mankind that such grand promises often come with hidden (and shockingly high) price tags.

Nostradamus frequently used ancient names for cities within his quatrains. I think he wanted to add layers of meaning within the name of the city or the city's principal association (as a port city, a trade city, what have you) and to provide a reference point for future readers. After all, Nostradamus didn't concentrate on what places were labeled on a map when he was searching his night visions for insights on the changing path of future people. The name would become a detail of lower importance, and he resorted to using ancient names out of convenience and poetic necessity.

In line 3, the help of *Pannonia* (sometimes interpreted as Hungary because much of that country's land is on the Pannonian Plains) is given to the *King of Kings.* This way of indirectly naming Hitler allowed Nostradamus to give a multi-layered reference to the ruler of everything in his realm, to the leader of the race that would run things (Aryans according to Hitler), and to the figure of Christ, who has the King of Kings as one of his many names. The reference to Christ may seem a little crazy considering that he and Hitler acted completely differently. But the reference was Nostradamus's way of subtly but firmly connecting the idea of Hitler as an antichrist figure (which I go into great detail about in Chapter 13).

In the end, Hitler's promises of a great nation were of no use, and he delivered quite the opposite of what he promised — death and destruction. Nostradamus marked the years when people blindly followed Hitler during the Third Reich (the dictatorship of Germany) as an example of the dangers of practicing faith without insight and thought. I believe Nostradamus struggled in Quatrain C IX – 90 with the issues of the change from the Age of Pisces (a period of time when the Zodiac sign of Pisces is believed by astrologers to have an influence on events), where things were built simply on faith, to the

Age of Aquarius, (beginning around the year 2050 after an overlapping transition period from the Piscean Age, see Chapter 19) where understanding and questioning are the buzz words of the day. I think he was trying to give voice to two warnings:

- ✔ **For his own time:** He saw blind faith as troublesome because it could lead to acts based on emotion or superstition rather than on thought, something that was coming to be valued in the Renaissance.

- ✔ **For future times:** Without religion (or morals), he saw a danger of losing respect for life.

Nostradamus struggled with these issues in this quatrain and didn't quite find his balance.

Devastation of unknown proportions

Weapons during the Renaissance were limited to one's own hands, swords, cannons, and the occasional musket. With this background, I'm amazed at the description Nostradamus gave of modern war, which is what I think he does in Quatrain C II – 6:

> Near the gates and within two cities
>
> There will be two scourges the like of which was never seen,
>
> Famine within plague, people put out by steel,
>
> Crying to the great immortal God for relief. (C II – 6)

Interpreters typically match this quatrain with the double atomic bomb drop on Nagasaki and Hiroshima during World War II. I tend to agree with this assessment. Numerologists even see in the dating of Quatrain C II – 6 a numerical code that predicted the dates the atomic bombs would be dropped. The 6th of August (for Hiroshima) and 9th of August (6 turned upside down — a real stretch of logic in my opinion for Nagasaki) were the days the bombs were dropped *Near the gates and within two cities.* This description is very accurate of the cities that experienced a new and strange kind of plague — nuclear fallout with its sickness, devastated land, and starving people.

To me, line 3's *Famine within plague* accurately identifies the radiation sickness that prevented people from gaining weight. The rest of line 3 says that the people are *put out by steel.* I take this phrase to be Nostradamus's description of the delivery method used for the bombs in airplanes.

Quatrain C II – 6 is loaded with very emotional words. I think Nostradamus attempted to describe the distress and confusion he felt at seeing these images in visions that he believed were divinely inspired. He'd seen devastation from traditional weapons, but the complete flattening of the land probably appeared to Nostradamus as a famine. And, indeed, after the bombs were dropped, the land was un-farmable around these sites. In addition, the radiation sickness probably appeared to Nostradamus as a plague that caused bleeding from the mouth, loss of hair, anorexia (that famine again), and all sorts of stomach upsets. I believe Nostradamus watched these events almost 400 years before they happened and worried that mankind and its technological toys could cause such disasters. Nostradamus's emotional words were his own personal expression and a way of (hopefully) getting the future's attention.

I think that in line 4, Nostradamus recorded the only possible solution he saw for the disaster: *Crying to the great immortal God for relief.* To me, this line — this humble, earnest prayer of the victims — represents a more emotional and personal response from Nostradamus than any other he gave about the wars and plagues of mankind. I believe this vision disturbed Nostradamus very much. As a doctor and human who cared about others, he was almost unable to imagine the situations that would bring this kind of destruction.

The Prophecies' Direct Impact on WWII

When recording his visions, Nostradamus had to consider just how powerful and influential the right prophecy could be if placed in the right hands. The people that lived during the Second World War weren't ignorant of Nostradamus and his writings. At certain important points during the war, his quatrains became more than just a voice from the past — they became a propaganda tool in the present used by Hitler to predict his ultimate victory by interpreting quatrains in his favor.

Nostradamus may have foreseen the events of the war, but he didn't hint as to whether he knew that the predictions themselves would begin to actually influence the future rather than just be a reflection of the events.

Influencing the invasion of Paris

Sometimes events just happen the way they're supposed to — or do they? Looking at Quatrain C IV – 80 and the events of the time period predicted, I have to wonder whether the quatrain manipulated the future. Take a look for yourself:

> Near the great river, great ditch, earth drawn out,
>
> In fifteen parts will the water be divided:
>
> The city taken, fire, blood, cries, and conflict,
>
> And the greatest part involving the colosseum [the collision]. (C IV – 80)

You may be interested to know that the people of France brought this quatrain to the attention of the French government and used an interpretation of the quatrain as an argument in support of building a very expensive wall of French fortifications along the border of France and Germany between 1930 and 1935. In this interpretation of the quatrain, Nostradamus seems to describe a wall that would help protect France from Germany.

The logic at the time suggested that if the wall was predicted hundreds of years ago, the French should consider building it, especially since others, like 19th-century Nostradamus commentator Torné-Chavigny and some people within the French government at that time, had proposed such a wall. Nostradamus seemed to voice his support through quatrains from the past.

This wall, called the Maginot Line after its major supporter, was built near the Rhine River *(great river)* and is crossed by rivers in 15 places *(In fifteen parts will the water be divided).* Even the most skeptical reader has to admit that the details about the river, ditch, and dug-out earth in the first line and the exact number of river crossings in the second line make this prophecy very specific in identifying the Maginot Line. These precise details and the fact that Nostradamus had written so many important prophecies for France convinced supporters that building the wall was the right thing to do.

Unfortunately, predicting the Maginot Line didn't make it any better as a defense. The remainder of the quatrain describes in detail the way that the Germans calmly went around the line of fortifications, met the French and British forces in a great battle *(collision),* and then captured Paris, the heart of France and its capital city. Interpreters of Nostradamus who lived around the time the Maginot Line was built (those who read the entire quatrain) actually tried to warn French officials that the tactic wouldn't work — Nostradamus said so. The interpreters used the harsh and devastating ending of Quatrain C IV – 80 as supporting evidence, but their efforts were useless. On both sides of this argument, Nostradamus's opinion (or what they interpreted out of his quatrain) held weight and was presented in serious discussions on the matter.

The hint and warning of Quatrain C IV – 80 seems clear — even the best-laid plans go wrong sometimes. The supporters who urged the building of the Maginot Line because Nostradamus suggested it made one large mistake: They believed that Nostradamus was incapable of making mistakes or of misleading. In other words, Nostradamus said that the Maginot Line would be built, so it *had* to be built. I don't think Nostradamus was infallible. He was a human quite prone to making the same mistakes you and I make. Nostradamus accurately prophesied about the Maginot Line and its effects, but doing so may have been an error because it turned into a self-fulfilling prophecy. Nostradamus's own words helped tip the scales and led to the direct invasion of Paris and France.

Giving Hitler a lucky break

"Hearye, hearye — there will be an attempt to kill Hitler!" Well, that was what Karl Ernst Krafft told the Nazis he had read in *The Prophecies* as well as the astrological chart he constructed (see Chapter 6). Krafft sent a warning to the Nazi party in the form of a horoscope, but the Nazi party was fairly superstitious and had outlawed horoscopes on Hitler. Krafft was arrested, but when his prediction turned out to be true, he was put to work with Hitler's private staff of psychics and astrologers where the story of his prediction gave him a distinction among his peers. The exact information contained in Krafft's horoscope was kept locked away in a cold, dark filing cabinet (and probably destroyed later), but Quatrain C VI – 51 remains open for all to see:

> People assembled to see a new spectacle,
>
> Princes and Kings amongst the bystanders,
>
> Pillars walls to fall: but as by a miracle
>
> The King saved and thirty of the ones present. (C VI – 51)

Nostradamus gave some obscure clues in this quatrain if you're just looking at the surface level. But taken all together, these pieces make for an attempted assassination pie (with whipped emotions on top).

Sometimes putting new words in place of the existing words in a quatrain alters it just enough to suggest a situation or meaning. Consider how I paraphrase Quatrain C VI – 51:

> When important people gather to see the intentional show, there will be only a few who escape the things falling about them.

The quatrain itself is a more exact match to the specific events of the Munich Beer Hall assassination attempt in 1939 on Hitler, but my paraphrase has a broader perspective. Following is the story of the actual event with the quatrain references included so you can see how closely Nostradamus managed to predict the trouble at the Munich Beer Hall, an old haunt of Hitler's from when he was a rising star in the younger Nazi party.

Every year, Hitler spoke at the Munich Beer Hall (a meeting place where *people assembled*). But in November 1939, Hitler had been in power four years, and the *new spectacle* (Hitler's new plan for the expansion of Germany) promised to be bigger and better than Hitler's attempt to take over the government in 1923 (which failed but he used the subsequent treason trial to his advantage for propaganda purposes).

I believe that the *Princes and Kings* are references to the leaders of Germany (members of the Nazi party) that Hitler addressed. The bomb (which was hidden in a *pillar wall*) intended for Hitler exploded and did a great deal of damage, but Hitler and his central group of men left the meeting just minutes before the explosion (possibly due to Krafft's warnings). Well — some call it luck, Nostradamus called it fate, and I call it a very unlikely outcome unless Hitler and his gang had a previous peek at Quatrain C VI – 51 and/or a very good astrologer like Krafft on their side. Fortunately for Hitler, he read Nostradamus *and* had his own staff of astrologers to predict the event and protect the leader.

Don't let it go unnoticed that the people in the Nazi party used Nostradamus's prediction about the attempt to kill Hitler to help prevent the assassination at the Munich Beer Hall. I believe that Nostradamus made a great leap of faith by putting his prophecies out for the future because he wouldn't have any control over how they'd be used. The fact that he put his predictions out there anyway shows his cautious vote of confidence in mankind.

Quatrain C VI – 51's description of the attempted murder of Hitler may seem like just a side note that doesn't deserve your attention, but I think there's something more to the eye here. Nostradamus gave a prophecy that was fulfilled completely, but the prophecy also had additional and unpredicted effects on the world. Without the prophecy of Nostradamus to clue Krafft to the dangers, he may not have looked closely at the events he saw outlined in the stars. I believe that astrology isn't the same as random guessing, and more than 350 years after Nostradamus predicted the assassination attempt, the German astrologer Krafft used the astrology chart for Hitler to produce a warning about the assassination that resembled Nostradamus's warning quatrain. The impact on you? Maybe a much larger situation is out there if you care to notice. Just look up in the sky.

Images of Terror

This section covers one of the hardest quatrains I've had to examine. With modern technology, plenty of easy-to-access images of World War II and the events surrounding it are available, but the visual images of Nostradamus's quatrains are just as powerful sometimes. To me, they're also more terrifying because they came from so long ago, and the warnings didn't seem to help at all. Quatrain C VI – 49 contains a brief slide show of imagery that represents many of Hitler's actions and the battles of the war:

> The great Pontiff of the party of Mars
>
> Will subjugate the confines of the Danube:
>
> The cross to pursue, through sword hook or crook,
>
> Captives, gold, jewels more than one hundred thousand rubies. (C VI – 49)

The untrained eye may not notice that the beginning two lines are rather intense. In line 1, the leader *(great Pontiff)* is named in relation to Mars, the planet associated in astrology most often with war, blood (because of its red surface), and aggression. Oddly enough, the warlike Mars is lead by a Pontiff, a term typically used to suggest a religious leader. I think Nostradamus used these words together to create a kind of verbal tension that would mirror the tension between the military and Hitler (who led with a very intense, emotional, and almost religious fanaticism).

Line 2 says that this leader will take control over the areas in the *confines of the Danube* River, and Hitler certainly did this effectively. Nostradamus displayed skill and cleverness when using words in unusual ways to get his meaning across, but he also managed to create a prophecy that was right on the button. As a former English teacher, I applaud.

Lines 2 and 3 bring my discussion to the symbols of Germany and the not-so-pretty aftermath of the conquering of countries. My interpretation of line 2 suggests that the war will happen with the aid of the *cross* (a reference to the legitimacy Pope Pius XII gave to Nazi and Fascist governments) and even by *hook or crook* (whatever means necessary, including illegal and immoral).

Other translations place the idea of something being crooked with the cross, an image that strongly resembles the bent and equal-armed cross called a *swastika,* which was the symbol and rallying point for the Nazi Party in Germany. Originally, the symbol represented the revolving sun (a connection to the power of the life-giving sun), prosperity, and good fortune and can be traced to times before the Egyptians. Hitler wasn't a fool, and he used that ancient symbolism for his own goals to help give the Nazi rulers a sense of timelessness, to increase the idea that he had the good of the people in mind (*swastika* translates from the Sanskrit word as "conducive to well-being"), and to suggest that as the ruler of the Third Reich (which translates as "Third Realm or Empire"), he was the life-giving force.

The Nazis took the time to plunder captured European nations and enrich Germany with the treasures, art, and decorations of other countries. Nostradamus predicted this Nazi practice in the last line of the quatrain, and he layered meanings in the *one hundred thousand rubies* reference:

- ✔ The first layer alludes to the jewels and valuables the Nazis took (especially from banks, businesses, and homes belonging to people the Nazi party considered unworthy).

- ✔ The second layer refers to the image of droplets of blood, which can often have the deep color of rubies. The loss of life was a kind of victory for Hitler because that meant more financial gain and fewer people to resist his rule.

In Quatrain C VI – 49, the voice of Nostradamus rings clear as a warning about the dangers of power.

Foreseeing Hitler's Final Solution

I struggled to get through this quatrain without falling into a state of stupefied horror. Nostradamus, who witnessed discrimination in his own time (related to the powers of the Church that I discuss in Chapter 2), opened his mind to divine inspiration and received some truly awful visions. I only hope the horrors he saw weren't as clear or as terrifying as the reality turned out to be:

> The unworthy one embellished will fear the great furnace,
>
> The elected one first, not returning some of the captives:
>
> Great bottom of the world, the Angry Female [Irale] not at ease,
>
> "Barb." Danube, Malta. And the Empty One does not return.
>
> (Presages 15, *Almanac 1557*)

Experts on Nostradamus don't always include *The Almanacs, Epistle to Henry II,* and *Preface to César,* and *Sixains* (the *Sixtains* are sometimes thought to be just good forgeries) as part of his prophecy work. *The Almanacs* are frequently left out depending on whether the interpretation links each of the quatrains to years contemporary to Nostradamus (in which case they're not helpful as prophecies for modern times) or to times in the future when studying these quatrains might prove more exciting. The *Epistle* and *Preface* are sometimes excluded from discussions because they're prose and even more convoluted than the quatrains, making them harder to understand. I've included pieces of these works in this book to give you an idea of the full scope of Nostradamus's work. You should know, however, that certain people will sniff and sneer if you bring up these sections of Nostradamus's work.

This quatrain reads almost like a history book description of what's sometimes termed Hitler's Final Solution to the problem of so-called inferior races and people. This time, Nostradamus addressed Hitler as the *unworthy one.* I think this term gives you Nostradamus's opinion that Hitler wasn't worthy of being human.

I believe Nostradamus foresaw one of the more tragic and horrific aspects of World War II and Hitler's campaign to purify the human race. The Nazis placed undesirables — mostly people who were Jewish or of an ancestry other than white Caucasian —in crowded trains like cattle (where these people began to lose their human identity) and hauled them off to concentration camps where most were killed. One of the notorious ways of disposing of these people was to place them in huge furnaces.

To better understand Nostradamus's vision, it's best to walk through the quatrain line by line:

- **Line 1:** This line says that the *unworthy one* will *fear the great furnace.* I think Nostradamus was suggesting that Hitler's doubt of his own worth (as a child of questionable birth with possible Jewish ancestry) would make him fear the great furnace. If his fanatical followers discovered that he was even possibly related to the Jews, he could've met a similar fate to all those he murdered. But the fear could also come as part of Hitler's realization that he would fail and lose the war. I also believe Nostradamus was suggesting that Hitler would fear what the furnaces symbolized — the deaths of millions of people ordered by one man. Layered on top of all this is the Christian idea of hell, where an eternal flame burns through your soul. I believe the visions Nostradamus saw convinced him that hell would be the appropriate end for Hitler and quite possibly the only thing that Hitler would fear.

- **Line 2:** The second line continues the vivid description of the concentration camps that Nostradamus must've seen in his visions very clearly. He described the *elected one,* which I believe is a reference to the Jews, Hitler's primary target in the campaign to exterminate the undesirables. Next Nostradamus gave the chilling prophecy that the Jewish people would never return to their homes. Line 2's words suggest a hollow and empty feeling in homes and streets — something Nostradamus might have seen when he looked into the future.

- **Line 3:** Nostradamus continued to express his opinion about this future time by calling the place (whether it was the real place of Germany or the place in time) the *Great bottom of the world.* He stopped just short of saying that this would be as low as people could possibly go, but he said outright that certainly Mother Israel *(Angry Female Irale)* wouldn't approve of these actions *(be at ease).* Nostradamus clearly identified the people of Jewish ancestry or faith as the object of this cleansing project that would end with the furnace of death.

- **Line 4:** The final line of the quatrain brings you to the end of Hitler's campaigns with a listing of places that were important to the war and then relief because *the Empty One* (meaning Hitler who is without a soul, without caring for people, or is even empty of the hope of winning) will not return with his inhuman war. *"Barb"* can be considered either a Nostradamian reference to Hitler (Barbarossa being one of the other names used for him in quatrains and a connection to the ancient conqueror by the same name) or a reference Hitler's campaign to invade Russia, code named Barbarossa. I doubt that Nostradamus would've seen the code name for the actions taken by Hitler as important, so I stick with the historical reference that would've been more likely to have meaning for Nostradamus way back in the 16th century.

Chapter 13

Telling the Tales of the Three Antichrists

Since the dawn of Christianity, a shadowy figure in the future has been waiting for the right time to jump out of the dark and scare humanity — the antichrist. The Bible contains only a handful of references to the antichrist, but the concept has grown beyond its roots in Christian belief and now sits firmly among society's vague idea of what the future holds. Nostradamus followed his faith, well, faithfully, and the idea of the antichrist was well known to him.

Other religions refer to similar figures who'll show up in the future, create mass changes and trouble, and ultimately hail the end of the universe. But they aren't all dressed in the same scary imagery that surrounds the Christian antichrist, especially as Nostradamus presented the idea. For Nostradamus, though, there wasn't just one figure who would hail the end of time. There were three. In this chapter, I help you determine just what Nostradamus meant by an antichrist, who he had in mind, and which people (or ideas) may be a better match than some of the standard interpretations.

Settling on a Definition

Yeah, I know, understanding what Nostradamus meant by *antichrist* should be easy because the word almost defines itself. But the trick here is that *almost* isn't enough. This is Nostradamus, after all. Sure, *anti* means *against,* and *Christ* is a figure from the Christian religion who was well known for acts of kindness, forgiveness, and spiritual nice-guy habits. You may be tempted to take the simple route — the antichrist is a figure who's simply against Christ — but the layer-loving Nostradamus didn't take the simple route so it won't work for understanding his perspective on this topic.

Nostradamus spoke to the future and had to cover all his bases to make his meaning clear. In my opinion, he hedged his bets by using images that some-body in the future would recognize. When trying to squeeze meaning out of a quatrain, go back to what Nostradamus might have known and see if you can find overlapping ideas from his religious, mystical, and social knowledge. (The biographical information in Chapters 3 and 4 will help.) And remember his overall goal: to *help* the people of the future.

Because Christianity has been one of the world's major religions for hundreds of years, and Nostradamus was a Christian, you can be sure that his meaning of *antichrist* was the same as what was described in the Bible (see the Book of John if you're interested in the nitty-gritty details). Nostradamus likely thought that regardless of how the times change, the Bible would still serve as a touchstone for future generations.

Ah, but that's as certain as it gets. In this case, the layers of meaning that Nostradamus so loved actually come right from the source. In a nutshell, the Christian version of the antichrist will seek to draw people away from the teachings of the Christian religion. In some descriptions, he'll be the formal announcement of the Apocalypse. (The Apocalypse can be anything from the day all people are judged by God to a day of revelation and new insight. But generally a little world destruction is thrown in with the antichrist and apoca-lypse to get your attention.) This person will also be recognized as a *false teacher,* or someone who will teach ideas that aren't in line with Christ. This last idea suggests that the antichrist may actually be the leader of a non-Christian religion — or even the religion itself.

I believe that Nostradamus built in a very real, identifiable layer of meaning that could be traced to an individual person for each antichrist. But I also believe that for each antichrist, he had an alternative meaning. Rather than being a person, the antichrist could be an idea, a social trend, or anything that would take away from Christianity and its major ideas, including faith, hope, and charity. Anything that went against the Church's basic beliefs would look like something anti-Christian to Nostradamus, who would've zeroed in on dangers to his own devout belief in the Catholic Church. Nostradamus knew, without a doubt, Christianity was the one true way to connect with the divine and he felt deeply about protecting this connection.

Introducing the First Two Scalawags

The people most often identified by Nostradamus interpreters as antichrist figures are Napoleon and Hitler, in that order. Granted, if you've been reading this book straight from Chapter 1 to here you already know what Nostradamus thought of those two characters. (If not, check out Chapters 10 and 12.) By using the antichrist slant, Nostradamus let the future know that the stakes were much higher than just who would rule over Europe. As antichrist figures, these two men would have the power to change the course of human events and bring about the beginning of the end of the world as we know it. For Nostradamus, these men were so important that he wrote quite a number of quatrains about them, but I can only touch on the most common ones (and some of their explanations) here.

Napoleon Bonaparte

For a man with one hand in his coat in most portraits, Napoleon sure had his hands in a lot of Europe during his day. He also had quite a hand in forming and reshaping the Europe that would follow his empire-building days.

If you're going to pick a future figure that'll have a lasting impression on the world, and you're French (like Nostradamus was), selecting a Frenchman as a powerful person isn't unreasonable. But Nostradamus had other reasons for identifying Napoleon as his first antichrist. The ruler who conquered most of Europe single-handedly began more campaigns and bloody battles than Europe had seen to that time. From Nostradamus's 16th-century viewpoint, Napoleon was an earth-shaking change.

It's frustrating when trying to pin down Napoleon as an antichrist, however, because Nostradamus hedged his bets. Instead of identifying Napoleon by his crimes against humanity (although some of the battles were described), Nostradamus simply fell back on the time-honored tradition of name calling, which made Napoleon stand out among the quatrains as more brutal, more unworthy, and simply more horrifying than dictators in other quatrains. Here's a tour of the creative ways that Nostradamus identified and condemned Napoleon as an antichrist:

- ✔ **Butcher:** *He is to be found less prince than butcher* (C I – 60). The idea of a leader being a *butcher* (who kills and keeps going without regard for the life he has just ended) suggests massive deaths, and Napoleon certainly fits the bill. The comparison between Napoleon and the *prince* also gives you an idea that Nostradamus separated Napoleon away from the idea of the Prince of Peace, as Christ has been called.

- ✔ **Great enemy:** *Great enemy of the entire human race* (C X – 10). For Nostradamus, Napoleon's lack of religious connection would've made him an enemy even if he hadn't destroyed the European countryside.

✔ **Destroyer:** *The old Destroyer the city will ruin: / He will see his "Romania" quite desolated, / Then he will not know how to put out the great flame* (C IV – 82). Nostradamus gave Napoleon the name Destroyer and then listed the places and realms that would be lost to his destructive power, a very similar description to the one given of the antichrist who brings destruction and devastation. I believe the *great flame* in this quatrain compares the fire in alchemy that changes the qualities of something to the great changes of the Apocalypse. If Napoleon started these changes, then he could certainly fit as the leading antichrist.

✔ **Wild:** *With a name so wild will he be brought forth / That the three sisters will have the name for destiny* (I – 76). Translators have long stumbled over the first line but finally discovered that the French "nom farouche" can be either a *ferocious name* or the Greek word *neapolluon,* which means *certain destroyer.* After untangling the wordplay, you discover that the wild, ferocious person is someone who's already associated with the word *destiny.* Regardless of how you bring these words into English, Napoleon brought with him a wild destiny. Oh, and I believe that the three sisters mentioned here are the three sisters of Fate from ancient Greek mythology who control the lives and destinies of everyone in the world.

Another title Nostradamus bestowed upon Napoleon is "of fire." In Century VIII – 1, he writes, "Pau, Nay, Oloron will be more of fire than blood." In Chapter 10, I identify the first three words of this quatrain as an anagram for Napoleon. But here I'd like to take a moment to show you how Nostradamus's word games may work in a bit more detail.

Pau, Nay, Oloron is the starting point, but then you need to rearrange the words. Nay Pau Oloron, scrunched together is naypauoloron. Split that up and you have Naypauolo ron, which is close to Napaulon roy (*roi* is the French word for king), or Napoleon the king.

Then, check this out: Naupoleone is the Corsican version of his name (Corsica being his birth place), which you can rearrange to form the final key.

✔ Drop the *N* and change *u* to *y.* You get Aypoleone.

✔ Drop the letters *e.* You get Aypolon.

✔ Move the y to follow the l. You get Apolyon.

Apolyon sounds similar to *Apollyon* (and the spelling is just one letter off) which is the name given to the Apocalypse described in the Bible's Book of Revelations.

Now that the word games are out of the way, look at the rest of this line. According to Nostradamus, this antichrist would be more connected with fire (change) than with blood. I believe this reference could be a comparison to the second antichrist, Hitler, who created much larger pools of blood (see the following section). The comparison of these two types of influence (change and blood) links these two figures together as the antichrists and also gives you a way to understand why Napoleon, whose crimes don't appear to be as tragic as Hitler's, may also be an antichrist.

The political, social, and legal changes Napoleon made during his European tour were dramatic and accomplished without (and sometimes in spite of) the Church. Nostradamus would've seen these changes as being against the nature of Christ, placing Napoleon neatly into the category of antichrist.

Today, Napoleon represents one of Nostradamus's versions of the antichrist, but his word isn't the final one. (Nostradamus was overly fond of focusing on the French and European side of things.) It's possible that as the world changes, different versions of the antichrist may threaten different people around the world in different ways. I'd have to say, though, that determining whether an up-and-coming leader will bring positive or negative changes in the long term is nearly impossible.

Note too that for some people, an evil force doesn't have to be a person but can be a thing. For example, some people view electricity as an evil force that distracts them from the path of spirituality.

So perhaps the first antichrist wasn't Napoleon but the Age of Reason which stripped many people of faith, leaving the Church with fewer followers. The pattern of looking, thinking, and evaluating without the emotional connection could certainly be devastating to the spiritual side of life and could qualify in my book as one of the first antichrist patterns (as opposed to people).

Adolf Hitler

Hitler had presence. He motivated and manipulated hundreds of thousands of people with the power of his mind and ideals. Through the use of propaganda and a huge army, he changed the direction of Europe as much or more than Napoleon. Nostradamus nominated him for a role as the second and possibly bloodiest antichrist. Scholars occasionally debate the identity of the first antichrist, but Hitler's role as a terrifying shift in the path of humanity seems fairly secure with both the scholars and Nostradamus.

Can you hear me now?

Hitler knew about Nostradamus, read his prophecies, and believed that the quatrains containing Hilter referred to him (see Chapter 12). So Hitler probably read the following quotes from Nostradamus and heard from the horse's mouth what he had to look forward to as the antichrist:

✔ *The Roman power will be thoroughly abased* (C III – 63). The seat of the Holy Roman Empire was in the area we know as Germany. Nostradamus apparently saw that Germany wouldn't fare well, because to *abase* something is to lower the rank, humble, or reduce to a state of worthlessness. Hitler should've

taken the warning, but he didn't and at the end of World War II, Germany was forced to accept responsibility.

✔ *Hunger, thirst, doubt will come to plague them very strongly / They will not have a single morsel of meat, bread or victuals* (C IV – 90). After noting the areas of Milan and Pavia, Nostradamus warned the people that the governments wouldn't pay the price tag on the war; the people would. They'd be the ones to suffer from starvation. The *doubt* would be the idea that maybe the leaders' promises weren't worth all the fighting.

I have a couple of doubts about Hitler's role, though, and I explain them as I walk you through Nostradamus's case against Hitler, which was most clearly described in the *Epistle to Henry II,* 44 – 46. Take a look:

> . . . In the Adriatic great discord will arise, and that which will have been united will be separated. To a house will be reduced that which was, and is, a great city, including the 'Pampotamia' and 'Mesopotamia' of Europe at 45, and others of 41, 42, and 37 degrees.

> It will be at this time and in these countries that the infernal power will set the power of its adversaries against the Church of Jesus Christ. This will constitute the second Antichrist, who will persecute that Church and its true Vicar, by means of the power of three temporal kings who in their ignorance will be seduced by tongues which, in the hands of the madmen, will cut more than any sword. (*Epistle to Henry II,* 44 – 46)

This translation suggests that the numbers 37, 41, 42, and 45 are latitude measurements on a map, but I get a stronger meaning out of this quatrain when the numbers are connected to years. All of the years (in the 20th century) were important for Hitler: In 1937, he announced his plans for expansion (and war), and beginning in 1941, Jews were required to be marked by wearing stars. The remaining years coincide with the wide-scale assault that would come to be known as the Holocaust.

The countries of *the Adriatic* include Italy, Yugoslavia, Albania, and Greece and match with the region Benito Mussolini (Italy's leader) expected to have under Italian control after World War II. These pieces help pinpoint Hitler's time, making him the lead suspect for antichrist number two. Also, Hitler did *persecute that Church* by continuing to harass the Catholics within his realm, and *the true Vicar* could be a reference to the pope, who struggled with being surrounded in Italy by Mussolini's Fascist power.

Nostradamus saw clearly when he recorded this prophecy, but I think perhaps most modern interpreters have left things a little on the simple side. Here are some of the clues that indicate Hitler as the second antichrist:

✔ The *three temporal kings* are commonly thought to be the secular leaders during this time: Hitler, Mussolini, and a third leader, perhaps Franklin Roosevelt or Pope Pius XII (rumored to have supported the Fascist cause personally not religiously). But if you read the section as connected thoughts, it sounds like the action of setting *adversaries against the Church* (something done by the *infernal power*) is actually what could be termed the antichrist, and the *temporal kings* are the ones *seduced by tongues*. Perhaps Hitler, Mussolini, and the third leader were seduced by the idea of their own power — with word of mouth being a way to represent reputation.

To really understand the fine distinction I'm getting at, you need to know that *who in their ignorance will be seduced by tongues* is a line typically used to point out that Hitler and Mussolini used the power of persuasion, speech, and even rumor (the voice and tongue) to manipulate the situation. But in the prophecy, the populace isn't seduced, the three leaders are, which means that some of the meaning has gotten confused. The leaders can't be the ones doing the seducing, unless Nostradamus allowed a little double meaning into his writing, which is very possible. (Luckily, that would make the other interpreters *and* me right.)

✔ *In the hands of the madmen, will cut more than any sword,* seems to indicate that the *tongues* will be the cause of the problem (the leaders will be a tool, not the problem). The result will be more death and destruction than any sword could possibly render. The propaganda of World War II which was impressive and motivated by evil *(infernal power)* becomes the major cause of the destruction being described in Nostradamus's 16th-century way.

The preceding points make up the doubts I have about Hitler's role as the second antichrist. Consider them carefully, because they form a slippery slope of thought and responsibility. Were the leaders responsible for their actions, or was the *infernal power* — whatever started this whole mess — responsible? Nostradamus seems to have written this section to indicate that Hitler, as the second antichrist, would be to blame for the events that would follow, especially the ones recorded in the quatrains (see Chapter 12). But I believe the actual responsibility started with the *infernal power* that ignited this process and led Hitler astray. The power of the human mind to ignore what it doesn't like, twist logic horribly, and ignore how events affect other people is one of my prime definitions of an evil force. Regardless, in my book, Hitler was still responsible for his actions and should bear the brunt of the responsibility for the events during World War II.

I have to admit that during my study of Nostradamus, I've struggled to find his reason for predicting such a figure as Hitler. If the purpose was for the future to prevent Hitler's influence, then people seem to have fallen down on the job. If the purpose was to give a second antichrist meaning, I find the prospect unappealing. Still, Nostradamus presented an overall view that humanity would be moving toward some goal other than the atrocities committed by Hitler, a hope at the end of things.

Some surgeons of 16th-century France believed that a process of letting the sickness out of a patient was necessary before healing could begin. Using that concept as a foothold, I believe that Nostradamus was diagnosing the future with an illness — one that looked an awful lot like an antichrist. The illness was a lack of empathy or caring for the condition of the world and its people. For example, the concentration camps weren't a well-hidden secret but a politely used propaganda tool for the "temporary removal" of the Jews to safety. The pope, people within the Nazi party, and many of the Allied leaders knew about the concentration camps and didn't act. These leaders became very much like Hitler when they ignored the humanity of these people. So I think Nostradamus was warning the future people of World War II — and warning us today — that a respect for life will keep people from these dark nights of the soul.

Three's Company: The Coming of the Third Antichrist

And now for the million-dollar question: Who's the third and final antichrist identified by Nostradamus, and when's he getting here? Unfortunately, you're not likely to find a clear answer on this one.

Seeing spots

Quatrain C II – 89 is often linked to the antichrist through the last line, where *the bloody one* ends up taking a count of what has happened. The antichrist is associated in other quatrains with spilled blood and massive death, so this quatrain seems to fall neatly into the same category and hits close to home:

One day the two great masters will be friends,

Their great power will be seen increased:

The new land will be at its high peak,

To the bloody one the number recounted. (C II – 89)

Look a little closer at line 3, and you notice that the *new land* is mentioned. America is suddenly in the picture! This reference is an easy connection to America because it was the new land explored and conquered around the time Nostradamus wrote (see Chapter 2).

The *two great masters* in line 1 could be the nations who influence the situation at hand. And because America is mentioned in line 3, I can fill in one of those two slots. The last line could possibly be a double-reference — one to the third antichrist and the other to Mikhail Gorbachev (whose forehead bears an irregular red birthmark), in which case I could fill in both slots: The *two great masters* (leaders) would be the president of the United States and the leader of Soviet Union.

If this last line identifies Gorbachev *(the bloody one)* as the third antichrist, then three possibilities exist regarding the accuracy of this quatrain's prediction:

- ✔ The human race has finally learned its lesson about respect for each other, and Gorbachev's impact was avoided.
- ✔ Nostradamus was wrong in predicting Gorbachev as the third antichrist.
- ✔ Interpreters are wrong in identifying Gorbachev as the third antichrist.

Wondering what my take is on these three possibilities? In a nutshell, I don't think Gorbachev is the third antichrist. I think that Nostradamus was referring to Gorbachev in a different capacity. And for what it's worth, in my mind, the events of this quatrain haven't happened yet. But the seeds of this antichrist's future may be sprouting now and may be too ordinary to be seen yet.

The quatrain says that the events will occur — *the number recounted* — when America is at its best. Defining the best of America is another book entirely, but I believe that America is still growing into its possibilities. Granted, my vision may be limited by my experiences in the same way that Nostradamus's visions were limited by his understanding. But if I'm right, and America isn't yet at its best, then this prophecy hasn't been fulfilled.

And here's a surprise ending for you: I don't see this quatrain as having a negative spin. Perhaps the third antichrist will bring drastic change — an end to things as people know them — but maybe the change will be for the better. Perhaps America will reach its peak and join with the world community.

Scheduling a date

With such an important event as the coming of the third antichrist (and possibly the end of the known world), Nostradamus tried to give some very accurate dates. He made direct references in Quatrains C X – 72 and C VIII – 77. This section helps you evaluate how close he got to pinning the tail on the antichrist. First, take a look at Quatrain C X – 72:

> The year 1999, seventh month,
>
> From the sky will come a great King of Terror:
>
> To bring back to life the great King of the Mongols,
>
> Before and after Mars to reign by good luck. (C X – 72)

Well, that seems clear enough: In July 1999, the *King of Terror* — a great name for an antichrist if I've ever heard one — will bring back Genghis Khan (an effective and frightening warrior-king of the Mongols). Mars, the symbol for war, destruction, and violent change, will be in control. The only problem is that Nostradamus seems to have missed the mark. July 1999 didn't reveal strong changes — and ol' Genghis was nowhere to be seen on the cable news networks.

But perhaps 1999 was the year and month the third antichrist was born, and the world will just have to wait and see.

Now take a gander at Quatrain C VIII – 77:

> The Antichrist three very soon annihilated,
>
> Seven and twenty years of blood will his war last:
>
> The heretics dead, captives exiled,
>
> Blood human body water reddened on land to hail. (C VIII – 77)

All doom and gloom, this quatrain predicts several pieces about the coming war of the third (and hopefully final) antichrist — mainly that the war causing such destruction will last 27 years. If you can find the beginning point of this war brought by the antichrist, pinning the tail on the date as well as on the antichrist himself is possible. But the beginning seems to have slipped under the radar so far.

Beyond just dating the war of the antichrist, however, this quatrain begins to give an outline of what events might be happening during this time. First and foremost is that the *Antichrist three very soon annihilated*. This phrase can be taken one of three ways.

- ✔ If translated slightly differently, the antichrist will kill three brothers and perhaps even predicts the death of the Kennedy brothers (this interpretation is really reaching too far in my opinion).

- ✔ The third antichrist will be *annihilated* quickly after he comes to power.

- ✔ There will be not one final antichrist but three people who will act together as the antichrist figure and that they'll die quickly.

For my money, I would select door number two because, in the grand scheme of time, 27 years isn't that long, and it might be the time for the antichrist's death meant by Nostradamus's prediction of *very soon.*

But after we've disposed of the antichrist there's still the matter of his 27-year war and some other losses Nostradamus is counting when there are *heretics dead, captives exiled. Heretics* for Nostradamus probably mean those who are without faith and not in touch with the Christian God. According to Nostradamus, they'll be gone. This would fit with Nostradamus's Christian view of the end of the world after the third antichrist. As for the *captives placed in exile,* I see these as the leaders who are captive to their own ideals that fail to help the world. These leaders are exiled (taken away by force or law) from their own thoughts by the facts that surround them, namely death and destruction. Idealism isn't going to help face the events in this war. These leaders in exile could also be real leaders, like the Dalai Lama, the Buddhist, religious, and political leader of Tibet who is in exile. This strangl hold over other countries and their leaders could be part of the antichrist's war.

Nostradamus sums up the effects of the war with a list of images meant to scare you a bit including *Blood human body water reddened on land to hail.* I believe that these images refer to:

- ✔ **Blood:** Nostradamus uses this word for both the literal blood of people as they die and as the life force of faith within people as it's spilled (lost).

- ✔ **Human body:** This refers to the staggering body toll that will wreck mankind during this war of the antichrist as well as to the focus (wrongly in Nostradamus's ideas) on what our bodies do rather than the mind or the heart do.

- ✔ **Water reddened on land to hail:** This phrase can be taken two ways. The first is that the rivers and lakes will become the reservoirs for the blood, thus polluting them and the rest of life, or second, that the rain will be reddened as it falls and become more damaging (as hail is more damaging than water) as it comes to Earth. The most likely explanation for this change is something stirred up in the atmosphere like dust, chemicals, or radiation from nuclear or chemical warfare.

Current areas of war and destruction — including Iraq, Palestine, Korea, Afghanistan, and even Russia — could be considered the beginning of larger struggles to come. Unfortunately, to mark this prophecy as accurate or not, you'll just have to see how things progress or whether the other elements of the quatrain begin to match events happening in the world.

Dealing with some sketchy details

I know, I know. You were hoping for some tangible details and clues about the mysterious third antichrist. Weren't we all, my friend? It'd be nice to pencil Armageddon into my busy schedule. Here are two possible reasons why Nostradamus was so sketchy on this topic:

✔ Some interpreters have suggested that Nostradamus struggled to iden- tify the date and person of the third antichrist because of the relatively low-profile nature of the antichrist himself. He could be an average person in a key position to make impressive changes.

✔ Part of the trouble Nostradamus had in making predictions about world- wide events came from his tendency to focus on events and people closer to home in Europe. It's possible that the antichrist could be from areas Nostradamus wasn't familiar with, including the United States and South America.

And while I'm speaking about clues, know that several of the quatrains that mention the final antichrist use a word that isn't a word — or at least it isn't one translators and interpreters have been able to decipher. "Mabus" is the term used where you might expect to find the name of the third antichrist. If you have lots of time on your hands, you can play with some of the word games Nostradamus enjoyed to discover who the antichrist might be. But so far, there isn't a firm theory that holds water.

Muddying the waters with another theory

Just when you think you have at least one thing figured out — you know the type of person to be on the lookout for as the third antichrist — I have to step up and change the picture. I simply don't feel that the third antichrist is a person at all. For one reason, the verbs in some of these quatrains are plural, not singular, and they aren't referring to individuals. For another, a single person rarely holds worldwide influence for more than 25 years. Even Napoleon and Hitler didn't manage that one.

There's no real reason why the third antichrist has to be an individual at all. From Nostradamus's 16th century viewpoint, one of the trends he foresaw in the future could create a definite problem for Christianity. That trend could be the scientific, prove-it-to-me attitudes of the people from the Age of Aquarius (you and me). Technology threatens to remove further the ideas of human life as being unique and powerful. It can lead people to lose their drive to find a direct connection to the divine, or worse, get lost in the multitude of theo- ries and religious concepts floating about.

Chapter 14

Taking a Technological Tour

1 believe that Nostradamus's predictions within *The Prophecies* have been incredibly accurate and very surprising. One way they're so surprising is that every once in a while, Nostradamus slipped in a prediction for technological advances alongside all his warnings. These predictions suggest the future may be a little brighter than some of the quatrains (and critics of Nostradamus) may have you believe. To me, Nostradamus's predictions about modern technological marvels serve as a reminder that the world is on the right track for the growth and improvement that Nostradamus foresaw. If the less than encouraging prophecies have marked the progress of humanity up to this point, and Nostradamus has been able to predict these unsettling events, then I'm encouraged that our future could hold more of these remarkable improvements in science and technology that Nostradamus included in the quatrains I explore in this chapter.

I believe that including these technology-focused quatrains within the larger scope of his prophecies allowed Nostradamus to soften the impact of the wars and broaden the overall perspective of humanity's future. He showed that the future isn't all that bad and that people have some redeeming values. When he finally looked somewhere beyond the people and places of Europe and issues like war and royal rule, he gazed upward at the sky and forward to the future and all its possibilities. He looked at the ways mankind would handle the wild and unimaginable power of electricity and the vast space above us.

Cataloging Modern Marvels

Nostradamus was more than just a man of spirit; he was a man of science and medicine as well. I think the quatrains in this section show just how astute he was at foreseeing the wonders the brightest minds would bring forth into the world.

Every prophet is limited by his understanding of the world and his knowledge of terms and words. I can't imagine more troublesome visions for Nostradamus than those of the new-fangled things that would surface in the modern era due to the Industrial Revolution and the widespread use of electricity. But Nostradamus gave his best shot in Quatrain C III – 44 when he tackled several inventions all at once with, I believe, a great deal of success:

> When the animal domesticated by man
>
> After great pains and leaps will come to speak:
>
> The lightning to the virgin will be very harmful,
>
> Taken from earth and suspended in the air. (C III – 44)

I love this quatrain. The imagery makes me smile because I can just imagine poor Nostradamus (essentially a country doctor) trying to describe our technology-driven world. (Granted, builders in Milan, Italy, used some assembly-line techniques in the 16th century to build boats, but they certainly weren't based on machinery.) As I understand it, *When the animal domesticated by man* is a reference to the automobile.

I believe that throughout the quatrains, Nostradamus gave machines animal-like qualities because they moved on their own and made noises, yet weren't quite human.

Here's a quick look at the other inventions I think Nostradamus was describing in this quatrain:

- ✔ **Will come to speak:** The telephone, which after *pains and leaps* to make the voice clear enough to hear, was a modern invention that changed the pace of life. However, another interpretation is possible, I think: If you read lines 1 and 2 together, then the car is speaking, or honking its horn, on the streets around the world.

- ✔ **Lightning to the virgin will be very harmful:** The original language that line 3 was written in has different translations, and this particular translation — especially the use of the term *virgin* — doesn't really work for me. I prefer the translation *lightning goes to the rod,* which makes more sense if Nostradamus saw TV antennas or lightning rods (to divert the dangerous discharge of electrical energy) in his visions.

✔ **Taken from earth:** Lightning taken from the earth could be Nostradamus's view of electricity when it's moved away from its natural environment. This interpretation makes sense when you finish the line and think in terms of the electricity (which is what makes up lightning) found in power lines hung in the air between houses (*suspended in the* air) or being used to power space stations and satellites that are *suspended in the air* above the earth's surface.

Some Nostradamus critics claim that by reading too much into these metaphors, you're simply making stuff up, but I feel that these metaphors and descriptions were the only way Nostradamus could communicate what he saw. Certainly there were no words in middle French, Latin, Greek, or Hebrew that described the images in his visions.

Shooting for the Stars: The Space Prophecies

With the desire to fly and the need to find a pattern of meaning for life in the stars, people have been looking up at the sky in wonder since they squinted into the first sunrise. It's only natural that Nostradamus wrote about, dreamed of, and even idealized the place that kept him transfixed night after night. In the peaceful quiet of space (and in the visions that showed him the future of space), Nostradamus found a great deal of hope.

Livin' la vida luna

For nearly three-quarters of a century, mankind has sought ways to find new resources and advance its place in the newest frontier — space. The race to conquer space included all the firsts: first man in space, first man on the moon, and even the first space station. Now it's a race to advance medicine and the sciences to find cures for disease and generally improve the quality of life here on Earth. The situation wasn't much different from when the countries in 16th-century Europe funded expeditions to sail around the world and find new trade routes, raw materials, and lands they could add to their growing empires. If you add in scientific curiosity, you can use the same explanation for the modern search to explore the uses of space. Fly on into Quatrain C IX – 65:

He will come to go into the corner of "Luna,"

Where he will be captured and put in a strange land:

The unripe fruits will be the subject of great scandal,

Great blame, to one great praise. (C IX – 65)

The key to this quatrain is the word "Luna," which is one name for the moon. The ability to go to the moon is a recent phenomenon, so this quatrain could reasonably relate to our own time period. By picking the quatrain apart line by line, you can more easily figure out the meaning:

- **Line 1:** The first line says *he* goes to the moon, but I think *he* in this case means both an individual and people in general who made it to the moon in the 20th century.

- **Line 2:** To me, line 2 says that mankind is enthralled by the idea of space travel (*captured,* like capturing someone's imagination) and must face new and different challenges in a world that people don't understand (*put in a strange land*).

- **Line 3:** Nostradamus pointed out some pitfalls of not understanding this new place called space in line 3. You can easily interpret the *unripe fruits* that are the cause of *great scandal* as a prediction about the parts for the space shuttle Challenger that were rushed into use before they were ready (which would make them *unripe*). This mistake caused the catastrophic Challenger explosion on January 28, 1986. All seven crewmembers were killed, but the one who received the most press coverage before and after the event (*great scandal*) was Christa McAuliffe, a schoolteacher who was the first civilian to be on a space flight. (The Columbia space shuttle disaster on February 1, 2003 was most likely not part of this prediction, because the cause of the disaster was linked to the break-up of the leading wing — a defect in parts rather than a part that wasn't ready for flight.)

- **Line 4:** The last line seems to suggest that the results from space exploration would be mixed. Nostradamus was right, of course. The disaster of the Challenger explosion slowed the United States space program and kept the U.S. out of space for the next three years while NASA fixed problems, answered questions (*great blame*), and tested systems. The slowing of U.S. flights into space helped improve the safety of the program but slowed the possible scientific advancements of experiments in space. Meanwhile, the Soviet space program, which lagged behind the U.S., continued to make advances and take impressive steps toward accessing space as a resource to enrich its knowledge and people (*great praise*).

I think Nostradamus discussed the quest to explore space in Quatrain C IX – 65 to point out that people should carefully prepare for the future and not rush into things before they're ready. By pointing out that the competition among countries for the resources of space would result in both praise and blame, Nostradamus reminded the world that only with patience and cooperation will people win the prize.

Finding solutions in the sky

Round and round the world goes, and we ride along without thinking about what lies beyond our home planet. I think Nostradamus saw the big picture, though, and he wasn't afraid to share. Quatrain C VI – 5 may be up in the sky interpretation-wise, but the point he made is very much down to earth to me:

Very great famine through pestiferous wave,

Through long rain the length of the arctic pole:

"Samarobryn" one hundred leagues from the hemisphere,

They will live without law exempt from politics. (C VI – 5)

I believe this quatrain's predictions belong to our century rather than Nostradamus's time. He tied the events together in one quatrain and mentioned something above the Earth's surface, which definitely brings this prophecy into the space age. Travel had advanced quite a bit in the 16th century, but only horizontally.

This quatrain is frequently divided into two separate predictions, and in this section, I continue that tradition with a twist.

The sickness of mind and body

Line 1 predicts *famine* as a result of a *pestiferous wave.* In other words, the cause of the famine is some sort of wave (maybe of water; maybe this wave is just imagery) that, to me, sounds like it's anything from bothersome to morally evil to contaminated with an infectious disease. You can approach this line a couple different ways:

✔ One way to look at this line is as a literal description of human starvation caused by a disease. Many interpreters associate this description with the AIDS (acquired immune deficiency syndrome) epidemic that has spread in wave-like patterns through Africa and into the world's population. Because the African nations are losing people so rapidly, food is difficult to produce, and the crisis in those countries is astounding. As a doctor, Nostradamus may have seen these events and been concerned enough to include them in a prediction for the future. I believe this is the major piece of Nostradamus's meaning in this quatrain, but it's not all of what he wanted to convey.

✔ Line 1 could also be a metaphor for something that isn't a physical sickness. *Pestiferous* can describe something that's morally wrong or ideologically offensive — like a disease of the mind rather than a disease of the body. If you use this interpretation as your starting point, the *famine* becomes a starvation of the soul, something Nostradamus feared with the changes in the world's view on religion. (Chapter 17 gives you the scoop on those types of predictions.) I think this meaning is a subtle part of Nostradamus's insights about events he predicted would occur near the time of the events higher up in the sky.

The sickness from outer space

Lines 2, 3, and 4 present prophecies about the relationship humans have with the sky. Line 2's *long rain* may refer to radiation in the 20th and 21st centuries that rains down through a hole in the ozone layer. (The *ozone* is a part of the atmosphere that protects the earth and the people inhabiting it from harmful ultra-violet rays.)

Nostradamus made a tiny mistake in this prophecy, however, because the ozone hole is over the Antarctic, not the *arctic pole*. Regardless, size matters, and Nostradamus said the rain would be the *length of the arctic pole,* which is correct because the hole in the ozone layer is about the size of Antarctica and is linked to the production of toxins from industrial plants, the burning of fossil fuels, and the release of chemicals into the atmosphere that deplete this important protective layer. It's like humans have been wiping off the sunscreen that naturally protects us from getting sick. So in this particular prophecy, I think Nostradamus did a great job of describing in 16th century terms the strange goings-on four and five centuries later.

The prediction in lines 3 and 4 is an example of a successful prophecy as long as you remember that Nostradamus wasn't familiar with modern technology or terms. Unfortunately, even knowing that he struggled with descriptions hasn't helped interpreters unravel the first word of line 3, "Samarobryn." Nostradamus used the word as if it were a noun and the name of the object, person, or thing that would be *one hundred leagues from the hemisphere.* Here are some ideas about this tricky word's meaning:

✔ Translate the word as Amiens, a city in Northern France without much connection to space travel and unlikely to be in space itself.

✔ Interpret the word as a combination of the names for two drugs related to AIDS research (and a tie-in to the disease of the first line). The two drugs are Suramin and Ribavrin. Added together as *Surabavrin,* they sound similar to *Samarobryn.*

✔ Look at the parts as a compound word, *samo-rabotin,* which means *self-operator* in Russian. This logic could connect the word to a Russian satellite that's capable of sustaining itself.

✔ Rely on Latin, the language of the ancient people so admired during the Renaissance, and this word is a description of a *samara* (winged seedpod) that is *obire* (orbiting).

✔ Take it as a word that people have yet to understand. It could possibly be the name of an unknown cure for AIDS or even the name of someone who'll influence space travel (Sam A.R. O'Brian has been suggested).

Taking all these possibilities (with a grain of salt because a better one may come along soon), I believe Nostradamus used a compound word to describe a compound and complex idea — the third and fourth options from the preceding list. I don't think Nostradamus knew much Russian, but I'm certain his Latin was strong, and the winged seed explanation makes the most sense. Look at Figure 14-1, which shows the Mir Space Station, for an idea of what Nostradamus could've seen in his gazing bowl of prophecy. Not knowing anything else, he may have described the space station as best he could using the images he had available to him — a typical *winged seedpod* like the ones I used to hurl from treetops as a child. The visual similarity to the space station is very strong.

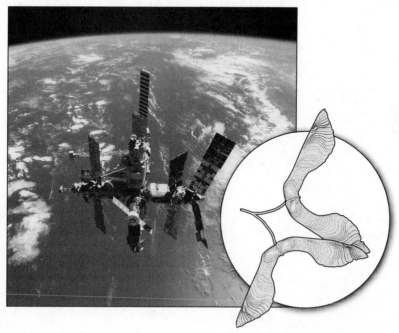

Figure 14-1:
The Mir
Space
Station and
a winged
seedpod.

Mir photo courtesy of NASA

Although translating the word "Samarobryn" as Amiens, a city in Northern France, doesn't seem like the best option to many interpreters of Quatrain C VI – 5, I believe Nostradamus made a connection and pun that many people have missed. Jules Verne was the town councilor of Amiens and happened to be one of the first science fiction writers to include travel to the moon, into the earth, and to other far-flung places in his writings. Some of his titles you may recognize include *Journey to the Center of the Earth, 20,000 Leagues Under the Sea,* and *Around the World in Eighty Days.* Nostradamus's prophecy may include a connection to this visionary writer and a description of the strange stories as a way of suggesting to folks of the future that the hints of what could happen would be all around them, if they'd just look.

Continuing with my space station take on the quatrain, line 4 says that these space stations will *live without law exempt from politics.* Word choice can tell a lot about meaning. For example, I think it's important that Nostradamus didn't say *lawless* in place of *living without law.* The word *lawless* tends to make people think of a wild lack of control and disorganization. *Living without law,* however, sounds like life on the Mir space station, as well as on the International Space Station, in which life continues outside of artificial controls of governments and countries — especially because the station and its people are *exempt from politics.* The issues faced in politics since the dawn of man seem to be set aside as the countries are brought together in these space stations without all the war and trouble addressed in Nostradamus's other quatrains.

In Quatrain C VI – 5, Nostradamus presented famine, disease (whether of the mind or the body), and environmental problems. Then, like a cameraman who controls your vision, he panned up to the skies. Nostradamus saw many of the answers to his own times in the stars, so it isn't too much to believe that he'd suggest people look up for the solution to their own troubled times. I think the ideal conditions of being without restrictions or politics seem to be his solution to the troubles mentioned earlier in the quatrain. And I believe the important piece he wanted you to take home is that the only way to solve global problems is to recognize the problems and place them in a neutral zone where humanity comes before any political, social, or religious system.

Chapter 15

Playing Politics: People and Events of the 20th Century

In This Chapter

▶ Identifying some famous folks

▶ Picking apart the politics in Nostradamus's prophecies

Nostradamus wrote nearly 1,000 quatrains and published his prophecies with the idea that humanity would benefit from knowing what was going to happen. He recorded events as he foresaw them, and like a good newspaper reporter, he followed the five Ws: who, what, when, where, and why.

This chapter takes you through some quatrains that I believe relate to a few famous modern-era people. I've hand-picked quatrains that I think involve people who are probably the most familiar to you or who influenced the path of history and major world events. In addition, I've included a smattering of political quatrains to give you an idea of how far Nostradamus's visions reached. So put on your travel clothes. You're going on a whirlwind tour of people and politics in the 20th century.

Rolling out the Red Carpet

History is a lot like great theater when you think about it. It includes some outstanding events (which I touch on in other chapters) and some really stunning people whose brilliance stands the test of time. I believe Nostradamus saw a clear picture of some folks who'd shake up the world stage with their entrances and exits. In this section, I introduce you to a few of his interesting cast of characters.

Counting out King Ferdinand of Bulgaria

Although royalty took a severe hit leading up to the 20th century, with revolutions (like the French Revolution, which I cover in Chapter 9) and democracy breaking out around the world, kings still held some power after the 1900s. One of these monarchs was a man known as King Ferdinand I, elected as *regent* (someone who rules on behalf of a monarch who's absent, too young, or sick in some way) of an independent Bulgaria in 1887 (and stepped down in 1918). In a rare show of clarity, Nostradamus actually named this man and predicted his actions in World War I in Quatrain C IX – 35:

> And fair Ferdinand will be detached,
>
> To abandon the flower, to follow the Macedonian:
>
> In the great pinch his course will fail,
>
> And he will march against the Myrmidons. (C IX – 35)

This quatrain describes a *fair Ferdinand* who *will be detached* and *abandon the flower.* I believe these statements clearly indicate that a person named Ferdinand will leave a place of beauty and his source of strength. Two leaders with the name Ferdinand could've shown themselves in Nostradamus's scrying bowl. But this quatrain's references to Macedonia, *detached* (which I believe means detached from allies and the truth), and *abandon* (which to me means left to his own devices by his so-called allies) leads me to think Nostradamus was talking about Ferdinand of Bulgaria, who was tricked and betrayed numerous times. As for Nostradamus calling him *fair,* I don't believe he was talking about Ferdinand being blond or light-skinned (which he wasn't). I think Nostradamus was referring to Ferdinand's preference for fair-skinned men — an extra detail to help identify him.

The goal that motivated King Ferdinand to *abandon the flower* was *to follow the Macedonian,* or to recapture Macedonia, a country which once belonged to Bulgaria and which still held a largely Bulgarian population. During the second year of World War I, Germany (who needed help) agreed to help Bulgaria regain control over Macedonia if Bulgaria would join the war. Unfortunately, when push came to shove in the *great pinch* (which I believe refers to the final battles in World War I), the German forces within Bulgaria were moved to fight in other areas, leaving Bulgaria weakly defended and open to invasion by the British and French. And as for the final line in the quatrain, I believe that the *Myrmidons* were the soldiers from southeastern Europe who were in Macedonia during Ferdinand's first attacks of the war. In mythology, Myrmidons are mindless and fiercely loyal to their leaders, and the soldiers in Macedonia were definitely loyal, which is what made them so difficult to conquer. I think Nostradamus's use of *Myrmidons* instead of just saying *soldiers* provides more interpretative depth as this word expresses an opinion about the quality of the enemies Ferdinand faced.

King Ferdinand of Bulgaria was an ambitious man who sought power. He pursued his dream of a larger empire, but in the end, he found himself alone and, ultimately, removed from the ruler's seat. This scenario describes how one man's ambition can lead an entire country and its people into useless wars — which is what I believe Nostradamus foresaw and warned humanity about here. Societies should note this pattern of one man's ambition put above the people's interests and be forewarned about today's leaders. I think Nostradamus hoped the warning about Ferdinand and its connection to Germany would be enough of a hint (especially with the other Hitler quatrains in Chapter 12) for people to look at leaders with a critical eye.

Reigning in British royalty

Many Americans are fascinated with the British royal family because, well, we don't have any of our own to watch for every little hiccup or drop of jelly on a royal tie. Americans have Hollywood and its stars, but that's not quite the same.

For Nostradamus, the royal houses of Europe were interesting because they held a great deal of power, money, and influence on future events on a global scale. He spent a great deal of time predicting the royal families' actions (check out Chapters 7, 8, and 9). But I believe that he gazed into the future long enough to know that royals aren't always shaping the future of entire countries — sometimes, they're just doing regular stuff. After all, they put on their pants one leg at a time just like everyone else.

King Edward the lovestruck

In only a few historical situations can the words *king, abdication, divorce,* and *Britain* be used in the same sentence, and almost all of those words involve King Edward VIII of Britain. To me, Quatrain C X – 22 gives a definite and amazing impression of what would happen to England's king:

> For not wishing to consent to the divorce,
>
> Which then afterwards will be recognized as unworthy:
>
> The King of the Isles will be driven out by force,
>
> In his place put one who will have no mark of a king. (C X – 22)

This quatrain reads like a fairy tale gone wrong. Nostradamus put the real action in line 3, where *The King of the Isles* (which I believe means a British king) is *driven out*. The reason he's driven out is given in line 1 — *For not wishing to consent to the divorce.*

Now compare those snippets with some real-life events surrounding King Edward VIII: Back in the 1930s, the British people didn't like the fact that King Edward was dating a twice-divorced American woman. Scandal! The people and government ministers of England disliked the idea of this arrangement so intensely that King Edward was forced to choose between ruling England and marrying the woman he loved. So King Edward VIII abdicated (willingly stepped down) the British throne on December 11, 1936. Afterwards, George VI ascended to the throne. He was the younger brother of Edward, and only a remarkable circumstance like death or abdication could've brought him to power, and therefore he had *no mark of a king* (line 4) — no one had planned on him being there.

Nostradamus wasn't a man who only wrote about politics and war; he also understood the power of passion. In Quatrain C X – 22, he predicted the influence of love over power in deciding who would rule a country. You and I can take note that life isn't always about power and wealth. Sometimes things happen a certain way because humans are ultimately motivated from within. Understanding the internal motivations of a person in a leadership position (which is the thinly veiled reason some tabloids use for digging up dirt on politicians) can help folks decide whether that person should be in office. I think that by sticking this quatrain in among the quatrains of war, deceit, and mistrust, Nostradamus also wanted to raise the point that people occasionally act on what they *believe,* and I think Nostradamus admired the strength of beliefs within King Edward VIII. I think the guy still held that royal glow by Nostradamus's standards, because Nostradamus referred to Edward as a king even though he wouldn't be one after abdicating.

Prince Charles and Lady Di

They're often considered the most royal of royals, and I'm guessing you've heard of them: Charles, prince of Wales, and Lady Diana Spencer. I think that had this couple read Nostradamus's prophecies and recognized Quatrain C X – 55 as relating to their lives, the path of history (and the heirs to the crown) could've been different:

> The unfortunate nuptials will be celebrated
>
> In great joy but the end unhappy:
>
> Husband and mother will slight the daughter-in-law,
>
> The Apollo dead and the daughter-in-law more pitiful. (C X – 55)

As the ages have moved forward, this quatrain has taken on several interpretations. The first historical event that seems to connect with this quatrain was the 1565 marriage of the widowed Mary, queen of Scots (her husband, King Francois II of France, died in 1559 after only a year of marriage) to Henry Stuart, Lord Darnley (a descendent of King Henry VII of England if you're keeping track). As for the husband and mother slighting the daughter-in-law, it was a well-known fact that Queen Catherine de Medici of France (Mary's mother-in-law from her previous marriage to Francois II) disliked Mary — but not nearly as much as Catherine disliked and distrusted Mary's cousin, Queen Elizabeth I of England. I see that Lord Darnley was a backstabbing snake in the grass of royal proportions (he became power hungry and helped organize a rebellion against Mary's rule) and that the ending of this marriage was most unhappy, but I don't think Nostradamus intended this in his prophecy. (Check out Chapter 8 for more on these folks.)

I believe that line 1's *The unfortunate nuptials will be celebrated* refers to an era much later than Mary's time in history and that Nostradamus's prophecy was finally fulfilled in 1981. During that year, Prince Charles married Lady Diana in a glamorous fairytale wedding, complete with an open-air coach to carry them away into the sunset.

Nostradamus didn't let the idea linger, though, and said in line 2 that the nuptials were celebrated *In great joy but the end unhappy.* After two children, many accusations of affairs, and rumors of royal instability, Prince Charles and Princess Di divorced. Both before and after the divorce in 1996, the queen and her son scorned Diana and criticized the way she lived and raised the two children. I think Nostradamus accurately predicted that both *Husband and mother will slight the daughter-in-law.*

The final line of this quatrain reminds me of the truly human nature of the tragedies Nostradamus described. Most of his quatrains are about the lives of countries, but these lines describe individuals and their personal tragedy. *The Apollo dead* is a typical Nostradamus reference to the ancient Greek god Apollo, who was the god of prophecy (a coincidence, I think not), purification, and healing. In this case, I think Nostradamus used Apollo to stand for prophecy — for the prediction of the happily-ever-after that comes with fairy tale marriages but is dead in this marriage.

While Diana was still alive, imagining anything more *pitiful* than the nasty and very public divorce she had just gone through was difficult. The tale continued just as Nostradamus wrote it, however, and the *daughter-in-law* died in a car accident in Paris, France, in 1997.

I believe Nostradamus knew the marriage of Charles and Diana would be tough. But the important thing to note is the impact these kinds of events can have on the rest of the world. Because the world insisted that Charles and Diana be ideal and not real, their particular fairy tale marriage didn't work. As time passes, it has become less important that Charles and Diana be a perfect model of royalty and more important that they are individuals who have importance beyond just their titles. Nostradamus predicted the demise of the elaborate fantasy of married life, but he didn't predict the death of marriage altogether. I think that in Quatrain C X – 55, Nostradamus predicted a shift in the changing image of marriage — something that fascinated and repulsed the man whose strong Catholic upbringing taught him a very clear definition of marriage. The stress Nostradamus described for the royal marriage can also be seen as a prediction for the stress other marriages will face. You and I should think about the 16th-century seer's concerns for the state of matrimony. (Check out Chapter 17 for more on Nostradamus's predictions for the future of marriage and the family.)

Saluting American royalty

Americans have never had their own royal family to obsess over, but we've gotten close. When Joseph P. Kennedy, a Boston businessman and local politician, married Rose Fitzgerald (the daughter of Boston's mayor), they began a strong family tradition of active political involvement during the early and mid-1900s, making the Kennedys as *nearly royal* as any American family can get. This political pair are the parents of a number of political children, including John F. Kennedy, the 35th President of the United States. In addition to having wealth and powerful connections, a large part of the Kennedy family's influence seems to have been rooted in the need to excel.

I figure Nostradamus probably foresaw the glint of the highly public and political lifestyle that would carry these people through history and was fascinated by their ability to make changes in how the world worked by holding public office (not just any office . . . senators, governors, and the presidency) and by encouraging both charity and the arts. I believe the Kennedys appeared in several quatrains because Nostradamus foresaw the numerous times they'd influence the fate of the nation and even the world.

Swimming against the tide with JFK

President John F. Kennedy shared a deep-rooted need with Nostradamus to help the people of the world live in peace with one another. I'm guessing Nostradamus thought writing about JKF was important because it was like one kindred spirit calling out to another across the years. I believe Nostradamus devoted several quatrains to this topic, including Quatrain C II – 57's tragic description of JFK's comet-like rise and fall from power:

> Before the conflict the great wall will fall,
>
> The great one to death, death too sudden and lamented,
>
> Born imperfect: the greater part will swim:
>
> Near the river the land stained with blood. (C II – 57)

Nostradamus's writing has a wistful and almost storylike quality in this quatrain. He began setting the stage with the phrase *the great wall will fall*. To me, Nostradamus meant a wall as an invisible barrier between those who rule or have political power and everyone else (kings and peasants for Nostradamus; the very wealthy and the everyday guy for you and me).

The invisible wall is the illusion that something is different about the people on the other side and that the difference (whether that is wealth, money, power, or royal blood) makes one person more special or important than another. But with John F. Kennedy, the wall appeared to fall away because people related to his seemingly ideal life with his wife and children and to the "good guy" image he projected. They were living in an ideal world that many wanted, and it was just kicked up a notch or two from regular life.

A quickie history lesson here to help you put into perspective why everyday people related so well to JFK: John F. Kennedy was born in 1917 and became the youngest elected president. His wife, Jacqueline, was a well-to-do woman who brought grace and fun (with the help of her young children) to the oval office. The period of JFK's presidency was nicknamed Camelot, a reference to the idea of knights in shining (or slightly rusted) armor who save the world and gentle ladies who show the world grace (the first lady encouraged arts and literature).

I believe JFK is the subject of line 2, where Nostradamus wrote the sad words *The great one to death.* These words accurately reflect the sudden assassination of Kennedy in Texas in 1963. As a charismatic leader, he had won the respect of many people worldwide, and they saw it as a tragedy that the man with so many ideas for change died so early in his career. JFK served 2 years and 10 months as president, or in other words, he lived through most of his term, or *the greater part.*

Other details within the quatrain seem to be very accurate — almost enough to make you suspect that Nostradamus had done a little time traveling (not really) to find out that JFK was *born imperfect,* with a bad back among other health problems.

Although the first lines of this quatrain seem to be a clear description about the life and death of JFK, the last line isn't quite as easy to bring into the light of understanding. But I'm going to explain my take starting with an extended *metaphor,* or a series of descriptions that use one item to stand for another:

- In the case of Quatrain C II – 57, I think the life of the Kennedy family is described as a river (the river of life is a common metaphor in literature). This river ties together the swimming in relation to JFK's life and the overall powerful changes a river can have on the surrounding land. Rivers mark and change the landscape where they exist, and the Kennedy family did the same with the social and political landscape.

- Surrounding the river of the Kennedy clan is a vision of *land stained with blood* that unfortunately matches the theme of untimely death and misfortunate birth defects. I think the blood on the land is a double pun for the following:

  - The blood of the Kennedys, who are said to be cursed and who have a tendency to die in dramatic ways.

  - The blood of the soldiers in Vietnam, a controversial war that caused riots in the United States and abroad. During his presidency, JFK helped momentarily diffuse the military tensions between the United States and the Soviet Union, which suggests he may have been handy when the Vietnam crisis boiled over if he'd lived to swim the full length of his life.

The words Nostradamus used in Quatrain C II – 57 aren't quite as harsh as the ones he chose for the war quatrains (the blood runs more freely in the beginning chapters of Part IV), and I think his word choice was intentional. To me, he wasn't trying to scare future generations into making a change; he was simply prophesying that an important leader would exist but die before he could further influence the world. I believe Nostradamus pointed out the lost opportunity for mankind as a reminder — a warning of sorts — that even though people are becoming more enlightened, overall, humanity still sometimes loses and misses people who could've been even more helpful.

Reliving dreams of Camelot gone

Quatrain C IV – 14 doesn't have the poetic ring of Quatrain C II – 57, and it also doesn't have the same impact on the heart. I think Nostradamus had a fairly good clue about events, and he predicted them with reasonable (although not amazing) accuracy in this quatrain. But the details don't focus the picture quite as clearly on John F. Kennedy as I'd really like:

> The sudden death of the first personage
>
> Will have caused a change and put another in the sovereignty:
>
> Soon, late come so high and of low age,
>
> Such by land and sea that it will be necessary to fear him. (C IV – 14)

To figure out the meaning of this quatrain, examine it line by line:

- ✔ **Line 1:** Certainly *the first personage* in this quatrain can easily be seen as the president (the first person in charge), but exactly which president it identifies isn't clear. *The first personage* can even apply to just about any head of a large organization or country. But I believe thinking in larger terms is safe here because Nostradamus wasn't likely to get a clear image of small, unimportant events. If you add a typical Nostradamus flair to the first line, then *personage* becomes a play on words that points to someone who rose to the top because of his personality. Some interpreters easily pin this quatrain on John F. Kennedy's life from the very first line, but I suggest you look at all the details.

- ✔ **Line 2:** The death in line 1 creates change and *put(s) another in the sovereignty* in line 2, which means that with the leader dead, another person steps up to be in charge. This idea fits neatly with the scenario of John F. Kennedy's death, which elevated vice-president Lyndon B. Johnson to the role of the 36th president of the United States.

- ✔ **Line 3:** As for line 3's *late come so high and of low age,* consider these facts:

- JFK came *so high* (gained respect) as a result of his delicate handling of the Cuban Missile Crisis (a situation in 1962 between the Soviets and the U.S. that nearly started that third World War Nostradamus predicted) so *late* in his short career as president.

- Compared to other U.S. presidents, JFK was *of low age* (very young) when he was elected.

✔ **Line 4:** To me, Nostradamus continued the reference to the Cuban Missile Crisis by remarking in line 4 that others would find it *necessary to fear him*. During the crisis, ships carrying nuclear weapons from Russia cruised toward Cuba, off the coast of Florida, before JFK's blockade of Cuba skillfully turned the boats around and sent them back, thereby avoiding nuclear war. I figure that to Nostradamus, turning that much potential destruction around was impressive, and that kind of power should be feared.

In Quatrain C IV – 14, I can definitely see a strong parallel between the life and influences of John F. Kennedy and the *great personage* described here. The trouble is, I can also see that the idea of a charismatic leader who dies, is replaced, and leaves his mark on the world isn't a particularly new and unique vision. With that in mind, I have an inspiring thought: Perhaps the point is that we often see value in people and things too little too late (like JFK) and the quatrain was written to demonstrate that people should be more aware of the good things as they're happening. Noticing the good parts of life can help us live with purpose and enjoy the benefits of our growth.

Two greats for the price of one

Nostradamus arranged his quatrains in a variety of ways to have different effects on his future audience, and I believe that Quatrain C IX – 36 pairs two U.S. presidents. Take a look at what the prophet had to say:

> A great King taken by the hands of a young man,
>
> Not far from Easter confusion knife thrust:
>
> Everlasting captive times what lightning on the top,
>
> When three brothers will wound each other and murder. (C IX – 36)

Even interpretations printed before 1981 indicated that the first two lines of this quatrain refer to an assassination attempt on someone other than JFK, so Nostradamus gets bonus points for conveying his message through multiple interpretations and times. As it happens, Ronald Reagan survived an assassination attempt by John Hinkley, Jr. *(the hands of a young man)* during the first 100 days of his presidency in 1981 by undergoing two hours of surgery — the *knife thrust.*

The *confusion* came in several places during this shooting:

- ✔ Initially, the president was believed to be unharmed because he thought that the pain in his side was perhaps a broken rib from being shoved into the limo by a Secret Service agent after the shooting. The confusion was cleared up when he coughed up blood and the driver redirected his route to George Washington University Hospital.

- ✔ The Secret Service escort was initially following the presidential limo to the White House and didn't catch the switch to George Washington University Hospital quickly enough to prevent getting separated from the limo (but after a slight detour they eventually arrived at the hospital).

- ✔ No one initially knew how badly the president was injured, because despite massive blood loss, he walked into the hospital. A chest X-ray showing the bullet 2 inches above his heart cleared up the confusion.

- ✔ The defense believed John Hinkley was insane, but the prosecution believed he was able to understand his actions. This confusion was never resolved and a jury found him not guilty by reason of insanity. Hinkley was confined to a mental hospital for the duration of his life.

Nostradamus used the phrase *Not far from Easter* to date this quatrain. March 30, 1981, was the date of the assassination attempt on Ronald Reagan, so to me, the first two lines of Nostradamus's prophecy gave in a few precise words the details of that very chaotic event.

Nostradamus said a lot in two little lines, but he had even more on his mind to share. The third line brings the focus to events on a more worldwide scale. *Everlasting captive times* may seem like a harsh description for the time Reagan spent in office, but the fact remains that a higher than usual number of hostage situations happened during his term in office. However, the negotiation efforts of the previous president, Jimmy Carter, were a strong factor in the release of captives in Iran after 444 days, shortly after Reagan was sworn in as the new president.

Most interpreters think that *lightning on the top* is a reference to the antennas used on televisions during the time of both the Reagan *and* Kennedy assassination events (both of which were highly televised — something that increased the public's feeling of involvement in both events). I agree that this idea seems the most plausible — that Nostradamus would've seen these strange items and described them as best he could.

If *lightning on the top* refers to a TV antenna projecting the assassination attempts, then I think lines 3 and 4 connect the *three brothers* to the Kennedy brothers, meaning that the Kennedy brothers *wound*(ed) *each another* by their deaths. Look at the facts: John F. Kennedy was assassinated during his term as president in 1963, and Senator Robert F. Kennedy was assassinated in 1968 while campaigning for president. The Kennedy family hoped that the third brother, Senator Edward Kennedy, would carry on the legacy of political power. But his political career was limited after a tragic car crash, in which a woman passenger died, and he was suspected of driving while intoxicated. I believe Nostradamus nailed these details down to the seemingly minor incident (historically speaking) of a car wreck, which turned out later to keep Edward Kennedy out of the White House.

I also think that line 3's *lightning on the top* may have an alternate meaning. Perhaps Nostradamus saw another important aspect of Reagan's life that influenced both world history and the ideas of individuals about health — his struggle with Alzheimer's disease, a degenerative nerve disorder that shows up mainly as increased memory loss of important and unimportant events and actions. The impact of this degenerative disease of the nerves (which run electrical charges like lightning) on a once very public figure brought the destructive power of this disease to the attention of the general public through reports on Reagan's health.

For a brilliant leader of a strong nation, I can easily imagine that his condition would've appeared to Nostradamus as *Everlasting captive times* — periods when Reagan was at the mercy and control of his disease and had to rely on people around him. If that was the case, then 16th-century Doctor Nostradamus may have also struggled to understand imagery related to neural pathways and misfired thoughts within the brain, and *lightning on the top* may have been his attempt at a description of the disease.

I believe that Nostradamus tied together the Reagan assassination attempt and the Kennedy assassination (along with mentions of JFK's brothers, who also followed a political path) to leave future generations a clue about how to change the world. Leading an entire country is a dangerous business. I think Nostradamus pinpointed these leaders, because, despite the risks, they tried to follow their ideals to make a change. I believe Nostradamus admired their determination and wanted people to notice them in the larger picture of history, so he included Reagan and JFK in *The Prophecies* to emphasize their importance among other movers and shakers in the modern world.

Playing Politics

I can't discuss politics over dinner, but Nostradamus seemed to think that anytime was the right time to talk about it. You may notice as you read through this section that the quatrains all involve major issues like war, peace, or alliances. I think the reason Nostradamus wrote prophecies about these issues boils down to one word: importance. I believe he looked ahead through time by *hundreds* of years, so the issues that showed up in his visions as important to the future had to be pretty big and go beyond the issues of daily life. Subtleties — like the average price difference between American and Chinese tea — weren't likely to appear in the prophet's visions.

The Hungarian Revolution

Nostradamus foresaw changes in the way the world would work, and most folks never notice that his prophecies have traced so many changes in the world. To me, Quatrain C II – 90 is a perfect example of the clues Nostradamus left about how the world would evolve into something totally new from the world he knew:

> Through life and death the realm of Hungary changed:
>
> The law will be more harsh than service:
>
> Their great city cries out with howls and laments,
>
> Castor and Pollux enemies in the arena. (C II – 90)

To get a good grip on this quatrain, follow along as I examine each line:

- **Line 1:** *The realm of Hungary* is very specifically named in this quatrain as something *Through life and death* changed. The way I see it, the quatrain isn't saying a person lives or dies, but rather freedom from communist control is living or dying. Hungary was a communist country. A revolt in 1956 attempted to shift the influence in Hungary, but the change wasn't quickly achieved. The Soviet Union sent troops and political leaders to quiet the revolt of the people who called themselves freedom fighters.

- **Line 2:** *The law* refers to the rule of the communists who try to keep very tight control over events, people, and the media. Nostradamus wrote that *The law will be more harsh than service,* which could be a reference to the idea that service (a way of working for something or someone else) seems more appealing than living under communist rules.

- **Line 3:** It's also possible that Nostradamus saw the Hungarians attack Soviet tanks with Molotov cocktails (glass bottles full of gas with a fuse made of a rag of cloth) in the 1956 revolt. These cocktails, and the mobs and fighting that surrounded them, could be applied to the phrase *city cries out with howls and laments.* The Hungarians were hurting physically, emotionally, and mentally from the struggle to maintain the war for independence. An additional layer of meaning in this line is that Hungarian leaders sent out radio pleas *(their great city cries out)* to the outside world to assist Hungary in repelling the Soviet troops.

- **Line 4:** I believe this line is a wonderful reference by Nostradamus to the Greek mythological twin characters of *Castor and Pollux.* These twins ultimately became the astrological sign Gemini (the on-again, off-again twin sign of the Zodiac). This sign is natural for the country of Hungary because the communists controlled this country until the underlying struggle with the opposite force, independence, gave way to a more democratic rule. In addition I think Nostradamus added another layer of meaning since the twins can also refer to the internal battle in Hungary between those people who wanted to remain part of the Soviet Union and those who wanted to become independent.

My interpretation of *the arena* is that it's a wide area used for conflict, like a playing field. In the battles of Hungary, the arena was the world, because the battlefield wasn't limited to Hungary — the struggle for freedom is something that many other countries have fought. During the 1956 revolt, Hungary called on other free countries — like the United States, France, and England — to assist them. Unfortunately, joining forces with Hungary would've meant a direct fight with the Soviets, and none of the bigger countries wanted to risk nuclear war over the smallish country. The struggle for freedom and the change from communism to a more democratic society and market-based economy traces a trend in the world of the diminishing rule of communism, something that would affect countries everywhere as Hungary joined this open market.

You probably haven't run a country lately or even had the opportunity to choose between democracy or communism. I believe Nostradamus used Quatrain C II – 90 to make the point that sometimes events in life aren't about the little people; they're about the bigger issues like maintaining personal dignity by being able to make free choices in an open society. Unfortunately, that idea doesn't really help the people who suffer for their ideas in situations that the world powers deem to be unimportant or too scary to handle.

The Spanish Civil War

Nostradamus sang a refrain from his favorite songs of France, Germany, and Spain in Quatrain C III – 8 with a foreboding twist that should've caught someone's eye:

> The Cimbri joined with their neighbors
>
> Will come to ravage almost Spain:
>
> Peoples gathered in Guienne and Limousin
>
> Will be in league, and will bear them company. (C III – 8)

I believe this quatrain tells the unfortunate prophecy of the growth of the Nazi (in Germany) and Fascist (in Italy) parties through the struggle of neighboring Spain. *Cimbri* is an ancient name for the race of people who ultimately settled in Germany. Nostradamus wrote that they would be *joined with their neighbors . . . to ravage almost Spain.* Many interpreters make sense of the last phrase of line 2 by translating it as *almost all of Spain.* That translation combines with the first two lines so that they read as "Germany and Italy will take control of Spain," which doesn't make sense unless you take a peek in the history books and see that Germany jumped into the Spanish Civil War during 1936–1939 to support the Fascist cause in that country (and to secretly test their war prowess).

Guienne and Limousin are adjoining areas of France. These regions ultimately became the retreat area for many of the French and Spanish soldiers who fought against the Fascists and Nazis during the Spanish Civil War, but these men found themselves under Germany's rule after the 1940 invasion of France. For the French soldiers, the men within these regions who had already fought Fascism would *bear them company* — the French were now in the same position as the Spanish had been at the end of the Spanish Civil War by losing the battles and coming under the control of the Germans.

The idea that Nostradamus predicted the Spanish Civil War and Spain's loss to the powers of the Nazi and Fascist parties should send shivers up your spine. I believe that Nostradamus saw, predicted, and told everyone that WWII was coming in a pre-prediction so clear that many could see the connection between Spain and France but couldn't see how these two ancient enemies would have something in common. The fact that France didn't learn from the fate of its neighbor and that the world didn't learn from the first World War (which set the stage for the second one by having a terrible peace treaty) show that humans tend to be a learn-it-themselves kind of group. That way of learning is both slow and painful, as is evident when Hitler was thrown into the mix. I believe Nostradamus was suggesting that people begin learning from history and from the actions of other people instead of repeating the same mistakes again and again.

The fall of the Berlin Wall

The original development of the Berlin Wall must've been something for Nostradamus to see in his nighttime visions, but the destruction of that same wall had to be even more striking. That monumental event is what I think Nostradamus recorded in Quatrain C V – 81:

> The royal bird over the city of the Sun,
>
> Seven months in advance it will deliver a nocturnal omen:
>
> The Eastern wall will fall lightning thunder,
>
> Seven days the enemies directly to the gates. (C V – 81)

With so many symbols in this quatrain, the best approach is to sort them out before putting the pieces together and gaining some meaning from this quatrain. Here's my take on the symbols:

- **Royal bird:** This bird is the eagle that was used as the symbol of the Nazi controlling party.
- **City of the Sun:** Nostradamus typically used this term to refer to Paris; the sun was commonly associated with the royal house of France.

✔ **Nocturnal omen:** This phrase either refers to a comet or to the Aurora Borealis, and it helps date the timing of the events.

✔ **Eastern wall:** Many interpreters insist that this term refers to the Maginot line (eastern boundary) of France from WWII. But the term could just as well refer to the wall that divided Eastern Berlin from Western Berlin.

✔ **Gates:** Gates typically symbolize the opening or closing of a space or time.

I believe that Nostradamus's prediction in Quatrain C V – 81 is a mixed bag of accuracy and confusion. Some of the elements, like those in the first line, sound very much like other elements within the *Prophecies* that I believe predicted events surrounding World War II and the struggles between Germany (bird) and France (sun). The time period is almost clear with a prelude *seven months in advance* of some sort of nightly sign — maybe a comet, a shooting star, or a significant astrological combination.

Lines 3 and 4, however, give me the impression that this quatrain is simply more applicable to the fall of the Berlin Wall in Germany. The wall that divided Berlin after World War II was intended to restrict access between residents of East Berlin (which remained under communist control) and free West Berlin. I believe the phrase, *the enemies directly to the gates,* was Nostradamus's warning that the act of separating people is an enemy of human development. I also believe that Nostradamus used *the gates* as a symbol for the opportunity that exists when a barrier between different groups of people is removed.

In Quatrain C V – 81, Nostradamus didn't clearly connect his message to just one event in history. But I think the message itself — that something is to be gained from dropping our walls (real or metaphorical) and working together — is clear and important enough for people to remember.

The changing face of communist China

Trade to and from China had been going on for hundreds of years by the time Nostradamus wrote his prophecies, but the government in China really didn't impact his life much. Fortunately for you and me, he wasn't limited completely by the knowledge of his own world, and I believe he recorded in Quatrain C IV – 32 the changes that would come to China in the 20th and 21st centuries and the power of individuals to make those changes:

In the places and times of flesh giving way to fish,

The communal law will be made in opposition:

It will hold strongly the old ones, then removed from the midst,

Communism put far behind. (C IV – 32)

Line 1 isn't a favorite among most interpreters — as far as I can see — because direct references to this line are few and far between. As for my interpretation, I see *places and times of flesh* as being one way of living and the *fish* as being a symbol of another, possibly Christian way of living. To Nostradamus, the *times of flesh* under *communal law* could've looked like a time without religion, or the spiritual cheerfulness of a connection with God. For those living under the rule of communism (*communal law* as it's called here), the freedom to express the inner beliefs becomes an almost religious experience, and it was a freedom people fought for very hard during the Tiananmen Square incident in Beijing, China, in June 1989.

It will hold strongly the old ones, then removed from the midst, is a phrase that so clearly sums up the attitudes toward communism within China that I must stand and give Nostradamus a round of applause. The people are very used to the control and influence of the communist government, so many of them fear change. These people are the ones who hold strongly to *the old ones* — the leaders, systems, and rules that have governed their lives for so long. In the end, however, these leaders, systems, and rules are declining, and many people in China believe it's time *Communism* (is) *put far behind.*

Quatrain C IV – 32 foretells the fall of Communist China. In recent years, the world has witnessed the first chinks in the Communist armor — from Tiananmen Square to economic and free market reforms. But it also relates a story from the past to the future about the power of the individual to make choices that can change history. During the Tiananmen Square incident, for example, one person stood in front of a line of tanks, and they miraculously stopped. In the face of the government and its military, one young man was willing to risk his life to try to prevent the useless killings of people protesting for a change in their government. For you and me, this quatrain is a reminder to keep a firm hold on the beliefs we've examined (the protesters at Tiananmen Square were mostly students seeking knowledge, but workers of every class were there) and step forward if a need arises to defend those ideas. Changes were coming, and I believe Nostradamus saw them ahead of time. I think that this quatrain offers solace to those people who struggle to change oppressive systems of government, whether it's communism in China or some other -ism in a newly formed country.

Chapter 16

Looking at Events in the New Millennium

*H*umans are a strange breed that tend to get worked up about the oddest things — like dates. By the amount of time news programs devoted to the topic of the millennium, you'd think it was something more than just the clock ticking from December 31, 1999, to January 1, 2000. It's as if the clock had been building tension for a thousand years, and at that culminating point, people were ready to . . . to do something.

The trouble was, nobody seemed sure whether the human population was going to become enlightened, explode, cease to exist, or simply have yet another New Year's Eve celebration. People were confused — that is, unless they read the works of Nostradamus, who predicted various events related to the millennium.

The quatrains presented in this chapter are some of the most engrossing because they refer to a time period you recognize as relatively recent. The events surrounding the end of the 20th century (the end of the 1900s if you're not good at keeping score), the change of the millennium, the September 11, 2001 terrorist attacks on the United States, and even the rapid spread of false Nostradamus prophecies have all made major headlines in the last 10 years — and again in this chapter.

Dating the millennium

Okay, from the looks of the title, I'm not suggesting you take the new millennium out for dinner and a movie. I'm taking a moment to talk about a touchy subject among the scientific community — the true, actual date of the millennium changeover. Because the current calendar began with year 1 (there was no year 0), the new millennium technically started on January 1, 2001 — at least that's what many folks say. For what it's worth, astrologically speaking, the millennium has been shifting for years now (Chapter 19 can give you more star studded details on the astrological ages), and neither 2000 nor 2001 was that spectacular or special in the grand cosmic scheme of things.

Millennium Madness

Remember how everyone acted just before New Year's Eve 1999 when we turned the corner to 2000 and the New Millennium? The fear of the changing millennium was almost like a sickness that only got worse as the event grew closer. For you and me, the millennium represented the challenge of making sure our computers would understand that time marches on after December 31, 1999 (which some shortsighted programmer in a dark room somewhere had failed to do). The millennium bug, or Y2K (year two thousand) bug, became the top story months in advance of the actual event as people raced to make sure they were ready.

Survival became a serious issue for many of the people who harbored doubts that the click of the clock's hands would come and go without much trouble. Some people stocked up on canned goods and fresh water in case widespread computer failure rendered everything from bank accounts to the electrical grid useless. And every charlatan and trickster used people's fear for profit by selling bogus items like charms to protect against the Apocalypse and special locators to guide alien ships on the day after.

With all the commotion, you may think the people in our generation were the only ones to ever worry about what tomorrow might hold. But, actually, the nightly news in 1999 could've just as well been the news from 999 AD, when farmers quit working the fields and all human industry came to a screeching halt after the Church said the end of everything was near. (Why work?) Every time a change of century or millennium has occurred, people have done some crazy things.

Nostradamus had some thoughts on the matter many years before as well. And he saw powers larger than your laptop at work. According to an astrological concept (which Nostradamus believed in), the year 2000 marked the point between the Age of Pisces (loosely 300 BC to about 1950 AD), when faith was most important and people lived by unquestioning trust, and the

Age of Aquarius (loosely 2050 AD to about 4300 A.D.), when reason, scientific explanations, and proven methods will be the most important, at which the influence of the Ages was *equal*. According to this concept, at the turn of the millennium, the world was balanced on a point of astrological significance.

The idea of a point in time is a little misleading, however, since the actual shift is more like crossing a street. You start on one side of the road called the Age of Pisces and cross the road until you find you are standing on the other side of the millennium called the Age of Aquarius. You've made a shift from one place to another, but it took some time. This makes pinning the date on the millennium prophecies very difficult. Regardless of the actual date of the millennium change, it seems only fitting that as the world slid into the age of science and questioning around the middle of the road (2000), people questioned the very science that controlled much of their lives (computers) but had a little bit of faith left over that everything would work just like the guys from the service departments said it would.

In times of trouble (war especially), people frequently look to religion, leaders, and anything else they can think of that seems official or has some sort of power. People want answers to their tough questions and are taught from an early age to turn to wise people. Many people turn to Nostradamus's prophecies for answers, and for some of those people, the idea that Nostradamus saw and predicted events hundreds of years ago suggests that the divine power he believed inspired him must have meant for these things to happen. Strange as it may seem, even in the middle of tragedy, it helps people emotionally (if not rationally) to think that a certain event was supposed to be that way.

Whether you believe people are born with certain abilities or learn everything as they grow up, a fact that rings true across all human nature is that when faced with a puzzle, people try to figure it out. For most of the world, the millennium was a great big, mysterious problem just waiting to be solved and Nostradamus gave it his best shot. Human nature, in turn, led to the millennium madness that ensued.

Weighing Whether 2000 Was the Beginning of the End

New Year's Eve, 1999. As some of us awaited Y2K glitches and others limited their expectations to monster morning-after headaches, still others spent time considering even larger issues that are still up in the air.

Many people associate the new millennium with the beginning of the end of time. And some people believe that in Quatrains C I – 48 and C VI – 44, Nostradamus gave today's world a heads-up on what to expect as the calendar moves from the 20th century to the 21st century. But controversy exists as to the true date of the millennium (see the sidebar, "Dating the millennium," earlier in this chapter if you care for the details), and astrologically speaking, the date is *really* fluid (one might even say it's watered down). Considering these obstacles, Nostradamus could've helped the world out by being a little clearer on his predictions for and date of the big event. But, alas, he wasn't.

As puzzling as the dark side of the moon

If you're seeing stars about what's going to happen as a result of the millennium change, relax, I can give you a few pointers and help you figure out what in the world Nostradamus was predicting. Some believe that his prophecies, this quatrain in particular, place the end of the world at the millennium, while other interpreters insist it's just a change of ages and nothing to get your blood pressure up about. Let's check out Quatrain C I – 48 for some prophetic answers:

> Twenty years of the reign of the Moon passed,
>
> Seven thousand years another will hold its monarchy:
>
> When the Sun will take its tired days
>
> Then is accomplished and finished my prophecy. (C I – 48)

Nostradamus went with astrology to date everything here. The *reign of the Moon* in line 1 refers to a cycle of the moon more along the lines of years (something called the *trithemian periodicities* if you really want to know) rather than its 28-day journey you'd typically think of. Nostradamus was probably referring to the cycle that began around 1535 (this lunar cycle is about 345 years). *Twenty years* into this cycle would accurately date the publication of *The Prophecies,* so methinks that in this quatrain, Nostradamus at least accurately predicted the publication date of his biggest work. (Nostradamus probably wrote this quatrain in 1554, so it still counts as predicting the future.)

Another layer of meaning is possible in line 1: Begin with the end of the lunar cycle in 1880 and add twenty years, making the date 1901 and the beginning of the 20th century. Nostradamus enjoyed his layers of meaning so much that I can't let this line go without pointing out one more possibility: The *reign of the Moon* could also refer to the beginning of his nighttime studies in prophecy where the moon was his companion.

As for the rest of the quatrain, the prophecy isn't crystal clear, and I'd like to find the predictions for the millennium simply by picking up a large, dusty astrology book and looking up the answers, but nothing is ever that easy with Nostradamus. You see, the trouble starts when you try to figure out when the *seven thousand years* (line 2) starts and ends. Several options are possible:

- ✔ Begin twenty years into the Moon's cycle in 1555, which puts the end of the new monarchy in 8555.

- ✔ Begin with the date of creation as 4184 BC (calculated by Nostradamus in the _Epistle to Henry II_), which puts the end of the monarchy in 2816 AD

- ✔ Begin with the current calendar's beginning, year 1, which puts the end of the monarchy in 7001 AD

- ✔ Begin with the date of creation as 5315 BC (a date suggested by Abbot Johannes Trithemius, whom that larger cycle of the Moon was named after), which puts the end of the monarchy in 1685, not nearly long enough to include all of Nostradamus's other predictions.

With so many options, making a decision is difficult. Fortunately, Nostradamus tried to narrow down the answer by adding in extra bits of information in line 3. His phrase, _the Sun will take its tired days,_ is perhaps a reference to

- ✔ The end of the sun's cycle, astrologically speaking, in the Age of Pisces as it begins to renew its energy in the Age of Aquarius (basically the time of today).

- ✔ The Christian ages, believed by the Christian mystic faithful to be watched over by angels. According to this belief, Gabriel is currently watching over us, and the next angel, Raphael, will begin his rule in 3652.

- ✔ The end of the sun's natural life span as a star, when it consumes most of its energy. The good news is the sun isn't supposed to get this tired for another 4 or 5 billion years!

Because Nostradamus focused on the influence of the stars on humanity, the change in the astrological ages (1950–2050 is the range and close enough to the millennium) may have been his meaning here. This meaning ties in nicely to the coming of the antichrist who shows up as the prelude to the end of the world predicted to begin in 1999 (see Chapter 13) and general superstition about the turning of the millennium. But Nostradamus mentioned in the _Epistle to Henry II_ that his prophecies predicted events through the year 3737, which is pretty close to the time for the angel Raphael. So Nostradamus may have been using his own date of creation as the timeline for this quatrain.

The question becomes whether the end times are associated with 2000 or 3737. Honestly, I don't think they're associated with either year, and for that matter, I'm certain Nostradamus didn't think the world would end at all. I believe that Nostradamus didn't prophecy the end of life but just life as we now understand it. How's that for a twist? The dates are intentionally broad to tell us that the changes will take time. The last line of Quatrain C I – 48 says that his prophecy will be finished, but he doesn't comment on the end of time, life, humanity, the stars, or anything else. Nostradamus placed a limit on his own knowledge and admitted that there was a limit to his own powerful visions — he couldn't see into forever. In the end, the shift of ages (the shift in astrological influences I discuss in Chapter 19) will lead to a powerful shift in people's perception of their own importance — which is most significant to you and me.

The monster beneath the rainbow

Nostradamus didn't stop with just one prophecy for the millennium. It was a big event, and he tried to cover it from every angle — especially the angle that gave him the most possibility of being accurate. Diving into Quatrain C VI – 44 ought to put some focus into your understanding of the big guy's vision:

> By night the Rainbow will appear for Nantes,
>
> By marine arts they will stir up rain:
>
> In the Gulf of Arabia a great fleet will plunge to the bottom,
>
> In Saxony a monster will be born of a bear and a sow. (C VI – 44)

Overall, this quatrain discusses the events associated with the third antichrist and the possible identity of one of the three antichrists, figures prophesied to make great change (for other quatrains about all things antichrist, check out Chapter 13). But it also gives some information about when the millennium will actually happen.

Since Christianity began, the antichrist has been the herald of the end of the world, the end of time, or the end of the millennium, depending on how you want to interpret the Bible. I leave that debate for the biblical scholars and just focus on the changes as Nostradamus pointed them out in the shift of the millenniums.

Line 1 is a very apt description of the Aurora Borealis, a display of brilliantly colored lights in the skies of the Northern hemisphere caused by solar wind (a stream of particles spit out of the sun like a geyser). The display of lights occurs about every 11 years and has been connected to and even blamed for strange events throughout history. Nostradamus would've been giving too many dates if he were referring to every time these lights would be visible. But he limited the date to the time when these lights would be particularly bright and seen in Nantes, France.

One of the brightest displays of the Northern Lights (as the Aurora Borealis is called) in France was on April 7, 2000. The lights have to be particularly bright to be seen clearly in Nantes because the lights are dimmer as you move away from the North Pole and toward the equator, so combining the city with the

Aurora Borealis was a clever way for Nostradamus to date the events in this quatrain to somewhere around 2000 — the time of the millennium. I believe the millennium date in this quatrain provided by the lights connects the third antichrist (who is due to arrive around 1999), as the introduction for the disastrous events in the quatrain predicted to occur after the monster's arrival. In this case, the monster is the antichrist.

Lines 2 and 3 discuss the wars and battles that will result from the changing of astrological ages (see Chapter 19) and the coming of the antichrist, but line 4 is truly the bearer of bad news. Nostradamus and the rest of the folks from the 16th century considered the birth of animals and humans with odd mutations (like two-headed children) to be signs of terrible events about to happen. They also believed the Northern Lights were a terrible omen of things to come, so technically, lines 1 and 4 were the bearers of bad news. Nostradamus connected the millennium to these strange portents to suggest that it will contain some unusual and possibly frightening things. What they are, the world will just have to wait and see, but I think Nostradamus gave these warnings to prepare people for the changes, which doesn't make sense if the world is just ending anyway. He gave the "be prepared because it's going to be rough, but we'll make it through to a better and brighter day" speech without so many words. The times they are a-changing, but he certainly doesn't say the times they are a-ending.

Sorting through September 11

Just mentioning *9/11* takes people's thoughts back to the date and events that kept them locked to TV sets in living rooms all over the nation. In addition to increased airport security (with the resulting delays) and increased military operations around the world, the attacks of September 11, 2001, led to other drastic changes. Americans now pay more attention to events and issues outside their own borders, and they have a different attitude (maybe not fully expressed, but still there) about the United States as a place safe from the dangers hounding other regions of the world each day. And although the events took place on one day instead of unfolding over the years, Nostradamus didn't miss a thing in that watery looking glass of his.

Following are quatrains that Nostradamus wrote in reference to the *new city*. With these prophecies, his voice was heard — as usual — after the fact. These prophecies require the same type of examination as every other quatrain, and for myself, I find that some of them hit close to home in predicting the events of September 11 while others are too vague — or just hoaxes.

A burning sky in New York

Most of the modern world probably knows the basic facts about what happened on September 11 in New York City, but how much Nostradamus saw becomes the question of the hour. You can find out by looking at Quatrain VI – 97:

> At forty-five degrees the sky will burn,
>
> Fire to approach the great new city:
>
> In an instant a great scattered flame will leap up,
>
> When one will want to demand proof of the Normans. (C VI – 97)

 First things first: Many interpreters agree that the *new city* in line 2 is New York City, but critics claim that the quatrains connected to September 11 (which largely involve the phrase the *new city*) aren't about New York. I believe in taking this on a case-by-case basis.

For Quatrain C VI – 97 the match between the *new city* and New York is a strong one. Having at least one agreed-upon point in this quatrain is important, because the rest of it seems to create some confusion. The confusion begins when someone presents Quatrain C VI – 97 as a prophecy that predicted the attacks on September 11. Whether this quatrain prophecies the attacks of September 11 depends on the individual interpretation of the pieces of the quatrain. I go through these pieces shortly, but overall, I believe that several pieces of the quatrain fall a little short of an accurate prediction if a literal interpretation of the quatrain is all you're using. If you're using a more figurative approach, then the prophecy has some strength, but not a great deal. After you begin to look at the facts and interpretations of Quatrain C VI – 97 you'll see that the literal connection is on shaky ground.

At forty-five degrees, which I believe is a reference to *latitude* (an imaginary line running around the Earth east to west that marks the distance from the Earth's equator), Nostradamus found a city on fire. But the *new city* of New York in line 2 isn't at forty-five degrees latitude. It's closer to forty degrees, but remember that Nostradamus's love for the stars didn't mean he was fantastic at astrology. He was occasionally mistaken in his calculations (see Chapter 6). Actually, no cities on the forty-five degree latitude line could be considered the *great new city* in Nostradamus's way of looking at things, so I believe he was just off by a few degrees on the location. Nostradamus's critics point out that as an astronomer, he should've been able to be more accurate. As an astronomer, perhaps he could've been more precise, but because he was also human and doing everything without a calculator, I'll allow him this error without deducting too many points from his grade.

The sky will burn seems to me a clear reference to fire above the earth, which is probably the best interpretation Nostradamus could find for towering office buildings on fire. The burning theme in the first line continues through lines 2 and 3, which makes me think that Nostradamus was drawing attention here for a reason. I believe Nostradamus used the repetition of fire to make the point that the changes starting in the sky (with real fire) would continue burning and would *approach the great new city* — meaning attempt to bring change and purification to the city. And then almost instantly, Nostradamus saw that a *great scattered flame will leap up* — meaning the same changes for the city would spark in other areas.

Viewed in this regard, this quatrain is a loose match for the attacks of September 11 and the changes in people's perspectives that resulted from the attacks within that city including a strong sense of patriotism, sympathy, and a realization of how quickly things can change.

For me, the effect of the *scattered flame* in line 3 of Quatrain C VI – 97 is important to comprehend. I think the fire that touched the Twin Towers in New York can symbolically be called vulnerability, fear, terror, or a simple adjustment of perspective. The terror part of this equation comes from not knowing when another attack might happen, along with the shocking idea that these attacks could (and did) happen. In addition, smaller sparks of fear and awakening went throughout the country and touched the far corners of the world. So I believe Nostradamus pointed out the *scattered flame* because he wanted the future to notice the impact one event can have. He wanted us to notice that our world is getting smaller and more connected. And if this interpretation is true, then in line 4, Nostradamus also suggested that we start making people answer for their actions *(one will want to demand proof of the Normans)*.

The busy man's guide to 9/11 quatrains

After the September 11 attacks, lots of folks did a fast and furious (and sometimes sloppy) reading of Nostradamus's prophecies to see whether he predicted the tragic events. Of the quatrains listed by the newly inspired readers, only a few have a vague hint of references that could apply to September 11.

Emotional reactions stirred up a furious search among *The Prophecies* for quatrains that matched and answers for why this kind of event occurs. I believe that in the case of Quatrain C I – 87 the connection is real, but in the other two quatrains I examine, people are trying too hard to make things match the prophecy and are ignoring major elements that Nostradamus would've probably included like the political and even the medical implications of the attacks. My interpretation of these three quatrains is relatively brief — compared to all the commotion — because space is limited and there are vast quantities of topics to be covered to provide an overall understanding of Nostradamus.

Making a connection to mythology

Here's one quatrain that may hit the mark:

> Volcanic fire from the center of the earth
>
> Will cause trembling around the new city:
>
> Two great rocks will make war for a long time.
>
> Then Arethusa will redden a new river. (C I – 87)

If you're working on a figurative understanding of this quatrain then the judgment of God (the *fire*) will surround New York *(the new city),* and the Twin Towers (one meaning for *Two great rocks*) will be the cause of a war lasting for many years. Arethusa is a mythological nymph (like a fairy) who was chased by a Greek god. To escape, she was changed into a fountain or river (depending on the story you read). In this quatrain, her waters are red, probably with blood.

In general terms, this could be seen as a prophecy of the attacks of September 11 and the subsequent wars as the *two great rocks* struggle for power. I tend to support this interpretation for two reasons.

- ✔ When Nostradamus brings rocks into the picture, they're typically a symbol of the religious ideas of a nation — the rock of faith as one common phrase puts it. In the case of the attacks of September 11, the rocks symbolize the religious differences between the two groups. I also see cultural differences in this struggle, but these differences aren't mentioned in the quatrain. Nostradamus was hitting the high points of the event, and I'm sure it's forgivable to skip some details.

- ✔ Arethusa ran from Alpheus (a Greek river god) to avoid being joined with him physically. But when she became a river, he swam underwater and mingled with her anyway. One of the reasons given for the attacks on America on September 11 was that Muslim extremists didn't want America's western culture mixing with their own strongly religious culture. By attempting to keep the two cultures apart (or even destroy one of them), however, the people behind the September 11 attacks produced the opposite effect. Troops and worldwide attention were brought into the countries where the extreme views originated, and the result has been a very real series of casualties, a river that is red with blood. The two worlds of beliefs, just like the two Greek gods, have mingled despite the intentions of the one running.

> The final piece of Arethusa's story includes her appeal to the goddess Diana to save her, and it's Diana who turns Arethusa into the river. One of the underlying tenets of the extreme faith of the group believed to have organized the attacks is a constant call on the power of God for help. I see a similarity between Arethusa calling on a Goddess and the extreme sect calling on their God. Nostradamus used the revived stories of the Greeks very effectively here to prophecy the events around 9/11.

Critics point out that Nostradamus could be discussing the eruption of a volcano called Vesuvius outside of Naples (originally called Neapolis meaning "new city"). A literal interpretation of these lines might give you that impression, but I believe Nostradamus included the Greek myth (originally used as teaching stories) as a clue that he intended this quatrain to be treated more like a figurative story than a literal one.

Be wary of the king

The September 11 interpretation for this quatrain relies on a figurative interpretation for the first part but the second part is pretty literal.

> The King will want to enter the new city,
>
> Through its enemies they will come to subdue it:
>
> Captive free falsely to speak and act,
>
> King to be outside, he will keep far from the enemy. (C IX – 92)

So, briefly, a man who believes he is better than others (the *King,* a terrorist leader) will try to take New York *(the new city),* and by working with America's adversaries *(through its enemies),* he will win *(subdue it).*

Lines 3 and 4 get a bit murkier, but I believe that the *Captive free falsely to speak and act* are people who believe themselves to be free but who act falsely anyway. The idea of the *captive* connects with the actual terrorists who were within America to carry out the attacks. They're portrayed figuratively as captives to the ideology that will lead them to commit the attacks on September 11. The *King to be outside* and *far from the enemy* is probably the same one from Line 1 and is the leader of the country or group wanting to enter the new city. This leader would look like a king from Nostradamus's 16th-century point of view.

I have my doubts about this interpretation of the quatrain. While the leader of the group that organized the attacks has been kept *far from the enemy,* I don't particularly see why he would want to enter New York if that's what the new city is supposed to represent. The leader and the groups behind the attacks on September 11 specifically want nothing to do with the commercialism and western culture of the *new city.* With this interpretive quandary in mind, I begin to suspect that the *new city* doesn't signify New York City, but rather a city like Naples. There are enough pieces within this quatrain that don't quite fit to make me doubt whether Quatrain C IX – 92 is really related to September 11. I believe Nostradamus may be concentrating on his own interests here by focusing on Europe.

Watered down meaning

Figuratively speaking, this quatrain may have a hint of prophecy about the September 11 attacks, but overall I think Nostradamus was pointing us in a different direction.

> Garden of the world near the new city,
>
> In the path of the hollow mountains:
>
> It will be seized and plunged into the Tub,
>
> Forced to drink waters poisoned by sulfur. (C X – 49)

Supporters of this quatrain suggest that the quatrain's figurative interpretation means that the World Trade Center in New York (a *garden* or market for the world) is the site of an event (water poisoning) leading up to the attack on the skyscrapers *(hollow mountains)* that will fall. But if you're trying to read through the quatrain, you'll notice that this interpretation takes things completely out of order.

Some interpreters find that the garden *near the new city* in Line 1 refers to the Garden State of New Jersey and the *hollow mountains* in Line 2 refer to the World Trade Center. These connections suggest that this prophecy is aimed at the 1993 attack on the World Trade Center when a truck loaded with explosives was left under one of the buildings. The *Tub* (or in some translations this is a Vat) could be Nostradamus's hint that there was something being cooked up or mixed, like the fertilizer and diesel fuel that was mixed to make the bombs. This would be one of those times that Nostradamus's knowledge of cooking and the apothecary (pharmacist) trade shows up in his writings. Line 4 can be interpreted several ways including as a hint that one bomb will poison the waters of New Jersey, that the people will be trapped in an underwater tunnel when additional bombs go off, or that the terrorists will find themselves in the death chamber.

There are enough connections here to the 1993 attack on the World Trade Center that I believe this was the event Nostradamus prophesied rather than the September 11, 2001 attacks. One of the things that leads me to strongly dismiss this quatrain as a September 11 prediction is that it doesn't contain information about the additional events surrounding September 11 such as the two other planes that crashed or the subsequent war that's part of the prophecy in Quatrain C I – 87. Nostradamus's visions were unpredictable, so making this kind of decision is a judgement call, but I think that despite the hype of fly-by-Internet interpreters, the connection to September 11 is overrated and this belongs with the 1993 events of the past.

Interpreters who match the *new city* with Naples have given an interpretation of this quatrain where the *garden* is understood to be the plain of fertile volcanic soil between Naples and Vesuvius. The quatrain is believed to prophecy the eruption of Vesuvius and the waters *poisoned by sulfur* are the result of this eruption. It's possible that Nostradamus was focusing on things closer to home (Italy and France being very much neighbors and connected economically and ecologically), but this interpretation doesn't provide a good explanation for the *Tub* in line 3 or the fact that the eruptions of Vesuvius have never reached all the way to Naples. In any case, although this interpretation makes a case for a volcanic eruption and terrorist attacks, it isn't a prophecy for September 11 and should be filed either among quatrains relating to the 1993 World Trade Center attack or to the collection of quatrains that have yet to be fulfilled.

Beware the hoaxes and hysteria

And now I find myself having to explain the strange behavior of my fellow humans. In the great drive to understand and find solace in Nostradamus's writings, unfortunately a great deal of *mis*understanding leads people to give Nostradamus a bad reputation for stuff he didn't write. This concept isn't something that just started. All the way back to Napoleon (see Chapter 10) and even to the court of Queen Catherine de Medici (you can meet her in Chapter 8) during Nostradamus's lifetime, people have rewritten the quatrains to suit their particular needs. Simply put, people have been borrowing and muddying Nostradamus's good name for hundreds of years.

One prime and particularly ironic example popped up all over the World Wide Web just hours after the 9/11 attacks:

> "In the City of God there will be a great thunder,
>
> Two brothers torn apart by Chaos,
>
> while the fortress endures, the great leader will succumb,
>
> The third big war will begin when the big city is burning.
>
> — Nostradamus 1654"

If you've read Chapter 3, you can probably pick out the biggest problem with this quatrain without any help. Nostradamus lived from 1504 to 1566, so any prophecies written after his death (like this one supposedly from 1654) either reflect a *really* unusual talent or just aren't real.

The truth is, this quatrain is a hoax, and a man named Neil Marshall wrote it while he was a student at Brock University in Canada. He wrote the quatrain (and then published it on his Web site) as part of a 1997 paper explaining that if a quatrain has enough vague language and general references, some event will eventually match it just by luck — not as a matter of prophecy.

Because it was freely available on his Web site, Marshall's quatrain found its way onto the gossip lines of forwarded e-mails. The people who copied the quatrain either meant to mislead people and stir up more controversy and trouble around the 9/11 attacks, or (and sadly I think this scenario is more likely) they searched the Internet randomly for quatrains related to New York and didn't bother to actually read the surrounding information.

I believe that hoax quatrains and other attempts to confuse the understanding of Nostradamus's prophesies are, at the least, disrespectful to a man who (whether he succeeded in prophecy or not) tried to leave a helpful legacy for humanity. Hoax quatrains should serve as a warning that not everything that glitters comes from Nostradamus.

Here are some hints to indicate that a quatrain isn't an authentic Nostradamus quatrain:

- Have doubts if the lines are entirely in English, with no reference of the original text exists. By this I mean quatrains that aren't numbered and where there's not even a glimmer of the original French. (I've kept to the English translations in this book simply for your benefit, but I've provided quatrain numbers for all, I reference the original French for discussion and interpretation at times, and I provide you with a list of additional resources in Chapter 22 in which you can find all the quatrains.)

- Check the date of the prophecy against Nostradamus's writing times (1554 to 1566).

- Check the quatrain number against a solid source to make sure the quatrain in question matches the same-numbered quatrain in the solid source. (See Chapter 22 for these kinds of resources.)

- Know and trust your source. The latest tabloid paper won't give you reliable information.

- Check the wording to see whether the quatrain uses a modern term that Nostradamus wouldn't have known like *(CD* or *rock 'n' roll).*

- Look extra carefully at any prophecy from Century VII, because it's the grouping that Nostradamus left incomplete.

- Question seriously any quatrain that isn't identified by both the century and the quatrain numbers.

Part V

The Prophecies of a Future Era

The 5th Wave   By Rich Tennant

"Let me give you a tip. Forget the racing form, try the quatrains in the third century."

In this part . . .

Part V goes where no reader (at least in this book) has
gone before — the future. Unfortunately time traveling
isn't possible, so instead, I take you through some quatrains
for the far future as I see them. In this part of the book,
you're probably anticipating the *denouement* — the big
event that ties up all those terribly annoying loose ends
from Nostradamus's other prophecies. If you believe
Nostradamus explained everything in his quatrains for
the future, you may be a little disappointed. Seems his
prophecies reveal our future lives as quite a cliffhanger.

Nostradamus's visions for the greatest changes to mankind
are framed by famine of the body and soul, diseases that
wipe out large portions of the world's population, issues
within the religions, floods a-plenty, and a few catastrophic
ecological disasters. But it's important not to get lost in the
details — or the downright danger — and to remember that
Nostradamus was looking at the big picture, which has a
happier ending overall than some quatrains may lead you
to believe. I'm personally betting on the treasure hunt of
clues within some quatrains that supposedly leads to
untold buried riches.

Chapter 17

The Future of Religion and the Family

In This Chapter

▶ Commenting on religion, again

▶ Evaluating changes in family values

▶ Examining attitudes about love and sex

*N*ostradamus was a learned man, but he was also someone who had a life and family of his own. He was inquisitive, and his interests went farther than just wars, royal family struggles, and politics. Nostradamus tried to discover as much as he could about *all* the topics that interested him, including the future of religious beliefs, marriage and the family, and the impact an individual's actions can have on himself and the people around him. The significance of the relationship between one man and one woman may seem small compared to World Wars, but Nostradamus (and the theorists of the Renaissance) knew that the smaller world (the microcosm) could be studied as an example of the larger world (the macrocosm). Knowing how to manage a healthy religious connection with God and emotional connection with family reflects on how society as a whole takes shape. The stronger the microcosm of the one-on-one relationship is, the stronger the larger world will be (in its relationships between different countries, religions, and ideological groups).

The topics in this chapter are personal, but they've remained on the top of people's lists of concerns throughout time. Nostradamus touched on these timeless topics in the quatrains within this chapter and went so far as to predict some struggles for the Church and for the family, and he ultimately gave some decent advice in the end.

Growing up, Nostradamus was exposed to a number of faiths and belief systems (see Chapter 4). With all these perspectives coloring his world, Nostradamus was motivated to seek out a sense of the divine and to continue his search for a connection to that greater power, or goodness. In addition to these personal influences, the power of the Christian Church was ever present in Renaissance society (see Chapter 2). For Nostradamus, all these influences were so strong that it was almost impossible for *The Prophecies* not to discuss the future of the religious life on Earth.

Seeing Religious Trouble on the Horizon

"May you live in interesting times." This phrase that most folks assume is a well-meant wish sounds close enough to a curse that I've always believed it to be one. After all, interesting doesn't necessarily translate as happy, productive, or even wealthy. The quatrains that apparently reference the 21st century fulfill this curse very neatly, but I don't think that's what Nostradamus had in mind when he wrote them. Put on your peril-sensitive sunglasses and look at one in particular — Quatrain C IX – 51:

> Against the red ones sects will conspire,
>
> Fire, water, steel, rope through peace will weaken:
>
> On the point of dying those who will plot,
>
> Except one who above all the world will ruin. (C IX – 51)

I see all the elements of a great spy novel: conspiracy, fire and explosions, deathbed confessions, religious strife, and the world in tattered pieces (which reminds me of the changes brought by the antichrist, which I discuss in Chapter 13). It's a good general description of the apocalyptic end of the world scenario and is very consistent with Nostradamus's other quatrains describing life during the great astrological change around the time of the millennium (right about now). Now all you need to do is identify the good guys from the bad guys. But if you think that's going to be easy, remember that Nostradamus's visions were colored with his opinions of the world.

For example, line 1 says the *red ones* will find themselves at the other end of a conspiracy by the *sects*. I take that line to mean that the world's major religions (other than Christianity, and I get to that next) will band together against the *red ones*. Now, don't make assumptions about what *sect* means; religions around the world have used the term to apply either to themselves or to newly formed religious groups. The world's major religions all started as small sects. Today, interest in religion has expanded and people are exploring the practices of ancient religious traditions from around the world. Many of these religions are considered smaller divisions or sects of one of the world's major religions, which include Islam, Judaism, Hindu, and Christianity.

Over time, the color red has represented anger, passion, blood, Mars, seriousness, and intensity — all of which I think Nostradamus saw in this color. Plus, I think Nostradamus saw in the color red the religious association of the blood of Christ and was indicating all the Christian churches (for the Catholic Church, he might have used Rome or the pope as a symbol).

The connection with the idea of Christ's blood confirms for me that Nostradamus saw trouble between the Christian churches and other world religions *(sects)*. Line 3 says that the non-Christian religious sects that band together will be *on the point of dying*. In other words, they'll lose followers or their leaders' power and influence will wane in the years to come. Some of these changes may, in fact, be the result of the shift toward the Age of Aquarius, an astrological time period that began its influence around the 1950s and will increase its influence until it's in full force around 2050. During the Age of Aquarius, the focus will be on valuing the ideas of science and personal knowledge over blind faith (see Chapter 19).

The end of line 2 suggests to me that peace will be present (presumably on the religious front) before the beginning of the religious struggles when the elements listed at the beginning of this line won't be faring so well under peaceful circumstances. These elements can hold a number of meanings:

- *Fire* can mean fast, dramatic changes (from alchemy), inspiration (from mystical traditions), and destruction (as a natural element).
- *Water* can mean emotion, insight (think of Nostradamus staring into his bowl of water, a tool he used for divination), meditation, and persistence.
- *Steel* can mean man's power to manipulate his environment by will, military might, armies, and personal power.
- *Rope* can mean connections (ties) to the past through necessity (rope is very useful to have) and the interconnected nature of things (rope twisted together to gain its strength).

Now let's put line 2 back together to understand what Nostradamus wanted us to see about the patterns of today. Together, these elements will be weakened through the period of peace. I think Nostradamus was pointing out the laid-back attitude people can have about religion during times of peace and that this way of thinking can weaken faith in the divine, along with our powers to seek improvement *(fire)*, personal insight *(water)*, will-power *(steel)*, and connection to the divine *(rope)*. People are more likely to try to improve these pieces of their lives when they're faced with financial or physical ruin rather than when everything is going just fine.

Line 4 falls victim to translation issues and has two valid interpretations:

- One person involved in this struggle will be ruined by the world or by the events of the world. If this interpretation is accurate, then I believe this person's ideas and faith have been ruined by the terrible acts humanity has committed.
- One person will rise above all others in the upcoming struggle and become the one who ruins the world. Nostradamus interpreters frequently see this figure as a leader of nations, a historical figure (like Hitler), or even a thought or idea that could undermine the ideas of people and bring everything crashing down.

I believe this quatrain records religious trouble for the time of the new millennium, and I see strong connections between the words in line 2 and the religious struggles in line 1, not to mention the rather depressing insight (someone ruined by the world, or vice versa) in line 4. Anyway you slice this quatrain, the religious unrest and lack of faith are part of the prophecy that Nostradamus intended as a warning for the dangers of a lack of faith.

Sometimes people need a good challenge to bring out the best within. Quatrain C IX – 51 warns that the coming of worldwide religious peace may not bring with it the ideal calm you may imagine. It's also a warning that the refuge most people find in religion may not be a great idea. I think Nostradamus used the battle between the religions to point out that people should take refuge in the individual's role in religion.

Meeting a Leader Who Will Shake the Foundations of Faith

The nightly visions that moved Nostradamus through his prophecy process were touched and inspired by the insight of God — or at least that was Nostradamus's intent. For another idea of the changes that Nostradamus saw coming down the pike, look at Quatrain C I – 96:

> He who will have charge of destroying
>
> Temples and sects, changed through fantasy:
>
> He will come to do more harm to rocks than to living people
>
> Because of the din in his ears of a polished tongue. (C I – 96)

He who will have charge was Nostradamus's way of identifying one man who, as a leader, will impact and change the path of human spiritual development. Pretty heavy stuff. I believe Nostradamus referred to one person and not an idea because he didn't beat around the bush with descriptions, and he used the reference to a single person throughout the quatrain. Recognizing this point makes a heck of a lot of difference in understanding this quatrain.

That person, who interpreters have identified as various leaders of several modern religious movements, will be *destroying / Temples and sects*. That's an odd thing for a religious leader to do because most spiritual paths teach tolerance. But Line 2, in its entirety, makes the reason for the destruction clear: The *Temples and sects* will have been *changed through fantasy*. I think the *fantasy* may be the belief that money or another person is necessary to connect the individual and God (or the name of the divine that works best for you). I believe this idea, along with the notion that churches will stray from the truth into a land of fantasy that no longer reflects the true beliefs of their religion, are the important ideas Nostradamus tried to convey here.

At first glance, this leader doesn't sound like he'll be on a good mission if he's going *to do more harm to rocks than to living people,* but Nostradamus was rarely that literal. I think the *rocks* in line 3 refer to the rock-solid foundations of the religious institutions that have existed through the centuries. The leader will damage these foundations (which will already be different from their origins because fantasies will have changed them) by undermining them, or bringing doubt and questioning to the faith.

I don't think Nostradamus meant that the leader will directly attack, so don't think in terms of guns and car chases. More likely, the leader will wear away established patterns of faith by asking questions that aren't easy to answer — a quality of the climb up the Kabalistic Tree of Life (an explanation of which is planted in Chapter 4) toward enlightenment and the astrological change into the Age of Aquarius (where knowledge is valued over faith; see Chapter 19). But Nostradamus left us with a comforting note that the damage (I know insurance agents are cringing) will be to the churches and not to the people — *more harm to rocks than to living people.*

What a relief! During the Age of Aquarius, faith will take a backseat while the focus will be on facts. I believe that the leader will ask questions about why religions exist and what purpose they serve when people can have a personal connection with the divine. The world may lose a bit of its enthusiasm for faith, and in this way, the churches will lose some followers as they begin to seek answers from science rather than from God — a recognizable shift into the Age of Aquarius. Facing these challenges may cause some struggle for the churches, but the Kabbalah teaches that these challenging times will help people to achieve a balance of thought and mind, something central to the idea of the Kabbalah.

The time period for exactly when this person will come to change the world's religions seems a little vague, but the reason for his appearance is clear to me: The modern advertising of churches through slick newspapers, television, flyers, and even bumper sticker art *(polished tongue)* will stir up a deep, troublesome idea that this isn't where religion started and isn't where the spiritual path should end up. I believe that Nostradamus timed the appearance of the leader with the change of the millennium and the Age of Aquarius because he saw that the state of religion would be in serious need of fixing, and the leader would be the one to *do more harm to the rocks* (religions) and hopefully straighten them out by challenging the false attitudes of churches.

So, lookout for religious leaders that question the status quo and insist on making changes. Forced change isn't a good idea, but introducing challenging ideas and reconsidering old habits can lead to personal and spiritual growth on many levels. Unfortunately, these leaders are often silenced because humans are reluctant to change. The polished tongues that are present in Quatrain C I – 96, however, don't sound like they're necessarily delivering the truth. Whether changing the status quo is good or bad depends on humanity's response, but we'll never know the possibilities if we don't try.

Following A New (Old) Path

Nostradamus's worry that the people of his time were only going through the motions of religious conviction pervades his writings. This concern was echoed in Quatrain C II – 8, and examining the contents can clarify a very surprising turn of religious events in Nostradamus's eyes:

> Temples consecrated in the original Roman manner,
>
> They will reject the excess foundations,
>
> Taking their first and humane laws,
>
> Chasing, though not entirely, the cult of saints. (C II – 8)

The exact nature of the temples mentioned in line 1 is ambiguous, so a quick history lesson is in order: During the last century B.C. (100 BC to about 31 BC), under the rule of Julius Caesar and Augustus, the Romans conquered one area after another to create their great empire, and they did something few conquerors ever did — they allowed the people to keep their native beliefs. The soldiers even brought some of those beliefs back to Rome so that the temples there represented the different people's religions.

Not only did this approach make the conquering easier (because not a lot changed from the people's perspective), but it also broadened the scope of religious understanding in Rome. (I should point out that the conquered areas did have to acknowledge and make sacrifices to the Roman gods as part of their payment for being a part of the Roman Empire.) Rome became one of the original homes for religious tolerance until the Emperor Nero (54–69 AD) began to show less tolerance for local customs. Early Christians faced persecution, but in 313 AD, Christianity became the official religion of Rome under Emperor Constantine I when he signed the Edict of Milan.

The native religions that returned to Rome with the soldiers (and were then later outlawed) were considered to be pagan. The term *pagan* originally meant any uneducated or unsophisticated farmer or earth-dwelling peasant (what we may call a hick or a redneck). Because many of the religions that Rome encountered were based on the seasons, and the gods of fertility and harvest came from the countryside, these religions' belief systems became intertwined with the original term *pagan* so that today they're used to mean the same thing. So I think *Temples consecrated in the original Roman manner* refers to the religions and temples of Rome and was Nostradamus's way of reminding people that a time existed before Christianity when all religions were sacred.

According to Nostradamus's visions, these original temples *will reject the excess foundations,* which I believe means that these ancient faiths won't follow the basic ideas that lead other religions (mainly the Christian

Church from the Renaissance) toward wealth and power — the foundations that kept the Church a major influence for so long. I think the *excess* mentioned in this quatrain can only be the opulence, wealth, and acquisition of material goods by some of the clergy. The Church itself had some great ideas, but the men within the organization — the cornerstone of the movement if you look at it that way — weren't immune to the seduction of power and money.

Lines 3 and 4 say that these temples will be *Taking their first and humane laws* and *Chasing the cult of saints*. I'm amazed that a man like Nostradamus, who was very devout in his own Christian faith, recorded and even foresaw that other religious paths would answer the needs of people in the future.

As for *Chasing the cult of saints,* I believe Nostradamus gave a clear prophecy of how he thought the Catholic Church would stray from the relationship to divinity through Jesus Christ (with *excess*) and instead begin to rely on a number of saints and other religious figures. From Nostradamus's point of view (with all that Renaissance influence), the saints and excess would act as a way of diluting the actual worship of God, which leads me to conclude that for him, faith was truly about the ability to connect with God without all the trappings of silk hangings, large churches, and heavy *tithes* (a percent of a person's annual income paid to support the church and it clergy).

The new world, Nostradamus suggested, will find itself facing older religions rather than newer ones. These older religions won't quite chase the new ones out of their place in society, but they'll probably give them a good run for their money, because the older religions emphasize the personal connection with the divine that was part of the early Church before the excess led to too many trappings and rituals in worship. Ultimately, I believe Quatrain C II – 8 suggests that whether your path is Christian, Jewish, Muslim, or pagan, the modern time is a good time to return to your powerful inner connections with the God that guides you.

Getting Back to the Basics

Although Nostradamus wrote many quatrains dealing with the major religion of his time — Catholicism — he couldn't escape a few parting comments about those other upstart religions, who I think he was referring to in Quatrains C III – 67 and C III – 76.

For this discussion, you just need to look at the first two lines of C III – 67, which say that *A new sect of Philosophers / Despising death, gold, honors and riches* will come to prominence in Europe. Interpreters have traditionally translated these new philosophers as a new religion or a resurgence of the Protestant and Lutheran sects that grew during Nostradamus's lifetime.

(Check out Chapter 2 for the religious rebellious scoop.) I believe, however, that Nostradamus used his love of layers to refer to two issues:

- ✔ The new forms of religion that would move into the world of the future.

- ✔ The world of *alchemy,* which by its very nature led people to avoid death (alchemists were at least partially seeking eternal life), gold, honors, and riches. In the traditional sense, alchemists sought the items identified in the quatrain only as part of the journey to the final goal of obtaining a divine connection (especially true for Nostradamus) and immortality.

Along with the growth of the purely religious sects that will guide mankind, I believe Nostradamus suggests that alchemy and some of the stranger arts will find a place in this new and strange world of the future. After all, the mystical traditions worked for him, so why wouldn't they work for everyone else? This is the dawning of a New Age.

But Nostradamus didn't seem able to maintain a straightforward opinion on how all these changes will occur. In Quatrain C III – 76, he appeared rather convinced that Germany will be the seat of some drastic changes that directly relate to pagan paths, which lead only into trouble:

> In Germany will be born diverse sects,
>
> Coming very near happy paganism,
>
> The heart captive and returns small,
>
> They will return to paying the true tithe. (C III – 76)

In lines 1 and 2, Nostradamus wrote that the *diverse sects* of religion that will be conceived and *born* will be *coming very near happy paganism.* The phrase *happy paganism,* however, seems ironic coming from a devout Christian. I can't help but believe that he was in fact talking tongue in cheek about the false happiness that he felt pagan religions promised. Through dealing with rural people, Nostradamus probably developed a certain respect for their ideas, but I also believe he viewed them as backward and distant from the true salvation of Christianity.

You can clearly see this concept in the last two lines, where Nostradamus pointed out that the *heart captive* (presumably the imagination, hopes, and dreams) will find that for everything the pagans have sown (planted the seeds of) in their religion, they will find *returns small.* In other words, the investment of heart and soul in the false paganism won't yield the answer to the people's spiritual needs, and the pagans will return to what Nostradamus calls *the true tithe,* giving homage and honor to the Christian Church.

On the surface, Nostradamus appears to have been truly confused about the future of religions, but I don't think he was. I think he was simply concerned and tried to use the images of his own time to give future generations a hint for fulfilling their own places in the universe and for finding a spiritual home.

Nostradamus's seeming admiration for the original Roman manner in which religious sects grew was just his way of saying that the time is right to get back to basics and quit concerning one's self with money and material wealth. True wealth, he believed, came from the search for closeness to God (sometimes through alternative means, like alchemy or even ancient pagan practices that honored God's creation), and his message to people of the modern era was that the key to getting closer to God isn't through the Church or society as they exist now.

Instead, some sort of change must occur before enlightenment can happen. And to him, people's enlightenment is tied to the Age of Aquarius, as well as to the pathways of the Kabbalah leading to the top of the Tree of Life. I think these are the ultimate goals Nostradamus saw for humanity, and he was warning future generations that the change isn't going to be easy. Some people who could help will probably be imprisoned and ignored, but eventually the people of the world will regain their senses and listen to the new ideas — even if they're frightening.

Changing the State of Spirituality

Ah . . . and now you get to the heart of the problem that Nostradamus saw in his visions. Although he had Jewish ancestry, Nostradamus was first and foremost an upstanding Christian kind of guy, and the Church was the major influence in his prophecy. He gave credit to the Christian God for all his humble prophecies, including the one about the troubled Catholic Church in Quatrain C I – 43:

> Before the change of Empire occurs,
>
> A very marvelous event will take place:
>
> The field moved, the pillar of porphyry
>
> Placed, transferred onto the knotty rock. (C I – 43)

I think *the change of Empire* is a phrase that refers to the general state of humanity or a country — especially because Noatradamus used a capital letter to spell *Empire.* In this case, I believe it's the state of man's spirituality, which for Nostradamus was tied closely to the state of the Church. The *very marvelous event* (that) *will take place* was something that Nostradamus seemed to be quite excited about. I believe he anticipated the *change of Empire* and the changes beforehand to be leading somewhere positive.

As for the rest of the quatrain, I can only find meaning through delicate guesswork, because I don't believe the great change has happened. The events listed, if taken literally, will be quite the engineering feats, because a field will move and a pillar will be created from a rare rock formation. *Porphyry* is a rock consisting of red, green, and purple crystals. These colors, and the reference to the crystal formations, may be an indication that Nostradamus was remarking on an alchemical change, or yet another way of removing the impure pieces of humanity and reaching the golden state of immortality — goals for both alchemy and Christianity. These colors are also present along the path of enlightenment or the Kabbalah.

Note that Nostradamus also associated porphyry with changes in the Catholic Church in Quatrain C X – 93. That quatrain says the pope will travel the world and may be forced to move the seat of the Catholic Church from Rome. The new location will be near *Arles, will retain the hostages, Near where two columns are found of porphyry* (Quatrain C X – 93). Placing the Catholic Church in Arles would mean a major move in religious power to within the borders of France, something that may be a pipe dream for Nostradamus who loved France and his faith. Still, it's something that Nostradamus saw such a major move in the central power structure of the Catholic Church.

So based on both quatrains' references, here's my take on the whole porphyry association: I believe the colors purple (the royal color used by some churches during Lent to represent penance), red (a color closely associated with blood and the sacrifice of Christ), and green (the color that represents Spring and the ever-present life after death) from the rare porphyry rock formation were clues from Nostradamus that people should pay attention to these aspects as the new spiritual Empire emerges (in a new location?) and begins to focus on the topics these colors symbolize.

For Nostradamus, the future of the Christian Church seemed closely connected to the idea of penance (although he didn't say for what exactly), the sacrifice of things people think give them strength, and the renewal of faith in the coming Age of Reason (the Age of Aquarius). I'm sure Nostradamus foresaw the wars and atrocities of the modern era (and the erosion of the ideals of the Christian faith) and found it necessary to tell the people of the world they're ruining their own futures. The colors red, green, and purple and their symbolism were important to Nostradamus. I believe he pointed them out so that when you and I see the drastic changes within and without of the Church, we know that ultimately they're for the best. Knowing which areas to concentrate on is also helpful to make the kinds of changes Nostradamus suggested.

Changing Family Values

As you've been reading this book, it probably seems as if Nostradamus's prophecies cover just about every imaginable topic. But I haven't even touched on all the topics Nostradamus addressed. I believe that Quatrain C VIII – 63 discusses one of the rarer topics for Nostradamus — the state of the family and the life of the average person within the 21st century:

When the adulterer wounded without a blow will have

Murdered his wife and son out of spite:

Wife knocked down he will strangle the child:

Eight captives taken, to choke without respite. (C VIII – 63)

Nostradamus's critics often level their attacks at the vague and general nature of his wording, and this quatrain gives these particular doubting Toms a good starting point because no pieces are specific to a time period or person. The ideas expressed, though, are adultery, murder, the death of a child (although I don't think death is literal), and people taken hostage. Unfortunately, history finds itself full of times like the ones described in this quatrain. The lines of the quatrain are a small story within themselves, telling the tale of betrayal and the consequences.

This quatrain begins with an ominous image in line 1 with the phrase, *When the adulterer wounded without a blow.* The actual identity of the adulterer is left to the imagination and could stand for a married man in general (a kind of archetype). But the idea of making promises or vows as you would if you were married and then breaking them with adulterous actions creates the tension between the people and their expectations in this quatrain. I believe the wound that's inflicted without a blow is against the adulterer, but not to the adulterer's body. The blow is to his pride or sense of self. You may find it strange that the adulterer would be wounded. But from the perspective of Nostradamus, a religious and family man, an adulterer probably has a need within himself that isn't met, which is why he commits adultery and thereby harms himself as one of God's children and his family.

In line 2, you witness the adulterer's emotional reaction as he finds a final ending *(Murdered his wife and son out of spite)* to the trouble within his life. The adulterer has already caused himself pain in line 1, and now he uses *spite* as a reason for his murders, which I believe are metaphorical and not literal deaths. The ideal of a wife and son are shattered when adultery destroys any notion of trust and honesty. Nostradamus certainly seemed to provide social commentary in this quatrain, because the man who has an affair is associated with crimes much worse than extramarital sex. Everyone is wounded in the process. The adulterer becomes a victim of his own crime by damaging his moral self and is then lowered even below adultery to the level of a criminal when he takes that rage out on his own wife and son.

The themes of disrespect and self-damaging behavior continue in line 3 as the man knocks down his wife and *strangle*[s] *the child* — both metaphorical actions rather than real actions in my opinion. In line 3, Nostradamus seemed to repeat the same events in the story in a slightly different manner. Repeating events within a quatrain wasn't Nostradamus's style, and I think he spoke about the archetype (ideal example of a type of person) of husbands and wives in line 3 as a way of commenting on relationships in general rather than on just one family's story. The struggle that starts the trouble is adultery — physically cheating on one's spouse — but cheating can be defined in multiple ways. Cheating can mean having a confidante who never touches you physically but has an intimate knowledge of your mind, or it can even involve not telling your spouse about your longing to take a pottery class. The consequences of cheating as laid out by Nostradamus's prediction are fairly severe. Not only do the adults in the situation suffer, but so do the children and, ultimately, so do the social standards.

Line 3 says that the adulterer *knocked down his wife,* but this happens after he murdered her (assuming of course that the events occur in chronological order as presented in the quatrain). It makes more sense that he's knocking down her station in life or her position as wife (the archetype) by having the affair and committing these other crimes. Along the same lines, Nostradamus also listed one of the crimes as *strangling the son,* something I think the adulterer accomplishes by creating a bad reputation that would limit (or *strangle*) the son's opportunities to earn a living or learn to be a decent man.

Beyond children having to deal with the uncomfortable results of adultery, I think Nostradamus attempted to point out a larger social issue for his own time and for the future. Simply put, the *child* reference doesn't have to be literal; it can be a layer of meaning that's more than what it seems — a metaphor for ideas and values that people pass on to the future as a kind of social child. The personal dishonesty that exists within and among people is a kind of adultery that can harm the metaphorical children of society, the next generation. Here's my thinking a piece at a time:

- Each person is responsible for her own actions and relationships (to other people, to God, and so on). When people don't admit to their true feelings, all their relationships fall downward.

- The metaphorical children of these unions — the ideas, products, and futures from any combination of these people — will naturally reflect the qualities of the parents.

- If people have negative and suspicious thoughts, the world and the future (which are reflected on and found in the children) will also have suspicion.

I sense that the final line was Nostradamus's way of making the quatrain distinctly related to the 21st century. The word *captives* would make a six o'clock news program in every city in America if the people are public figures or international figures. But I believe that the people who are captive are everyday people trying to have regular relationships. I believe that the people in this quatrain symbolize the families around the world that struggle with the issue of adultery, honesty, and integrity. They're captives within potentially harmful relationships.

Eight captives could be any number of things, including real people, nations, or my personal favorite concept — the idea that the seven deadly sins, along with the general viciousness of wars (which Nostradamus described in other quatrains), will *choke without respite* the people who live in these times. Nostradamus was fond of using numerology (dial up more info about this topic in Chapter 6), so the fact that he mentioned the number eight adds a layer of meaning to the quatrain. Eight can be associated with infinity (Christian mysticism), receptivity or the true name of god (Jewish mysticism), or someone who is money-oriented or stern (alchemy and other mystical traditions). For my dollar, I'd bet that Nostradamus used eight to indicate that the money-oriented and stern concepts from alchemy (a mystical practice) would contribute to keeping people captive in the situation (especially the family) and choking out religiously loft ideas of infinity or of being receptive to the true name of God from the marriage, the people, or the situation.

I believe that Nostradamus's point in Quatrain C VIII – 63 was that understanding the message is more important than knowing the history of the people who created the state of affairs concerning present day family values. The values people live by each day will continue to follow them farther than they may imagine — quite a reminder to remember the larger picture beyond daily events. Nostradamus also reminded us that everything we do, like having an extramarital affair or not living up to our own moral standards, affects us and the people around us. We're part of a community, and every action has a ripple effect through the people around us. My version of this warning: Think before you act.

Shifting Attitudes Toward Love and Sex

Okay, just a little over the risqué edge is Quatrain C VIII – 25, which I believe is about changes in relationships that Nostradamus foresaw:

> The heart of the lover opened by furtive love
>
> Will cause the Lady to be ravished in the brook:
>
> The lustful woman will feign half a hurt,
>
> The father will deprive the body of each of its soul. (C VIII – 25)

I don't hear the divine inspiration of Nostradamus's nightly visions in this quatrain, but I do hear the long, consistent story of love and mistrust among men and women and Nostradamus's concerns about how these relationships are handled. Nearly every famous person (and lots of people who aren't famous) has had or has been accused of having a *furtive love* that the public wants to discover. The *Lady to be ravished in the brook* may seem quaint, but she's a *lustful woman,* and during Nostradamus's time, this kind of sexual activity would've meant the ruin of the woman's life and livelihood. The *lustful woman* isn't without her share of the blame, however, and she commits a kind of crime to *feign half a hurt,* which denies her true feelings. The end of line 2, in which the woman is *ravished by the brook,* may not be quite as literal and lecherous as it sounds. A lady's reputation could be metaphorically ravished or even ripped to shreds by the babbling brook of gossip during Nostradamus's time and even into modern times.

Here, each of the lovers is responsible for his or her actions within the event, but Nostradamus only mentioned the woman. The reason was probably because women were much less likely to find a decent living (or marriage — it was the same thing back then) if they were known to be sexually active or if the protective seal of a family's guardianship had been broken.

The final line brings the story of lovers caught to a close. The statement *deprive the body of each of its soul* tells me that Nostradamus thought this kind of outside influence to keep these lovers apart was a really good idea. The loss isn't just love, according to Nostradamus. It's the very soul of the people involved, something his devout heart and mind would've been concerned about.

I view this quatrain as Nostradamus's commentary on the slippery nature of relationships and reputations and the care that must be taken to protect both. For Nostradamus, the responsibility to protect these things lies within *The father* from line 4, which could be a reference to the guidance a priest may offer before a wedding or in marriage counseling. Some interpreters relate this quatrain to specific ladies and their lovers who have been denied a relationship or marriage by protective fathers, but I can't find enough detail within this quatrain to make it stick to a specific lady and her love. I think the quatrain is speaking about relationships through time, which I don't think Nostradamus saw changing much over the centuries.

A man from the 16th century believed he was able to send messages to the future about behavior, war, disease, and even natural disasters, but he chose to comment just for a moment on the relationships among men and women. Why? Who knows? Nostradamus brought this matter to attention in Quatrain C VIII – 25 and pointed out that troubles are to be had in the system of courtship and marriage as it exists. But he didn't make any real suggestions about solutions that might equalize this situation. The only possible suggestion he made for the future relies on *The father* being interpreted as a religious figure that becomes involved in the relations between men and women and adds divine guidance and advice for the relationships' success.

Chapter 18

Foreseeing Disasters in Our Future

....

In This Chapter

▶ Fearing famine

▶ Watching for changing weather

▶ Facing new plagues

▶ Getting struck by natural disasters

....

*W*e're all self-absorbed when it comes to the whole survival thing. And I think rightfully so. Since man first stood upright and tried to take his first steps (no cameras or cooing parents there), he has had an ever-present desire to hold power over the universe. People want to know that their lives are in their own hands and that they have the power to make changes. What scares me and seems to have scared Nostradamus, though, is that when given choices that could significantly alter the fate of the world, people have walked some pretty scary pathways that have clearly posted "Don't go there" signs. Even so, I don't think Nostradamus foresaw that people would be the only cause of major events happening on Earth during the next several hundred years.

This chapter walks you through quatrains covering elements of nature that (along with mankind's own destructive tendencies) could spell the end of the human race as we know it. According to Nostradamus, mankind seems to be facing a number of dangers, including starvation, flooding, drought, a plague that kills even the most Godly among men, and an Earth-shaking beginning to the rule of the third antichrist. I have to admit, this world scares me a bit.

Connecting Overpopulation and Famine

It's a trait written in the deepest part of your brain: Find food and survive. Yet nowadays, the fight for survival doesn't even enter into the thoughts of most folks in the developed world. People assume they're above all that nonsense. The world has modern medicine and advanced agricultural techniques that fight disease and allow people to produce an abundance of food. But regardless of all the technological advances humans have made, Nostradamus still issued a warning that has been picked up, verified, and then echoed loudly throughout ecological conservation groups — Earth can't support many more people and their technology. If people keep going at their current rate of growth, the results will be disastrous for the natural world.

Born to devour

Nostradamus was a storyteller of sorts, and this particular skill often showed up in his quatrains about the future. The stories that catch our interest are the stories that talk about events and people we care about, and we care about ourselves. Quatrain C III – 42 tells the story of human survival and how close we can be to starvation.

> The child will be born with two teeth in his mouth,
>
> Stones will fall during the rain in Tuscany:
>
> A few years after there will be neither wheat nor barley,
>
> To satiate those who will faint from hunger. (C III – 42)

Certainly in Nostradamus's day, a *child . . . born with two teeth in his mouth* (line 1) would suggest that something just wasn't right. Nostradamus and his colleagues would've looked to the heavens to determine what catastrophe was on its way after the birth of such a child. I can also see another layer of meaning in line 1, because a child born with teeth is ready to eat and devour — something humans have done for quite some time, as we've learned to grow more crops and eat larger and larger portions. I believe this child represents mankind and its voracious ability to consume whatever lies before us — even if by consuming a large meal our health is endangered or by consuming firewood, we'll cause deforestation.

In his visions, Nostradamus saw *stones fall during the rain in Tuscany* (line 2), which I take to be a reference to rains filled with stones, which wouldn't be wet or helpful for the crops. These stones are a metaphor for judgment or accusations directed at Tuscany. Stones are a typical biblical reference to the troubles people can receive at the hands of Nostradamus's God. And because the rain isn't really wet or relieving, *neither wheat nor barley* (line 3) will be available, and *a few years after,* there will be many *who will faint from hunger* (line 4) without any bread. This kind of judgment and punishment (by creating a situation with no crops) makes me think that Nostradamus saw something wrong within the region of Tuscany for the people to deserve this kind of treatment. It's also important to note that in line 4, Nostradamus said there won't be enough to satiate the people — not that there won't be food, but that there won't be enough to satisfy the people. This suggests that people's appetites will be too much for what the Earth could bear.

In Quatrain C III – 42, Nostradamus seems to have clearly outlined the devastation as far as the land is concerned. But to truly make his point, he brought in the starvation of the people. I believe Nostradamus saw the natural disaster of overpopulation as a kind of disrespect for the Earth for which men were judged (with stones being thrown). I think he warned future generations — in a quatrain without a date because population is difficult to predict — that humans would become the next form of plague to cover the planet, eating everything in sight like locusts. And I think Nostradamus relayed an underlying message that the hunger people would seek to fill wouldn't necessarily be one of the body but rather one of the soul.

Starvation on a universal scale

Most of Nostradamus's quatrains have been identified as dealing with people, places, wars, and events. But the ones that are harder to pin down to a time period are those that deal with natural catastrophes, like the famine prophesied in Quatrain C I – 97 that contains an unusual feature:

> The great famine that I sense approaching,
>
> Often turning, then becoming universal,
>
> So great and so long that one will come to pull out
>
> Roots from woods, and babe from breast. (C I – 97)

Although Nostradamus discussed his own insights within the quatrains, he didn't frequently use a reference to himself as "I." Using a reference to yourself adds strength to your comments, and I think Nostradamus intentionally used the personal reference as a signpost that the ideas in this quatrain concerned him greatly.

Nostradamus was often concerned about lack of food and fresh sanitation, but I look at line 1's *great famine approaching* and see two closely linked ideas. The literal translation is that a lack of food will starve many people and force them to *pull out / Roots from woods, and babe from breast* (line 4). I believe Nostradamus used the images of people returning to the gathering ways of their ancestors and pulling a small child from the only source of food it knows to show the kind of desperation that will become the norm if the famines from his visions come to pass.

For me, the key to understanding this famine is in line 2, where Nostradamus wrote that it's *Often turning, then becoming universal:* The reference to *turning* brings to my mind the simple understanding of the universe and the turning of the seasons. I think Nostradamus was saying that variations in crops happen naturally, because seasons go through harsh and mild phases regionally, but these will become changes on a global scale, causing starvation from the shortage of food. By opening up the famine with the word *universal,* Nostradamus included the entire universe and all of God's world.

So I believe that the *famine* — if you stop thinking literally for just a moment — can represent the starvation of the human spirit for the freedom to connect with the divine as well as a physical starvation. Ironically, connecting (eating) with the world created by the God of Nostradamus's beliefs will ultimately help to connect the person with the divine presence.

I see Nostradamus as a powerful seer and doctor who knew what it took to sustain and encourage life. In the future of life within his visions, I think he saw that mankind would be unable to view the big picture ecologically (the toll of so many people on the Earth) and control population growth. But there's more. I believe that with the quatrains about religions, wars, famine, and power struggles, he was asking that people evaluate a larger issue than just what's happening in the quatrain at hand. My take is that together, these types of quatrains point out that people of the world are seeking something to satisfy them, to feed both their physical and spiritual hunger. I think Nostradamus presented a peek at the solution to this insatiable hunger with references to the universal energy and a connection with the divine.

A Flood of Problems

When it rains it pours, and Nostradamus knew that floods (probably caused by heavy rains or even by global warming melting the ice caps) weren't a good sign from the heavens above for the future of the world. But he recorded what he saw, and his prophecies contain numerous floods. For Quatrain C I – 17, I believe that the divine inspiration Nostradamus requested showed up, because he accurately prophesied about the changing seasons — something modern weathermen and women still struggle with on a day-to-day basis:

> For forty years the rainbow will not appear,
>
> For forty years it will be seen every day:
>
> The parched earth will wax more dry,
>
> And great floods will accompany its appearance. (C I – 17)

To wring out the meaning of this quatrain, the following three sections break down the imagery Nostradamus used in this quatrain relating to the weather, the forty years, and the floods. Knowing that weather-related events predicted by Nostradamus are going to happen is just like knowing whether it'll rain tomorrow. You can't stop the rain, but you can take an umbrella. Likewise, you can find some comfort in the idea that these changes are part of a much larger pattern (if you remember that Nostradamus asked for divine guidance in his visions, and you believe he got it). For those people who worry about the effects of global warming, relax — it's been coming for years.

Predicting El Niño

From a scientific point of view, I feel that in Quatrain C –17, Nostradamus predicted the cycle of El Niño or La Niña (an opposite pattern) — the seasonal warming of the Pacific climate that causes drastic flooding in some sections of the world (especially South America) and droughts in other areas. For example, the torrential downpours of rain and mudslides in South America and some of the droughts in the southern and western United States have been blamed on the effects of El Niño. The peoples of South America named this weather pattern that causes so much trouble El Niño because it typically begins around late December, the time when Christians celebrate the birth of Christ (*el niño* is Spanish for a young male child).

These drastic climatic changes are similar to the *parched earth* (line 3) and *floods* (line 4) described in this quatrain. These dramatic changes in weather would've been difficult for a local French doctor of the 16th century to imagine, so a connection to the floods of Noah was about as close as he could get to describing it.

As good as Nostradamus may have been at foreseeing the weather, he may not have had the dating on this El Niño thing correct, because it happens approximately every 3 to 7 years, not every 40. Scientists don't understand exactly why El Niño happens or when the next one will occur, but it's still well off the 40 years mentioned in Quatrain C I – 17. But Nostradamus may've been pointing out that a particularly serious cycle will encompass 40 years of these weather patterns.

Waiting for another 40 days and nights

Many scholars favor the idea that Nostradamus was referencing the biblical 40 days as an important symbolic number to connect the 40 years from line 1 in Quatrain C 1 – 17 with the same kind of life-altering changes associated with the flood that kept Noah afloat. According to the story of Noah, he spent 40 days in his ark full of animals while flood waters washed away life on Earth. If I understand the interpretation of this Bible story correctly, God believed mankind needed to reset, and a massive flood was his way of managing the change. Nostradamus seems to suggest that the same kind of change is due to happen again in the future.

I believe Nostradamus's visions of war, famine, and other horrors were surely enough to suggest to him that a start-over for the future of man was also necessary. The trouble with this version of restarting things is that there isn't a reference to battle, starvation, or disease (Nostradamus probably would've mentioned the affects of this on the body since he was a doctor), or any other events other than the weather.

In line 3, *The parched earth will wax more dry,* but Nostradamus then states in line 4 that rains that will flood the earth. The on / off fluctuation of rainy seasons is one of the things associated with El Niño and gives me the impression that Nostradamus may have started out with a teaching story from the Bible again, but by mentioning real weather he brings it back down to events that impact our lives. But relax, the rains and flood seem to happen in Nostradamus's vision only when the rainbow has been seen for 40 years.

The rainbow from line 1 symbolizes the happier, gentle rains that can be seen with sunshine and a light heart, but in line 4, Nostradamus predicted that *great floods will accompany its appearance.* The dry period and the floods that come with the rainbow are part of great changes for the world, like the 40 days on a boat (due to flood waters) were very changing for Noah.

Although he predicted for the future, Nostradamus also wrote for his own contemporaries, and I believe he used yet another layer of meaning with this traditional Bible story of Noah. I think he was emphasizing the Renaissance Church's position that the people in the pews should be focusing on the life of Christ and the plans laid by God, not man. Noah's ark and the saving of the animals is a great image of a God who both judges and is merciful.

The rains that God sent to cleanse the earth (which is a familiar Nostradamus theme) lasted 40 days and nights — a reference to Noah that the contemporary reader wouldn't have missed. Another powerful connection to the number 40 comes from the number of days between when Jesus Christ rose from the dead and when he was taken into heaven. Christians consider the sacrifice of his life and then his resurrection to be a payment for the sins of all mankind and the miracle that saves people from a very unhappy fate without a divine connection — something very close to Nostradamus's heart.

Divining a future drought

Nostradamus uses Quatrain C I – 17 to comment on the future of mankind, and quite a bit of detail needs to be sorted out to understand all the pieces he included in this quatrain. Line 3 seems to be a little on the depressing side when you realize that even though the rainbow *will be seen every day / The parched earth will wax more dry.* I don't think that's a good thing. In fact, for the survival of humans, I'm really certain that's not a good thing.

After the parched earth reference, mention of a massive flood that *will accompany its appearance* is in line 4, but Nostradamus didn't stop to identify what exactly *it* is. Not identifying the cause of the great flood was either a serious oversight on the part of the prophet, or he was referring back to *the rainbow* in line 1. The rainbow can refer to a number of things:

✔ A literal bright and shiny collection of colors in the sky

✔ The country-folk associations of the colors for the changing seasons

✔ The rainbow of colors associated with the Kabbalah's progression toward connecting with the pure divine (part of the teachings of Jewish mysticism; see Chapter 4 for info on the Kabbalah)

I feel that Nostradamus used the country-folk and Kabbalah associations. They would've been more familiar to him. I think he used the dangers of the changing seasons to point out that looking up at a rainbow — to something that typically inspires wonder even if you know the process that creates a rainbow — will help humans through an upcoming drought. Droughts and famines certainly test the quality and determination of people everywhere, and they're also great equalizers.

No End to Illness

Look at the whole of Nostradamus's life, and you can see two strong threads that run all the way through it — medicine and prophecy. It's not a big surprise then that several quatrains focus on the health of people in the future. I'm sure he was distressed by the fact that deadly diseases continued to appear in his visions of the future.

Same cough, different day

Nostradamus was certainly familiar enough with contagious diseases to give a clear description in Quatrain C IX – 55 of the next plague-like disease he believed the future needed to know about:

> The horrible war which is being prepared in the West,
>
> The following year will come the pestilence
>
> So very horrible that young, old, nor beast,
>
> Blood, fire Mercury, Mars, Jupiter in France. (C IX – 55)

For this quatrain, I want to start from the bottom up, because the last line gives a time frame for the rest of the events. Mercury, Mars, and Jupiter are only together in the same portion of the sky (in the same astrological sign) every two or three years. These planets were aligned in February 1998, July 2002, and September 2004, and they'll be aligned again in February 2009 and April 2011. Keep this info in your back pocket for a bit.

According to lines 2 and 1, in that order, the time of the disease *(pestilence)* will follow a *war which is being prepared in the West.* You should notice that this wording means the war isn't fought in the West; it's simply prepared there. For Nostradamus, *West* meant starting in France and looking toward the setting sun — countries like Spain, the U.S., and Canada. The general world, however, views the U.S. as a representation of life in the western world, and I feel that Nostradamus would've picked up on those details in his visions.

Although there was an influenza outbreak in 1918 (following the U.S. entrance into World War I in 1917) when all the planets mentioned in line 4 were aligned, I think Nostradamus's point was that a pattern of war followed by disease outbreaks would occur. The astrological alignments repeat, and so does the opportunity for disease to spread.

The undeniable connection between astrology and the body in 16th-century medicine makes the link between the planet alignments and people's ailments a reasonable prophecy coming from Nostradamus. I believe this prophecy can be right over and over again. For example, after World War II, the number of malaria cases in the U.S. rose dramatically after the return of soldiers. Too many interpreters try to pin a quatrain to one event when, to me, the event mentioned clearly repeats — and Nostradamus wrote it that way on purpose.

I believe that in Quatrain C IX – 55, Nostradamus pointed out for our benefit that during certain times (like after wars in line 1), diseases are likely to run rampant. Knowing about them won't necessarily help, but at least they won't come as a complete surprise. Maybe he even meant this quatrain as a warning against wars.

As for the kinds of diseases Nostradamus may have foreseen, the terms *blood* and *fire* in line 4 suggest to me that the diseases burn you from the inside and are carried in the blood rather than through contamination in the environment (like the common cold spreads). Diseases of the blood are hard to treat, and so are diseases of the life-giving flow of energy — an alternate interpretation for the *pestilence* that will affect people *young* and *old,* as well as animals *(nor beast).* Diseases that have been identified as possible matches with this quatrain's descriptions include the Ebola virus, influenza (the flu bug as I call it), AIDS, and perhaps even cancer.

AIDS: A plague with far-reaching effects

Like the plague of Nostradamus's time, the modern era acquired immune deficiency syndrome (AIDS) has exacted a mind-numbing toll. AIDS is a worldwide epidemic that continues to spread death and destruction, especially in poorer countries where folks are unable to take necessary preventive measures or receive medical treatment. Sometimes I think Nostradamus, the intuitive country doctor, had his pulse on the nature of such diseases more than modern scientists with their slow and scientific methods.

I believe Nostradamus foresaw the coming of AIDS, and his commentary on this plague brought several other issues to the surface. Unfortunately, I can't deal with all of them given the scope of this book, so forgive me for just touching lightly on one or two issues within this quote from *The Epistle to Henry II,* paragraph 33:

> Then will commence a persecution of the Churches the like of which was never seen. Meanwhile, such a plague will arise that more than two thirds of the world will be removed. One will be unable to ascertain the true owners of fields and houses, and weeds growing in the streets of cities will rise higher than the knees. For the clergy there will be but utter desolation. (*Epistle to King Henry II,* 33)

Nostradamus began by identifying a *persecution of the Churches* that would happen during the time when a *plague will arise that more than two thirds of the world will be removed.* I think that for Nostradamus, these events were two of the most serious that could happen, and tying them together in a paragraph in *The Epistle to King Henry II* suggests that a connection exists between the two. I'm going to try to unravel this connection for you.

Persecution of the Church, at least by Nostradamus's standards, could come in many forms:

✔ New religions that threaten Christianity, which Nostradamus believed was the only way to redeem people's souls.

✔ Lack of faith in general by people — those who don't seek a connection with the divine.

✔ Political persecution through which the Church loses its power and influence over the laws and directions of nations. (For an example of political persecution, see Chapter 10 on Napoleon, who made the Church take a back seat in his drive to conquer.)

✔ A plague (a term I believe Nostradamus used both literally as in a disease of the body and metaphorically as in a disease of doubt or misguided actions) that does damage to the Church as well as to the entire population of mankind.

My belief is that in this case, Nostradamus went beyond drawing attention to a lack of religious faith to focus and talk about a plague now known as AIDS that has affected every segment of the population, even priests on occasion. I have to hand it to Nostradamus on this one. Without a specific name, I believe he predicted exactly the kind of danger mankind would face.

The danger for the Church may not seem obvious, but issues have plagued the Church recently, including scandals and the struggle to maintain the elements of faith in this new age of science. The scandals have involved the abuse of religious power for personal gain and the recent cases of sexual abuse as reported in the news *(persecution),* all of which undermine the goals of the Church. Nostradamus would've also viewed these events as detrimental to the Church's goals of bringing people to trust Christianity and Christ.

In modern times, the Christian faith already faces trouble from alternative religions and people who doubt something not based in experience and science. The modern Christian movement has struggled with how to maintain its strength of spiritual connection while connecting with people who want to ask questions.

The proper place of sexuality within modern daily life and within the Church has also been called into question (something of concern if a sexually-transmitted disease is about to wipe out parts of the population). From Nostradamus's point of view, the shift in how all aspects of sexuality are approached by the Church (including priests marrying, families that aren't traditional, birth control, and more secular lives of the priesthood) could be a real threat to the power of the Church and its priests who were removed (at least in theory) from these everyday issues to focus on spiritual guidance. For Nostradamus, such issues for today's world would be seen as directly challenging the Church and suggest that the standards of the church will be tested by the lives of its members.

I think paraphrasing the last part of this prediction helps straighten out how Nostradamus felt about things. Here's my take:

- ✔ After the plague hits and the Earth has lost most of its people, there won't be enough people left to appreciate or properly use the lands (for crops, housing, and so on) that are left unattended by the dead. The *weeds growing in the streets of cities* will simply be the signpost that very little hope is left for religion and humanity after the AIDS plague.

- ✔ Weeds that *rise higher than the knees* was Nostradamus's way of revealing that the suffering will go on for a long time, whether from the illness AIDS or from the scandals surrounding it (notorious bedroom scandals, open social sexuality, as well as the overall scandal to the Church itself of sexually-active priests). Of course, the prophet was clear that by the time AIDS finishes affecting the population, the garden of people will *have more weeds than flowers.*

The example presented by the AIDS epidemic is that people aren't always what we expect (as Nostradamus expected celibate priests), and even those people in religious leadership positions are vulnerable. If the priesthood, with its scandals and lawsuits, sets the standard for the rest of us, and they're unable to lead by example, then Nostradamus warns we're all in for the plague of our lives.

In paragraph 33 of *The Epistle to Henry II,* Nostradamus mentioned that nearly two-thirds of the population would be affected by the illness (figuratively, the loss of faith, and literally, the plague). I don't know about you, but Nostradamus now has my attention, because suddenly my chances of survival are slim to none, and slim just left town. To me, corruption, reasonable expectations, and an awareness of the rampant sexual desire of humanity with the power to destroy or create is the curious message Nostradamus gave to the future. Sexual power can carry with it a heavy price.

Changing the World One Natural Disaster at a Time

You never know quite when things are going to change, and the biggest of life's transformations aren't ever listed on your calendar. Nostradamus seemed to want to alter that trend, at least in part, by predicting a change in the future of natural events around the world. One of the most drastic changes that can affect a region is a natural disaster, and Nostradamus mentioned more than a few of them in his quatrains.

Earthquake, rattle, and roll

If you've ever experienced an earthquake, you know just how unbelievably frightening one can be. Earthquakes are almost impossible to describe in words, but I believe Nostradamus tried in Quatrain C IX – 83 to give you an idea of these trembling terrors. Unfortunately, the critics don't all agree:

> Sun twentieth of Taurus the earth will tremble very mightily,
>
> It will ruin the great theater filled:
>
> To darken and trouble air, sky and land,
>
> Then the infidel will call upon God and saints. (C IX – 83)

The Sun, astrologically speaking, is the center of everything, no matter what 16th century astrologers thought. That said, the Sun's position in Taurus (the astrological Zodiac sign of the Bull during late April through mid-May) gives this quatrain a very specific-feeling time period. Each of the twelve Zodiac signs represent a section of the 360-degree sky, giving Taurus 30 degrees total. In line 1, Nostradamus listed about two-thirds of that time *(twentieth of Taurus),* which makes the math complicated. So just go with the guesstimate that, according to line 1, an earthquake will occur somewhere around the 10th of April or the 10th of May.

Nostradamus wrote that *the earth will tremble mightily,* and I've never seen a clearer prediction of an earthquake, especially because Taurus is considered the sign of the Zodiac that rules the Earth and is connected strongly with it. I believe that in the charts and figures that guided Nostradamus's nighttime observations, there was a hint that the Sun (a sign of life and renewal) would come around again to shake things up in a very literal way.

There's just one tricky bit to figuring the timing on this quatrain. Nostradamus didn't provide any clues for identifying the year — just a time period during the cycle of Taurus, which rolls around every year at the same time. Some ingenious interpreters have looked at the quatrain number and tried to make a guess that way. If you use the century number (IX, or 9 for those of us who don't use Roman numbers all the time) to fill in the century and use the quatrain number (83) to fill in the last two digits of the date, then the year becomes clear as can be. Nostradamus predicted an earthquake between April and May in 1983.

The closest earthquake I can figure for this quatrain is one that occurred in Greece, where there'd be an ancient *great theater filled* with tourists and the ghosts of the Roman and Greek men who were so admired during the Renaissance. Although the earthquake in Greece during 1983 measured 7.2 on a scale of 10 (causing some minor damage and being felt in Yugoslavia), I don't believe this prophecy has found its match among the events of history. For one, the earthquakes don't match the scale of the ones Nostradamus described, and two, none of the major ancient theatres were damaged.

In line 4, Nostradamus revealed who would be the one *To darken and trouble air, sky and land* (line 3). I think Nostradamus was describing his third antichrist here (flip to Chapter 13), and the passage almost sounds like he was warning that things were about to get worse.

Of course, other interpretations place this event in a major theatre — namely in Hollywood on vulnerable California's Andreas fault. In a sense, Nostradamus just made a good bet that an earthquake would be felt somewhere that was viewed as a major place — whether it was a movie theatre in Hollywood, a political theatre in the Middle East, or an historical theatre in Greece. Earthquakes happen all the time, and I think that for once, Nostradamus simply used a convenient event to give the doomsday arrival of his third antichrist an interesting entrance. He was fairly close on this prophecy, but that's largely because he hedged his bets and placed the idea of an earthquake in an earthquake-prone region. It's sort of like saying you're going to find fur at the local dog pound.

Just because Quatrain IX – 83 is a prophecy, and just because Nostradamus wrote it, doesn't mean that common sense has to go out the window. For example, the panic that ensued in California during a 1988 earthquake scare was unnecessary and downright unhealthy. Many people feared that the reports of the Big One shaking California for all it was worth were real. They left their homes and headed East. The cities experienced some problems, yes, but they were related to people, not earthquakes. My take on the warning from Nostradamus's time? Always look at things with the entire sky in mind. One star isn't going to give you an accurate and tell-all horoscope.

A river of change, a mountain of comfort

No matter how you chop, slice, or dice Quatrain C VI – 88, it talks about some drastic changes in and around the Ebro River (in Spain mostly), and those changes just might have something to do with an earthquake. Then again, they may not. Take a look:

> A great realm will be left desolated,
>
> Near the Ebro an assembly will be formed:
>
> The Pyrenees mountains will console him,
>
> When in May lands will be trembling. (C VI – 88)

The poetry of Nostradamus may stand in your way on this one, so paraphrasing the first two lines is the best way to start so you can begin to understand this quatrain. Here's my take:

> A country or region near Spain will suffer and collect together in a formal group.

The cause of the distress seems to be mentioned in line 4: *When in May lands will be trembling.* First, I present the more widely known interpretations of this quatrain, and then I guide you through a new perspective.

The traditional view

The *great realm will be left desolated;* this much, many interpreters agree on. Here are some of the general interpretations that are associated with the components of Quatrain C VI – 68:

- ✓ **World War II:** Line 1's *realm desolated* may be a reference to the destruction after World War II when the German tanks trembled the land and caused massive damage.

- ✓ **Famine:** Line 1's desolation may be a reference to the idea of a country being lifeless or empty — perhaps a place where the lands have failed to produce crops (lifeless lands unable to support people) or events like war have damaged the land. Crop failure happens in regions around the world, but the Pyrenees aren't known for this problem.

- ✓ **Political reorganization:** The *realm* in line 1 may give birth to the *assembly* that forms in line 2, resulting in major changes — as severe as the earthquake suggested by the *trembling* in line 4.

✔ **May events:** Line 4 says that May (or at least springtime) will be the time-frame during which the events prophesied in the quatrain will occur. The astrological sign of Taurus, which rules during May, is associated with the element of Earth.

✔ **Earthquakes:** Earthquakes are the most frequent interpretation due to the *trembling* in line 4, which would be an easy explanation for the desolation of the realm in line 1. If Nostradamus was talking literally about earthquakes, some very devastating ones have occurred in the past during the Spring. But to me, none of them match the clues in this quatrain closely enough, so I believe this quatrain has yet to find its own time as a prophecy of earthquake devastation.

A new perspective

I'd like to offer a slightly off-the-beaten-path view of this quatrain that's a little more up to date than just interpreting a tremble as an earthquake. Nostradamus was limited in his imagery by his experience and time period's ideas, but that shouldn't limit your interpretations. Maybe Nostradamus (who was familiar with the monarchy and strong governments of the early 1500s) foresaw the independence of the cities in the Ebro area and felt it may actually begin to shake the old monarchy system so much that the whole foundation (Earth) of politics and industry may change. Certainly cities independently governing themselves would be an earth-shaking idea for Nostradamus, a fan of the queen of France. Within the region of the Ebro are many manufacturing centers, and these very modern and machinery-driven factories (whose powerful engines may shake the Earth) could've definitely given Nostradamus the idea that changes would occur swiftly.

Line 3's *him* seems to be the most important word, and it's the one that presents some of the most interpretation trouble. To me, Nostradamus was saying that through all the shifts, including social and ideological changes, *The Pyrenees mountains will console him.* In other words, change is frightening, and for *him,* the mountains (or maybe the *assembly* from line 2, probably made up of regional people who have experienced the desolation) will bring some kind of internal peace and comfort.

I just can't help but think that instead of referring to an individual (which seems kind of odd considering the scale of the changes — either natural or social — being discussed in Quatrain C VI – 88), Nostradamus was referring to mankind finding peace within the Pyrenees mountains, which form a natural boundary between Spain and France. Perhaps in a subtle way, Nostradamus was agreeing with the old saying that good fences make good neighbors, or that all people have a place of their own and that personal space (even on the level of a country) is a good way to avoid conflict.

Chapter 19

Looking Toward the Age of Aquarius

*Y*ou've just turned to the chapter that covers a topic lots of folks are interested in — predictions for what'll happen sometime around the year 2050-ish, if you're figuring by the stars. According to astrologers and Nostradamus, the world will make a monumental shift. The clock is ticking — believe me — and Nostradamus had his eye on the second millennium hand. I believe Nostradamus saw that the future would be both serious and exciting. Of course he warned of a few floods and earthquakes to keep people on their toes, but he also glimpsed hints of a grand hidden treasure just waiting to be found.

The Dawning of the Age of Aquarius

If you've read the chapters up to this point, you may realize that Nostradamus seemed to be working up to something, some kind of big change that mankind will experience, and — *ta da* — the year 2050 (or so) is it. It's the time when, according to an astrological concept, the Zodiac sign of Aquarius will rule the planet's overall mood.

Nostradamus's astrological studies included the *Zodiac*. In addition to each influencing a certain portion of every year, as I discuss in Chapter 6, each of the 12 signs of the Zodiac also influence an entire chunk of years (about 2,100 of them). These 12 sections of years, or ages, follow the Zodiac in reverse order (in Chapter 6, I list all 12 in order). Astrologers determine when we're in one age or another by finding out which constellation the sun is in when it crosses over the celestial equator, which is formed by simply extending the Earth's equator into the sky, on the Spring Equinox (around March 21).

Pisces is a rather long constellation. Right now we're in between Pisces and Aquarius. The completed shift to the Zodiac sign of Aquarius won't technically happen (by the actual stars in the sky) until the year 2600, but astrologers feel that the full influence will begin around 2050. Think about a transition between ages like the Earth bouncing from one stepping-stone in the sky to another. The transition time between ages is when Earth is mid-bounce between one sign of the Zodiac and the next. In 2050, we'll be on the down side of that bounce, headed toward Aquarius, and we'll begin to feel the influence of Aquarius more than the sign of Pisces we just left.

From astrological schools of thought, here are some tidbits to keep in mind when you think about Aquarius:

- The sign of Aquarius is now ruled by Uranus, a planet very fond of change, the unconventional, and modern science.

- When Aquarius is exerting its influence, maintaining intellectual independence and finding answers through examination will be the preferred way of doing things.

- The symbol for Aquarius is two horizontal wavy lines representing the flowing of gifts equally to all.

- People born under the Zodiac sign Aquarius (and possibly those who live during the time of Aquarius) lean toward being idealistic and concerned with humanitarian affairs.

- Aquarius is the 11th sign of the Zodiac, a particularly important number in alchemy (a mystical tradition that Nostradamus studied and that you can find out more about in Chapter 6). For alchemists, 11 meant enlightenment and a reflection of the power of one (or The One, the divine being), with victory in the end through knowledge.

For me, it's like Nostradamus took the Earth and did a giant horoscope for all the years past 2050 that he could see. And I think he determined that the product of all the other times have been leading humanity to this point. Through trouble and strife, people have been building themselves (nothing like a little adversity to develop character) to face the challenges of a new age that Nostradamus felt would be like nothing ever seen before.

Flooding the Future with Problems

Although many quatrains touch on the theme of floods, Quatrain C III – 12 sticks out in my mind because of the volume of rivers that seem to be included:

> Because of the swelling of the Ebro, Po, Tagus, Tiber and Rhône
>
> And because of the pond of Geneva and Arezzo,
>
> The two great chiefs and cities of the Garonne,
>
> Taken, dead, drowned: human booty divided. (C III – 12)

Taken as a story of floods and their aftermath, this quatrain sounds almost like it's straight from the Bible, which isn't surprising considering that Nostradamus studied biblical stories, as well as some of the more mystical stories of destruction and creation. But I think this quatrain is a good example of a couple issues Nostradamus found worrisome.

The effects of global warming

In a very literal sense, floods drastically reorder the world as you see it. Nostradamus watched in his visions as the waters of different rivers swelled, but he didn't see a random collection of rivers overflowing their banks. I believe he was sharing his insights through hidden language and veiled references:

- ✔ **Ebro:** One of the main rivers of Spain made up of a collection of tributaries throughout the land that end in the Mediterranean Sea. Interestingly enough, many of the cities along this river are *autonomous,* meaning they have the power to make their own laws according to the local people's wishes.

- ✔ **Po:** The longest river running through Italy (west to east). This river touches many provinces in Italy and creates a river valley known for its industry. In this quatrain, I think Nostradamus used it to represent Italy's industrial power.

- ✔ **Tagus:** Yet another large river, running from Portugal and Spain through the Iberian Peninsula in southwest Europe and ending in the Atlantic Ocean in a nifty lagoon.

- ✔ **Tiber:** A really large Italian river with a silt bottom that occasionally makes it unusable for trade boats. The Tiber has flooded several times over the years, causing dramatic changes.

- **Rhône:** A large river running swiftly through France and Switzerland. This one flows southwest through Lake Geneva (probably the *pond of Geneva* mentioned by Nostradamus), turns back northwest, and then finally heads south.

- **Pond of Geneva:** Possibly a reference to Lake Geneva, where the city is based. I believe Nostradamus was referring to the city of Geneva, which is central to Europe and has long been desired as a prime location for a central European government.

- **Arezzo:** Not a river or body of water, Arezzo is a city in central Italy that was originally independent in its government.

Together these pieces represent some of Europe's major strengths and the natural links that connect countries from the Atlantic to the Mediterranean. But I think something else links these pieces together: the independent nature of their governments and the strength of the industry in the areas. Flooding in these regions would indeed be a catastrophe, because the largest part of mainland Europe relies on these rivers and the regions they represent.

Flooding in Europe would be horrible, but not an event that would end the world, unless you remember that for Nostradamus, Europe was the majority of the civilized world, where art, religion, science, and trade were centered. For Nostradamus, who possibly didn't completely get the full picture of the nations of the future, destroying Europe was destroying the known world.

Although some of the rivers mentioned in this quatrain have been known to overflow somewhat during especially rainy seasons, these rivers have never joined forces to create one massive water slide across Europe. That kind of catastrophe would require some incredible waterfall — *much* more water. Where on Earth would it come from?

Try the polar ice caps. As they melt, they add water to the oceans and change the dynamics of life on Earth by adding to the amount of water that evaporates, rains down, and then flows into the rivers. This kind of polar melting has been happening over the past 100 years or so, along with a slow and imperceptible (to you and me anyway) rise in temperatures. The term *global warming* generally refers to the increase in temperatures humans cause with industrialization (like that in the Po and Ebro regions mentioned in the quatrain), electric heating, cars, and other modern conveniences.

I believe that Nostradamus clearly foresaw changes in the overall global temperatures and the effects of the industrialization and the ecological changes, but to make the point that the effects would be devastating, he needed to make the point that the important centers of the world would be destroyed. So I think he used the information he had, and at the time, Europe was the place to be — unless you were expecting a flood.

An alternative theory: The rivers as a metaphor

If you don't take Nostradamus completely literally about the rivers and the cities, there's an alternative to the theory that Quatrain C III – 12 is about a flood. Line 3's *Garonne* may represent a gathering place similar to a large river that's formed where tributaries all gather together. The final connection, then, would be *The two great chiefs* in line 3 who come together in the *cities of the Garonne* (in southwest France).

The fact that Nostradamus mentioned two cities is important, because it gives the idea that somehow a split still exists among people. Nostradamus didn't tell whether this division of people is because of politics, religion, or for other reasons. In this scenario, the people (like the rivers) come together from different regions with different purposes, and they join with each other to work (like the rivers in Quatrain C III – 12 flow) in a unified direction until the two leaders become involved.

Continuing with this interpretation that the rivers represent people, *The two great chiefs* in line 3 represent the leaders of these people. Unfortunately, something happens in line 4 where the cities are *Taken* and the people are *dead, drowned: human booty divided.* The idea of a city or its people being taken suggests to me that Nostradamus saw the action of one man against another becoming the force that creates trouble in the end for everyone. With the flood of people (possibly refugees from a war started by the two great chiefs in line 3), there's death, destruction, and ultimately a division of people — an ending that's almost completely counter to the beginning of the quatrain, when the rivers were *swelling* in unison.

Although this is an interesting theory that I've studied, I still think the idea of a catastrophic flood is a more likely interpretation of Quatrain C III – 12. All the rivers combine at the beginning, resulting in devastation at the end. I think my reasoning especially holds up because the alternative theory of the rivers as just a metaphor has the people coming together (overflowing like the rivers), and they're overwhelming the situation that develops between the two leaders. Ultimately everything ends up in a state of trouble.

Although I can't give that theory my full support, it raises the question of whether the rivers are a kind of metaphor for mankind coming together in many aspects. The river as a metaphor works only so far and begins to break down when I try to find a parallel idea for overflowing people (that just doesn't sound like fun), so I think the literal interpretation of global warming and raging rivers is more likely. Working this one out would take serious study and more of a library than you really need to worry about.

The bottom line about the fate of mankind

The prophecy from Quatrain C III – 12 seems to hinge on the bountiful waters of the world overflowing and flooding known civilization. According to the prophecy, the devastation wrought by nature will be impressive. But Nostradamus made a point of reminding people that the devastation created by the hands of men (the *leaders* mentioned in line 3) who might use tragic events like natural disasters to their advantage can be just as terrifying.

He showed this particular devastation by using emotionally loaded words in the final line of the quatrain. In line 4, *Taken* and *human booty* both suggest a lack of respect for human life, and *drowned* presents a grisly image of the death of people in the path of the destruction. Nostradamus used all these words to get an emotional and intense response from you, the reader, so that you'll take heed of this warning prophecy.

As the Piscean age of mankind was coming to a close (its run was roughly from 300 BC to about 1950 AD, and we're now in between the ages), I believe Nostradamus saw the floods of change moving across the landscape with such swiftness that he could only imagine them as natural disasters. Whether he was referring to figurative natural disasters — radical changes in how things work — or literal flooding due to global warming, it's still up in the air, because I think this prophecy has yet to be completely fulfilled. I personally believe that the answer lies in both the figurative and literal versions, because the increase in industry, people, and other machines that create heat (or deplete the ozone) contribute to the fulfillment of the flooding prophecy by causing global warming.

The impact of Quatrain C III – 12 on today's world is easy to understand: Watch where you put your foot; mankind has a while yet to live on Earth. Whether you're a granola-crunching tree-hugger or a city-loving consumer, everyone shares the same planet, and the effects of these changes can be very personal. Everything's related, and I believe Nostradamus was very clearly aware that with all the divisions in people's lives (tributaries), you might forget the delta at the ocean — the goal that keeps you going, whatever that might be. For what it's worth, my soapbox speech is this: Ecologically, we're endangering ourselves in a very reckless way, almost like a 4-year-old who plays with chemicals just to see how they smell.

Trouble Spelled Out in the Stars

At night, Nostradamus received visions through serious meditation, with aids from mysticism of just about every variety. During the day, he had his apothecary practice making cosmetics, along with his astrology practice (sometimes accurate, sometimes a little questionable), which is what he relied on to tweak and perfect the prophecies he recorded in his mysterious quatrains.

Quatrain C VIII – 48 contains many astrological references that Nostradamus hoped would help date the event he predicted, but I'm not sure those references have been as helpful as he intended. Either we're not as good at deciphering astrology as Nostradamus gave us credit for, or the quatrain itself is flawed with missing info or very hidden meanings. Or maybe Nostradamus just made this one up. Take a look at the quatrain, and I'll walk you through it line by line:

> Saturn in Cancer, Jupiter with Mars,
>
> In February "Chaldondon Salvaterre,"
>
> The Sierra Moreña assailed from three sides,
>
> Near "Verbiesque" conflict mortal war. (C VIII – 48)

Under the influence: An astrology lesson

When astrologers say that Saturn is *in* Cancer (line 1), they mean that the planet Saturn is moving through the part of the sky where the Zodiac sign of Cancer resides (where the stars for Cancer show up in the sky). In a bit more straightforward speak, the events in this quatrain could happen in cycles every 2½ years according to Nostradamus, because the events are connected with Saturn when it's in Cancer, which just happens to be once every 2½ years. (Bonus tidbit for those of you who are really into this stuff: Because Saturn moves so slowly and spends a long time in each sign, it doesn't finish its turn around the sun for 29½ years.)

In addition to studying the placement of the planets among the stars, astrologers also study how the planets influence people. I believe this influence is the aspect Nostradamus wanted to include in this prophecy. Consider first that the influence of the Zodiac sign of Cancer can be summed up with the word *emotionalism*.

Now consider that when Saturn is in Cancer, the planet influences people to feel pessimistic and insecure, but these people are also facing obstacles (like poor communication) and tests of their resolve that Saturn places in their way. These obstacles are Saturn's special way of teaching people to persevere and grow from new experiences; no other planet teaches in quite this way. So Cancer under the influence of Saturn isn't the best way the stars can align, and it tends to lead to overly emotional trends like extreme nationalism or a sense that you need to protect your home at all costs.

In line 1, Nostradamus also used a second astrological reference — *Jupiter with Mars* — to explain the trouble of the upcoming years. Followers of astrology believe Jupiter is the planet that controls business success and tends to encourage new experiences. Mars is the planet of physical energy and aggression, both sexually and physically. If any planet is bold, Mars is the one, but it also represents unleashed energy.

Followers of these concepts believe that combined, the planets are unfortunately some dangerous influences, and they've shown up over and over again. Believers say that nearly every time Saturn and Cancer have gotten together, wars and civil unrest have occurred all over the world and that the violence of these fights has been the result of Jupiter and Mars clashing heads.

A clue about time

Line 2 seems to give a specific hint about time. Nostradamus wrote that the great events would happen *In February,* but the astrological time period of Saturn in Cancer (a repeating event) stated in line 1 is spread out and isn't easy to pinpoint. Even expert astrologers can't understand exactly what Nostradamus may have been calculating. Between the translation problems and the small nuances of interpretation on both the words and the stars, the final interpretation is still somewhat questionable. Various experts, for example, have made different conclusions:

- ✔ The event (I'll get there momentarily) is too vague to be determined.
- ✔ The trouble will happen on February 10, 2189.
- ✔ The trouble will happen on February 1, 2769.

I don't know about the exact date, but it does appear to me that the fights and struggles of mankind occur in cycles that follow the stars.

During Nostradamus's day, views of the sky were limited because the telescope wasn't invented and used for sky gazing until around 1608. The sign of the Zodiac known as Aquarius was considered to be ruled by Saturn (a serious taskmaster) until Uranus (a planet in astrology that tends toward heightened spirituality with insight, realization, and a changed world view) was discovered in 1791 and the Zodiac sign was re-a-signed (get it?). Nostradamus probably viewed the new age with a little trepidation, because the Age of Aquarius sounded like a lot of work and trouble which, as far as he knew, would be ruled by the aggressive, harsh, and lesson-teaching Saturn. I believe part of Nostradamus's overall hope for the future came from his intuitive under-standing that the future (and the Age of Aquarius) would be guided by a more spiritual force like Uranus.

A vague warning

"Chaldondon Salvaterre" (line 2) is certainly one of the more mystifying phrases within Nostradamus's work, and in this quatrain, it's the piece that seems tied closest to February. "Chaldondon Salvaterre" is one of the unfor-tunate victims of Nostradamus's fun-loving word games and is only somewhat revealing in the overall meaning of the quatrain:

- ✔ I think "Chaldondon" is a reference to the Chaldean oracles, a group of prophecies studied by early Christian theologians.
- ✔ "Salvaterre" seems to be a combination word — *salva* (which is the first part of *salvation*) and *terre* (for *Earth*).

I believe Nostradamus was giving the world hints that the future will need both the mysterious (prophecies) and faith (Christian salvation for the people of Earth) in the future time he was predicting.

Line 3 begins to describe the location of at least some of the future trouble. *Sierra Moreña assailed on three sides* seems like a clear enough reference to the Sierra Morena mountains in California. This range of mountains has been the dividing line for a number of nationalist conflicts, including the Spanish Civil War (thanks to Saturn in Cancer, in my opinion), and it lies along the very large and active San Andreas Fault, a division in the Earth's crust that occasionally shifts and creates violent earthquakes. So I think Nostradamus warned of future earthquakes, and between them and the *mortal war* in line 4, I believe the world is definitely in for some trouble in the far future. As for *Verbiesque* in line 4, I must agree with other interpreters that not enough information is available to decipher this word into anything meaningful.

Although I want to enjoy this quatrain and understand the depths of the description and prophecy, this kind of insight is just not meant for me. What starts out as a seemingly specific prophecy (based as it is on astrological mea-surements) turns into a vague warning. I don't necessarily blame Nostradamus for this dim prophecy for the far-future — after all, he'd been staying up late for many years by the time he wrote this. But I'm disappointed in it, especially after reading the more precise prophecies about events before the millennium.

With only a vague timeframe of February over a span of many years and a reminder of both prophecy and faith before a mortal war, the final message from Quatrain C VIII – 48 is wide open for interpretation. I believe Nostradamus wrote this quatrain as a hint for people to prepare for a great war and as a reminder of his belief in the constant need for faith and prophecy to guide the world in future struggles.

Cracking the Code: A Treasure Hunt

It appears that Nostradamus had a hint of a sense of humor. Scholars and amateur sleuths alike have found several quatrains in which Nostradamus made mention of that wonderful childhood dream — hidden treasure. This section covers two of those quatrains.

I believe Nostradamus may have known the location of hidden treasures that were removed from the world for safekeeping — including art, literature, gold, and the special minerals and elements required to produce the elixir of life (essentially an immortality potion). Either that, or he just threw in a few quatrains to keep you and me on our toes and guessing, no matter what the serious matters of life. Regardless, get ready. You're going on a treasure hunt.

A rewarding journey

Quatrain C VIII – 29 displays some of Nostradamus's best puns within *The Prophecies,* as well as a great interweaving of myths, religions, and opinions. The so-called experts have opinions on what he meant here, and agreement isn't easy to come by. Here's what all the fuss is about:

> At the fourth pillar the one dedicated to Saturn
>
> By earthquake and flood demolished
>
> Under the Saturnian edifice an urn found,
>
> Of gold carried off by Caepio and then restored. (C VIII – 29)

I think paraphrasing this quatrain is the best way to start so you can get the overall idea before looking at the individual pieces. Here's one possible paraphrase:

> At a place dedicated to Saturn and devastated by natural disaster, Caepio's gold will be found and restored.

With some of the awkward poetry phrases out of the way, you can clearly see that a treasure is involved.

Capering Caepio

The biggest key to understanding this quatrain lies in knowing who this guy Caepio is and what he was doing with the gold in the first place. Q. Servilius Caepio, according to history, was a Roman procounsel (kind of like a governor that Rome appointed to rule over a distant region of the empire) who had a fairly scary run-in around 103 B.C. with a group of people known as the Cimbri (whom you might call the forefathers of the Celtic people). Caepio was a successful general, and the whole treasure thing started when he marched to Toulouse, France, where an uprising was occurring at the time. (Toulouse was also a place where Nostradamus spent much time studying during his wandering years, so he would've come across stories about Caepio's adventures.)

After Caepio captured Toulouse, he and his men hauled off large sums of gold and treasures, especially the offerings that the Cimbri had previously stolen from the Temple of Delphi during their raids. But Caepio never made it to Marseilles (his intended destination) with the golden goods. No one is quite sure whether the Cimbri stole the gold back or whether another group of desperados relieved Caepio of his loot.

In Quatrain C VIII – 29, Caepio is the leader of the theft of the gold, and Nostradamus used him to clue you in to the story (which many people consider to be a legend, I must add) of the sacking of Toulouse and all the riches involved. I believe part of the reason Nostradamus tied Caepio into the quatrain's overall treasure theme was to remind people who may wish to receive the riches of the world that cooperation is simply a must. Caepio's eventual downfall within the Roman empire had everything to do with his inability to cooperate with other generals (who were noble, as opposed to his own standing in society) operating at the same time.

Achieving the prize in the end

The key to understanding the position of the treasure is to know what a fourth pillar and Saturn (*fourth pillar the one dedicated to Saturn*) have to do with this whole mess of stolen goods and bad guys.

Some interpreters think line 3 is a reference to the ancient Church of St. Saturnin-du-Taur (now called Notre Dame du Taur), a church in Toulouse, rumored to have been built over a sacred lake. The church was the original resting place of Saturnin (a leader in Toulouse before Christianity became the official religion). Nostradamus uses his typical method of referring to places by their ancient names to add layers of meaning to this quatrain.

But wait a minute, you say. Isn't the pillar *By earthquake and flood demolished?* Why yes, yes it is. But despite its destruction, line 3 says, *Under the Saturnian edifice an urn found,* so whatever of value is under the pillar isn't destroyed. So, undeterred, these interpreters view this pun on the word *Saturn* as Nostradamus's very clever way of hinting that the Cimbri treasure is buried either beneath or near the church that used to be called St. Saturnin-du-Taur or the St. Sernin Basilica (a church of special rank) where the remains of Saturnin are said to have been moved (and the church which still rhymes with the quatrain's words). But I think there's more going on here than just a gold-digger's treasure hunt with two possible places to dig.

The number four in *fourth pillar* carries some powerful symbolism:

- **Thought:** In Christian mythology, the number four represents the power of the intellectual mind to discern and evaluate.

- **Imagination:** In Kabbalistic (Jewish) mysticism, this number represents the power of creative thought and the four base words that form Kabbalah.

- **Death:** In the basic understanding of the alchemical use of numbers, four was associated with completion (like death), where the four seasons bring the end of a traditional year. In this way, the number is viewed as representing practical and traditional ideas rather than ones that are more elevated and divine.

- **Revelations at death:** The Zohar is a series of books related to and commenting on the Torah and Kabbalism. The faithful believe that the *fourth* book of the series, a book of revelations, was divinely revealed to and then written down by the author, Rabbi Shimon bar Yochai, on the day he passed away.

I believe that the emphasis placed on the *fourth pillar* shouldn't be ignored. The *fourth pillar,* if you take all those layers of meaning into consideration (and they're just *some* of the possible layers), isn't just the place where Caepio's gold is found but is also the thought, imagination, and the quest itself — all of which become the treasure.

I believe the *fourth pillar* is also a place of enlightenment — where mental riches are revealed — and that it's founded on all the symbolism the number four entails. I also believe that Nostradamus was letting the world know that the journey to this place of enlightenment is one of thought. In other words, I think Nostradamus was, as usual, commenting on how people should go about living their lives and getting what they want — or even reaching the treasure.

I believe Nostradamus used the lure of Caepio's gold to support his own idea (well, it wasn't originally his because it was a basic part of alchemy studies) that much is to be learned and improved upon along the way before all the riches are rewarded at the end. Even within the Christian Church, there's much to be said for improving your life and following the Bible before the final reward after death.

Take a hint from the prophet who sought out wisdom night after night: You have much to gain by learning along the way of your journey in life. It's even possible (in my opinion) that the journey itself — not getting what you want (even if it's the mythical gold, stolen and re-stolen, in Quatrain C VIII – 29) — is the reward. Plus, knowledge can't be taken from you; you always have wealth if your journey is one of thought and learning.

The search for understanding

Nostradamus gave another clue for finding the treasure in Quatrain C VIII – 30:

> Within Toulouse not far from "Beluzer,"
>
> Digging a deep pit, palace of spectacle:
>
> The treasure found will come to vex everyone,
>
> And all in two places and near the Basacle. (C VIII – 30)

In this quatrain, I think Nostradamus was getting to the actual directions for the treasure. According to line 1, it's supposedly *Within Toulouse not far from "Beluzer."* Toulouse is a town in southwestern France, halfway between the Mediterranean Sea and the Atlantic Sea. But unfortunately, few people have been able to figure out where "Beluzer" is — or even whether it's a place, person, or one of Nostradamus's word games. Some interpreters have pointed out the rhyme between *belousar* (Provençal French for a particular kind of rock formation) and the term "Beluzer," so the final word of line 1 may indicate a marker in the form of a large rock or even a standing rock of some kind. This interpretation isn't far-fetched when you think about it, because Nostradamus spent a great deal of his time outdoors during his youth, and he may have used the scenery to help give this quatrain a rocky twist.

Although I believe that "Beluzer" may indeed be a rhyme or pun in French for a stone formation, I don't think it's a very accurate hint about the treasure's resting place, because no one seems to have found the treasure. And, I hold out that the possible pun in French isn't all there is to this word. I think the word is in fact an anagram, a word that Nostradamus twisted and rearranged to obscure the details from those people who shouldn't know them.

I believe line 2 brings in the first human hands of modern times seeking out the treasure, because they're *Digging a deep pit, palace of spectacle.* The *deep pit* makes sense at first glance; the people are digging for treasure and have to go fairly deep. But Nostradamus didn't mention whether these people are digging for the sole purpose of finding the treasure. I don't think they are. To me, Nostradamus was saying that people will find the treasure when they're *digging a deep pit, palace of spectacle* (line 2), which suggests that the digging is related to the palace rather than the search for treasure. In other words, it'll be found as an accident connected with *a palace of spectacle.* So the digging may be started as part of another project — building a foundation, for example.

Although you and I may think a palace that creates (or holds) a spectacle has to be something big like a sporting arena or a grandiose house, Nostradamus's ideas of a spectacle were from the 16th century, and even a small theatre or richly decorated church (showy but not deeply religious perhaps in his eyes) would've seemed a spectacle for this man.

Two hints are left in this quatrain, and neither one provides a clear, satisfactory answer. Line 3 tells you that the *treasure found will come to vex everyone,* which seems to be quite a bold statement. Maybe some people won't care about the gold or the insights. But everybody's different and hard to please, so believing that one treasure (which doesn't start off sounding bad at all) will become a problem for absolutely *everyone* is hard for me. This line leads me to conclude the treasure isn't a physical one of gold, jewels, and precious items but a treasure made of information that will upset the current understanding of the world.

Nostradamus planted the final piece of the puzzle in this quatrain by identifying that the treasure (whatever it really is) won't be found in one place but *all in two places and near the Basacle.* It's easy to see why the treasure would be split up for protection's sake (like all computer geeks will tell you, it's good to have a back-up plan), but Nostradamus threw yet another rock at our pile by introducing *the Basacle,* which was the name (actually, Bazacle) of a protective castle in Toulouse, as well as the name of the region's milling section.

Most interpreters still focus on the shiny treasure that Nostradamus promises as the accurate interpretation for these lines; here are those interpretations:

- Nostradamus was adding a third place near the Bazacle castle (or its general vicinity) as a location for a piece of the treasure or as a marker to find the second piece.
- Nostradamus was simply creating a diversion for easily distracted treasure hunters.
- Nostradamus was reminding searchers that protections will be in place and that the treasure won't be in the middle of nowhere and easily found.

Treasure hunts inspire the imagination and fire up those people who seek out adventure — unless you read between the lines and notice that for everyone seeking the treasure in Quatrain C VIII – 30, there's some trouble at the end. Just ask Roman General Q. Servilius Caepio, who lost his career and his money after trying to gain wealth and riches without working for them. I believe Nostradamus was truly just giving hints and rhymes about his own confounded riddles, which are, as he treated them, golden treasures of information. The treasure you find today is that the search for understanding and knowledge — for the riches of the past — will improve the current times. Look to history, Nostradamus seemed to say, and discover something along the way.

Part VI
The Part of Tens

The 5th Wave   By Rich Tennant

1544—A confusing time for Nostradamus as he roams the countryside and briefly tries writing quatrains that predict the past.

Well, that *never* happened...

This neither.

Oddly, his predictions turn out to be less than 5% accurate.

In this part . . .

The Part of Tens provides some additional ways to
access Nostradamus. I give some trivia about the very
human person who was Nostradamus. I guide you through
some easy steps and suggestions for approaching the quatrains to find your own meanings. And finally, if you've just
gotten your appetite whet with the quatrains presented in
this book, and you're hungry enough to chow down on the
rest of the quatrains in *The Prophecies* (or to partake in
some truly chewy research), then you'll like the suggestions I have for continuing your walk into the future with
Nostradamus.

Chapter 20

Ten Insights into the Life and Mind of Nostradamus

In This Chapter

▶ Getting up close and personal with Nostradamus

▶ Focusing in on facts about his career

▶ Discovering interesting info that has emerged after his death

*N*ostradamus's works have remained in nearly continual publication. Yet even if you've read this book or other books about him, you may still feel like you don't know the actual man who was first known as Michel de Nostredame and then later known, like a rock star, by his last name alone, Nostradamus.

Knowing some of the everyday-life details about Nostradamus can help you understand him better, even if you don't understand his quatrains. So I've collected 10 (okay 11 if you want to get technical) pieces of interesting information about Nostradamus and his life as a kind of get-to-know-him-better chapter that will hopefully make him seem more alive. If some of the material seems to be a little negative, don't take that too hard. I believe he wasn't perfect, and for me, that gives him a kind of charm.

Life in Provence

Ah, what a life it was in Provence! Not a man alive then (or now for that matter) could argue the beauty of the region, although occasionally harsh winds swept through the region and left only the hardiest of plants and people. The gentle valleys created near-perfect places for the development of fine wines, olives, fruits, and a variety of local cheeses.

The flavor of Provence for Nostradamus would've been one of variety and temperance. The people who lived in the region kept both the local seasonal traditions and the religious traditions of invaders who had hounded the shores of Provence for hundreds of years. The people Nostradamus met on the street may well have taken an attitude of simply adapting to changes and holding their own against the harsh winds of the seasons and the seasonal fighting. Although Provençe itself was more tolerant of Jews, the cities like Salon and Aix in Provençe were hotbeds of religious troubles as part of the Religious Wars that occupied France for years.

Stepping outside of the Nostradamus household door, however, you probably wouldn't find much to indicate this struggle of ideas. Tending to the daily activities of living, people would venture down streets to the cobbler or clothes-makers, or for vegetables on the market street. Food was a minor passion for Nostradamus, so I imagine he was particular about some of what was prepared for him. But meals in his home would be based on the basic natural ingredients from Provençe, including local cheeses, nuts, olives, goat cheeses, and a bit of meat that could be ox, cow, lamb, fish, or fowl. It's also likely that with his knowledge of plants and access to slightly exotic sources for spices, the use of herbs in his home was more like something you'd see on a cooking show than you'd see in the typical Renaissance peasant (who did have tasty herbs, just not such a variety). Stews, pies, and vegetables were a probably a tasty treat in the Nostradamus home.

Traveling in the 1500s

Nostradamus was certainly a traveling man, but how he traveled and what it took to manage all that traveling may surprise you. During his wandering tours of France to cure plague victims, he frequently walked carrying only one bag full of a necessary change of clothes (just one), a notebook or two, and perhaps some items for casting the astrological charts of the patients. A small pack was necessary because he walked from town to town, hopefully finding a home that allowed him space in trade for his services. But he had to be careful not to stay where he might become a victim of the Black Plague.

Part of the wear and tear on Nostradamus's body came from walking about 10 kilometers (that's 6 miles) per day. So to go from his hometown in Saint Rémy de Provençe to Avignon for school was a two or three day journey of 20 kilometers, or about 18 miles.

When the queen summoned Nostradamus from Salon to Paris, he made amazing speed and reached her Majesty's presence in just under one month. The distance was 368 miles if he were flying by crow, but he traveled by horse, so the actual distance was more likely to be well over 400 miles. To keep his trip speedy, the queen arranged for a fresh and rested horse to be stationed at every town along his route; otherwise, Nostradamus would've taken nearly twice as long to cover the distance.

The Family Man

Nostradamus wasn't just a prophet and astrologer. Among the many hats he wore were the ones called Father and Husband. His first marriage in Agen was brief, and from the stories, he was a man who enjoyed home life with a young and beautiful wife and two children. The comforts of a wife and children were very inspiring, but the depth of Nostradamus's feelings showed after their deaths (for that story, see Chapter 3) when he gave himself over to despair and left his home for the life of a wandering doctor.

With Anne, Nostradamus's second wife he nested with in Salon, there was less of the new love feeling he'd experienced with his first wife and more of the solid, lasting partnership that would see him through long nights of visions and the trying life of a prophet. Anne was a widow, he a physician, and their family eventually extended to include six children who certainly watched their father's clients consult the charts created for them and listen intently to his advice. This was the daily work that kept his family fed and maintained their lives.

His children would've been educated in the traditional Renaissance topics that were taught to Nostradamus, like Latin, Mathematics, the Greek and Roman philosophers, and certainly astrology. These children probably received more encouragement to listen to their inner selves than most children of the age.

Among the six children, Nostradamus seems to have had two favorites — César and Madeleine. César, the son to whom the first section of the *Prophecies* is dedicated, became a poet, painter, historian, and even Consul of Salon. His favorite topic — dear ol' dad — got him into trouble, though, because César had a rather liberal imagination, and the lines between reality and fiction sometimes faded in favor of making Nostradamus seem better in the eyes of the reader. When Nostradamus died, César received (via a special addition to the will during the last hours of the prophet's life) a brass astrolabe and a large gold ring. These gifts were quite special, considering the fact that money inheritance wasn't typically given to sons until they were 25 years old.

Despite the favoritism of sons over daughters, Nostradamus definitely favored Madeleine. As daddy's girl, she was given (along with César) special gifts in Nostradamus's will, including a larger sum of money than her sisters or even her mother received and two walnut cases with jewelry. She didn't even have to wait until marriage to receive the gifts, which was standard procedure during this time. Madeleine and her husband were also involved in the continued publication of Nostradamus's material.

A Doctor with Good Intentions

No one who has researched Nostradamus has ever denied that he gave his all as a doctor while traveling from village to village in the countryside treating plague victims and folks suffering from other ailments. A few critics disparage his skills as a doctor and apothecary (what we call a pharmacist today), but I'm inclined to cut him some slack. Although his avant-garde treatments of fresh air and clean water did nothing for those people actually afflicted with the plague, they likely helped prevent the spread of the disease.

The truth is that as a doctor of the plague, even Nostradamus acknowledged a troubled career. As an apothecary, Nostradamus researched and tracked the influences of many plants on the human body. He produced facial creams and salves (rub-on gooey stuff) that were supposed to cure certain ailments and reduce the appearance of age. The price of these creams was often dependent upon the patient's ability to pay, and the more costly the ingredient, the better the cure supposedly was in Renaissance days. I guess I'm willing to let some doubtful cosmetic creams slide when you figure that all his doctoring and apothecarying — as misguided as they were at times — helped him earn a living while he wrote *The Prophecies,* which have ultimately benefited many.

An All-Star Astrologer Only in His Dreams

Nostradamus practiced the art of astrology from his early learning until his death. Unfortunately, though, if you look at some of the details in his work, you see that he needed even more practice, especially when doing math and working with the angles of the stars in the sky.

Many of the astrological charts Nostradamus drew up contained errors, inconsistencies, and even two suns. So the man we consider an influential voice from the past took quite a bit of bad mouthing from his fellow astrologers. Eventually, Nostradamus even stopped calling himself an astrologer and simply referred to himself as a lover of stars.

You have to admire a man who maintains his own ideas in the face of criticism from his peers. He may have given in and admitted that he wasn't the best of the best, but Nostradamus continued to believe he was divinely connected with the patterns of the stars, and he followed his passionate interest despite the nay-sayers in the crowd. For that bit of bravery, I give Nostradamus two thumbs up.

Comfortable at Home but Not Filthy Rich

During Nostradamus's own time, he was a published author and recognizable person, but those perks didn't seem to help his finances much. Information from his last will and testament reveals that although Nostradamus was living very comfortably (in modern money, he died with almost $1 million in assets and money from his travels), he certainly wasn't rolling in dough like true royalty or those people who had high-ranking government jobs. And, well, obviously he hasn't received any money from the books published about him after his death. Nostradamus was a man who had to work for his living but could afford to write for months and then get paid in lump sums as his writings were published and sold.

His stone-front house in Salon was on a narrow street (much like the rest of the houses) and fell within the circular barricade walls of the city, which kept the daily world Nostradamus lived in fairly small. On the narrow first floor, you may have found Anne, his wife, preparing dinner for the young children who sat on benches (a chair was reserved for important people like Nostradamus or the head of the household). On the second story were bedrooms with no closets (closets were a waste of space). Clothes were scented heavily with perfumes (only the inner garments were washed) and stored in trunks, wardrobes, or other furniture built for this purpose.

On the third floor, Nostradamus had the personal luxury of his own study with long benches to hold his equipment and charts and a desk and stool for his deepest work of prophecy. This upstairs prophet's workroom was where he produced his cures, creams, and astrological charts and read as many books as he could get his hands on. Compared to the peasant who owned nothing and slept together with an entire family in one room, Nostradamus lived in the lap of luxury. But he was still well below the queen's standard of living. Each time she dressed, several maids were needed to arrange her outfits and her hair.

Quarrelsome with Common Folk

Although I believe Nostradamus recorded and published his prophecies out of a genuine concern for the world he lived in and for future generations, that doesn't mean he loved, or was loved by, everyone in his time. Being a published and reasonably well-off man didn't buy him any particular respect while he lived in Salon, France. The lower classes and Nostradamus seemed to have had a kind of running feud.

During peasant revolts against the general way France was being run, specifically between the Catholic and the Protestants (persecution of the Protestants at various times became intense under the Inquisition), Nostradamus went so far as to rent his home to someone else for a few months and take his family out of Salon. Because he was a Christian who'd converted from Judaism (which always made people suspect you were up to something), and because of his association with Queen Catherine de Medici (you can meet her in Chapter 4), who was known to the peasant class as "that Italian woman," Nostradamus ran into conflict with people of the lower classes. They apparently resented the queen as an outsider, and Nostradamus felt the heat of guilt by association. After the rebellion calmed down, he returned to Salon and continued writing, but events like that had to shake the guy up.

Although historical records don't prove the story that Nostradamus had quarrelsome relationships with the peasants, some historians still report that for his part, Nostradamus wasn't overly kind to the common people. I don't think he's much to blame, though, because he was born into a world where the place and manner of your birth determined what you'd do in life. If you were born a peasant, you were chained to the land; if you were born a noble person, you were responsible for protecting both the peasants and the land.

As part of the almost-noble professional class of physicians, Nostradamus probably felt a strong sense of responsibility for his plague patients, but I doubt he identified with them much at all because they weren't like him. They weren't educated and backed by family members in positions of power (like Nostradamus's brother, the prosecutor).

Artistic Differences

Like many artists and writers today, Nostradamus experienced what we label "artistic differences" with company executives and editors — both in life and in death. A potential downside to being published is that at some point, the author's writing ends up in the hands of other people that just mess with it and mess with it.

While publishing *The Almanacs* and later the original pieces of *The Prophecies* (in 1555), Nostradamus had several heated discussions and disagreements with the publishing houses and moved his manuscript from one place to another. The publishing houses seem to have gotten a bit of revenge, however, by printing unauthorized and slightly altered copies almost immediately after the original was out the door. The collected printing of all ten centuries in *The Prophecies* (he set up an arrangement for the second half of *The Prophecies* to be published after he passed on) was subject to the same printer errors and typos as the originals had been, but they probably also suffered through some editing by Nostradamus's wife and his secretary, Chavigny.

Favorite Pickup Line: "I'm a Capricorn. What's Your Sign?"

Although Nostradamus probably didn't use his sign to court women, he was a Capricorn (what a coincidence, so am I), having been born on December 14, 1503. (The time of birth wasn't typically recorded, so the exact moment of birth is still debated, especially by those people who've drawn up Nostradamus's astrology chart to see whether he lived up to his own stars.) Nostradamus followed these typical Capricorn tendencies:

- **Motivated to achieve personal goals.** Nostradamus was determined to listen to his intuition and prophetic insights, and he established a life that allowed him to do that.

- **Sense of responsibility to self and others.** *The Almanacs* and horoscopes Nostradamus carefully wrote showed that he felt a responsibility to be honest with his info. The whole doctor thing also accurately demonstrates this Capricorn trait.

- **Attentive to details.** Throughout his life, Nostradamus studied and kept notes on everything of interest to him, even cooking. He was a lifelong student who wrote for hours on end and drew up chart after astrological chart to try to pinpoint events from his visions.

- **Hardworking, patient, and tireless.** Nostradamus was known to stay up late into the night working on his quatrains and seeing visions. By some accounts, he needed very little sleep each night to keep going.

- **Altruistic.** *Altruism* is an unselfish concern for others, and I believe that the time and energy Nostradamus spent writing for a future he'd never see is a perfect example of this trait. He wrote the prophecy quatrains out of concern for humanity, not himself.

- **Reserved with a touch of humor.** Most of the quatrains deal with serious and world altering events. But occasionally, the puns, wordplay, and treasure hunt themes Nostradamus incorporated make me certain that behind his serious face was a sense of humor that peeked out.

- **Somewhat fatalistic.** Okay, so if you've read the quatrains, you may see this one coming, but Capricorn people tend to go with the worst case scenario, and then if something better happens, great.

December 14 isn't actually part of the normal range of dates for the Zodiac sign of Capricorn. But when the Church realized that Easter and other dates were drifting because the years weren't the right length, the Church shifted from the Julian calendar to the Gregorian calendar. That shift to the new calendar system moves Nostradamus's birthday to December 24 — the very beginning of the Capricorn time of year.

A Wiz with Jams and Jellies

A little known but very interesting fact is that Nostradamus was an accomplished cook. He didn't make dinner or anything, but he did dabble in jams and jellies and even published a small book of recipes entitled *Excellent er Moult Utile Opuscule a tous necessaire qui desirent avoir connaissance de plusieurs exq uises recettes*. Don't let the title scare you. In English, it means *An excellent and most useful little work essential to all who wish to become acquainted with some exquisite recipes*. Nostradamus was known to make tasty jams, a fine sweetmeat, jams for women with difficulty in the love department, and even jams to be used as prevention for the Black Plague.

Faithful to the End

Stories about Nostradamus say that he walked daily to and from the local church where he'd sit quietly and reflect. There aren't any daily records of who attended church services, but his will also strongly suggests that he was deeply religious. After his death, the importance he placed on religion and on his connection with the Christian Church remained evident in monies he left to two Franciscan Friars, a Franciscan monastery (the chapel he frequented), and 13 beggars.

Nostradamus made religion a strong part of his daily life and consistently gave credit for his skills — astrological and otherwise — to God's blessings and guidance. Interestingly, the very first thing Nostradamus gave away in his will was his soul into the care of God. If that doesn't sum up his opinion on the matter of his faith, I'm not sure anything could.

Nostradamus's wife and children (when they reached a certain age) attended services with him, and the children most likely received some religious instruction from both their father and the local friar. One of the kids, André, seems to have been the troublesome son, but after a brush with the law, he took monastic vows and changed his life — probably due in part to the strong sense of salvation and forgiveness he'd heard at home as part of the Christian faith. At any rate, historians know that André passed away and was buried in a monastery.

Chapter 21

Ten Tips for Exploring *The Prophecies* on Your Own

. . . .

In This Chapter

▶ Taking *The Prophecies* one step at a time

▶ Untangling the codes again and again

▶ Sitting down with your inner prophet

. . . .

Perhaps you've seen a show on television where various experts share their interpretations of *The Prophecies*. In addition, you've probably read bits and pieces of this book, taking in my interpretations of Nostradamus's predictions. Now you'd like to try to get meaning out of Nostradamus's words by yourself. I know how that feels; the hidden future can be *very* alluring. I hope this chapter helps your endeavor by giving you ten tips for pulling apart the nonsense of the quatrains and putting everything back together with some meaning for yourself and your corner of the world.

Get a Game Plan

The most natural mistake readers make is trying to take in everything Nostradamus wrote at once. He was a very deep guy with a lot to say, so don't try to get your PhD in Prophecy in one day. Whether you begin by selecting a topic, person, or idea that you find interesting and then finding a specific quatrain to match (you can look at what other people have said about a specific quatrain as a starting point for your own ideas), or you begin by simply choosing quatrains at random, there should be a method to your madness. And the method should go something like this:

1. **Read the entire quatrain in English all the way through *several* times, and jot down general ideas about what you think the topic may be (a war, a person, a church-related matter, and so on).**

Don't get attached to your original ideas; they may change by the time you're done.

2. **Note if your quatrain's translation from French to English matches word for word with other people's translations. (Sometimes tiny word changes by one translator can make a difference in how you interpret Nostradamus's meaning.) Pick a translation that makes the most sense to you.**

After you have a translation you like, try briefly reading over other people's understanding of the quatrain so you get a broad view of possible meanings that other people see within the quatrain.

3. **Pick out what seem to be the most important or key pieces — names, places, and other things necessary for making any kind of sense of the quatrain.**

Remember any relationships that exist between items. These relationships could be important later to understanding the text.

4. **Examine these pieces of the puzzle from many different angles, and let your search be free form, but don't expect it to go in one direction.**

Exploring the Internet and libraries, as well as brain storming to find ideas associated with the items in the quatrain, are some of your best bets for unraveling these mysterious pieces. Try to find locations on maps and see what's nearby or whether there were important people around or events that happened in or near that town. For people, begin with their biographies and the important ideas and people associated with them. Often Nostradamus used a person to represent either an idea or a country.

If a word or place seems to lead nowhere, try rearranging the word (in English and in French if you can) to form other words. Remember that Nostradamus loved word tricks like the ones discussed later in this chapter, so you need to be familiar with these techniques in order to unravel the tricky words in some quatrains.

Take notes on what you find for each piece. After you've gathered the pieces, look to see whether any of the pieces are related to each other. Do they all talk about Germany? Is everything about struggle or war-torn areas? These are the kind of general questions you should ask to try and tie the pieces together.

5. **After you get the background information on who, what, and where the quatrain is discussing, reread the quatrain, and try to put it all back together as a story with more details.**

This is the time to go back and really look at the relationship among the pieces in the original quatrain. Try rewriting the quatrain using summarized versions of the words you've researched. This kind of paraphrasing can help because it takes the sometimes awkward words of the quatrain and simplifies them. You may find that with your background knowledge of the previously mysterious pieces, the quatrain will begin to give up its answers.

6. **Try to figure out when the events are supposed to shake down, using quatrain dating (I touch on that concept in Chapter 10), history, and current events to help you.**

Sometimes just knowing who's involved gives you an idea of time because you can look at the person's lifespan. Be careful, however, not to make assumptions. Just because Nostradamus used an older name for a place doesn't mean the events being discussed happened when the place was known by its ancient name.

7. **Reread the quatrain and the information you've gathered about the pieces to see whether Nostradamus may have hidden an overall trend or pattern within the words.**

This is the time to rely on what you know about Nostradamus's favorite topics and see whether he has reverted to old habits by discussing politics, religion, France, or the like.

If the past just doesn't seem to match up with the pieces of your quatrain, you may need to look at more recent events. Keep an eye on the news, especially beyond the first headlines, on the topics of science, natural disasters, slow changes in political power, and issues that seem connected to the items in your quatrain. Even if nothing matches, you may still be able to find the beginning of a pattern (like the changes from Communism to free trade in Eastern Europe that have taken decades) that may be a future prediction. Don't toss out that quatrain just because the answer isn't in the past.

These steps form the basic outline for examining Nostradamus's quatrains and prophecies, but they aren't the definitive guides. Add your own steps as you find that they become necessary.

Keep in Mind Nostradamus's Secret Techniques

Reading Nostradamus's works is like wearing someone else's prescription glasses — things may not really be as they appear. Nostradamus was fond of using secret techniques from his time and from the mystical traditions he studied, and he added a fair amount of intentional confusion to keep the Church from showing too much interest in his works. Here's a short (and necessarily incomplete) list of his techniques to keep in mind as you look at specific words:

- **Anagram.** A word in which the letters can be rearranged to form a new word (the real one Nostradamus intended). (See Chapter 10's discussion of PAU, NAY, LORON as *Napoleon King*.)

- **Apocope and apheresis.** The omission of a letter or syllable at the end or beginning of a word. Depending on his mood, Nostradamus used other techniques, including adding letters and syllables rather than dropping them. (See Chapter 12's discussion of World War II for an example of this technique).

✔ **Connotation.** An implication from a word. Nostradamus used words simply to give the reader a beginning point, because he actually made references to ideas associated with a word rather than to its actual definition. This technique is used throughout the quatrains.

✔ **Antique reference.** The most ancient term available for a person, place, or item. For example, rather than using the 16th century term for a town, person, or place, Nostradamus used the oldest name for it.

✔ **Homonyms.** A word that's spelled the same or has the same sound when pronounced as another word with a completely different meaning.

✔ **Synecdoche.** A way of using one piece of something to represent the whole, like a hand for the entire person or a king for the entire country.

Find Out How to Speak in Symbols

Symbols are words used to represent something else, and they're used because they effectively add depth of meaning to what they represent. For example, using the symbol of the cock (rooster or bird) to represent France adds meaning because it brings along some of the symbol's own characteristics. France takes on the ideas associated with that animal, such as its ability to fight and defend its territory, persistence, and a very graceful display of feathers (not to mention the fact that the rooster generally runs the barnyard). For more details on Nostradamus's use of symbols, flip over to Chapter 6.

Nostradamus used symbols within his writing to add depth and give you additional ideas about events. Look to see whether he used a word that has extra symbolic meaning rather than just literal meaning.

Remember the Frame of the Quatrain

One man with one perspective from the 16th century wrote all the quatrains. Even as well-read and widely educated as he was, Nostradamus was just one person trying to make a difference. Keep in mind that your ideas may not match his ideas about anything, especially the complex topics of astrology (Chapter 6), alchemy (Chapter 6), medicine (Chapter 2), the Kabbalah (Chapter 4), and religion (Chapter 4), which were the foundations of his writing. If you're going to get a hold on Nostradamus, understanding these concepts as they existed in his time is important. These areas of study have gone through periods of growth and change since Nostradamus wrote his last quatrain, and he couldn't possibly have known every little detail of these topics, even if he foresaw the changes in methods and usage through the years (which I think he did).

Read Between the Lines

After you've looked at a quatrain, read between the lines to see whether Nostradamus used a *metaphor,* a form of speech where one thing is used to represent another thing, and the two things are compared. Instead of talking about a literal war between two leaders, for instance, Nostradamus may have been discussing a battle of ideas between two sides in an argument.

Metaphors are one of the ways Nostradamus snuck in layers of meaning in his quatrains. When using the term *plague,* for example, he may have been talking about a real and bonafide sickness that will attack people's bodies. But he may have also been talking about a more generalized sickness (apathy or the general lack of religious faith) that will behave and look just like a plague. Many times, the multiple interpretations of words in a quatrain clue you in to the fact that Nostradamus gave you a parfait (layered dessert) of a quatrain.

Know Your History

History speaks for itself, or so the historians would have me believe, but I don't hear much talking. In fact, you have to do quite a bit of reading just to get part of the story straight about events in the past.

If you really want to understand the quatrains, you need to know the past, so do some reading and a little bit of research. This kind of work will help you put the pieces together as you read the quatrains.

Nostradamus lived in 16th century France, and the sights, smells, and intellectual movements, had a great deal to do with his understanding of the world. Think of those factors as the prescription for his glasses. You try to use your own modern prescription to see what he saw. Having background info on some of the events around his time is very helpful. Plus, you're not going to be able to identify a quatrain on World War II or the fall of the Soviet Union, for example, without a basic knowledge of events — and, for that, you need to be familiar with historical resources where you can find out more information on topics beyond France and the 16th century. A fun and easy place to start are books in the *For Dummies* history series like *World History For Dummies* or *World War II For Dummies.*

Tune Into Current Events

In addition to knowing the past, you also need to bone up on general ideas and events — the major movers and shakers — of your own time. Doing so can help you interpret quatrains relating to the present day and the future. Keep an eye on developing technologies, medicine, and politics around the globe (not just in America), with a special focus on France and Europe. (Nostradamus was French and European, so many of his prophecies are focused there.)

And in today's world of global markets, the Internet, real-time news, and fast food, there's no telling what can happen in a very short period of time. If you keep the general topics of the prophecies you've studied in the back of your mind while reading the paper or watching the news, the patterns may begin to make sense before something happens — and recognizing events beforehand is one of the perks of learning to understand prophecy.

Listen to the Prophet Within

I believe Nostradamus was a man with a connection to the wider universe (and maybe even to the divine), and this connection let him see that certain events were going to happen and certain patterns in human behavior could be avoided. I also believe he wasn't the only person to ever have the gift of prophecy and that the connection to the universe is available to everyone, although not everyone uses his or her abilities. Nostradamus was a doctor and a man of his times — not so different from you and me. But I believe Nostradamus was different because he took the time to study and practice his gift of prophecy.

As you read through a quatrain or a section of Nostradamus's writings, make sure you don't tune out the feeling that there's a deeper meaning to what he has written than just the words you see or that he's talking about a particular event you may know about. Sometimes intuition can be a fabulous guide to understanding just the right meaning.

One of the layers Nostradamus intentionally placed in his quatrains was meant for the adept — people who naturally find meaning — and with the vast amount of information people see on a daily basis (the statistics are astounding), you and I count as adepts. The layers he placed for the adepts aren't straight-out prophecy; they're more like build-your-own-prophecy starter kits. These are seeds for finding your own inner prophet, even if this inner profit disagrees with the so-called experts (who, by the way, still haven't dug up Nostradamus to ask him some very important questions).

Let Go of Expectations

Of all the things you must do to understand Nostradamus's prophecies, letting go of your expectations may be the hardest one. But I'm here to tell you it's gotta happen, or you'll be stuck in a mire of confusion.

Here are some expectations that have to go:

- ✔ **Everything Nostradamus wrote should make sense now.** Wrong. Quatrains begin to make more sense as the images become more evident. Rockets and modern machinery, for example, were confusing to early interpreters but were eventually pretty easily identified. I believe not all the prophecies have come true and that modern day people aren't completely prepared to understand them all, so some of the quatrains may remain obscure.

- ✔ **Nostradamus was always right.** Oh, so wrong. I believe that Nostradamus could indeed see the future, but only from his point of view, and everybody has bad days now and again. If you add the idea that the future can change when people make decisions in the here and now, then Nostradamus's predictions can only have a limited amount of accuracy. People are very difficult to predict after all.

- ✔ **Nostradamus has written a prediction for me.** I know this one sounds very appealing, and if you're a person who'll influence larger world events, you may be right. Overall, however, Nostradamus wrote prophecies about large events, big catastrophes, wars, and religious troubles.

- ✔ **I don't believe in any of the mystic traditions or religions he studied, so these quatrains don't apply to me.** Okay, remember that these things did matter to Nostradamus, and whether you believe in them or completely understand them isn't the point. The point is he believed in them, understood them, and put them in his writings. So understanding them will help you get to his larger meanings, which weren't limited to a specific religion or mystical tradition.

- ✔ **Every major event has its own quatrain.** When world events change, or nature brings on a particularly strong season of storms, looking to Nostradamus to see whether he predicted the event and told the world what they should do is tempting. Even if an event is very large on your scale, from the viewpoint of humanity and Nostradamus, the event may not have even registered.

Just because a quatrain doesn't exist for a particular event, don't get all droopy and assume that the event isn't important. You could waste valuable time looking for a quatrain when you could be handling the crisis yourself — something I think Nostradamus would've approved of.

Look at the Big Picture (and on the Bright Side)

You find quatrains about war, plague, famine, desolation, the barrenness of the human heart, and other equally depressing subjects throughout *The Prophecies,* and they can really bring you down — trust me. I've had to resort to more than one walk in the park to brighten my perspective after studying Nostradamus for hours on end. The key to avoiding this kind of malaise is to look to the larger picture that includes all of humanity, not just that event or quatrain's topic.

Keeping things in perspective is important. Nostradamus was a healer, an astrologer, and a religious man. He saw what he believed were divine paths that humanity would follow, and I think he believed that the pathways would lead to growth, change, improvement, and hopefully the brighter future of the Age of Aquarius, a time after the final wars of the third antichrist are done. He saw a light at the end of the tunnel.

Most important to ask about any quatrain is this: What lesson can I find here that will help me deal with the next crisis or event that will challenge me? This kind of questioning will keep you in Nostradamus's footsteps and always looking to the future.

Chapter 22

Ten Tips on Finding Quality Resources

*O*ften people who read about Nostradamus find that the intricate details of his life and work and the puzzling quatrains keep their brains spinning for a long time — and they hunger for more. If you're one of those people, you'll love this chapter, which dishes up ten (more or less) resources for further info. And here's a bonus, folks: Reading and studying literature about Nostradamus, his quatrains, and the concept of prophecy are excellent ways to keep your mind sharp and your powers of observation in good shape. So if you're eager to step up and go beyond the level of the beginner, I have a few suggestions that I've developed over the years on how to spot sources with potentially helpful insights or opinions on Nostradamus, and how to avoid the others.

For the most part, you have two paths to take — the Internet and books. The truth is that most of what you find on the Internet is common-knowledge biographical information and some limited quatrain interpretation. Serious work on the quatrains seems to be reserved for published books, which are for sale on every Web site corner.

Strike a Balance

I recommend you go for a balanced view — from reviewing those Internet sites and books that discredit Nostradamus to checking out the ones that claim he was a powerful prophet. I even suggest you dive briefly into those scary sites that say that Nostradamus's writings explain the entire existence of everything (which I don't believe is true), just so you get an idea of the variety out there.

Check the Freshness Date

Maybe checking the freshness date sounds silly, but many of the truly serious Nostradamus researchers continually work to untangle problems in translation, evaluate new texts that are discovered molding in old French town halls, or just reexamine their theories to see whether they still make sense. These are the researchers who aren't simply resting on their laurels and who deserve your reading time.

Evaluate the Source

Your chances of getting valid interpretations are good if someone with a history in prophecy or Nostradamus research wrote the book or Web site. Material written by your average math teacher probably isn't going to yield too much useful information. If the author isn't mentioned at all, or is mentioned without any clue as to whether or not he knows what he's talking about, turn your attention to another source.

Consider a Bilingual Approach

Look for publications and Web sites that include both the original French text and the English translation, or at least make references to Nostradamus's original text. For example, although I've kept the French to a minimum in this book, I do go back to the original text when there's a difference in translation or a word that isn't supposed to be translated at all. Having both versions of a word allows you to recognize when one translation is different from another one you've seen or even whether the book or Web site is using a different version of the original Nostradamus text. (Errors in printing and assumptions about what abbreviations mean can change the words of the original document from one version to another.) Differences in either the original or the translation can ultimately change the meaning the author extracts from the quatrain and what you get from your reading.

Question Shocking Openers

Any Web site or book jacket that starts off with the shocking and most controversial quatrains — like those linked with Hitler or the attacks of September 11, 2001 — isn't likely to have an unbiased view of Nostradamus's writings. Dramatic pictures of horrific events connected with the quatrains (or their pieces) are simply used for shock value and don't give you an in-depth understanding of Nostradamus's writings.

Check Out These Web Sites

Here are some of the good Web sites to check out:

- **Internet Sacred Text Archive** (www.sacred-texts.com) is a collection of many texts that have influenced the world, including Nostradamus's quatrains and at least one interpretation.

- **Prophecies Online** (www.propheties.it) is a not for profit site that includes scans of Nostradamus's original texts (French and English), his horoscope, historical information, and more. It includes very limited interpretations to relate the quatrains to you in the here and now.

- **Internet FAQ Archives** (www.faqs.org) is just a large listing of frequently asked questions (FAQs) that have been compiled for easy access. A search for Nostradamus leads you on a wandering trail of other people's research and ideas.

- **Morgana's Observatory** (www.dreamscape.com/morgana) discusses prophecies and other topics from around the globe and from many cultural and religious backgrounds. The information about Nostradamus is limited to a few quatrains, but fairness seems to be applied to the ones that are discussed.

Pick Up a Good Book

Here, in alphabetical order, are some authors who can most likely add something to your understanding of Nostradamus:

- Erika Cheetham
- John Hogue
- James Lemerurier
- Edgar Leoni
- David Ovason
- James Randi

Each of these writers has books by several titles and publishers, so I won't bore you with the individual details for each one. I will point out that these authors have different opinions, translations, interpretations, and approaches to the Nostradamus puzzle, so you'll get a variety of viewpoints. It's up to you to pick the aspects that resonate with your own thoughts on the matter.

The business of translating and interpreting Nostradamus's prophecies is more like an art than a science. There are truly no hard and fast rules, and most of what's written is opinion. Some of the opinions are held up by vast quantities of research and decoding, and although those opinions are perhaps a little more valid, there are no final answers that explain exactly what Nostradamus meant.

Avoid Online Sales Pitches

Every time you try to access more than just a general biography of Nostradamus online, you run into an ad for someone's book or lecture series. This is a clear indication to run for the local bookstore instead.

Beware of Extreme Opinions

Sites that use headlines and quotes out of context to denounce Nostradamus as a useless fraud or to announce that he should be studied by everyone everywhere for all the answers are probably more focused on winning the contest of who's more right than on the actual investigation of Nostradamus's works. Books and Web sites alike can fall victim to the temptation to place Nostradamus on a pedestal and forget that he was, in fact, a man of his times with biased opinions who may have occasionally made mistakes in the course of writing nearly 2,000 years worth of prophecies. Beware of sites with something to prove.

Question Metaphysical Writers (Yes, Even Me)

Question what you read from metaphysical writers, because they generally assume from the beginning that prophecy works and that Nostradamus had the ability to foretell the future, with a little help he claimed from God. Web sites using metaphysical writers may provide you with more interpretation, but the writers aren't likely to look at a quatrain and admit they don't know what it means.

Research Topics that Influenced Nostradamus

If *Nostradamus For Dummies* has inspired you to delve deep into the mind and inner workings of Nostradamus, then you have a long road ahead, and I wish you well. As a parting gift before you set out on this quest for knowledge, let me suggest that you demystify the mystic by reading up on astrology (both the modern and the 16th century version), the mystical traditions of the Kabbalah, the path of alchemy, and the mysticism of the Catholic Church. These topics should keep you busy for quite some time. Together, they circulated around in Nostradamus's mind as he composed his prophecies, and understanding them will give you a better framework for bending the quatrains into some sense.

Astrology:

- *The Only Astrology Book You'll Ever Need* by Joanna Martine Woolfolk (Madison Books)
- *Astrology For Dummies* by Rae Orion (Wiley)
- *Kabbalistic Astrology* by Rav P.S. Berg (Research Centre of Kabbalah)

Kabbalah and Jewish Mysticism:

- *The Essential Zohar: The Source of Kabbalistic Wisdom* by Rav P.S. Berg (Bell Tower)

- *The Way: Using the Wisdom of Kabbalah for Spiritual Transformation and Fulfillment* by Michael Berg (Wiley)

- *Pico Della Mirandola's Encounter with Jewish Mysticism* by Chaim Wirszubski (Harvard University Press)

Alchemy:

- *Alchemy: An Introduction to the Symbolism and Psychology* by Marie-Louis Von Franz (Inner City Books)

- *The Philosopher's Stone: A Quest for the Secrets of Alchemy* by Peter Marshall (MacMillian Publishing)

Christian Mysticism:

- *The Essentials of Mysticism* by Evelyn Underhill (Oneworld Publications)

- *Teachings of the Christian Mystics* by Andrew Harvey (Shambhala)

- *Lost Christianity: A Journey of Rediscovery to the Centre of Christian Experience* by Jacob Needleman (Element)

A Brief Chronology of Nostradamus's Life and Times

The timeline in this appendix reflects information from a variety of sources and historical records, some of which may be questionable considering the authors' knowledge at the time. The timeline of many events in Nostradamus's life invites speculation and debate because there simply aren't accurate dates or records of his activity. My advice is not to focus on the specific dates involved but rather on the overall development of events during the Renaissance and unfolding of Nostradamus's life and work.

Some Key Early Renaissance Events

The Renaissance began around the mid-1300s in Italy and spread throughout Europe over the next 200 years, give or take a few years, so it's nearly impossible for me to cover everything important that happened. The following list of dates and events is a sampling of events that were important to the developing times and to Nostradamus on his way to being a prophecy writer:

1454 Johann Gutenberg uses his last monies to develop the printing press in Germany, but after his bankruptcy, his creditors print the first mass-produced book, the *Gutenberg Bible*.

1461 The Hundred Years' War between France and England comes to an uneasy end with England limping home and abandoning all of its French possessions except Calais. The king of France is tempted to continue the winning streak to expand the territory for France.

1468 The Catholic Church establishes the Inquisition to persecute Jews, Muslims, and heretics.

1473 Astronomer Nicolaus Copernicus is born.

1486 Humanist philosopher Pico della Mirandola, decried as a heretic by the Catholic Church, publishes his 900 treatises on all subjects, including the idea that humanity's only limitations are self-imposed, and people are capable of great achievements.

1492 Columbus sails the ocean blue and returns with a bountiful claim in the New World for his financers, King Ferdinand and Queen Isabella of Spain. Industry and empire-building become all the rage across Europe as the news spreads and ships begin to travel between the worlds. Although Spain is expanding its conquests, at home it's expelling all people of the Jewish faith.

1494 King Charles VIII of France invades Italy, specifically to gain control of Naples. This act begins a long-running struggle called the Italian Wars that involves much of the larger countries in Europe until 1559.

1498 Louis XII succeeds Charles VIII in France. Louis XII was the monarch who was popular with the people and ruled during Nostradamus's childhood until 1515. Louis XII helped set the stage for the true beginning of the Renaissance in France.

Chronology of Nostradamus's Life and Times

October 31, 1503 Pope Julius II assumes the Papal throne, rebuilds Rome (and St. Peter's Basilica), and initiates the Roman Golden Age.

December 14, 1503 According to most reports, Michele de Nostredame (you know him by his Latinized chosen name, Nostradamus) is born around noon in Saint Rémy de Provence to Jacques Nostredame and his wife, Reyniere. Jacques (or Jaume, as some biographers believe he was called) is recorded as a well-to-do grain merchant.

1509 Henry VIII begins his rule as king of England, and the intrigue and backstabbing among the rulers of Europe increase dramatically during this period.

1512 At the age of 9, Nostradamus begins his education with great-grandfather Jean de Saint Rémy, learning all the basics of Latin, Greek, Hebrew, Mathematics, and the celestial sciences (astrology).

1513 French forces leave Italy with their tails tucked and losses fresh in their minds, but as soon as they get home, France is invaded from the north by an Anglo-German coalition. French King Louis XII agrees to peace terms but is still a pretty effective king in other areas.

The Medici family, who later produces Catherine de Medici (future queen of France), returns to power in Florence.

1515 French King Louis XII dies, and François I inherits the throne. He promptly captures Milan.

1517 The school at Avignon receives the young student Nostradamus (although there are no official school records of this that survive) with mostly open arms. His lack of respect for authority and his overly enthusiastic interest in astrology give him some reputation troubles.

1517 Martin Luther nails his 95 statements to the door of the castle's church in Wittenberg, beginning the Protestant Reformation and one of the largest threats against the Church (later known as the Catholic Church to distinguish it) that Nostradamus later writes about in *The Prophecies.*

1519 Charles, archduke of Austria (and king of Spain), becomes emperor Charles V, the most powerful ruler in Europe.

1522 Nostradamus's parents, concerned about his reputation and his future, send him to the University at Montpellier to study medicine.

1525 The Black Plague engulfs the French countryside, and Nostradamus, a star medical pupil, leaves his studies to wander the countryside and assist the dying and ill.

1529 Enrollment records at the University at Montpellier record that Michele de Nostredame re-enrolls on October 23.

1530 François Rabelais (who later becomes a humanist, physician, and writer) joins Nostradamus at Montpellier.

Roman Emperor Charles V, newly crowned, names Alessandro de Medici as the hereditary duke of Florence.

1529–1534 After about a year of study, Nostradamus receives his doctorate but leaves the University at Montpellier to wander again among the plague victims. While in Toulouse, he receives a letter from philosopher César Scalinger, so he moves to Agen, France, and becomes friends with the philosopher. While there, he also establishes a medical and apothecary practice.

1533 England's King Henry VIII nullifies his marriage to Catherine of Aragon and marries Anne Boleyn, who gives birth to Elizabeth, future queen of England.

Catherine de Medici marries Henry, duke of Orléans, who will become king of France in 1547. Both Catherine and Henry (later Henry II) were 14 years old.

1534 Henry VIII passes the Act of Succession and then the Act of Supremacy, effectively breaking away from the Catholic Church and establishing the Church of England.

1534 In Agen, Nostradamus marries Henriette d'Encausse, and the newly married couple celebrates the birth of two children.

1536 John Calvin publishes his major theological work as part of the Protestant Reformation.

1537 The Black Plague resurfaces. Nostradamus loses his new family (and as a result, his medical reputation) when they most likely succumb to this old enemy. He picks up his travel bags and heads out again without answering questions of the Inquisition of Toulouse regarding a passing remark he made previously about a statue of the Virgin Mary.

1538 Mount Vesuvius erupts in a mighty display of earthly power and strangeness. I believe reports of this grand event probably stayed with Nostradamus and helped shape his idea of natural disasters and later resurfaced as topics of concern within *The Prophecies*.

1541 John Calvin sets up a very stringent form of Protestantism in Geneva.

1542 Pope Paul III establishes the Universal Inquisition (also known as the Roman Inquisition to distinguish it from its counterpart in Spain), a hunt for people who work against the Catholic Church.

1544 Catherine de Medici gives birth to the future king, François II, and ensures the future of the Valois line in the French royalty.

1545–1563 Council of Tent. Catholic Church responds to calls for reform from the Protestant Reformation.

1546 The people of Aix and Salon in Provençe call on Nostradamus to heal those people afflicted with the plague, and he's hailed as a near miracle worker.

1547 On November 11, Nostradamus and Anne (nicknamed Gemelle) Ponsard marry and settle in Salon.

Ivan the Terrible crowns himself Tsar of Russia and begins his violent expansion of the Russian empire.

1550 Nostradamus publishes the *Almanac* of 1550, the first of yearly Almanacs published until his death.

1551 Nostradamus celebrates the birth of his daughter, Madeline, as well as the publication of his second Almanac during this year.

1552 Nostradamus publishes *Moult Utile Opuscule,* or *Very Useful Little Treatise,* which contains medical and cosmetic recipes.

1554 Nostradamus's son, César, is born, and Jean Aymes de Chavigny, a former town mayor, resigns his job to study under and work with Nostradamus.

1555 In April, Nostradamus's book on cooking, cosmetics, and apothecaries called *Traité, des fardemens et confitures* is printed.

May 4 brings the first publication of *The Prophecies* by Nostradamus, or at least the first 353 verses. Hearing that his prophecies refer to the royal family, Queen Catherine de Medici summons Nostradamus to consult in Paris, where he arrives on August 15. After dealing with a serious and painful bout with gout, he reports that all the queen's sons will be kings, which turns out to be mostly true.

1556 Nostradamus invests in a canal project, a move which demonstrates his concern for the health and development of the people around him, as well as the political and economic development of his region.

Hundreds of people are burned to death for heresy by the Protestants in England.

Charles V of Spain abdicates the thrown, and his son, Phillip II, assumes the thrown and rules until 1598.

1557 The second edition of *The Prophecies* is printed with 642 verses, and a few months later, the first pirated version of the publication appears.

Nostradamus and his wife celebrate the birth of their second son, Andrew.

1558 Nostradamus and his wife again find reasons to celebrate, this time with the birth of their second daughter, Anne.

Queen Elizabeth I takes over the English thrown.

1561 April brings disturbances among the common people of Salon, and Nostradamus and his family flee until July when things calm down.

France isn't the only place in upheaval. England's Queen Mary dies, leaving Queen Elizabeth to take control of the country. She's a Protestant, which creates unrest among the Church of England followers who don't believe that an illegitimate, Protestant woman could be the head of the Church of England. During her time on the throne, however, she did encourage religious tolerance.

In September, Nostradamus's wife gives birth to their youngest child, Diane.

1562 The Wars of Religion begin in France between the Catholics and the Protestants, continuing until 1598.

1564 Catherine de Medici travels through France trying to increase her general popularity. She stops in Salon and meets with Nostradamus. During the visit, Nostradamus predicts that a young boy among the royal grouping will be a future king. He is correct, because Henry IV is among the group.

November finds Nostradamus in Arles for even more royal consultations, and he's given the title Royal Councilor.

1566 *The Almanac* Nostradamus publishes for the next year claims that a "strange transmigration" will occur in November 1567, an intentional misdirection and accurate description of his own death later in June of the publication's year.

Nostradamus draws up his will, verbally predicts his own death to his assistant, Chavigny (the only source of this info), and is then discovered dead on July 2 of dropsy, or what you call edema (painful swelling and retention of water).

Index

• B •

BUSINESS, CAREERS & PERSONAL FINANCE

0-7645-5307-0

Home Buying

0-7645-5331-3 *†

Also available:

- Accounting For Dummies †
  0-7645-5314-3
- Business Plans Kit For Dummies †
  0-7645-5365-8
- Cover Letters For Dummies
  0-7645-5224-4
- Frugal Living For Dummies
  0-7645-5403-4
- Leadership For Dummies
  0-7645-5176-0
- Managing For Dummies
  0-7645-1771-6

- Marketing For Dummies
  0-7645-5600-2
- Personal Finance For Dummies *
  0-7645-2590-5
- Project Management For Dummies
  0-7645-5283-X
- Resumes For Dummies †
  0-7645-5471-9
- Selling For Dummies
  0-7645-5363-1
- Small Business Kit For Dummies *†
  0-7645-5093-4

HOME & BUSINESS COMPUTER BASICS

0-7645-4074-2

0-7645-3758-X

Also available:

- ACT! 6 For Dummies
  0-7645-2645-6
- iLife '04 All-in-One Desk Reference
  For Dummies
  0-7645-7347-0
- iPAQ For Dummies
  0-7645-6769-1
- Mac OS X Panther Timesaving
  Techniques For Dummies
  0-7645-5812-9
- Macs For Dummies
  0-7645-5656-8

- Microsoft Money 2004 For Dummies
  0-7645-4195-1
- Office 2003 All-in-One Desk Reference
  For Dummies
  0-7645-3883-7
- Outlook 2003 For Dummies
  0-7645-3759-8
- PCs For Dummies
  0-7645-4074-2
- TiVo For Dummies
  0-7645-6923-6
- Upgrading and Fixing PCs For Dummies
  0-7645-1665-5
- Windows XP Timesaving Techniques
  For Dummies
  0-7645-3748-2

FOOD, HOME, GARDEN, HOBBIES, MUSIC & PETS

0-7645-5295-3

0-7645-5232-5

Also available:

- Bass Guitar For Dummies
  0-7645-2487-9
- Diabetes Cookbook For Dummies
  0-7645-5230-9
- Gardening For Dummies *
  0-7645-5130-2
- Guitar For Dummies
  0-7645-5106-X
- Holiday Decorating For Dummies
  0-7645-2570-0
- Home Improvement All-in-One
  For Dummies
  0-7645-5680-0

- Knitting For Dummies
  0-7645-5395-X
- Piano For Dummies
  0-7645-5105-1
- Puppies For Dummies
  0-7645-5255-4
- Scrapbooking For Dummies
  0-7645-7208-3
- Senior Dogs For Dummies
  0-7645-5818-8
- Singing For Dummies
  0-7645-2475-5
- 30-Minute Meals For Dummies
  0-7645-2589-1

INTERNET & DIGITAL MEDIA

0-7645-1664-7

0-7645-6924-4

Also available:

- 2005 Online Shopping Directory
  For Dummies
  0-7645-7495-7
- CD & DVD Recording For Dummies
  0-7645-5956-7
- eBay For Dummies
  0-7645-5654-1
- Fighting Spam For Dummies
  0-7645-5965-6
- Genealogy Online For Dummies
  0-7645-5964-8
- Google For Dummies
  0-7645-4420-9

- Home Recording For Musicians
  For Dummies
  0-7645-1634-5
- The Internet For Dummies
  0-7645-4173-0
- iPod & iTunes For Dummies
  0-7645-7772-7
- Preventing Identity Theft For Dummies
  0-7645-7336-5
- Pro Tools All-in-One Desk Reference
  For Dummies
  0-7645-5714-9
- Roxio Easy Media Creator For Dummies
  0-7645-7131-1

* Separate Canadian edition also available
† Separate U.K. edition also available

Available wherever books are sold. For more information or to order direct: U.S. customers visit www.dummies.com or call 1-877-762-2974.
U.K. customers visit www.wileyeurope.com or call 0800 243407. Canadian customers visit www.wiley.ca or call 1-800-567-4797.

SPORTS, FITNESS, PARENTING, RELIGION & SPIRITUALITY

0-7645-5146-9

0-7645-5418-2

Also available:
- Adoption For Dummies
  0-7645-5488-3
- Basketball For Dummies
  0-7645-5248-1
- The Bible For Dummies
  0-7645-5296-1
- Buddhism For Dummies
  0-7645-5359-3
- Catholicism For Dummies
  0-7645-5391-7
- Hockey For Dummies
  0-7645-5228-7

- Judaism For Dummies
  0-7645-5299-6
- Martial Arts For Dummies
  0-7645-5358-5
- Pilates For Dummies
  0-7645-5397-6
- Religion For Dummies
  0-7645-5264-3
- Teaching Kids to Read For Dummies
  0-7645-4043-2
- Weight Training For Dummies
  0-7645-5168-X
- Yoga For Dummies
  0-7645-5117-5

TRAVEL

0-7645-5438-7

0-7645-5453-0

Also available:
- Alaska For Dummies
  0-7645-1761-9
- Arizona For Dummies
  0-7645-6938-4
- Cancún and the Yucatán For Dummies
  0-7645-2437-2
- Cruise Vacations For Dummies
  0-7645-6941-4
- Europe For Dummies
  0-7645-5456-5
- Ireland For Dummies
  0-7645-5455-7

- Las Vegas For Dummies
  0-7645-5448-4
- London For Dummies
  0-7645-4277-X
- New York City For Dummies
  0-7645-6945-7
- Paris For Dummies
  0-7645-5494-8
- RV Vacations For Dummies
  0-7645-5443-3
- Walt Disney World & Orlando For Dummies
  0-7645-6943-0

GRAPHICS, DESIGN & WEB DEVELOPMENT

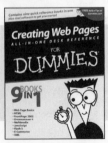

0-7645-4345-8

0-7645-5589-8

Also available:
- Adobe Acrobat 6 PDF For Dummies
  0-7645-3760-1
- Building a Web Site For Dummies
  0-7645-7144-3
- Dreamweaver MX 2004 For Dummies
  0-7645-4342-3
- FrontPage 2003 For Dummies
  0-7645-3882-9
- HTML 4 For Dummies
  0-7645-1995-6
- Illustrator CS For Dummies
  0-7645-4084-X

- Macromedia Flash MX 2004 For Dummies
  0-7645-4358-X
- Photoshop 7 All-in-One Desk Reference For Dummies
  0-7645-1667-1
- Photoshop CS Timesaving Techniques For Dummies
  0-7645-6782-9
- PHP 5 For Dummies
  0-7645-4166-8
- PowerPoint 2003 For Dummies
  0-7645-3908-6
- QuarkXPress 6 For Dummies
  0-7645-2593-X

NETWORKING, SECURITY, PROGRAMMING & DATABASES

0-7645-6852-3

0-7645-5784-X

Also available:
- A+ Certification For Dummies
  0-7645-4187-0
- Access 2003 All-in-One Desk Reference For Dummies
  0-7645-3988-4
- Beginning Programming For Dummies
  0-7645-4997-9
- C For Dummies
  0-7645-7068-4
- Firewalls For Dummies
  0-7645-4048-3
- Home Networking For Dummies
  0-7645-42796

- Network Security For Dummies
  0-7645-1679-5
- Networking For Dummies
  0-7645-1677-9
- TCP/IP For Dummies
  0-7645-1760-0
- VBA For Dummies
  0-7645-3989-2
- Wireless All In-One Desk Reference For Dummies
  0-7645-7496-5
- Wireless Home Networking For Dummies
  0-7645-3910-8

HEALTH & SELF-HELP

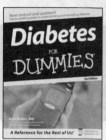

0-7645-6820-5 *†

0-7645-2566-2

Also available:

- Alzheimer's For Dummies
  0-7645-3899-3
- Asthma For Dummies
  0-7645-4233-8
- Controlling Cholesterol For Dummies
  0-7645-5440-9
- Depression For Dummies
  0-7645-3900-0
- Dieting For Dummies
  0-7645-4149-8
- Fertility For Dummies
  0-7645-2549-2
- Fibromyalgia For Dummies
  0-7645-5441-7
- Improving Your Memory For Dummies
  0-7645-5435-2
- Pregnancy For Dummies †
  0-7645-4483-7
- Quitting Smoking For Dummies
  0-7645-2629-4
- Relationships For Dummies
  0-7645-5384-4
- Thyroid For Dummies
  0-7645-5385-2

EDUCATION, HISTORY, REFERENCE & TEST PREPARATION

0-7645-5194-9

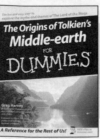

0-7645-4186-2

Also available:

- Algebra For Dummies
  0-7645-5325-9
- British History For Dummies
  0-7645-7021-8
- Calculus For Dummies
  0-7645-2498-4
- English Grammar For Dummies
  0-7645-5322-4
- Forensics For Dummies
  0-7645-5580-4
- The GMAT For Dummies
  0-7645-5251-1
- Inglés Para Dummies
  0-7645-5427-1
- Italian For Dummies
  0-7645-5196-5
- Latin For Dummies
  0-7645-5431-X
- Lewis & Clark For Dummies
  0-7645-2545-X
- Research Papers For Dummies
  0-7645-5426-3
- The SAT I For Dummies
  0-7645-7193-1
- Science Fair Projects For Dummies
  0-7645-5460-3
- U.S. History For Dummies
  0-7645-5249-X

Get smart @ dummies.com®

- Find a full list of Dummies titles
- Look into loads of FREE on-site articles
- Sign up for FREE eTips e-mailed to you weekly
- See what other products carry the Dummies name
- Shop directly from the Dummies bookstore
- Enter to win new prizes every month!

* Separate Canadian edition also available
† Separate U.K. edition also available

Available wherever books are sold. For more information or to order direct: U.S. customers visit www.dummies.com or call 1-877-762-2974.
U.K. customers visit www.wileyeurope.com or call 0800 243407. Canadian customers visit www.wiley.ca or call 1-800-567-4797.

Do More with Dummies

Products for the Rest of Us!

From hobbies to health, discover a wide variety of fun products

• Games
• Software
and More!

SARATOGA SPRINGS PUBLIC LIBRARY

SARATOGA SPRINGS PUBLIC LIBRARY, NY

0 00 02 0478623 0

GAYLORD

Check out the Dummies Speci

WILEY